S0-EXV-576

TRANSACTIONS

OF THE

AMERICAN PHILOSOPHICAL SOCIETY

HELD AT PHILADELPHIA

FOR PROMOTING USEFUL KNOWLEDGE

NEW SERIES—VOLUME 51, PART 3

1961

THE MONGUORS OF THE KANSU-TIBETAN FRONTIER

PART III. RECORDS OF THE MONGUOR CLANS

History of the Monguors in Huangchung and the Chronicles
of the Lu Family

LOUIS M. J. SCHRAM, C.I.C.M.

THE AMERICAN PHILOSOPHICAL SOCIETY

INDEPENDENCE SQUARE

PHILADELPHIA 6

MAY, 1961

Copyright © 1961 by The American Philosophical Society

Cum permissu superiorum

Library of Congress Catalog
Card No. 54–6120

This third and last part of the study about the Monguors primarily intends to present the history of the Monguor clans in Huangchung during the Ming and Ch'ing dynasties, based on the *Annals* of Hsining and the *Annals* of Kansu.

In order to make the history understandable, it has had to be put in the historical framework of the Huangchung country in which it evolved during five centuries.

In Ming times it is mostly the history of inroads into the country by Tibetans and Mongols; during Ch'ing times it is the history of the revolts of Mongols, Tibetans and Mohammedans, which several times ruined the country. Revolts and invasions were fought by Chinese troops unequal to coping with the situation, aided by the Monguor troops.

Part III is the history of the Monguor t'u-ssu clans,[1] called not only to defend their own country in combination with the Chinese army, but also to participate with the Chinese armies in wars in the provinces of Liaotung, Shensi, Shansi, Szechwan, and Yunnan, in Mongolia proper, and in the Tunhuang regions in Turkistan.

The hardships the Monguors endured during these five centuries were terrific, but their faithfulness toward the empire stood as strong as a rock, and is nowhere equally encountered among tribes which had submitted and pledged allegiance to the empire. However, this is overlooked in the official history. The number of Monguor soldiers who died in the wars is not known, but it is known that in each of the Monguor clans one or more of the chiefs died on one or another field of battle. The glorious military achievements of the Monguors are many.

The history of these five centuries is also the history of the development of the country and its thorough Sinization. The Monguors who had once controlled much of this country saw Chinese officials gradually take into their hands its civil and military administration, trying to relegate them to their own poor country. The Monguors felt that they were barbarians, but they admired the Chinese civilization and aspired to share its benefits. These five centuries are the time of the Sinization of the Monguors, which started with their chiefs, as among all the nomads. The boys of the

t'u-ssu clans attended Chinese schools and many among them obtained literary and military degrees, became Confucianists and officials in the Chinese administration. Meritorious t'u-ssu were rewarded with honorary titles, and the growing standard of civilization in the families of the t'u-ssu chiefs spread among the subjects.

This history also describes the amalgamation of many tribes of diverse origin, among themselves and with the few Chinese of the country, in a compound which constitutes a notable part of today's Huangchung population.

Long times of distress and suffering endured at the hands of a common enemy bring destitute people close together. Tribes come to shelter together, share each other's houses and land, try to talk together, marry, etc., and if the circumstances last for a long time, as was the case in Huangchung, the customs and languages become unified and an amalgamation takes place.

It is in order not to obliterate the different elements of the compound which constitutes the Huangchung population that the study starts with notes relating to the tribes which lived in Huangchung—T'u-fan, Tanghsiang, Tibetans, Shat'o Turks, and several thousands of Uighurs—with notes about the time and the circumstances of their arrival, the country in which they were settled, and the part they played in the history of the country of Huangchung.

The notes have not only an ethnographical importance, but also a bearing on the administration of these people, the study of their customs and the religions they practiced.

The history of the Monguor clan of the Lu family, according to its family chronicles is discussed because the Lu clan is the only clan which has been able to keep its chronicles. The chronicles of all the other clans have disappeared during the revolts which ravaged the country many times. The chronicles of the Lu clan, however, shed light on the organization of the other clans, their administration, their relations with the empire, the process of Sinization, the peculiar mentality of the families of the chiefs of the clans, etc., and complement our knowledge of the Monguor t'u-ssu families.

The history of the Lu family is significant also in the way it shows the interest of the emperor in the Monguor clans which rendered so much help in the time of the inroads of brigands and the wars with the barbarians. This interest is displayed by the granting of titles and promotions; by inviting the chiefs to the capital, offering dinners and entertainments, making them admire the splendor of the palaces, gratifying them with honorary distinctions such as the peacock plume and the jade girdle, and with gifts of clothing, silks, satins, and porcelains; by ordering the civil authorities to build honorific arches in the cities to honor

---

[1] A *t'u-ssu* was the "local chief" of a clan who had been appointed to his office by the sovereign state of which the Monguor clans were quasi-feudal frontier dependants. When the Ming dynasty invested a Monguor clan chief with the title of T'u-ssu he became a Chinese official while continuing to be also the chief of his clan. The institution of t'u-ssu was one that had been developed for the special purpose of administering non-Chinese tribal groups on the frontier of the Empire. See Louis M. J. Schram, The Monguors of the Kansu-Tibetan Frontier. I. Their origin, history, and social organization, *Trans. Amer. Philos. Soc.* 44 (1): 45–52, 1954 (hereafter referred to as Monguors I).

the eminent chiefs of the clan; and by delegating high officials to present official burials and sacrifices to the deceased chiefs and to read the sacrificial oration composed by the emperor himself as a farewell to the meritorious deceased.

These were some of the means used by the emperor to win the hearts of the Monguors and to make of them defenders of the empire.

It is a pleasure to acknowledge with the appearance of the last part of the study, my indebtedness to the Carnegie Corporation and the American Philosophical Society for the grants which enabled me to complete the work, and to Professor and Mrs. Owen Lattimore for the help they rendered and for their assistance in the preparation of the study.

I cannot conclude without remembering with gratitude the special debt I owe to Miss Theresa A. Tims, and without expressing my sincerest appreciation of her considerable help, graciously rendered, in correcting and preparing the English draft and the editing of the publication with wonderful patience and good humor through long hours.

NOTE ON THE CHINESE SOURCES

In the pages that follow frequent reference is made to three Chinese compilations, the *Annals* of the *Fu* or Prefecture of Hsining, and of the Province of Kansu. The full titles of these three works are:

1. *Hsining fu hsin chih* (New annals of Hsining prefecture) in 12 volumes containing 40 *chuan* or chapters, compiled between 1755 and 1762 and probably published soon after 1762. The editor of these "new" Annals had before him the original edition of 1595 and a corrected edition of 1657. I have never had access to either of these older editions.

2. *Kansu hsin t'ung chih* (New collected annals of Kansu) in 100 *chuan,* printed in the Hsuan-t'ung period (1909–1911). The edition is called "new" because it is based on an older original the compilation of which was begun in 1728 and completed in 1736. The older edition has been inaccessible to me.

3. *Wu liang k'ao chih* (Annals of the prefecture of Liangchow), printed in 1749, including the Annals of the subprefecture of P'ing fan.

L. M. J. S.

A NOTE ON TRANSLITERATIONS

OWEN AND ELEANOR LATTIMORE

As the main significance of Father Schram's work is its presentation of historical and sociological material, no attempt has been made, in editing his text, to be over pedantic in the transliteration of Chinese and Mongol names of people, places, institutions or titles. We have adopted instead what we hope are rules of common sense.

For Chinese, the system of transliteration with the widest international acceptance is that of Wade, and we have used it except in the case of geographical names where there is a well-established English spelling. For instance the strict Wade transcription for the name of the city of Lanchow would be Lan Chou, but we use Lanchow because that form is internationally well established. Similarly we write Szechwan (the name of a province) instead of Ssu Ch'uan.

For transcribing Mongol (and Manchu) there is no widely accepted system, but fortunately the sounds of these languages can be indicated with reasonable accuracy by the use of ordinary letters and without diacritical marks, as in the name Monguor itself. Monguor, Mongol, and Manchu names are therefore written in this straightforward way when they can be readily identified. There is however a special problem when names in these languages have come down through a Chinese phonetic transcription. The sounds of Chinese match those of Mongol and Manchu very badly, and it is therefore frequently difficult to restore the original. In such cases we have simply written out the name in its Chinese form, using the Wade system, with hyphens between the syllables. As an example of the choices that have to be made on an *ad hoc* basis, take the name (or title) that is usually written Jenghis or Genghis. A closer rendering of the Mongol sound and spelling is Chinggis. In Chinese this becomes Ch'eng-chi-ssu.

Titles, ranks, and names of offices are here rendered in the same rule of thumb way.

THE MONGUORS OF THE KANSU-TIBETAN FRONTIER
PART III. RECORDS OF THE MONGUOR CLANS
History of the Monguors in Huangchung and the Chronicles of the Lu Family

Louis M. J. Schram, C.I.C.M.

CONTENTS

I. HISTORY OF THE MONGUOR CLANS IN HUANGCHUNG

The Mongols, commanded by General Subudei, invaded the region of Huangchung in 1227 and invested the city of Hsining, which they conquered (*Annals* of Hsining **31B**: 8a and *Annals* of Kansu **46**: 20a).

In order to understand conditions in Huangchung at the time of the Mongol conquest it is necessary to take notice of the peculiar geographical conditions of the country, and to bear in mind the circumstances which had caused the presence in Huangchung in 1227 of the remnants of so many T'u-fan and Tang-hsiang tribes, of many thousands of Uighurs and of many Shat'o tribes. The social organization of this heterogeneous population and the ways in which it behaved will explain the policy adopted by the Mongol dynasty, followed by the Ming dynasty (1368), continued during the Ch'ing dynasty (1644) and even during more than ten years under the Republic (1911).

GEOGRAPHICAL CONDITIONS

The Province of Kansu is divided geographically into three parts: West Kansu, Huangchung, and East Kansu, separated from one another by the range of the Southern Mountains (Nan Shan) and the Yellow River, both running in a northeasterly direction. The Nan Shan range separates West Kansu from Huangchung, and the Yellow River separates Huangchung from East Kansu.

West Kansu, a long narrow strip, a corridor situated between the bases of the Nan Shan range and the Gobi desert, is of primary importance because through that country runs the old transcontinental silk trade road, already opened in the second century B.C.[1] and because

this road was the only one which secured communication between the Chinese capital and its western colonies. Until 1882 Turkistan was a part of Kansu Province. Military colonies had been established along this long corridor between 140 and 86 B.C. in order to protect the communications against the turbulent Turkish barbarians of the Gobi and the savage Tibetans. Passes running through the Nan Shan secured communications between West Kansu and Huangchung.

In A.D. 872 Kanchow, one of the oldest colonies situated in the corridor, became the seat of the Uighur Khanate.[2] Uighur princes ruled in Kanchow until 1028. At that time their realm was conquered by the Hsi-hsia. The Mongols occupied the country in 1227.[3]

East Kansu is separated from Huangchung on the west by the Yellow River, on the east it is bounded by

---

[1] Louis M. J. Schram, The Monguors of the Kansu-Tibetan Frontier. II. Their religious life, *Trans. Amer. Philos. Soc.* **47** (1): 9, 1957 (hereafter referred to as Monguors II).

[2] James Russell Hamilton, *Les Ouighours a l'époque des Cinq Dynasties, Bibliothèque de L'institut des Hautes Études Chinoises* **10**: 14, Paris, Imprimerie nationale, 1955. Uighurs (called Huei-hou, Hue-ho) of Hunnic origin belong to the group of the Tolos tribes (p. 1). Their empire in Mongolia, which lasted from 745 until 840, controlled the region from Manchuria to the Altai and the territory of the Karluk in the T'ien Shan; its capital (Karabalgason) was situated on the Orkhon River. At the time of the destruction of their empire at the hands of the Khirgiz, a group of Uighurs fled into the region situated between Ku Ch'a and Besbalik in Turkistan (p. 18). It offered its offices to the Chinese army (Kuei-yi-chun) of General Chang Yi-ch'ao, garrisoned in the prefecture of Sha Chou. It fought the Tibetans in combination with the Chinese (p. 13), and in 872 these Uighurs, allies of the Chinese, settled in Kanchow. Others settled in Shi Chou (Karakhadjo), and so the northern part of Turkistan had become an Uighur country (pp. 14, 15, 16). The Uighurs were converted to Manicheism in 762–763. They were the educators of the Turco-Mongol peoples from the ninth to the thirteenth century (p. 6).

[3] Edw. Chavannes, *T'oung Pao* **5**: 215, 1904. O. Franke, *Geschichte des Chinesischen Reiches* **2**: 493, 501, Leipzig, Verlag Von Walter De Gruyter, 1936.

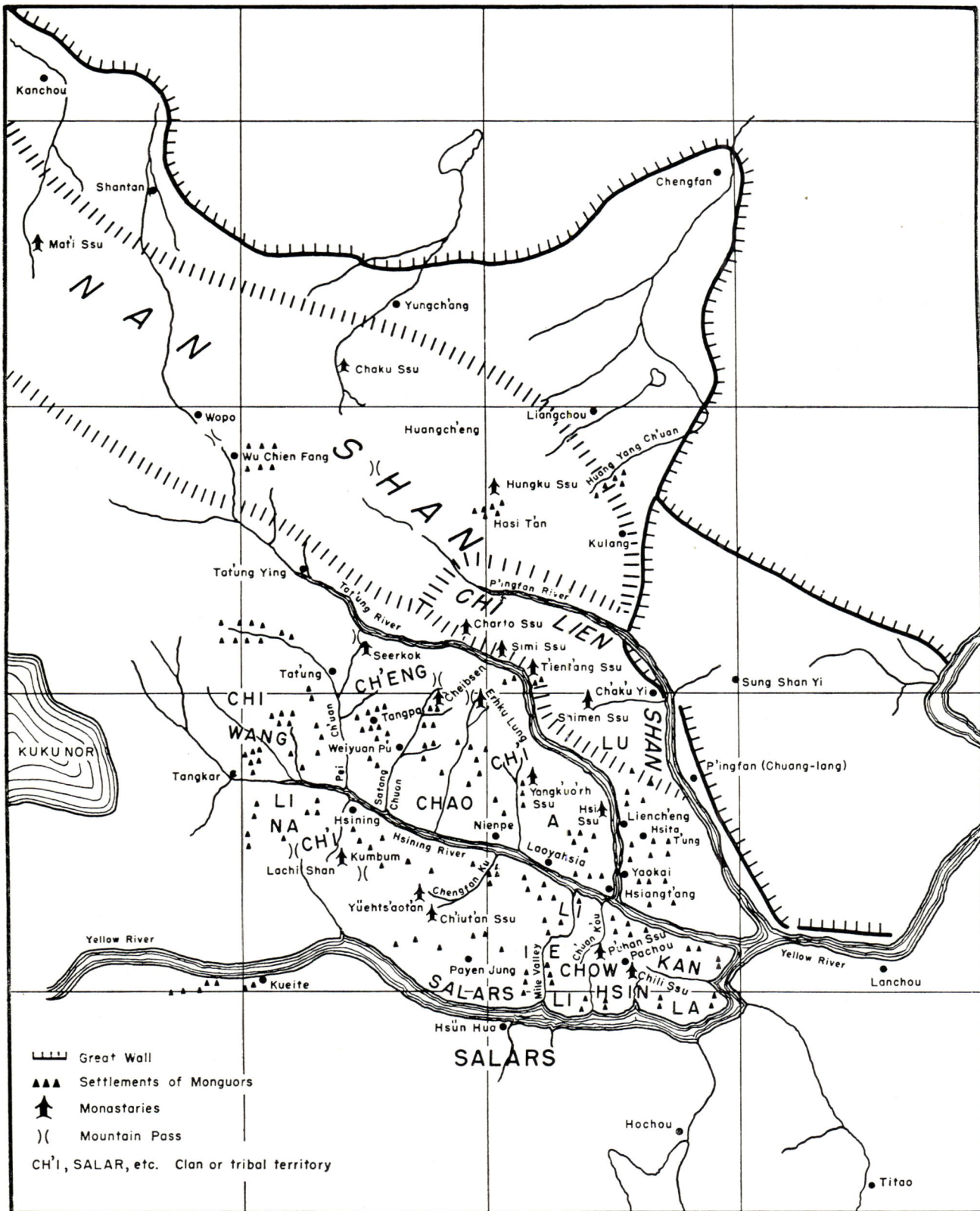

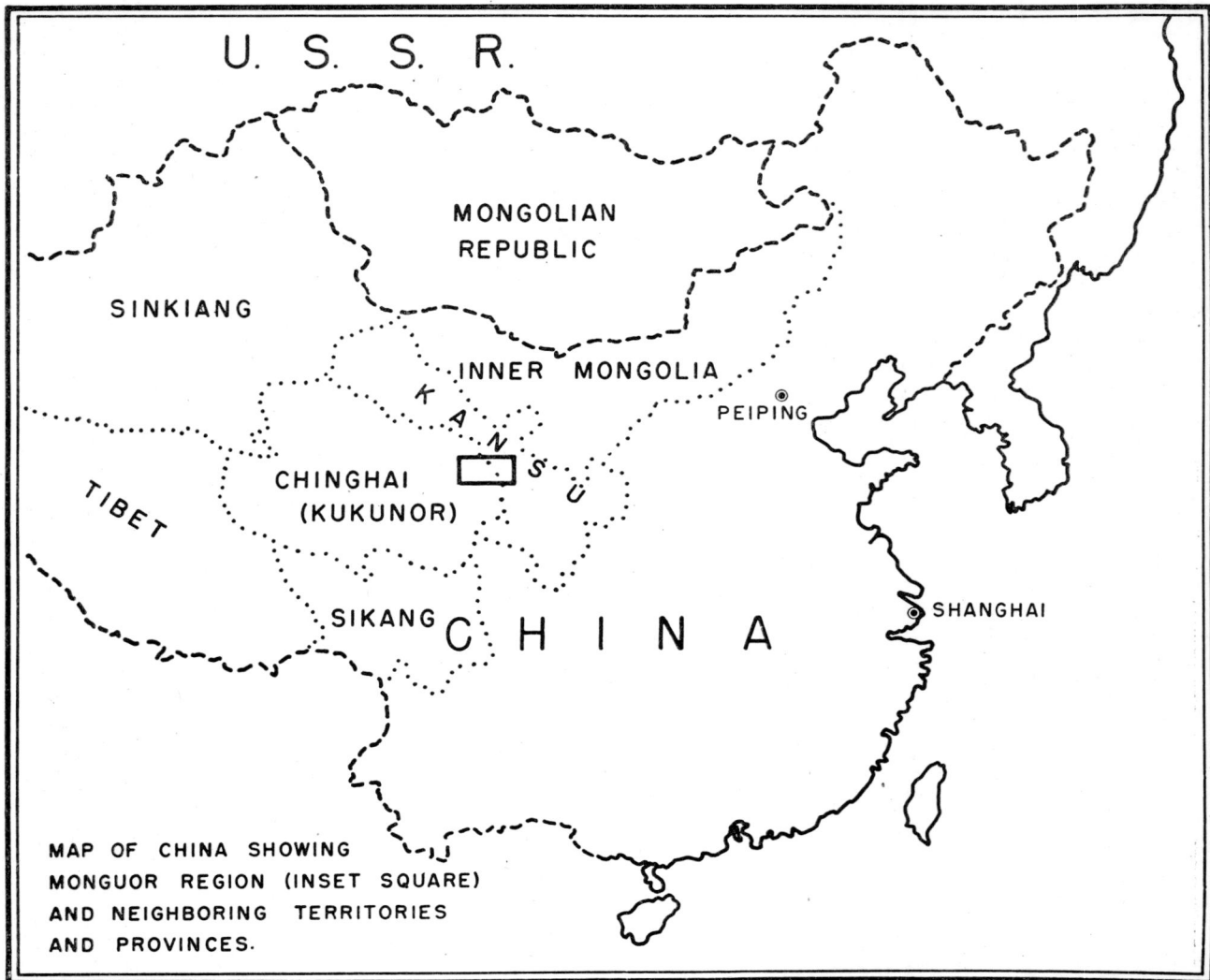

MAP OF CHINA SHOWING
MONGUOR REGION (INSET SQUARE)
AND NEIGHBORING TERRITORIES
AND PROVINCES.

the province of Shensi, and on the south by the province of Szechwan. During the period of the Han Dynasties, 202 B.C. until A.D. 220, Ch'iang (Tibetan) tribes roamed with their herds in the northern part of Tibet and Kokonor, in large parts of Shensi Province and East Kansu, and on the borders of Szechwan, Hupei, and Shansi Provinces.[4]

East Kansu had always been a region of momentous military importance, on account of its proximity to the city of Sian, situated in Shensi Province, which many times had been the capital of the empire, and on account of the impending threat of invasions on the part of the Tang-hsiang (Tibetan) tribes, whose cradle was situated in Sung P'an in North Szechwan, along the southern boundary of Shensi, where practically no boundaries were defined. The forays of Tibetans used to pass through East Kansu. Today, a city still exists called

Ti Tao, which means "the way of the barbarians," and is a reminder of these fateful days.[5] It was in order to cope with this crucial problem that so many Chinese military colonies had been established in East Kansu during the Tang dynasty, the Wu Tai (or Five Dynasties), and the Sung and Ming dynasties, and that intermittently new colonies and fortresses had to be built in order to stem the invasions and revolts of Tang-hsiang, T'u-fan, Hsi Hsia, and Mongols.[6] The Mongols at the time of their conquest of China had a lot of trouble in East Kansu and West Shensi, subduing the Tibetan and Uighur tribes which during the previous dynasties had submitted to China but whose loyalty and dependence always remained questionable.

[4] Wolfram Eberhard, *Kultur und Siedlung der Randvölker Chinas*, 67, Leiden, Brill, 1942.

[5] See the remarkable study of Owen Lattimore, *The frontier in history*, X Congresso internazionale di Science Storiche, Roma, 4: 11, Settembre 1955. Relazioni 1: 106, Firenze, 1955.
[6] Franke, *op. cit.* 3: 22, 1937. *Annals* of Kansu 45: 12. In 1096 more than fifty forts and colonies had been built against the Hsi Hsia in one year.

Huangchung is bounded on the north by the Chi Lien Shan, a range of lower mountains which constitutes the northern end of the Nan Shan range. Being less high and abrupt, it provides an easy access to the countries of Ninghsia, Ordos, and Mongolia. In order to prevent the junction of the barbarians of Mongolia with those of Huangchung, the Chinese General Ho Ch'u-ping, in 116 B.C. (Monguors I : 19) established the first colonies in Huangchung. It was along the natural depressions in the Chi Lien range that the Tibetans many times invaded the country of the Ninghsia, Ordos, and Shansi borders, and that Mongols made inroads from Ordos into Huangchung and Kokonor. On the south side no high mountains or large rivers separate Huangchung from Kokonor and Tibet, through which many roads provide access to Central Asia.

Geographically, Huangchung, bounded by the large Yellow River on the south and east, by low mountains on the north, and spreading wide open toward the southwest facing Kokonor and Tibet, seems to be a peninsula of Kokonor and Tibet protruding into China. Huangchung being more remote from the capital of the empire than East Kansu, the threat of inroads from the empire was apparently less imminent; and the importance of its trade being not comparable with that of the colonies situated in the corridor of West Kansu across the Nan Shan range, fewer colonies had been established there than in East Kansu. Every time rebellions or dynastic troubles occurred in China, the Tibetans of Kokonor helped their brothers of Huangchung destroy the colonies; however, as long as the empire was at peace and its military power intimidated the restless Tibetans, Chinese officials could proceed with collecting the tribute of horses from the tribes governed by their own chiefs, and the ways leading to Kokonor could be guarded.

The whole of Kansu, populated by barbarians, was for centuries considered as a colony and not as a province proper. Only in 1665 was the province of Kansu established, and even up to the Republic (1911) Kansu was ruled together with Shensi by a viceroy. Only since 1928 has the province of Ch'inghai been established, encompassing Huangchung and a part of Kokonor.

THE POPULATION OF HUANGCHUNG AT THE TIME OF THE CONQUEST BY THE MONGOLS

HUANGCHUNG DURING THE TANG PERIOD

In 1227 when the Mongols conquered Huangchung, the country was inhabited by depleted tribes of Tibetans, Uighurs, and Shat'o, without cohesion among them. The country had passed through the ordeal of centuries of wars, and the Chinese colonies had long since vanished.

The Tang dynasty (620–906) had been unable to cope with the turbulent empire of the T'u-fan contemporaneously founded in Lhasa, whose floods of untamed hordes had poured ceaselessly into the regions of Sung P'an in northwest Szechwan, and up into Kokonor, Shensi, and Kansu Provinces. Srong-btsan sgam-po, who had united the T'u-fan tribes into a nation, died in 650. He is credited with having initiated his subjects in Buddhism and in the Indian and Chinese civilizations.[7] Three times, in 730, 783, and 821, the Tang emperors had made treaties with the T'u-fan, fixing the limits of both empires.[8] The text of the last treaty, chiseled on a slab, is still preserved in Lhasa.[9] In Huangchung, in the village of Topa, 60 li west of Hsining (Annals of Hsining 7 : 7) and northwest of the city of Tatung (Annals of Hsining 7 : 17) still exist steles fixing the western limits of Huangchung. The texts are now indecipherable, except for a few characters.

The T'u-fan hordes smote upon the region of Sung P'an, in northwest Szechwan, the cradle of the Tibetan Tang-hsiang tribes. In 627 two groups of Tang-hsiang tribes, for fear of the invaders, fled to East Kansu. One group, called Tung-shan-pu, settled in the region of the modern Ch'ing-yang fu in East Kansu; the other group, called P'ing-hsia-pu, settled in the region of Mi Chih, in northwest Shensi. The leading tribe of the last group was the Topa, formerly pressed by the T'u-fan, which had submitted to the T'u-yu-hun.[10]

The P'ing-hsia-pu tribes of Shensi, during the revolt of Nan Lu Shan (756–764), had helped save the tottering throne of the Tang dynasty. Their chief had been rewarded with the name of the dynasty, Li, and the administration of some districts had been granted to the group. During the internal troubles which several times beset the empire, the P'ing-hsia-pu group had laid the foundation of its own Hsi Hsia Kingdom, and from 982 on it had considered itself strong enough to antagonize the Sung dynasty (960–1280), openly embarking on the conquest of Kansu and Shensi Provinces. The Hsi Hsia realm vanished at the hands of the Mongols in 1226.[11] Not only did these groups of Tang-hsiang tribes submit to China but, in A.D. 631, 300,000 more Tang-hsiang surrendered, pressed by the T'u-fan, and were settled in East Kansu and on the Shensi borders, where sixteen districts were established by the emperor in the countries assigned to them, garrisons established, and Chinese military officials appointed (Annals of Kansu 45 : 53a).

---

[7] Franke, op. cit. 2 : 373.
[8] Franke, op. cit. 2 : 437, 480, 484.
[9] Franke, op. cit. 2 : 484. Li Fan-koei. Inscription of the Sino-Tibetan treaty 821–822. T'oung Pao 64 : 1 sq., 1956.
[10] Franke, op. cit. 4 : 132. R. A. Stein, Mi-nag et Si-hia. Bulletin École Française Extrême Orient 64 : 228, Paris, 1956. Peter Olbricht, Die Tanguten und ihre Geschichte bis zur Grundung von Si-hia, Central Asiatic Journal 2 : 143. The T'opa founders of the Hsi Hsia might be of Sien-pi origin, 154.
[11] Franke, op. cit. 4 : 133, 134.

In Kokonor T'u-fan hordes attacked the T'u-yu-hun in 634, and drove them out of the country in 672. The T'u-yu-hun, nomad tribes of Sien-pi origin, had been settled in Kokonor since A.D. 280 and, facing extermination after decades of savage wars with the T'u-fan, succeeded in being transplanted by the Chinese in 672 into the region of Ling Wu (Ninghsia) in Ming-sha hsien.[12]

Huangchung (Hsining region) was already invaded by T'u-fan in 629. The T'u-fan administered several crushing defeats to the Chinese troops on the Kokonor borders, in Huangchung and in East Kansu. After the resounding victory of the T'u-fan in 678, the Tang-hsiang tribes settled previously in East Kansu, despairing of the aid and protection of the emperor, submitted to the T'u-fan, and with them fought the Chinese troops, devastating the country. These disastrous events continued indefinitely. The emperor having fled from his capital in 756 on account of the rebellion of An Lu-shan, T'u-fan and Tang-hsiang of East Kansu combined, captured in 763 the capital of the empire, burned the palaces, and looted the city and the neighboring country. The whole of Kansu was lost. The Tsan-p'u of Lhasa appointed his T'u-fan officials and military commanders in Huangchung and East Kansu.[13] The rebellion of the Chinese governors against the emperor had started in 783 and lasted until 787. In 783 the thread of destruction hanging like a Damocles sword over the dynasty, the emperor concluded the negotiation of a treaty with the Tsan-p'u, already initiated in 780. The T'u-fan would help the emperor out of his difficulty and be rewarded with four more prefectures situated southeast of P'ing-liang in East Kansu. The T'u-fan and Tang-hsiang had helped recover the lost capital in 784, but the Chinese refused to give up the four prefectures. The enraged Tibetans furiously invaded the Wei Valley, occupied Yen and Hsia Chou in Shensi and the whole region inside the Yellow River bend, looting and laying waste the countryside. Adding to the frustration of the Chinese, Tibetan armies administered the most crushing defeat to them in Turkistan in 791. Except for Turfan, Turkistan was lost to the Chinese. In 822 there followed the humiliating treaty by which China renounced its rights over Turkistan, over the whole of Kansu and some parts of Shensi. However, forays by savage Tibetan tribes did not cease.[14]

In 842 the Tsan-p'u Ta-mo died without issue, whereupon bitter feuds and sharp cleavages appeared among the T'u-fan governors and military commanders in East Kansu, Huangchung, and Tibet. The doom of the Tibetan nation was sealed, and the time seemed propitious to the Chinese for the recovery of East Kansu and Huangchung. But already in 842, Lun K'ung-jo, a T'u-fan military commander, proclaimed himself supreme chief of all the tribes settled in East Kansu and Huangchung. However, in Hsining there was a T'u-fan governor, Chang-pe-pe, appointed by the former Tsan-p'u. The two groups fought until 850. Chang-pe-pe, betrayed by some of his commanders, was forced to flee across Kanchow to Turkistan with 2,000 men of his group, pursued by Lun K'ung-jo and his 5,000 soldiers to Kua Chou. Before his flight, Chang-pe-pe had entrusted the defense of the city of Hsining to his faithful commander T'o-pa-huai-kuang. Lun K'ung-jo, hearing that the city of Hsining was occupied by T'o-pa-huai-kuang, hurried back and in a rage savagely laid waste the whole of Huangchung and eight cities and districts in East Kansu. After his brutal behavior his troops refused to follow him. He settled in Kuo Chou in Huangchung with the last 200 of his followers. He was beheaded in 866 by the T'u-fan commander of Hsining, T'o-pa-huai-kuang, who sent his head to the emperor. During these troubles Chinese troops had recovered nearly the whole of East Kansu and accepted the submission of the Tibetans of East Kansu (*Annals* of Kansu **45**: 65a, 66b. *Annals* of Hsining **30**: 30, 30a, 31a).

The *Annals* of Kansu record (**45**: 66b) that in 851 the independent Chinese commander Chang I-ch'ao received the appointment of military commander of the Chinese Kuei-i troops garrisoned in Sha Chou. Formerly he had occupied on his own account ten cities, and had sent his brother to offer them to the emperor. The *Annals* of Hsining (**30**: 30, 31a) record that Chang I-ch'ao pacified Hsining and Kuo Chou in 851 and in that way East Kansu and Huangchung were completely recovered after ninety years (763–852).[15] The *Annals* of Hsining (**30**: 30, 31a) also note that the Uighur commander Pukukun of Besbalik occupied the fateful city of Hsining in 866 and both *Annals* finally note: "at these times China was beset with many problems and its orders were not obeyed by the Kuei-i troops." The *Annals* of Kansu add: "in 872 the Uighurs captured Kanchow and many more districts." The history of Huangchung and Turkistan is very confused for this period.

The point of ruin and disintegration was reached among the Tibetan tribes, in East Kansu and Huangchung, after ten years of bloody fights between Lun K'ung-jo and Chang-pe-pe. The havoc savagely wrought among the tribes, tearing asunder their own tribes, transferring allegiance from one chief to another,

[12] Franke, *op. cit.* **2**: 397. Schram, Monguors I: 19. *Annals* of Kansu **45**: 55a. R. A. Stein, Mi-nag et Si-hia, *Bull. École Française d'Extrême Orient* **44**: 223.

[13] The Tsan-p'u was the representative of the T'u-fan hierarchy; he presided over the tribes who had pledged allegiance or had been subdued; he was the arbiter of the frequently conflicting interests arising among them. The stronger the repute of the Tsan-p'u the richer the pillages to be expected, and the stronger were the bonds which tied the nation together.

[14] *Annals* of Kansu **45**: 51, 62. Ch'u T'ang Shu, **146**: 3–5. Franke, *op. cit.* **2**: 398, 399, 438, 439, 466, 469, 480, 484. *Annals* of Hsining **30**: 25–30.

[15] Hamilton, *op. cit.* **10**: 13–16, 94–95, 128–129.

and systematically devastating the country in which they lived, explains a fact unique in history. The slaves possessed by the tribes (victims of wars apportioned to the chiefs) being without lords or depending on proprietors who could no longer control them or afford to nourish them, were able to abandon their chiefs and to establish a tribe of their own, called in history the Slave Tribe, "Hun-pu" or "Wu-mu." The slaves submitted in a group to the emperor in 862; they were settled in several districts of Kansu and even of Tunhuang, where they engaged in farming. A group of them was settled in Kuo Chou in Huangchung (*Annals* of Kansu **45**: 66*b*. *Annals* of Hsining **30**: 30, 31*a*).[16]

However, China was not able to pay much attention to East Kansu and Huangchung during the next twenty-five years (852–875). In 875 the terrible revolution of Huang Ch'ao started which lasted for nine years, followed by the disastrous armed competitions among the Chinese generals, and the end of the effete Tang dynasty in 906.

Then five insignificant dynasties, called Wu Tai, or the Five Dynasties, succeeded one another, accompanied by ruthless wars and destruction (907–960).[17]

HUANGCHUNG DURING THE WU TAI (FIVE DYNASTIES) PERIOD, 907–960

Three important facts have to be recorded concerning Huangchung during the Five Dynasties (907–960). First, the presence in Huangchung in 939, in the country situated between Kanchow and Hsining, of Shat'o Chu-hsieh tribes belonging to the group of the founders of the petty Shat'o Hu Tang dynasty (923–936), attested in *Wu-tai shih-chi* (**74**: 10*b*, 11*a*). At what time or in what circumstances these tribes had settled in that part of Huangchung is not known (*Monguors,* **I**: 30). However, the powerful Monguor clan of the Li t'u-ssu originated later from among the Shat'o Chu-hsieh tribes of that country.

DISINTEGRATION OF THE SHAT'O NATION AND HUANGCHUNG AND EAST KANSU

The second fact is the disintegration of the Shat'o nation. In 947 K'ai-p'ing fu the capital of the Shat'o Hu-tsin dynasty was taken by the Ch'i-tan. The Shat'o emperor and his family were deported to Huang Lung in northern Manchuria. The Ch'i-tan emperor, for fear of the revolting governor of Szechwan Province, had decided to garrison the numerous defeated Shat'o troops on the frontiers of Szechwan, and to send their wives and children into north Shansi as security for the fidelity of their husbands, promising to relieve them every year for a visit to their families.

Ho Chien, of Uighur origin, governor of the three districts of Chin, Chieh, and Ch'eng Chou in East Kansu, faithful retainer of the Shat'o dynasty, distrusting these promises and enraged on account of the ruthless behavior of the Ch'i-tan, refused to surrender his troops to them and to defend their frontiers. He offered his troops and the districts he controlled to the governor of Szechwan. During these fateful times of wars and slaughter, the petty Hu Han (947–950) and Hu Chu (951–960) dynasties had succeeded successively to the Hu Chin dynasty of the Shat'o, and in 955 the governor of Szechwan and the troops of Ho Chien were defeated by Emperor Shi Tsung of the Hu Chu dynasty.

Now was the propitious time for the Shat'o troops to vanish with their families in Kansu among the Tibetans, for east, north, and northwest China were troubled by wars. Kansu, during the time of the ephemeral Shat'o dynasties (923–947) had constituted an integral part of their empire, and the Shat'o officials were cognizant of the chiefs of the Tibetan tribes living in East Kansu and Huangchung. The poor and destitute Shat'o having no way to move, many individuals and minor and major groups among them must have been happy to enlist and to disappear among the Tibetan tribes, acknowledging the authority of the chieftains and accepting the name of their tribe. They must have preferred to flee to the most remote mountainous southern part of East Kansu. Incidentally, it is noted among the 520 tribes of the powerful Tibetan chief, the later t'u-ssu Yang settled in the remote T'ao Chou, a tribe called the Shat'o tribe (*Annals* of Kansu **42**: 64). A group of Ongutt Shat'o had fled to remote Lin T'ao, the region of the Tibetans. "They were Nestorians, they were taken prisoners by the Chin (1125–1235) and settled in Manchuria in the beginning of the twelfth century."[18]

Many groups among them fled to Huangchung and settled in the region between Kanchow and Hsining, joining the Shat'o who were living there in 939 (Monguors I) for at the time the Monguors conquered Hsining the entire region 60 li north and northwest of Hsining was inhabited by Shat'o.

That in 947 the Shat'o easily dispersed among the Tibetans, acknowledging their chiefs as their own, is quite normal, for their national pride must have been at very low ebb. Their petty first dynasty (923–936) had been controlled by three emperors of three different families and by a fourth whose mother only was known. The second dynasty (936–946) had been controlled by a Shat'o commander who had usurped the imperial power. The protracted wars had exhausted the discontented tribes, who did not know for whom they were fighting. The family of the founding ancestor of the nation had been obliterated and its doom sealed.[19]

[16] Stein, *op. cit.* **44**: 228.
[17] Hamilton, *op. cit.* 108, 128–129.

[18] P. Pelliot, Chrétiens d'Asie centrale et d'Extreme Orient, *T'oung Pao,* **15** (5): 630, 1914.
[19] Franke, *op. cit.* **4**: 42, 55, 58, 68, 1948.

FIRST DATA ABOUT BUDDHISM IN HUANGCHUNG

The third fact is the foundation in 940 of the monastery of Dantig (Sha-ch'ung) situated southeast of Hsining, on the northern bank of the Yellow River. It was founded by dGeba rab-gsal, a lama of the Zin-dpon hermitage, who had been ordained by three lamas who had fled from Tibet on account of the persecution of Buddhism in Lhasa, and had arrived in Hsining, via Khotan, and the country of the Hor (Uighurs). At that time in the region of Dantig there already existed great hermitages. The three learned men of Tibet were buried in a temple at Hsining. In sPari (the region between the Tatung River and the Nan Shan to P'ing Fan), there exists a stone pillar with the names of the three men chiseled on it. Later six more celebrated lamas fled from Tibet to Hsining. Probably the building of these hermitages happened during the span of time between the introduction of Buddhism in Tibet by Sron-btsan sgam-po who died in 650 and its persecution in 841 and especially during the years 756 until 842, when the Tsan-p'u of Lhasa controlled the entire Huangchung and East Kansu and appointed his officials. Lamas must have followed the invading T'u-fan tribes and built the hermitages and the temple in Hsining.[20] However, we have to take stock of the very judicious remark of Professor Tucci that at that time Buddhism was spread by single lama hermits and not by groups of organized monks as was the case after the reform of Tsung Khapa, born in 1354.

HUANGCHUNG DURING THE SUNG PERIOD, 960–1280

The Sung dynasty succeeded the fateful Five Dynasties in 960. However, it could not interfere effectively with Huangchung before 1086. Its action was limited to granting titles to Tibetan chieftains. During one and one-half centuries (875–1036) Huangchung was a no-man's-land inhabited by depleted predatory tribes each of them obeying a chieftain and having troubles among themselves (*Annals* of Hsining **30**: 1, 2). Several inroads were made by them on the frontiers. They used to lie athwart the trade roads, pillaging traders and ambassadors coming to court with wares and tribute, making them prisoners and selling them and their wares and tribute.[21] Nobody could cross their country without taking his life in his hands.

The waxing power of the turbulent Hsi Hsia and their inroads into East Kansu and persistent threats of invasions in Huangchung after 982 must have seriously intimidated the scattered Tibetan tribes in Huangchung and East Kansu, facing extermination one after another,

because in 1008 Wen-pu-ku,[22] chief of the important T'u-fan tribe of Mao-ch'uan (the actual subprefecture Nien-pe), went to court to surrender, leading forty-five other T'u-fan and Tang-hsiang tribes of Ho-shi.[23] However, perspicacious T'u-fan leaders should long since have considered a wrong policy the reliance upon the protection of the Sung dynasty, which had to contend with serious troubles from inside and to fight the empire of the Liao barbarians in north China and at the same time to repell the invasions of the turbulent Hsi Hsia in East Kansu and Shensi. Therefore some of them must have considered that the genuine solution of the problem would be not to rely upon China, but upon themselves, rebuilding a T'u-fan Kingdom and welding the tribes in a unit under the chieftainship of a descendant of the founder of the kingdom.

Ho-lang-yeh-hsien, T'u-fan chief of Ho Chou tribes in East Kansu, was by accident or design in Kao Ch'ang in 1008 as the guest of the T'u-fan tribes of the petty Mo-yu kingdom. There he met a handsome and intelligent boy of twelve years of age, called Chiossulo, a genuine offspring of the imperial Tsan-p'u family of Lhasa.[24] He invited the boy to Ho Chou. The lama Li Li-tsun, chief of the important tribe of Tsung K'o [25] and Wen-pu-ku the powerful chief of the tribes of Mao Ch'uan made an agreement with Ho Chou, and succeeded in moving the boy to Kuo Chou in Huangchung, acknowledging him as their chief. Confidence revived among the federated tribes in Huangchung and Ho Chou. Chiossulo was moved into the city of Tsung K'o and Li Lama appointed as minister. As cohesion among the tribes increased, the old predatory instinct was revived. In 1015 the lama, puffed up with pride, went plundering with the T'u-fan of Niku (region of the actual Lanchow) but was defeated by the Chinese general Ts'ao Wei in San-tu-ku and in the region of Hsi Liang. After these disastrous expeditions Chiossulo dismissed his minister, abhorred by the tribes. He left Tsung K'o, moved to Mao-ch'uan, and appointed Wen-pu-ku his minister.

In 1016 Chiossulo deputed chiefs of his tribes to convey to the court excuses for the inroads made by Li Lama, presenting his submission and a gift of 583 horses. At the same time, on account of the persistent

---

[20] George N. Roerich, The Blue Annals by 'Gos lo-tsa-la, *Jour. Royal Asiatic Society of Bengal,* **2** (1): 63, 1949. E. Obermiller, *History of Buddhism* by Buston Rin-po-che, **2**: 201, 1931. Monguors II: 12, 13.

[21] Hamilton, *op. cit.,* 108.

[22] Stein, *op. cit.,* 232.

[23] *Sung Shih* **492**: 8, 9, 10.

[24] "The T'u-fan dynasty founded in the 7th century by Sron-btsan sgam-po, consisted of tribes, not always on good terms with one another, welded into temporary unity. When king Lang-dharma started the persecution of Buddhism in 842 and was murdered the same year, the dynasty fell, never to rise again, and its military power vanished. However, the royal family was not wiped out with the end of the dynasty. Indeed Lang-dharma's descendants succeeded in founding some new petty kingdoms in the farthest regions of Tibet" (Giuseppe Tucci, *Tibetan painted scrolls* **1**: 3, Roma, 1949). The Mo-yu kingdom in Kao-ch'ang must have been a kingdom of the same pattern (*Sung Shih* **492**: 2b).

[25] Tsung K'o is the region situated southwest of P'ing-jung-i which is located 80 li east of Hsining.

inroads of Hsi Hsia on the Huangchung borders and in East Kansu, the deputation proposed to the emperor that he fight Hsi Hsia in combination with the 60,000 troops Chiossulo commanded. The proposition was hotly debated among the ministers. The emperor, afraid of the revival of a new and terrible Tsan-p'u power, and distrusting the inconstancy and predatoriness of the barbarians, refused the offer. Thereupon the embittered Chiossulo invaded Fu Ch'iang in South Kansu with his troops of Huangchung and Ho Chou, but suffered a striking defeat at the hand of General Ts'ao Wei (*Annals* of Kansu **46**: 6*b*). The commander of the troops of Ho Chou abandoned Chiossulo and submitted to the emperor, enfeebling the position of Chiossulo. In 1028 Hsi Hsia, invading West Kansu, liquidated the kingdom of the Uighurs in Kanchow and so the threat of invasion became more imminent.

Chiossulo and his minister submitted to the emperor in 1032 and were bestowed with titles. However, the Minister Wen Pu Ku revolted against Chiossulo, who killed him and later moved to Hsining. Chiossulo having troubles in his own backyard, Li Yuan-hao, King of Hsi Hsia, seized the opportunity to invade Hsining in 1035, but Chiossulo administered a tremendous defeat. This victory rendered him the master of all of Huangchung.

Li Yuen-hao conquered the districts of Su, Kua, and Sha Chou in West Kansu, commanding the trade roads to Central Asia, in 1036, and started moving T'u-fan and Uighur tribes into his kingdom of Hsi Hsia. Then many T'u-fan tribes, among them the tribes of Niku and several ten thousands of Uighurs preferred to flee to Chiossulo, pledge allegiance to him and settle in Huangchung. The scant population of Huangchung increased to the point where Chiossulo became the ruler of 600,000 subjects and Hsining started flourishing. The Uighurs, reputed traders, used to travel between Central Asia, China, and the Liao empire, and were familiar with the roads running from Hsining through Kokonor and the passes in the Nan Shan leading to Kao Ch'ang[26] and Central Asia. "The traders from all the kingdoms of Central Asia came to Hsining." Hsining thrived with trade; wealth and riches poured into the country and at the same time agriculture developed.[27]

SEVERAL TEN THOUSANDS OF UIGHURS FLED TO HUANGCHUNG

Now the emperor was in a hurry to send an official to congratulate Chiossulo for his resounding victory over the Hsi Hsia, bringing him the titles of military governor of East Kansu and supreme chief of Mao-

ch'uan (i.e., of the entire Huangchung), a gift of 20,000 pieces of silk and a salary, making him understand that he was an official of the empire. At the same time he enjoined him to attack Hsi Hsia in Liangchow. Chiossulo judged his troops too feeble to risk the venture. Another official arrived with the same order. This time Chiossulo treated him very roughly. His behavior was not that of a subject treating with the emperor, but rather that of a nephew talking about an uncle,[28] because two Chinese princesses, Wen Ch'eng in 643 and Kin Ch'eng in 710, had been married to princes of the imperial Tsan-p'u house of Lhasa. The Chinese official readily understood the attitude of Chiossulo and informed the emperor (*Annals* of Kansu **46**: 8*a; Annals* of Hsining **31B**: 2*a*). During thirty years Chiossulo did not care for the empire which intermittently waged war with Hsi Hsia in East Kansu and Shensi with varied fortune, nor did he care for the Chinese officials whom the emperor tried to appoint in Huangchung; he cared only for his own kingdom, appointing his officials in Huangchung and on the East Kansu borders. Huangchung was the only country where people lived peacefully engrossed in agriculture and where trade boomed.

HSINING IN THE HEYDAY OF ITS GLORY

Chiossulo was in the heyday of his glory. He rebuilt the city of Hsining. According to the notes recorded by a Chinese official who at that time had been sent to confer with Chiossulo,[29] the circumference of the city was 20 li. The city was protected by a strong, high wall dotted with towers, and eight gates secured access to the city. In the center of this enormous city was constructed a large fortress having four strong towers at the corners. This fortress must have corresponded to the actual city of Hsining and the enormous outer city must have been built to secure a refuge for the surrounding people and their herds at the time of inroads from invading tribes. Chiossulo resided in the fortress in a sumptuous palace, whose roofs were covered with glazed tiles. In this city was a large hall built on a terrace having eight steps and a sumptuous entrance supported by huge pillars. The administration buildings were constructed inside the city, two small palaces for the princesses of the Ch'i Tan and of the Hsi Hsia, and a splendid temple in which was throned a gilded Buddha statue, ten feet high, adorned with strings of pearls and a precious

[26] Kao Ch'ang is also called Turfan, Hsi Chou. In that region must have been the kingdom of Mo-yu where Chiossulo was born.

[27] *Sung Shih,* **492**: 8, 10, 11, 13. *Sung Shih* 251: 13. *Annals* of Kansu **46**: 6, 7, 8. *Annals* of Hsining **30B**: 1, 2, 3; **33A-B.**

[28] A. Rona Tas, Social terms in the list of grants of the Tibetan Tunhuang Chronicle, *Acta Orientalia,* V, 5: 266, 1955. Relationship between the Chinese emperor and the Tibetan king, of uncle and nephew on the maternal side, essentially reflects the Tibetan avuncular system; this relationship, which used to determine the mutual position of the two rulers, is rooted in social history.

[29] Enoki, *op. cit.,* 90, 91. Oshono kika keiryaku ni tsuite (On the *Hsi-ho ching-lueh* of Wang Ch'ao) in Mokoga Huho, Tokyo (*Meng-ku hsueh-pao,*) I, Shuo fu, **15**: 12 *a–b*.

mantle. Trade was transacted in this city, where shops had been built and traders, artisans, and well-to-do people lived. In the outer city was a large terrace with three steps where every three years Heaven and Earth were worshipped, and also two smaller fortresses. More than one thousand houses were built in the outer city and many Buddhist temples with glazed tile roofs, and abodes for the lamas. Half of the buildings in the inner and outer cities were Buddhist buildings. Lamas presided at all the public ceremonies and participated at the councils of the chief. Five li outside the outer city, to the west, was built a very large lamasery with abodes for five hundred lamas and a splendid temple.

These notes written by the Chinese official prove that Chiossulo was fond of display and munificence, that his realm was flourishing and opulent and that he was a very fervent Buddhist, reigning over a Buddhist people and surrounded by lamas whom he revered. Hsining seems to have been a small Lhasa. Chiossulo was a descendant of princes who had lived in Lhasa, and the old traditions prevailing in Lhasa must have been fresh and living in his family and among his officials.

It is worth noticing that in the description of the opulent city written by the Chinese official, after many thousand Uighurs had surrendered and pledged allegiance to Chiossulo, not a single mention is recorded of a Manichean temple or Nestorian church. The Uighurs are known to have been professing Manicheans although many among them must also have been fervent Buddhists or shamanists or perhaps Nestorians. The Uighurs at the time of their arrival at Hsining must have been accompanied by their religious leaders and would normally have built some temples.

In the *Annals* of Hsining (**15**: 2*b*), however, is noted a Pei-i-ssu the Temple of the White Clothes,[30] the stereotypical designation of Nestorian temples. This temple was situated north of the outer city and is the only Nestorian temple recorded in the *Annals*. The date of its construction is not recorded.

Chiossulo died in 1065 having had to defend twice more his independent kingdom against the Hsi Hsia, in 1058 and 1065 (*Annals* of Hsining **31B**: 2*a–b*, 3*a*, 33*a*).

This history of Chiossulo is of overriding importance for the study of the Monguors. Unfortunately, I overlooked it at the time I prepared Part I of the study. It reveals how at the time of the conquest of Huangchung by the Mongols (1227) and the Ming (1368), the population of the country had come to consist of T'u-fan tribes already mixed with Tang-hsiang tribes, a group of the Slave tribes and strong groups of Uighurs and Shat'o. It sheds light on names of tribes of Monguor commoners pointing to their Turkish and Tibetan origin. The fact that several thousand Uighur Turks had fled to Huangchung in 1038 from the corridor of West Kansu and pledged allegiance to Chiossulo,

seems to justify and to explain historically my former hypothesis: "It seems a reasonable inference that a fair number of the subjects in the Monguor clans are Turks, but not all of them Shat'o Turks" (Monguors I: 54). "A majority of Turkish elements is probably to be assumed among the commoners of the Monguor clans ruled by the *t'u-ssu*" (Monguors I: 55). That many Uighur Turks are encountered in the clans of the Monguor Shat'o seems normal, for tribes of Turkish origin must have preferred to live together. The fact that all of Huangchung had been occupied by T'u-fan Tibetans since 629 explains that T'u-fan tribes preferred to join the T'u-fan of Hsining rather than to be moved among the Tang-hsiang tribes of Hsi Hsia.

MOSLEM TRADERS IN HSINING

The history of Chiossulo points to the problem of the first appearance of Moslems in Huangchung. The *Sung Shih* (**492**: 13*a*) notes explicitly "that Hsining Uighurs went to Kao Ch'ang along Kokonor and that traders from all the kingdoms of Central Asia came to do business." That the Hsining Uighurs were very well acquainted with those of Turkistan is no wonder, even as the T'u-fan of Hsining were acquainted with those of Kao Ch'ang, for Chiossulo was born in Kao Ch'ang. However, traders did not travel only from Hsining to the oasis east of Tarim, but they traveled also along Kokonor to the oasis of west Tarim, Khotan, Yarkand, etc., and further into India. This last route was already well known in the sixth century A.D.[31] and lamas fleeing the persecution of Buddhism in Lhasa came over Khotan to Hsining. Since 943 the Karakhanids,[32] of Turkish origin, as were the Uighurs, had founded petty realms in the oasis of West Tarim. Their chief had been converted to Islam in 960 and forced his subjects to become Moslems. These Turks, being as sturdy traders as the Uighurs, were very cognizant of the booming trade of Hsining, through which territory they traveled bringing tribute to China,[33] and relations existed between Khotan and the house of Chiossulo itself, whose son Tung-chen had as a concubine a lady born in Khotan, and had adopted her son A li ku and appointed him as his successor in 1086.

Traders, according to the time-honored custom practiced all over China, were federated in guilds, protected by the local officials. They had their own business quarters, their own caravansaries and their permanent agents caring for the interests of the trade. Most of them had their families with them, and it seems very probable that during the booming period of 1038–1086, Moslem traders from West Tarim appeared for the very first time in Huangchung. No wonder that Marco Polo two centuries later noted explicitly the presence of Moslems in Hsining during the Mongol period in

---

[30] Referring to the white clothes worn at the time of baptism.

[31] Chavannes, *op. cit.* **6**: 333, 341.

[32] Hamilton, *op. cit.,* 94, 95.

[33] *Sung Shih* **490**: 7*b*. Franke, *op. cit.* **2**: 501.

1274 and also of Nestorians, probably traders as were the Moslems, originating from Kao Ch'ang.

BUDDHISM IN HUANGCHUNG

The history of Chiossulo has an important bearing upon the history of Buddhism in Huangchung and upon the specific character of Shamanism in the country.

In Part II (8–14) it is noted that, according to the *Annals* of Hsining, the first Buddhist temple in Hsining, the Ta Fo Ssu, had been built during the Yuan period (1280–1368). Since I was conversant with the history of Chiossulo, I suggested on page 12 that most probably during the occupation of Kansu by the Tsan p'u of Lhasa from 763 until 842, lamas would have followed the conquerors and spread Buddhism in Kansu. However, the first historical data are recorded in the *Blue Annals* translated by Roerich, where is noted the foundation of the monastery of Dantig in 940, on the northern borders of the Yellow River in Huangchung, and at the same time that in that country great hermitages already existed. These annals also note the existence in the city of Hsining of a Buddhist temple where Buddhist monks had been buried. These are the first historical data which prove that Buddhism was practiced in Huangchung before 940. Since the description of the city of Hsining during the reign of Chiossulo, who died in 1065, is available, we know that the city of Hsining was a Lhasa in miniature, where lamas stood at the helm, and that therefore, long before the Yuan period, Buddhism flourished on a very large scale.

SHAMANISM AND MANICHEISM

The Uighurs were converted to Manicheism in 762–763 and professed Buddhism and Nestorianism at the same time. At the time of their khanate in Kanchow in 872 their official religion was still Manicheism. Manicheism is based upon the doctrine of the existence of two distinct principles of good and evil, and of two distinct beings impersonating good and evil, both eternal, independent, and mutually antipathetic.

The shamanism of the Monguors (Monguors II: 94–97) has been explained on the one hand by the overwhelming fear of evil spirits existing among the shamanists, and on the other hand by the recognition of their dependence on good spirits in all the circumstances of life. The struggle between both groups of spirits has been recorded during the typical rite against hail. Then the people carry all their good spirits into the fields in the direction of the threatening clouds, and cry to them to fight the evil hail spirits, which they curse awfully. If it happens nonetheless that the crops are destroyed, the people sigh with despair saying: "the good spirits could not match the evil ones."

Professor Wolfram Eberhard,[34] reviewing the chapter on shamanism, suggested judiciously that there

[34] Wolfram Eberhard, *Jour. Amer. Oriental Soc.* **4**: 284, 1957.

might be reason to think seriously of the thesis of the influence of Iranian dualism upon the shamanism of the Monguors and upon that encountered in west China in a contact zone of Tibetan and Chinese populations. He notes that attention has already long ago been drawn to the Iranian elements in Central Asian shamanism. Since it is known that several ten thousands of Manichean Uighurs pledged allegiance to Chiossulo in 1036 and that they were settled in Huangchung and in East Kansu up to the borders of Szechwan, it is easy to agree with the suggestion. Without doubt Iranian elements had had time enough to influence the shamanism of Kansu, for my notes were recorded in 1910–1920, after these Manicheans had lived in the country for six centuries. Iranian influence upon the shamanism of Central Asia may be explained in the same way. The Uighur kingdom was liquidated in 840 by the Kirghiz, after the Uighurs had been converted to Manicheism eighty years earlier. Then they roamed in Turkistan and on the China borders carrying with them their Manicheism and came in contact with the shamanism of Central Asia.

SETTLEMENT OF THE UIGHURS

The arrival of thousands of Tibetans and several ten thousands of Uighurs all fleeing at the same time into Huangchung, driving before them their herds, carrying their belongings, etc., should have created a tremendous and delicate problem for Chiossulo to cope with. All these turbulent people had to be settled without hurting the feelings of the Tibetan tribes subject to him and already living in the country. This tremendous number of tribes must have upset the whole country, as many groups must have tried to occupy the territories which seemed fitting to them and have caused endless troubles.

The *Annals* of Hsining (4: 19a) dealing with the geography of the country note incidently that five thousand T'u-fan horsemen arrived at the well of Fu-t'i, and drove Uighurs who had settled there back to their own country. This well is situated near the well-known old fortress of Shih-pu-ch'eng (*Annals* of Hsining 7: 3a–b). This reveals how delicate a problem Chiossulo had to contend with, and indicates the attitude of the Tibetans toward the Uighurs intruding into their country.

It is impossible to find out which among the numerous tribe names recorded in the *Annals* for the first time in Ming times (1368) are Uighur, Tibetan, or Shat'o names, because all the tribes are generally recorded as being Tibetans.

What tribes were settled in Huangchung in 1008 when the twelve-year-old Chiossulo arrived in the country?

In Mao Ch'uan, the actual subprefecture of Nienpei, is recorded the presence of the important Tibetan tribe, T'u-fan mixed with Tang-hsiang, controlled by Wenpuku; and another important tribe controlled by the lama Li Li-tsung settled in the region of Tsung K'o. A third group is also noted, the group of the Slaves (Wu-mu) who settled in Kuo Chou, 150 li south of Nienpei, in 862.

To be sure, more insignificant tribes must have settled in Huangchung, but their names and the areas occupied are not recorded. Next to the Tibetan groups is recorded the Shat'o chu-hsieh tribe [35] living in a region 100 li south of Kanchow in 939, stretching from the Nan Shan to Hsining (Monguors I: 13b) and encompassing the region of the Tat'ung River. Many Shat'o, after the collapse of their dynasty in 955, had joined this group. These Shat'o were the southern neighbors of the Uighurs of Kanchow for two hundred years, who were a mixture of many tribes blended and fused into the compound that founded the Khanate of Kanchow in 872. Its predatoriness is attested in the history of Turkistan and Kansu.[36] Shat'o and Uighurs, according to the circumstances, had lived congenially together in former times, had combined their forces to fight a common enemy, but had fought against each other every time divergences of interest had arisen. What the relations had been between the Hsining Shat'o and the Kanchow Uighurs in 1036 is not known. The leading tribe among the Kanchow Uighurs was the Lung tribe.[37]

In what areas of Huangchung and east Kansu were these Uighurs and Tibetans settled by Chiossulo in 1036?

Scanning chapter 19 of the *Annals* of Hsining, dealing with the tribes settled in Huangchung in Ming times (1368) (three hundred years after their surrender to Chiossulo) one is amazed to read names of such tribes as Lung-pu, Lung-pen, Lung-wang, and To-lung. One thinks unwillingly that these names might point to tribes which had constituted the important Lung tribe of Kanchow, which might have divided into smaller tribes after the surrender to Chiossulo in 1036. One is surprised to read also that in 1071 the most powerful among the tribes depending on Hsining was the Lung-k'o tribe noted also as the Yu-lung-k'o tribe.[38] In the Lung k'o tribe there were numerous chiefs. The tribe was wealthy and opulent. It was settled in East

Kansu, in Yen Ch'uan Chai, which is Chang Hsien, situated 50 li southwest of Kung Ch'ang (Enoki, 158). The tribe surrendered to General Wang Ch'ao in 1071 with its 120,000 people. The *Annals* of Kansu 97: 14, record that Wang Ch'ao notified the emperor about the submission of the Lung-k'o tribe and petitioned to reward it with the name Pao (thankful). The request was granted and the emperor added the word Shun to the name, Pao Shun (thankful-faithful). Enoki (p. 111) noted also a Lung-po tribe living in East Kansu in 1071. It had troubles with the Tibetan To-chih tribe. However, the Lung tribes recorded in the *Annals* of Hsining were settled in Huangchung. The Lung-pu, numbering two thousand families, divided into two tribes, was settled south of Hsining on the northern borders of the Yellow River. Its people lived mostly in tents (*Annals* of Hsining 19: 3 a–b). The Lung-pen tribe numbering 873 families was settled 60 li west of Hsining. Its people lived partly in a city (fortress), partly in tents. The tribe controlled the Pen-pa-erh [39] tribe numbering one hundred families settled in the Hsi-shih-hsia (Tsamalung) on the rapids of the Hsining River between Hsining and Don Kir (*Annals* of Hsining 1: 12a, 15a). The small Lung-wang and To-lung tribes numbering eighty families were settled 80 li east of the city of Tatung on the borders of the Tatung River (*Annals* of Hsining 19, 20a) in the region occupied by the Shat'o at the time of their surrender. This seems to suggest that this group was congenial with the Shat'o group.

UIGHURS AND SUBJECTS OF T'U-SSU

In discussing the commoners, the subjects of the Monguor t'u-ssu (Monguors I: 31–53), it has been noted that during the Mongol period (1280–1368), Ch'i Kung-k'o hsing-chi, a member of the imperial family, had been appointed guardian of the region situated 90 li south of Hsining. He discharged the office of myriarch and evidently controlled his own 10,000 soldiers and their families. However, it is recorded that he governed also eight tribes of Tung Ku and vicinity, descendants of western Ch'iang (western Tibetans). Tung Ku was situated between Hsining and the Tatung River, in the region of Tatung, where during the Five Dynasties (907–951) Shat'o tribes lived, joined by other groups of Shat'o after the collapse of their dynasty. These western Ch'iang seem to be Uighurs of the khanate of Kanchow who had settled there in 1036. The Uighurs of Kanchow had come from the west, from Turkistan, and so are called western Tibetans, for all the barbarians are called Tibetans in the *Annals*. For what reason these eight tribes had been moved and put under the control of the myriarch

---

[35] Wolfram Eberhard, *Conquerors and rulers*, 89, Leiden, Brill, 1952.

[36] Hamilton, *op. cit.*, 128–129.

[37] *Wu-tai-shih* 74: 4a. Stein, *op. cit.*, 256. The Lung is a branch of the Uighurs of Kanchow whose customs differ little from those of the other Uighurs. The Lung came from Karashar (Yen-ch'i). Lung was the name of the clan chiefs of Karashar. They had settled in Kansu and Yi Chou (region of Hami). Hamilton, *op. cit.*, 128.

[38] Biography of General Wang Ch'ao in *Sung Shih* 87: 20 a–b. *Annals* of Kansu 46: 10b. *Annals* of Hsining 31: 3a, and the important study of Enoki Kazuo, entitled *Osho no kika Keiryaku ni tsuite* (on the Hsi-ho ching-lueh of Wang Ch'ao) in Mokoga Huho, 1, Tokyo, (Meng-ku hsueh pao) 1: 88–167.

[39] *Anthropos* 52: 560 sq., 1957. Dominik Schroder writes a very interesting article: Uber die Chia-Fandse von Bengbar, Tsing-hai (the Pen-pa tribe), und ihre Hochzeitssitten.

is not recorded. Friction between Uighurs and Shat'o? Not room enough in Tung Ku for the herds? A device to increase the military power of the myriarch?

It is also noted that twelve Pai-tieh tribes and others were controlled by the three Shat'o officials Li, Na, and Chi, who guarded the country 30 li south and west of Hsining. To these three Shat'o chieftains who controlled their own Shat'o subjects, the Pai-tieh tribes and others had been entrusted by the Mongols. Probably they were Uighurs, for they were moved from the Tung-ku region also, and it is noted that their customs and clothes and adornments were the same as those of the western Ch'iangs of the myriarch.

It is further noted that the Shat'o official Li Nan-ko originally controlled the tribes of Tung Ku and the Hula tribes. Probably being a prominent and powerful chieftain, he had enrolled among his Shat'o subjects these Uighur tribes, at the time they fled from Kanchow. At the same time it is recorded that the t'u-ssu Ah, Chao, Yeh, Kan, and Chu controlled the Lu-erh-chia tribes and others, which were in the main similar in customs, clothing and adornments, according to the *Annals*.

It is noted (Monguors I: 56) that only one large group of Chinese is known to have enrolled in the t'u-ssu clans. The group bears the surname of Pao and is usually called the Yuan Pao group. They are subjects of the Lu t'u-ssu. We were at a loss to explain satisfactorily the name Yuan Pao. The fact had been noted above that the strong Lung K'o tribe, with its 120,000 people, had received, in 1071, from the Sung emperor the name Pao for its faithfulness toward the dynasty. Is it not possible that, during the period of troubles, which lasted for nearly two centuries, the clan disintegrated, that a group moved to Huangchung and lost its language, conserving the name Pao, but, knowing that they were Uighurs, that they preferred to be enrolled in the t'u-ssu clans, as so many Uighurs during the Yuan period? Because this had happened during the Yuan period, they are still called the Pao group of the Yuan time, Yuan Pao chia.

It seems conclusively that these tribes were Uighur tribes which, during the Mongol period, had been divided in small units and entrusted to these petty military officials, and appointed as guardians of definite territory and mountain passes in Huangchung in order that they might be able to defend the country more easily.

SETTLEMENT OF UIGHURS AND SHAT'O IN EAST KANSU

The preceding notes explain the settlement of only a relatively small number of Uighurs. But where has the remainder of the several ten thousands of Uighurs been settled? Since the very important Lung K'o tribe was settled in East Kansu, and another Lung-po tribe is rooted in the same region, and on the map a

Lung village is noted near Ming Chou in East Kansu, our investigations are turned in that direction.

From 1086 on, the entire population of Huangchung and parts of East Kansu controlled by the descendants of Chiossulo was intermittently involved in troubles with the Chinese empire, and in 1096 it arose as one man against the Sung empire, combining its forces with those of the Hsi Hsia. The cities of Huangchung were taken and retaken alternatively by Chinese troops and Tibetans, and the whole country was devastated and ruined. The flourishing empire founded by Chiossulo had lasted for only about fifty years. The fateful Huangchung was again controlled by the Sung emperor. After another period of fifty years, during which Chinese and Chin empires fought the Hsi Hsia and then fought among themselves, the Chin empire occupied Huangchung in 1131 and appointed Kuan Shih Ku to control the Ho Chou area and all of Huangchung (*Annals* of Hsining 31: 8a).

What happened to the Uighurs from 1086 until 1227? Having been settled in the territories of Chiossulo since 1036, mixed with the Tibetan tribes depending on him, and having pledged allegiance to him, inevitably they had endorsed the policy of the tribes of Huangchung and had a desperate time. During the fifty years of wars and destruction many of these Uighur tribes must have disintegrated and mixed with others. In 1369, at the time the Ming dynasty conquered Kansu, organized the country, and established the régime of the t'u-ssu, the disaster was wrought among the tribes, especially in East Kansu.

Tang-hsiang tribes, in which T'u-fan tribes had mixed, had been settled in East Kansu since 627. Shat'o groups, in 955, had scattered into the remotest southwestern parts of East Kansu, in the region of the upper T'ao River and near the borders of Szechwan. In 1036, in the same region, a large number of Uighurs must have been settled and at the débacle of the Mongol dynasty (1368) many Mongol groups also remained in these countries.

Scanning the list of the t'u-ssu established in that region in Ming times, one wonders to see in the *Annals* of Kansu the clear distinction established among the subjects of the t'u-ssu. Every time, their subject Tibetan tribes are accurately noted as Tibetans, and next to them their native subject tribes. This intended distinction seems to point at genuine Tibetan tribes and at the mixture of Shat'o Uighurs and Mongols qualified as natives.

SARO AND SHERA UIGHURS

In the remote country of the mountainous Ming Chou Hsien at the source of the T'ao River is recorded the T'u-ssu Ma Chin-tung, of Chinese origin, controlling 26 native tribes (*Annals* of Kansu 42: 27a). In the same region T'u-ssu Hu Ch'eng controlled 41 villages of natives, inhabited by 440 families (*Annals* of Kansu **42**: 29*b*). This means that the natives of Hu T'u-ssu were no longer organized in tribes as were the subjects of the first Ma T'u-ssu. Still, in the same Ming Chou T'u-ssu Chao Tang-chih-kuan-pu controlled three tribes of Tibetans and eight villages of natives, who later became Chinese (*Annals* of Kansu **42**: 30*a*). Also in the same Ming Chou region, another *t'u-ssu,* Chao Cho-ssu-shieh, a chief of nomad Tibetans controlled 43 tribes of Tibetans and 48 tribes of natives. His subjects joined the revolt of the Yellow Tibetans (Uighurs),[40] their neighbors, during the Yung Cheng period (1723–1724). The t'u-ssu lost his office and his subjects were forced into the framework of the Chinese administration and became thoroughly Chinese (*Annals* of Kansu **42**: 31*a*). This important text proves definitely the presence of groups of still autonomous Yellow Tibetan (Uighur) tribes controlled by their own chiefs, in whose revolt the forty-eight native tribes joined. It may be supposed that they also were Uighurs still organized in tribes but controlled by the t'u-ssu. In Ti Tao along the same T'ao River the Mongol T'u-ssu Chao T'o-t'ieh-mu-erh controls three tribes of Tibetans and fifteen tribes of natives. In Choni region situated on the same river, between T'ao Chou and Ming Chou, the well-known T'u-ssu Yang controls 520 tribes called Tibetans (*Annals* of Kansu

---

[40] *T'oung Pao* 14, **1**: 149, 1913, records "the Yogur tribes in Kansu are separated in two groups, whose languages are entirely different. The Saro Yogurs (Yellow Tibetans) are Turks, the Shera Yogurs (Black Tibetans) are Mongols. This note is written according to articles of G. F. Mannerheim: A visit to the Saro Yogurs (*Journal de la Société Fino Ougrienne* **28**: 2, 1911, and to the article of S. E. Maloff: Restes de Chamanisme chez les Yogurs Jaunes (Saro Yogurs) en Russe, extract de la revue *Jivaia Starina,* 61–74, 1912. Concerning these two groups, the *Annals* of Kansu **42**: 87*a*, 88, 89, record: 15 Hsi-la-ku-erh tribes called Huang-fan (Yellow Tibetans, Saro Yogurs) live in the southern mountains (Nan Shan), five in the district of Kanchow, eight in that of Suchow and two in that of Kao T'ai, and also seven T'ang-wu-t'e tribes called Hofan (Black Tibetans, Shera Yogurs). The proper name of the Yellow group is Tan-chih. Formerly it inhabited the commandery of Han-tung (Sha-chou) and is of Mongol origin. It was looted by T'ulufan and moved by Governor Wang Chih into the southern mountains of Kanchow in 1518; it is usually called the Yellow Mongol group. The sources of the Ho River are 100 li southwest of Kanchow. (The sources of the Ho River are far from the regions of the T'ao River, Ming Chou, Ling T'ao.) The west side of the river is entirely inhabited by Yellow Tibetans, the east side by Black Tibetans, also called people of the northern way. The Black Tibetans called T'ang-wu-t'e originated from the Hsi-ch'iang (Western Tibetans) of the Han time (200 B.C.–A.D. 200). In 1696 they were forced to follow Galdan. After the defeat of Galdan, those among them who were engaged in farming, surrendered. In 1698 they received hereditary titles, with official documents and seals, on which were written and engraved Manchu, Mongol, and Chinese characters. Six tribes inhabit Kanchow territory, one inhabits Kao T'ai. These notes, excerpted from the *Annals* of Kansu, deal only with tribes living in the Kanchow territory and in the Suchow area, not with those of Ming Chou.

42: 32 *a–b*). Among these tribes one is called Shat'o tribe (*Annals* of Kansu **42**: 64*a*) and several are called Black Tibetans (Uighurs) (*Annals* of Kansu **42**: 67*a*). Also is noted a revolt of Black Tibetan tribes in 1712 in which the Black Tibetans of Yang T'u-ssu joined. The t'u-ssu helped subdue the revolt and titles were granted to thirty-seven tribes of these Black Tibetans (*Annals* of Kansu **42**: 32*a*). There are only recorded the most important t'u-ssu. Finally two important groups of Yellow and Black Tibetan tribes (Uighurs) are recorded in that remote mountainous region, which during the Manchu dynasty still lived independently, controlled by their own chiefs, and to which joined the Yellow and Black Tibetans who had submitted to local chieftains.

The Black Tibetans (Uighurs) living in the T'ao Chou district, depending on the Yang T'u-ssu of Choni, revolted during eleven years from 1868 to 1879.

Since 1822, the rebels of the old White Nenuphar groups, incessantly changing the name of their groups and moving from Szechwan Province, had invaded East Kansu and wrought tremendous havoc among the people of all of East Kansu for more than fifty years. The Tibetan, Uighur, and Shat'o tribes revolted at the same time. All the revolts were directed against the hated Manchu dynasty, a dynasty of barbarian origin which ruled China.

In 1868 the revolt of the Black Tibetans of Yang T'u-ssu had been more or less quelled. It broke out in full swing in 1879 again. According to the *Annals* of Kansu **46**: 70*a,* a Black Tibetan, subject of the Yang t'u-ssu, called Cho yang-jen-chieh, living in the Kua-tse-ku, was a shaman by profession. In 1879, during the devastating earthquake of the fifth moon, his wife gave birth to a boy, whom he insidiously had called to be a Living Buddha. The baby was brought to the monastery and the lamas with the shaman, intending to make money, spread the news. During the feast prepared to honor the Living Buddha, attended by a huge crowd making offerings, the shaman, a piece of red cotton rolled on his head and a sword in his girdle, performed the shamanistic rites. Enraptured in a wild trance, he disclosed what his spirit had just imparted to him: the Living Buddha was chosen, the spirit said, to become the emperor of China. All the Black Tibetans of the four tribes were enrolled in the army of the Buddha, weapons were prepared, and the Uighurs attacked the villages of Ah Ho T'an and Yung P'ing and others. At that time the revolt of the White Nenuphar, called by the Chinese the "Hairy brigands," was still raging in East Kansu. Troops soon arrived. The Black Tibetans were beaten and pursued.

The Governor General Tso Tsung-t'ang sent more troops, ordering them to capture the chiefs of the revolt. The shaman, the Living Buddha, and twenty other men were captured and killed, and T'ao Chou district was at peace. This typical incident depicts the true mentality of the barbarian tribes at that time, and the impact of shamanism and Buddhism upon these old Manicheans.

MA-T'I SSU, THE HORSESHOE MONASTERY

In the southern mountains of the subprefecture of Yung Ch'ang, in 1912, Fathers Essens, Selosse, and I visited a small group of Uighurs, living in the Ma-t'i Ssu-ku, the valley of the monastery of the Horseshoe. We saw two temples built in the rock. The upper temple was administered by lamas, the lower one by a couple of Chinese monks.

In the red sandstone of the mountain was a deep cave, where the lamas pointed to a large horseshoe imprinted on the floor. It was said to be the print of the shoe of the horse mounted in time of war by the legendary Gesar, who later became a Chinese god of war. Maybe for that reason Chinese monks live there. An iron stake was also planted in the cave on which two heavy chains were attached, said to be the chains with which Gesar restrained his terrible mastiffs. Legends were told claiming that Gesar had lived in the valley and built the temples.

At present the temple is an affiliate of the monastery of Erh-ku-lung belonging to the Living Buddha T'u-kuan. In one of his previous existences he had bought some land in that country, the revenues from which were used for the support of the lamas and the payment of yearly interest on the capital invested by the Living Buddha. The lama director of the monastery is responsible for the administration of the monastery and is appointed by the Living Buddha (Monguors II: 52).

The monastery of the Horseshoe seems to have existed long before the T'u-kuan Living Buddhas and the monastery of Erh-ku-long existed (1604), for we read in the *Annals* of Kansu 97: 37, that a lama from Tibet living in Ma-t'i Ssu, named Pa-shih-ha, was appointed by the Dalai Lama to collect from the Uighurs of the country the *t'ien-pa*, the yearly field tax, and to send it to Lhasa. It is noted also that the Uighurs of the country, every time they killed an ox or a sheep, had to offer to the lamas of Ma-t'i Ssu some meat or a skin for the support of the lamas. Did the Horseshoe monastery or hermitage already exist before the Khoshot Kushihhan had conquered Tibet and offered it to the Dalai Lama in 1642? It seems to be a very old hermitage on account of the legends claiming its origin date from the time of Gesar.

The *Annals* of Kansu claim also that the Uighurs living in the Horseshoe region were Yellow and Black Tibetans (shera saro Uighurs). When these Uighurs had settled in that country is unknown. They were engaged partly in farming but mostly in cattle breeding. Their daughters married Tibetan boys; their boys married Tibetan girls. The clothes of the women were partly Tibetan and partly Mongol. In not too long a time they would have become thoroughly Tibetan.[41]

ETHNOGRAPHY OF HUANGCHUNG AND EAST KANSU

The preceding notes have an important ethnographic bearing. It has been noted that in 625, for fear of invading T'u-fan of Tibet, several thousand Tang-hsiang from the region of Sung P'an in Szechwan had fled to East Kansu, submitted to China, and had been settled in East Kansu and Mi Chih in Shansi; also that T'u-fan hordes chased the T'u-ku-hun from Huangchung and the Kokonor region and settled in Huangchung in 629. From 763 until 842 the whole of Kansu had been lost to China; the Tsan-p'u of Lhasa controlled the country and appointed his officials. Consequently, the bulk of the population of East Kansu consisted of Tang-hsiang and T'u-fan subjects. In 955 the Shat'o nation disintegrated and many Shat'o groups were incorporated in the Tibetan tribes in East Kansu and many fled to Huangchung, joining the Shat'o group which was living there in 939. In 1036 tens of thousands of Uighurs surrendered to Chiossulo who settled them in Huangchung and in East Kansu. In 1368, in the Ming dynasty, some Uighur groups had still kept their tribal organization but, under the leadership of t'u-ssu, others had become mixed with Tibetans and Shat'o in village formations and two groups had conserved their autonomy under the leadership of their own chiefs. When in 1712–1723 these groups revolted against the Ch'ing dynasty, many small groups of Uighurs controlled by t'u-ssu followed the people of their race in the revolt. During the Mongol period (1280–1368) many groups of Mongols settled in East Kansu and Huangchung. After the collapse of their dynasty most of them submitted to the Ming and remained in the country. Some of their chiefs became t'u-ssu and other groups disintegrated and dispersed in the country.

These notes explain what specific tribes constitute the base of the present population in Huangchung and East Kansu and at what time these tribes had arrived in Kansu. During centuries they lived one next to the other, feuding and blending with the few Chinese of the country, forming the compound called Kansu Chinese.

COLLAPSE OF THE T'U-FAN KINGDOM OF HUANGCHUNG

Chiossulo had three wives. The first, belonging to the Ch'iao family, bore one son, Tung-chan; the second, the daughter of the lama Li Li-tsun, the dismissed minister, bore two sons; no notes concern the third (*Annals*

41 Mathias Hermann, S.V.D., *Uiguren und ihre neuentdekten Nachkommen*, *Anthropos*, 78–99, 1940–1941.

of Hsining, 31*b*, 33*a*. *Sung Shih* 492: 14*a–b*). In 1065 Chiossulo appointed Tung Chan chief of the tribes. He governed 600,000 subjects. The emperor ratified the appointment in 1068, granted to the new chief the titles previously bestowed upon the father, and seized the opportunity to send Chinese officials to help him administer Huangchung. Tung Chan was a faithful defender of the empire. When the Hsi Hsia in 1070 invaded East Kansu, he attacked them, thus breaking the impact of the invasion. In 1081, 120,000 of his troops fought the Hsi Hsia at the side of the imperial armies. He and his wife were repeatedly bestowed with more and more honorific titles. The Hsi Hsia tried to persuade him to transfer his allegiance to them, but he refused the offer. Thereupon the Hsi Hsia invaded Huangchung and laid siege to his city of Mao-ch'uan. He raised the siege making peace with the Hsi Hsia against the orders of the emperor. He died in 1086 (*Annals* of Hsining, 31*b*, 33*b*. *Annals* of Kansu 46: 11*b*. *Sung Shih* 492: 16*b*).

Jealousy and hatred long smoldered among the wives of Chiossulo. At the death of the lama Li Li-tsun, the dismissed minister, Chiossulo, to humiliate his daughter, had moved her to Kuo Chou, and then a large number of tribes of the Li clan had seceded and moved to the southern part of East Kansu. In 1057, advised by her brother, she had left Kuo Chou and fled with her sons to the city of Tsun K'o, situated in the main territory of the Li clan. Chiossulo, in order to avoid more trouble with the powerful Li clan, appointed her sons as chiefs of the tribes of Ni-ku and T'ao and Ho-chou in East Kansu and the emperor granted them official titles.

However, hatred was already too deeply embedded in the hearts of the Li clan, and Mou Cheng, son of the second wife of Chiossulo, started trouble in East Kansu in 1064, conniving with the Hsi Hsia. The Hsi Hsia were defeated and Mou Cheng submitted to the emperor and received new important titles. At the death of Chiossulo in 1065, Mou Cheng, the leader of the opposition, followed by an important number of clans and in connivance with the Hsi Hsia, was again on the warpath in 1072 in East Kansu. More Chinese armies arrived, cities were taken and retaken, and the wife of Mou Cheng and his children were taken prisoner by General Wang Ch'ao. East Kansu was laid waste. Finally after two years of destruction, Mou Cheng with eighteen chiefs of tribes submitted to China. Again more new important titles were granted to him and even the name of the Sung dynasty, Chao, was bestowed (*Annals* of Kansu 46: 10, 12. *Annals* of Hsining 31B: 33, 3, 4, 5. *Sung Shih* 492: 14, 16).

The legitimate son of Tung Chan having died, he appointed in 1086 as his successor, A li ku, the son of his beloved concubine, a boy born in Khotan from an unknown father, causing forever the ruin of the T'u-fan kingdom built by Tung Chan. The emperor ratified

the appointment despite the memorial presented to the throne by minister Su Shih (*Annals* of Hsining **33B**: 9, 10). The emperor preferred the time-honored policy of his predecessors sowing discord among tribes threatening the empire. He anticipated the annihilation of the tribes by themselves, and the easy recovery of East Kansu and Huangchung. The tribes in favor of the legitimate offspring of the second wife of Chiossulo started a murderous struggle with the tribes following A li ku, backed by Chinese troops. Again the savage propensity for self-destruction among the tribes was soon in full sway and tribes tore themselves to pieces. The emperor granted titles to A li ku and his son and also to the offspring of the second wife of Chiossulo. A war of destruction went on until the death of A li ku in 1096, who had appointed his son as his successor. The appointment was again ratified by the emperor. This time all the T'u-fan, Uighur, and Shat'o tribes revolted against the empire. A strong army of 100,000 invited Hsi Hsia troops came to rescue them in Mao Ch'uan. A tremendous blow was administered to the Chinese. Then the Chinese general, in desperate straits, made an offer of settlement and invited some T'u-fan chiefs to appoint the son of Mou Cheng as chief of the tribes because, he said, he was the genuine offspring of Chiossulo!

But it was too late. The tribes did not abide by the decision of the chiefs and had become the irreconcilable enemies of China. Murderous fighting continued, the cities in Huangchung were taken and retaken several times and delivered to sack and slaughter by Chinese troops and then by the rebel tribes indulging in acts of gratuitous cruelty. Villages became clusters of ruined hovels. Many tribes disintegrating, groups of them fled to the southern part of East Kansu and to the borders of Kokonor, but the Chinese troops continued fighting against the Huangchung tribes associated with the Hsi Hsia until 1115, laying waste the whole country (*Annals* of Kansu **46**: 1, 14; *Annals* of Hsining **31B**: 6, 7). At that time, the Chin empire embarking upon the conquest of China, the Chinese troops were ordered to leave Huangchung. Chin armies peacefully occupied Huangchung in 1131. Huangchung had enjoyed a period of glory and unusual wealth during fifty years (1036–1086) followed by forty-five years of internecine wars among the tribes and savage destruction of the country (1086–1131).

From 1131 until the conquest of Huangchung by the Mongols in 1227, the history of Huangchung is a blank page. The conquest of East Kansu and the war with China and the Hsi Hsia absorbed the whole forces of the Chin emperor. An official appointed in Ho Chou in East Kansu by the Chin cared for the uninteresting, exhausted, and depleted tribes of Huangchung, with its ruined cities and villages and starving T'u-fan, Tanghsiang, Uighur and Shat'o population. It may be assumed that in these circumstances the pitiful tribes started making a living, tilling the soil, tending their few animals, and hoping for a better future. These were the circumstances of the country and of the population which the Mongols encountered in Huangchung in 1227.

HUANGCHUNG DURING THE YUAN DYNASTY

General Subudei conquered Huangchung and occupied Hsining peacefully in the third moon of 1227 (*Annals* of Kansu **46**: 20a–b; *Annals* of Hsining **31B**: 8b).

The choice of a new emperor after the death of Chingis Khan (1227) caused a lull in the military operations. The Mongols, according to the time-honored pattern prevailing among nomads, never overcame this hurdle without trouble and rivalry among the princes, and several times the dynasty would be on the brink of collapse at that fateful time.

Ogodei, third son of Chingis, having been appointed by him as his successor, became emperor in 1229, and from the first days of his reign he vigorously resumed the war with the Chin empire in East Kansu and middle China, and conquered the cities of East Kansu and Shensi occupied by the Chin. The laborious conquest of the Chin was achieved in 1234 and in 1235 Ogodei started with the conquest of the Chinese empire, while in the meantime Mongol armies were fighting in Korea, in Central Asia, and Persia. The turbulent Mongols, still eager for more and more conquests, did not spend much time on the organization of the conquered countries, and Yeh-lu Ch'u-ts'ai, their wise minister, had to remind them again and again that empires could be conquered, but not governed, on horseback.[42]

Again a lull was created in the military operations, this time by the death of Ogodei, December, 1241, for trouble arose in the imperial family regarding the succession to the throne. Ogodei had chosen as his successor his grandson Shiremon, son of his third son Ku-ch'u who had died in 1236. The widow of Ogodei, Toragana, taking the regency from 1242 until 1246, preferred to see elected her oldest son, Guyuk, despite the opposition of the family. Unfortunately, Emperor Guyuk died in 1248. This time, descendants of the first and fourth sons of Chingis in 1251 elected Mongka, oldest son of Tului, the fourth son of Chingis. Peace was seriously disturbed. Malcontents of the second and third branches were killed, among them the widow of Guyuk, Chiremon,[43] and seeds of discord and hatred were planted forever in the imperial family. In 1251 until his death in 1259, Mongka resumed vigorously the conquest of China, which had slackened since the death of Ogodei in 1241. Then his brothers, Kubilai and Arik-boga, were both elected emperors in 1260 by

their respective factions, Kubilai in China, Arik-boga in Mongolia. War started among these two brothers and the descendants of all the sons of Chingis, and even the offspring of the brothers of Chingis participated in the struggle. Kaidu, son of the fifth son of Ogodei, was the leader of the endless revolt; he conquered Central Asia and at the death of Kubilai in 1294 he was still in possession of both Turkistan and the part of Mongolia west of the Khanghai Mountains. After the death of Kaidu in 1301, his son continued the revolt during the reign of the grandson of Kubilai, until 1309. During these times of disorganization and hatred in the imperial family, several princes transferred their allegiance many times from one to another of the leading chiefs of the revolt, even brothers taking sides in opposite camps.

No wonder that very little was done relating to the organization of the conquered countries. During their reigns Ogodei (1229–1241), Guyuk (1246–1248), and Mongka (1251–1259) eagerly engaged in more and more conquest. Fortunately Kubilai, more cognizant of Chinese civilization than his predecessors, reigned thirty-four years (1260–1294). However, during all this time he had to face disastrous revolts against him inside the imperial family and at the same time lead the conquest of China, Japan, Indo-China, etc. Consequently, the first notes concerning Hsining and the united Kansu are encountered during the reign of Kubilai.

Yuan Shih **60**: 27b records that from the beginning of the Yuan Hsining had been the assigned appanage of Chang Chi,[44] imperial son-in-law.

In 1275, Chang Chi and two other commanders were ordered to send their Mongol troops to Ao-lu-ch'ih,[45] the seventh son of Kubilai, Prince of Hsi P'ing,[46] who was engaged in a war with the T'u-fan. The country where the trouble occurred is not indicated (*Yuan Shih* **8**: 20b; *Hsin Yuan Shih* **114**: 7a; *Annals* of Hsining **32B**: 8a). Chang Chi received a seal in 1282 (*Yuan Shih* **12**: 2b) and money for his troops in 1283 (*Yuan Shih* **12**: 13b).

---

[42] René Grousset, Histoire de L'extrême Orient, 431, Paris, Geuthner, 1929.

[43] Grousset, *op. cit.,* 441.

[44] Louis Hambis, Monographies du *T'oung Pao* **3**: 108. *Yuan Shih* **1**: 160–162, Brill, Leiden, 1954. He was the great-grandson of Ch'i-ku of the Konggirat, who had married Tumalun, daughter of Chingis and Bortai. Chang Chi married the Princess Mangkotai.

[45] Hambis, *Monographies du T'oung Pao Supplément,* **38**: ch. 107 du Yuen shih, 114.

[46] The title of Prince of Hsi P'ing, and all similar titles, does not imply that the region of Hsi P'ing was appanaged to the prince, nor that he resided in Hsi P'ing. Hsi P'ing is Ling Wu near Ninghsia, and not Hsining. Chao Pao-chi, ruler of Hsi Hsia, having conquered Ling Wu in 1002, changed the name of Ling Wu into that of Hsi P'ing and established his capital there.

In 1013 his successor Chao Te-ming was appointed by the Chin emperor, Prince of Hsi P'ing, and in 1016 the Sung emperor Chen Tsung conferred upon him the same title. Hence the origin of the title. At the time the Mongols had conquered Hsi Hsia (*Annals* of Kansu **46**: 5b, 6a), they granted the title of the conquered city to their own commanders.

Sixty years after Huangchung had been conquered by Subudei (1227) the civil and military organization of the country was started. We do not know who cared for Huangchung before that time. Only *Hsin Yuan Shih* **48**: 5*a* records that for the first time, in 1269, after forty years, in Ho-chou (East Kansu) a bureau for the pacification of the T'u-fan (T'u-fan hsuan-wei-sse) had been established, and it may be presumed that Ho Chou kept an eye on Huangchung from that time on. However, Ao-lu-ch'ih controlled the Tibetans (*Annals* of Hsining **23**: 3*a*). Finally in 1286 Hsining was created a district (chou) depending on the military commandery (Tsung-kuan-fu) of the circuit (Lu) of I-chi-nai, situated 500 li northeast of Suchow in the Gobi. Regular civil and military officials were appointed (*Annals* of Hsining **22**: 5*a*) and the institution of the graneries established, from which we can infer that land taxes were imposed (*Annals* of Hsining **31B**, 8*b*; *Hsin Yuan Shih* **48**: 24*a*). In 1287 Chang Chi received the title of Prince of Ning P'u, prince of the second degree, with the duty of military commander and governor of Huangchung and with the order to garrison the country (*Annals* of Hsining **32B**: 8*b*; *Yuan Shih* **14**: 13*b*, 27, 60; *Ming Shih* **330**: 1*b*). This seems to indicate that Chang Chi, before that time, had not resided in his appanage and had not administered it, although he had been entitled to receive some revenues from it. He had been a simple commander of his own troops, always available to be sent by his superiors where emergencies arose. It was in that way that his troops had fought under the command of Ao-lu-ch'ih in 1275, that in 1288 he was ordered, in combination with other commanders, to fight Kaidu, who attacked the frontiers of Kansu (*Yuan Shih* **15**: 1*b*) and that in 1289 he helped to quell the revolt of Shiliemen (*Yuan Shih* **15**:14*a*). The date of the death of Chang Chi is not recorded. It is only noted that his wife received a title in 1317 and a gift in silver and cash (*Yuan Shih* **26**: 2*b*, 3*a*, 26).[47]

The fact that in 1286 the granary offices were established and land taxes imposed proves that in Huang-chung land was tilled. Consequently, the country must have recovered more or less from the tremendous devastation wrought by the disastrous wars, which had lasted for forty-five years preceding the conquest of Huang-chung by the Chin (1131) and during their peaceful occupation of the country, which lasted for a century (1131–1227). The depleted tribes of T'u-fan, Uighurs, and Shat'o, having lost most of their herds, would have been forced to concentrate on farming in order to earn a living, and to indulge in some trade and manufacture according to the circumstances. It may be supposed that, since the time of the conquest of Hsining by the Mongols (1227), troops, accompanied by their families as was the rule, occupied the country and practiced agriculture as did previous Chinese colonists, for no

granaries existed before 1286, and no officials to provide for the subsistence of the soldiers. Moreover, it is a fact of common knowledge that Kubilai ordered the Mongol troops to farm and to defend the country at the same time.[48] This is borne out also by the fact that at the time the Ming dynasty (1368) started establishing Chinese colonies in Huangchung (*Annals* of Kansu **42**: 55; *Annals* of Hsining **24**: 14*b*, and Monguors I: 30, 33), the conquered Mongol troops had to leave the irrigated country around the cities and were relegated to side valleys. The memory of this fateful decision, made by the Ming, was still fresh among the Monguors in 1910, and their tradition went so far as to claim their ancestors as the initial diggers of the irrigation canals and the inaugurators of agriculture in the country.

We get the confirmation of this fact from the celebrated Marco Polo, who with his father Nicolo and his uncle Matteo, went to Hsining in 1274, on his way from Venice to Peking. He writes, "the population of this country consists chiefly of idolators (Shamanists, lamaists) but there are also some Mohammedans and Christians (Nestorians) . . . the inhabitants employ themselves in trade and manufacturing. They have grain in abundance." [49]

Probably Marco Polo made this statement because the Mongol troops and the Tibetans, Uighurs, and Shat'o farmed in Huangchung. This text proves also that probably during the century of peace preceding the conquest of Hsining by the Mongols, some Mohammedans and Nestorians from Turkistan had returned to Hsining, which they had known since the time of Chiossulo (1038), to engage in trade.

However, because the note of Marco Polo dates from 1274, we have to consider that during the campaigns of Chingis Khan in Turkistan, which had started in 1209, the Mongols had come in close contact with Mohammedans and Uighurs.[50] The influence exerted at court by the Mohammedan Yalavach is well known. It was so striking that Empress Toragana had to remove and demote him at the time he tried to impede the succession of Guyuk to Ogodei, planned by the empress.[51]

According to H. F. Schurmann, in the early years of the Mongolian rule in North China a great number of Central Asiatic merchants had moved into China and organized in the corporation known as "Ortaq." Ortaq means "partner" or companion. These merchants were financial "partners" of members of the imperial family and nobility, from whom they received sizable amounts of silver as loans. This capital they used to expand their trade activities. In addition, many of them func-

---

[47] Hambis, *op. cit.* **108**: 160–162.

[48] Franke, *op. cit.* **4**: 562.
[49] *The travels of Marco Polo,* translated and edited by W. Marsden, reedited by Thomas Right, 135–138, Everyman's Library, J. M. Dent, London, 1950.
[50] Grousset, *op. cit.,* 483.
[51] Franke, *op. cit.* **4**: 276, 306.

tioned as tax farmers who collected revenues and taxes from the appanages of their benefactors. The financial administration of the appanages prior to the year 1260 was in the hands of the feudatories and not in the hands of the imperial government. After 1260 the situation changed radically; the newly established central government by Kubilai took over the financial administration of all parts of the realm. The revenues of the feudatories from their appanages were collected by officials of the central government and then turned over to the feudatories.[52] Consequently, Mohammedans must have lived in Hsining since 1260, caring for the control of the appanage of Chang Chi, and it is quite possible that other Mohammedans and Uighur Nestorians would have moved to Huangchung to indulge in trade during the Mongol period, even long before 1260. Later it will be noted that during the Mongol period Mohammedan Salars and the clan of the later Yeh T'u-ssu moved into Huangchung.

In the *Annals* of Hsining **31B** : 8*b,* is still noted the appointment in 1303 of the Prince of Hsining, Ch'u Pei,[53] as commander of all the troops of Kansu. However, no movement of troops is noted.

Also it is recorded in 1324 that Ch'u Pei rescued from famine the troops of the Prince of Hsi-p'ing (*Annals* of Hsining **31B** : 8*b*). Ao-lu-ch'ih, Prince of Hsi-p'ing, had died soon after 1303 in Ninghsia, his son Pu-ti-ma-ti-chia had inherited the title of his father, and later in 1337 the grandson Kuan-pu-pa. Thus Pu-ti-ma-ti-chia received help from Hsining and his troops were garrisoned in Lan, Kuan, and Lingwu.[54]

The *Annals* of Hsining note that in 1329 to Sulaiman[55] was granted the title of Prince of Hsining (and not of Hsip'ing), and that in 1332 on account of his military achievements, the emperor created four appointments of "preceptor of the prince." A seal was cast and bestowed upon the prince by the emperor. However, Sulaiman never lived in Hsining.

Two names of pacifiers of T'u-fan are also mentioned in the *Annals* of Hsining **22** : 3*b,* Chin-ch'a-t'ai[56] and Cho-chi-ssu-pan.

[52] H. F. Schurmann, reviewing Herbert Franke's Geld and Wirtschaft in China der Mongolenherrschaft, in H.J.O.A.S., Vol. 15, June 25.

[53] *Yuan Shih* 21 : 6*a;* Hambis, *op. cit.* 108 : 113 and 107 : 92, 8.

[54] *Hsin Yuan Shih* 114 : 7*b,* 8*a, b*; Hambis, *op. cit.* 108 : 141–143.

[55] *Yuan Shih* 36 : 4*b; Annals* of Hsining 31B : 9*a*; Hambis, *op. cit.* 108 : 103.

[56] Chin Ch'a-t'ai was the second son of Kochkar, great-grandson of Barchug, idukut (chief) of an Uighur tribe, which pledged allegiance to Chingis Khan in 1209 in Turkistan. The tribe remained faithful to the Mongol dynasty. Chin Ch'a-t'ai in 1318, refused the titles of Idukut and of prince of Kao Ch'ang, granted to his nephew T'ieh-mu-erh-pu-huo, who asked the emperor to bestow them upon his uncle (Hambis, *op. cit.* 8 : 132, note 3; *Hsin Yuan Shih* 116 : 7*b*).

Francis Woodman Cleaves, The Sino-Mongolian inscription of 1372 in memory of Prince Hindu, *Harvard Jour. Asiatic Studies* 12 (142) : 1 sq., June, 1949.

In Kuei Te, south of Hsining, on the bank of the Yellow River, a fortress had been built and a garrison established by the troops of Huangchung during the period Chih-yuan (between 1335 and 1340), in order to prevent inroads in Huangchung by T'u-fan or Tang-hsiang from East Kansu. Terrible famines, started in 1337, desolated East Kansu for years, and T'u-fan plundered East Kansu, pillaging more than two hundred cities and villages (*Annals* of Hsining 9 : 11*b; Annals* of Kansu 46 : 21*b*). Another important fortress was built 140 li west of the city of Yung Nan, northwest of Hsining, called the triangle city (San-chiao-ch'eng) and a strong garrison established. It controlled the routes leading from Kokonor to Suchow, Kanchow and Liangchow, I-chi-nai and Ch'ih-chin (*Annals* of Hsining 7 : 18*a–b*) and prevented inroads of T'u-fan and attacks of Mongols during the terrible revolt of Kaidu against Kubilai.

In both *Annals* nothing is noted relating to lamas traveling through Huangchung troubling the people, as is noted concerning lamas traveling through East Kansu on their way from Lhasa to Peking. Maybe the lamas knew that the country was too poor and entirely devastated and so they preferred to travel through East Kansu.

These are the poor records collected in the *Annals* of Hsining and of the province of Kansu, concerning the history of Huangchung during the period of the Yuan. No records are available, as is the case for the Ming and Ch'ing dynasties, relating to the distribution and amount of land, salt, and mill taxes, or relating to the exchange of tea against horses, bureaus for which were established in East Kansu, in T'ao Chou and Kung-ch'ang (*Annals* of Hsining 17 : 36). No records are available concerning the size of the population, the number of tribes living in the country, or the economic situation, or even the building of a single school or of Confucian or Taoist temples. There is only noted the existence of the Buddhist temple Ta Fo Ssu (*Annals* of Hsining 15 : 1*b*) built by the ancestors of the Li t'u-ssu clan during the Yuan period (Monguors II : 14). However, in the *Annals* it is carefully recorded that the Ming started with the erection of schools, the building of cities and hotels for the officials (*Annals* of Hsining 14 : 4*b,* 6*a,* 10*a*), and so we may conclude that during the last years of the Sung dynasty and the ravaging wars waged by tribes for forty-five years, enraged against the Chinese, taking and retaking and destroying cities, etc., few public institutions and buildings would have been left in the cities, and that nothing would have been done by the Yuan for the reconstruction of the country. The Mongol troops engaged in agriculture guarded the thinly populated country. That the country was thinly populated is borne out by the fact that the Ming rewarded lamas for alluring Tibetans to settle in the country (Monguors II : 16, 17), and also by the fact that two cities, situated south of Nienpei, Kuo Chou and Mi Chou, had been disestablished (*Annals* of Hsining 7: 12, and 7: 14).

During the Yuan dynasty a military organization had been elaborated in Huangchung providing for the defense of the strategic and vulnerable points of the country. Only two Mongol officers had been sent with their troops to occupy the country: the myriarch Ch'i Kung-k'o-hsing-chi, who controlled 10,000 soldiers with their families, and Ch'i-T'o-erh-chih-shih-chieh, a Mongol officer, who commanded twenty tribes of Chi-pen Mongols. Surrendered tribal local chieftains were enlisted in the cadre of the regular army; they received a title, and were assigned other tribes as subjects, in order to strengthen their military power. Each of them had to defend a definite area and was responsible for the peace of the area. To be sure a high officer controlled this military organization, but only the name of Chang Chi is known, Governor of Huangchung. At the time of the collapse of the Yuan dynasty, this group of officers submitted to the Ming and all of them became t'u-ssu and the founders of the Monguor clans of Huangchung.

It is easy to understand that the troops of Huangchung submitted to the Ming dynasty, in view of the dissensions existing among the Mongol princes at that time, the pitiable flight of the emperor from his capital, the defeat of the Mongol forces and the disintegration of the Mongol nation—all things which were known in the minutest detail by the officials in Huangchung. All the more, what were the conditions in the homelands of the soldiers of Hsining, who long since had been enlisted in the Mongol armies and who had their families following them in Huangchung? They had no way to move. Guarding the country of Huangchung, they had practiced agriculture, and knew they could make a living remaining in the country. There seems to have been no alternative for them, except to wait for the arrival of the new lords of the empire, and then to make the best of a bad situation, offering to remain guardians of the country in behalf of the new masters, as defeated troops in the Orient often used to do for centuries. That the officers, originating from Huangchung, agreed with the decision is not difficult to understand.

CONQUEST OF HUANGCHUNG BY THE MING

CONQUEST OF KANSU

After the death of Emperor Ch'eng Tsung, grandson of Kubilai (1295–1307), no capable emperors succeeded to the throne of the Yuan. During the reign of Emperor Huei Tsung (1333–1368) the provinces situated south of the Yangtse River were lost in 1360 and occupied by several groups of rebels who looted the country of its wealth. Chou Yuan-chang, chief of a group of rebels, succeeded in establishing a provisional government. He defeated or received the allegiance of one rebelling chief after another, and proceeded with his army for the conquest of the northern provinces of the empire. The emperor fled from the capital in 1368 toward Ying ch'ang, northwest of Jehol, and Su Ta, general of Chou Yuan-chang, occupied Peking in September, 1368. Chou Yuan-chang was proclaimed Emperor of the Ming dynasty. He established his capital in Nanking and adopted "Hung-wu" as the designation of his reign.[57] The last Mongol army, commanded by K'uo K'uo Timur, was defeated by General Su Ta and the province of Shansi was conquered. K'uo K'uo Timur fled to Kansu hoping to mobilize a new army, but Su Ta sent officials all over the country announcing the end of the Yuan dynasty and the accession of the Ming dynasty, and requesting submission (*Annals* of Hsining 31: 9a).

SURRENDER OF MONGOL PRINCES AND OFFICIALS

According to the family chronicles of the Lu t'u-ssu clan of Lien-ch'eng (the country contiguous with Huangchung), T'o Huan, Prince of Anting, descendant of the fifth generation of Kolgan, sixth son of Chingis Khan, had arrived in Kansu, with a small retinue, on his way back from Peking. T'o Huan discharged the prominent office of P'ing-chang Chengshih. He had defended the capital with the imperial guard against the Ming troops, but had failed to accompany the fleeing imperial family. He had assisted in Peking at the lamentable collapse of the Yuan dynasty and the piteous flight of the imperial family. He understood the uselessness of any further resistance against the victorious armies of the Ming. Having received in 1369 the invitation of the Ming emperor, conveyed by General Teng Yu, to come and see him, he went to call on the emperor, and surrendered, complying with the proposition of his reappointment as chief of his tribes in the territory he had occupied at the time of the Yuan. He controlled 3,245 families, totalling 21,686 persons. T'o Huan knew very well that the transfer of allegiance to new lords entailed the duty to fight in their behalf. Consequently in the third moon of 1370, the chronicles of the Lu clan note his participation in the resounding victory of General Su Ta over K'uo K'uo Timur.[58]

The surrender of such a notorious Mongol prince, living in Kansu, an eyewitness of the collapse of the

---

[57] Franke, *op. cit.* 4: 549–550. Grousset, *op. cit.,* 495–496.

[58] The problems of the origin and history of the Lu clan are discussed in the chapters dealing with the translation of the family chronicle of the clan. The name Lu was bestowed upon the clan by Emperor Ch'eng Tsung (Yung-lo) after his campaign (1410) against A-lu-t'ai, in which the son of T'o Huan, Kung-pu-shih-t'ieh, was killed. The Lu clan was a genuine Monguor clan and the close neighbor of the Monguor clans of Huangchung, speaking the same language, and called Monguor by the Monguor clans of Huangchung. Its history was closely connected with that of the Huangchung Monguors. Therefore it is included in the study.

dynasty, must have deeply impressed the other Kansu princes and officials, who had also received the same invitation to surrender. In the same year another Monguor prince of Huangchung, member of the imperial family, Ch'i Kung-k'o-hsing-ch'i, surrendered. He had been appointed by the Yuan emperor guardian of the region 90 li south of Hsining, had discharged the office of myriarch with golden badge and purple tassel, was official of the Li-wen-so of the province of Kansu and enjoyed the title of duke. His subjects numbered 800 families organized in four tribes, scattered in many villages in the region south of Hsining, noted for the forays of savage and predatory Tibetans (Monguors I: 53; *Annals* of Hsining 31: 9a; *Annals* of Kansu 42: 35). He was the first among the Monguor t'u-ssu of Huangchung who surrendered.

In 1370, on the third moon, K'uo K'uo Timur attacked with a new army the Ming troops in the Lanchow region, but suffered a crushing defeat at Shenerh-ku, at the hand of Su Ta. Here 1,800 princes and officials were taken prisoner and 80,000 soldiers died on the field of battle (*Annals* of Kansu 46: 22b). General Li Wen-chung, moving from Peking in pursuit of the Yuan emperor, reached in the fifth moon of the same year, the imperial family in Yin-ch'ang, where the last emperor of the Yuan had died a month before. He took prisoner the grandson of the emperor, the empresses, and princesses, etc. Only the heir apparent to the throne escaped toward Karakorum.

Su Ta seized the opportunity of his victory to send all over the country, Hsiu Yung-te, secretary general of the administrative organ of Shensi province, again inviting the officials to submit, while he continued the conquest of the cities and regions situated in the southeast of Kansu. Here the Yuan had established Hsuanwei-sse (pacification commanderies) and many myriarchies and chyliarchies, with Mongol incumbents endowed with hereditary titles, commanding a thousand or ten thousand soldiers with their families. The administrative center of the country was Ho Chou (*Yuan Shih* 60: 10a,b; *Hsin Yuan Shih* 48: 8–11).

The invitation to submission reached fruition, for in the sixth moon the Tibetan Suo-nan-pu, who had filled during the Yuan the important office of pacification commander and controlled forty-eight Tibetan tribes, arrived at the headquarters of General Teng Yu, offering the emblems and documents of his office, received from the Yuan. Later the name Ho was granted to him and the office of assistant commander of the commanderies of Ho Chou and Wei Chou. Together with the powerful Suo-nan-pu the Tibetan tribes living in the districts of Chi Ch'eng, T'ao Chou, and Min Chou, and the eighteen tribes of Chieh and Wen Chou surrendered.

In the same sixth moon, the Prince of Wu Ching, Bu Ma La, pacifier of the western regions, descendant of Ao-lu-ch'ih, the seventh son of Kubulai, following in the wake of the Lu and Ch'i princes, surrendered with all the Tibetan tribes subject to him.[59]

In the eighth moon, after receiving the invitation conveyed by the "interpreter introducer" Kung-k'o Sonan, the prince of Kao Ch'ang, Huo Chang, and the prince of Ch'i, Sang Ko, and Dorjibal, surrendered with their subjects.[60]

In 1371, on the third moon, another conquered Mongol prince, T'o-li-pe-lai, was sent to the still unconquered Mongol officials in Kansu with summons to transfer their allegiance to the new Ming dynasty. The repeated sending of messengers with summons for peaceful surrender, and the ceaseless surrender of Mongol princes and officials in Kansu, point to the presence of the tremendous number of Mongols living in that province at that time, mixed with Tibetans, Uighurs, and Shat'o, and at the number of officials who still seemed to "wait and see."

GENERAL SURRENDER OF THE MONGUOR OFFICIALS IN HUANGCHUNG

The Monguor officials in Huangchung still waited, despite the two summonses they had received in 1369 and 1370. To be sure an atmosphere of dark apprehension and portent must have hung over Huangchung after the flight of the imperial family, the capture of the capital, the creation of the new dynasty, the crushing defeats of the armies of K'uo K'uo Temur and the daily surrender of Mongol princes and officials east and west in their neighborhood. They must have realized that no peg remained on which to hang a last shred of hope for the restoration of their crumbled dynasty, and that a return toward Mongolia boded hopeless ills. In many councils there must have been discussed on the one hand all those fateful circumstances, and the presence at their very door of the victorious armies of Su Ta. On the other hand they must have appreciatively considered the fact of the reappointment in their former offices of the conquered officials. Then unexpectedly, in the third moon in 1371, was delivered the last summons to surrender, by the Mongol Prince T'o-li-pe-lai. This time the decision was readily taken; the officials would submit and remain the guardians of the country in behalf of the new emperor.

On the fifth moon the Mongol, T'o-erh-chih-shih-chieh, who controlled twenty tribes of Chi-pen Mongols composed of 700 families settled near Nien-pe in Ta-tse-

---

59 *Ming Shih*, 331, 1b; *Ming Hung-wu Shih-lu*, 53, 15.

60 Huo Chang is a descendant in the eighth generation of the Uighur chief Barchuk, who submitted to Chingis Khan in Turkistan in 1209. From Nanuril, his descendant of the fourth generation, who died in 1318, and was the first Prince of Kaoch'ang, the list of successions is confusing. The same is true of Sangko and Dorjibal. Sangko is noted as Prince of Kaoch'ang and Dorjibal as Prince of Ch'i!

Hambis, *op. cit.* 108: 7, 50, 132, 133; *Hsin Yuan Shih* 116: 5b, 7a, 9b; F. W. Cleaves, The Sino-Mongolian inscription of 1362, 25 sq., H.J.A.S., Vol. 1949, N. 1–2.

wan (the bent of the Mongols), and who was assistant official of the administrative body of the province of Kansu, representing all the officials of Huangchung, went to court to surrender (*Annals* of Hsining 27 : 9b). Together with him, Li Nan-ko, of Shat'o origin, vice-chairman of the administrative body of Hsining, surrendered with the officials of the entire district (*Annals* of Hsining **31** : 9; *Annals* of Kansu **42** : 46b), and all the officials received appointments.[61] T'o-erh-chih-shih-chieh, Li Nan-ko, and all the officials who had surrendered, became the founding ancestors of the t'u-ssu clans[62] in Huangchung (Monguors I: 31). To them is to be added Ch'i Kung-k'o-hsing-ch'i, member of the imperial family who had surrendered in 1369. In that way all the officials of the region of Hsining and Nienpei had surrendered and in the next year, 1372, Hsining was created a commandery (*Annals* of Hsining **31** : 9b). In the first moon of 1373 the emperor sent the edict to T'o-erh-chih-shih-chieh:

I govern the empire; with prominent people of all the world who love justice, I deal with courtesy, granting them offices, in order that they might have the opportunity to manifest their qualities. You, T'o-erh-chih-shih-chieh, who have lived long in the western country, have heard about our highly developed culture and have come to my court. I appreciate your intention. Now at the beginning of the establishment of the commandery of Hsining, I especially request your help. I hope you will devote yourself whole-heartedly to the submission of the tribes and the strict observance of the law, in order that the country may enjoy peace. I hope you will respond to my desire to give you this appointment. Have the title of Hsuan-wei chiang-chun (general who manifests his military qualities) and be commander of the commandery of Hsining. Edict, First moon, Sixth year, Hung Wu period. (*Annals* of Hsining **32** : 16a.)

The *Annals* note that he had received at the time of his surrender in 1371 the hereditary function of secretary commandant. The imperial edict of the first moon of 1373 granted him the function of commander of the commandery. The clan of T'o-erh-chih-shih-chieh was rewarded in 1401 by the emperor with the name Ch'i, when his son Chuan Chou had died on the field of battle.

WHO WERE THE OFFICIALS WHO SURRENDERED IN A GROUP IN 1371?

The Mongol T'o-erh-chih-shih-chieh and his 700 families, the Shat'o Li Nan-ko with his 4,000 families, the Shat'o Li Wen nephew of Li Nan-ko, controlling 963 families, and the Shat'o chiefs Na-sha-mi and Chi

Pao with their 150 and 90 families, respectively, all surrendered. At the same time five clans surrendered who were recorded in the *Annals* as Monguors: the clans Wang, Kan, Chou, Hsin, and La, with 150, 300, 62, and 100 families, respectively. The Mongol clan Ah with its 150 families surrendered, whose chief discharged during the Yuan the office of secretary of the province of Kansu, and also the Yeh clan with 70 families, Mohammedans of Turkistan, recorded as being of Ch'an-t'ou origin (turbaned heads). The chief of the Yeh clan was secretary of the administrative organ of Kansu during the Yuan. These are the twelve clans which surrendered in a group in 1371.

The date at which the Ch'eng clan, with 150 families, settled in Hsining during the Ming is not recorded. Its clan chief is of Chinese extraction and originated from Shan Yang in Chiang Nan (Chiang Nan became later the Nan Huei and Kiangsu provinces), and its subjects are called "natives."[63] The date at which the Chao clan, 120 families, settled in Huangchung during the Ming also is not recorded. Its chief during the Yuan discharged the duty of myriarch of Chao Tsang, and is noted as being from Min Chou and of Mongol origin. Li Hua-no, an offshoot of the Li Nan-ko branch, and so normally a Shat'o, received from the clan 100 families and became t'u-ssu only in 1645. To this list of 15 t'u-ssu clans is still to be added the clan of the Mongol Ch'i Kung-k'o-hsing-chi with his 800 families, who had been the first among the Huangchung t'u-ssu to surrender in 1369. Among them 13 clans were settled in Huangchung in the beginning of the Yuan period in definite territories, and the mountain passes to be guarded by each of them had been indicated. This seems to suggest that all of them were large or minor groups of soldiers, with their chiefs, wardens of the country in behalf of the Yuan. They continued during the Ming, and later during the Ch'ing, to occupy the territories they had occupied during the Yuan, except the two cities of Hsining and Nienpei, and to be charged with the same duties, because the

---

[61] *Ming Shih* **330** : 2a.

[62] I use the term "clan" to refer to a group sharing a common territory, a common surname, and a common chief. Monguor clans consist both of persons who recognize real or traditional kinship ties with the chief, and persons who do not recognize such ties but who have, nevertheless, adopted the surname of the chief and his kinsmen at the time they were integrated in the group.

[63] In Huangchung the subjects of the sixteen t'u-ssu clans living in the country are commonly called Monguors, by the Monguors themselves, whether they are of Mongol, Shat'o, Uighur, Tibetan, or Chinese extraction. The Chinese call them *t'u-jen*, i.e. "natives." Among these natives are people of Mongol, Shat'o, Uighur, and Tibetan stock and even some Chinese who entered the t'u-ssu clans. Tibetans settled in Huangchung, with their own tribal chiefs, are called Hsi-fan, and Mongols living outside Huangchung are called Ta-tse, Ta-ta, T'u-ta, Meng-ku, but never Monguors. The present study deals with the Monguors of Huangchung who speak a peculiar Mongol dialect, not understood by the other Mongols. In Ho Chou region lives a group of Mohammedan Mongols, whose language is very similar to that of the Monguors. However, the group is not called Monguor but Sant'a. The group of Mongols of the Lu t'u-ssu clan of Lien Ch'eng are genuine Monguors and recognized as such by the Monguors of Huangchung. In Chinese studies dealing with the natives of Huangchung, they are all indiscriminately called Meng-ku, Ta-tse, T'u-ta, Ta-ta, Hsi-fan, T'u-jen, and T'u-ming (Monguors I: 31, 32).

Ming fixed the number of both foot and horse each of them had to keep ready for emergencies and indicated the mountain passes they had to defend.

An interesting fact is that all the subjects of the 16 *t'u-ssu* are called *t'u-min* or *t'u-jen* in the *Annals* and by the people. Soldiers in the Yuan time were accompanied by their families. At that time no Chinese lived in Huangchung. Huangchung was the land of the barbarian Monguors, controlled by Monguor chiefs. It is no wonder that when the Chinese started founding Chinese colonies in Huangchung, the colonists called the Monguors natives, and called Hsi-fan the few uninteresting small Tibetan tribes having their own petty chiefs, for their language and customs differed entirely from those of the Monguors.

Still in Huangchung, on the borders of the Yellow River, but not in the prefecture of Hsining, are encountered two groups of Salars (Muslim Turks of Samarkand) who lived in Huangchung during the Yuan time, having no or few relations with the Monguors. They had already surrendered to the Ming on their own account in 1370, and their two chiefs had received an incumbency. The clan chief Han Pao-yuan had received the office of centurion. He controlled the four upper Salar clans (Kung) who had adopted the surname Han and inhabited the region west of Hsun Hua (*Annals* of Kansu 42: 43a). The clan chief Han Shan-pa had also received the office of centurion. He controlled the four lower Salar clans, which had adopted the surname Ma, and inhabited the region east of Hsun Hua (*Annals* of Kansu 42: 43b). The four upper and four lower Salar clans are called the eight inner Salar clans (Nei Pa-kung). There still remain five outer Salar clans (Wai Pa-kung) depending on and controlled by the subprefecture of Pa-yen-jung (Monguors I: 22, 23).

It is not known at what time the Salars settled in Huangchung. A legend is still spread among them relating to their arrival in the country during the Tang dynasty, 620–905. Anyway, the Salars were settled in Huangchung during the Yuan time (1280–1368) and surrendered to the Ming in 1370.[64] Consequently, in the fifth moon of 1371 the entire population of Huangchung with its chiefs had surrendered to the Ming.

MING POLICY TOWARD SURRENDERING TRIBES

The policy adopted by the Ming in Kansu, in order to promote the surrender of the numerous groups of Mongol officials living in that country who still commanded a fair number of soldiers and tribes of Tibetans with soldiers subject to them, which was to appoint the Mongol officials and tribal chiefs officials of the newly established dynasty, retaining control over their

[64] William Woodville Rockhill, *Diary of a journey through Mongolia and Tibet in 1891 and 1892*, 80, Smithsonian Institution, 1894.

own troops, seems at first sight to have been a dangerous one. The Mings must have known that many armed groups of Mongols had fled to Mongolia; they must have surmised that the heir apparent of the Mongol nation would try to invade China and recover his lost empire, and that in such circumstances the faithfulness of the surrendered Mongol officials in Kansu still commanding their own troops would have been questionable. However, without hesitation and apprehension they went ahead, using from the very beginning the surrendered officials to induce other Mongol officials and Tibetan tribes to surrender. Even from the very beginning they ordered their troops to follow the imperial armies fighting unconquered or revolting tribes of Mongol officials, even ordering their troops to fight Mongol armies at the side of the Chinese armies in expeditions to Mongolia. Several t'u-ssu and hundreds of their soldiers died on the fields of battle; even t'u-ssu were sent with their troops to other provinces to quell revolts. But after every military achievement the emperors never omitted to bestow upon the t'u-ssu awards and titles of which they were unusually fond. In Kansu the number of Mongol officials who rebelled after their surrender was small. Many t'u-ssu later on, remaining chiefs of their clans, at the same time entered the framework of the civil and military Chinese officials and fulfilled their duties in Chinese territory, receiving the rewards or punishments proper to the office. It may be said that the policy of the Ming in Kansu promoting the surrender of Mongol officers and tribal chiefs was successful and of enormous profit to the dynasty.

ANCESTORS OF THE LI T'U-SSU CLAN

The tradition all over the country and confirmed by both the *Annals* of Kansu (42: 38a, 46b) and the *Annals* of Hsining (27: 9a–b), claims the Li t'u-ssu clans to be the descendants of the Shat'o Li K'o-yung, who had received from the Tang emperor the name Li and been created Prince of Chin in 895. At the time the Tang dynasty had run its course, the Shat'o founded in China, successively, two ephemeral dynasties: Hu Tang (923–936) and Hu Chin (936–947) (Monguors I: 131 appendix, the Shat'o Turks). Among the t'u-ssu in Huangchung are encountered two Li branches: that of Li Nan-ko, to whose son, Li Yin, had been granted in 1425 the title of Earl of Huei Ning, and that of Li Wen, son of Li Shang-ko, on whom had been bestowed the title of Earl of Kaoyang in 1459. During the Yuan, the Li Nan-ko branch guarded the territory of San Ch'uan Valley (since 1930, called the subprefecture of Ming Huo) situated 120 li southeast of Nienpei, and controlled more than 4,000 families, scattered in many villages. The Li Wen clan controlled 963 families scattered in 48 villages and guarded the territory 30 li south of Hsining (*Annals* of Kansu 42: 39a, 48a). During the Ming and Ch'ing dynasties both branches still occupied and guarded the same territories.

On account of the fact that the original family chronicles were lost during the troubles which beset the Ming dynasty, the most fantastic legends have come to be spread among the Li Monguors and even among their t'u-ssu, relating to the history of the clan ancestors preceding the Ming period (1368). Some of them circulating among the Li Wen clan have been noted in Monguors I: 26, 27. Concerning the Li Nan-ko branch we possess two recent documents of 1937 and 1941 which Chinese scholars obtained, one from the Li t'u-ssu himself, and one from a clan member.

The first document, *Studies on Frontier Areas of Kansu, Ch'ing-hai, and Tibet,* by Ma Ho-t'ien [65] records, on page 179, the personal visit of Ma Ho-t'ien to the residence of the Li t'u-ssu in the subprefecture of Ming Hua and his trip to the ancestral cemetery at Hsiang T'ang.[66]

The Li t'u-ssu was so kind as to show the chronicle of his clan. The size of the chronicle is two feet square, the image of the ancestor is depicted on the first page. On the next page is elaborated his history, and so on for each of the ancestors. However, the only trustworthy part of the chronicle is that starting with the surrender of Li Nan-ko to the Ming and relating the succession of the t'u-ssu from 1371 until the present time. The entire text concerning the history of the ancestors preceding Li Nan-ko is unreliable. Then we left the t'u-ssu and went to the ancestral cemetery of the Li Nan-ko branch at Hsiang T'ang.

On page 180:

The cemetery occupies a terrain as large as six acres, enclosed by a mud wall. The central alley, bordered by stone sheep and tigers in a sad state of decay, leads to a big stele, behind which is said to be the tomb of Li Nan-ko, and in front of which is built a stone table for the offerings to the dead. On the stele are engraved the text of the ratification by the Ch'ing emperor, of the appointment granted by the previous Ming emperor to the incumbent to the office of t'u-ssu, the text of a funeral oration granted by an emperor at the death of a t'u-ssu, also the glorious achievements of the clan and the names of the t'u-ssu who died on the field of battle. On both sides of the avenue are erected the steles of the t'u-ssu of the Li Nan-ko clan dating from the Ming and Ch'ing periods, the most recent dating from the Kuang-su period (1875–1909). Outside the enclosure, at the entrance of the cemetery, are erected two big steles, "the spirit way steles." On the one erected on the eighth moon of 1427 is chiseled: (this is) the spirit way stele of Sir Li (Nan-ko), who posthumously received the titles of Yung-lu ta-fu, Yu-chun tu-tu-fu, Pen-chun tu-tu. He is a descendant of Li K'o-yung, whose original name was T'o-pa, to whom was granted the name Li by the Tang emperor. During the Yuan dynasty, Li Shang-ko was functionary at the offices of the prince of Ch'i. To him succeeded consecutively Li Mei-chi-lu, Li Kuan-chi-lu and Li Nan-ko who was T'ung-chih (vice-chairman) of the district of Hsining. He received during the Hung-wu period of the Ming the hereditary duty of Tu-chih-huei-shih (High Commandant). To his son Yin was granted, on account of his merits, the title of Earl of Huei Ning,

and posthumously were bestowed (upon Li Nan-ko) the titles of his son: Yung-lu ta-fu, Yu-chun tu-tu-fu, Tso-chun tu-tu-fu. On the second spirit way stele erected on the third moon of 1475 is chiseled: (this is) the spirit way stele of Sir Li (Li Yin) to whom was granted the title "official who sincerely manifested military achievements" to whom were bestowed, in a special way, the titles of Yung-lu ta-fu, Chou-kuo Huei Ning-pei (Earl of Huei Ning, pillar of the empire).

The second document is encountered in Shuo-wen-yueh-k'an 3, 10, 1942 (Ch'ung-ch'ing Shuo-wen Yueh-k'an shih). There we meet with the article "Genealogical record of the tribe of the descendants of Li K'o-yung" by Wei Chu-hsien, who passed through the sub-prefecture of Ming Hua (San Ch'uan Valley) in October 1941. He visited Li Pao-ch'ing, a clan member of the old Li Nan-ko branch, who told him that during the Shun-chih period (1644–1661) a genealogical chronicle had been composed based on all available sources, by Yueh-Nai, secretary of the t'u-ssu for fifteen years, well read in the history of the clan, and that Yueh Nai was a contemporary of T'u-ssu Li T'ien-yu.[67]

I copied the present part of the chronicle composed by Yueh Nai. The original name of the Shat'o tribe of Li K'o-yung was Chu-yeh. The Tang emperor granted him the name Li and the title of Prince of Chin (895). He saved the Tang dynasty during the rebellion of Huang Ch'ao. Li Ssu-kung moved into Hsi Hsia, Li Chi-feng followed the Sung dynasty, offering the four districts of Yin, Hsia, Suei, Ning.[68] From the Sung until the Yuan, during generations, they lived in Hsi Hsia and were renowned for their military presentations. At the time of the Yuan, Li Shang-ko was T'ung-chih tu-tu-chih (Vice-Chairman of the protectorate office) in Hsining. Then the Li clan divided into six sub-clans, each having its t'u-ssu. The most important among them was the Li Nan-ko clan. During the Ming, Li Nan-ko surrendered with the officials of Huangchung. Then follow the names of the descendants of Li Nan-ko who fulfilled successively the duty of t'u-ssu during the Ming. Finally a genealogical scheme is elaborated, starting with Li Shang-ko, succeeded by his son Li Mei-chi-lu, his grandson Li Kuan-chi-lu, who had two sons Li Nan-ko and Ch'a han Timur. The son of Li Nan-ko was Li Yin, the son of Ch'a Han Timur was Kuan Yin-pao. The son of Li Yin was Li Ch'ang, the son of Kuan Yin-pao was Li Wen. Further the names of the successors of Li

---

[65] *Kan, Ch'ing-hai, Tsang pien-ch'ü K'ao-ch'a-chi,* Shanghai, Commercial Press, 1947.

[66] Hsiang T'ang is the name of the locality where the cemetery is situated, and means the Hall of Sacrifice, the room where the corpse is laid out.

[67] The shift of the Ming dynasty to that of the Manchu was preceded by a period of troubles. The rebels in Huangchung looted the country of its wealth. T'u-ssu Li T'ien-yu, still faithful to the Ming, tried to restore order in his territory. In 1644 his wife, concubine, two brothers, and three hundred of his subjects were killed. He himself was taken prisoner by rebels and sent to Sian to the Manchu court. He was accredited in his former duty of t'u-ssu and died as a faithful official of the Manchus (*Annals* of Hsining 28: 2b. *Annals* of Kansu 42: 47b).

[68] *Annals* of Kansu 46: 3b, happened in 982.

Ch'ang and Li Wen correspond with the names encountered in the lists of the *Annals* of Hsining and Kansu.

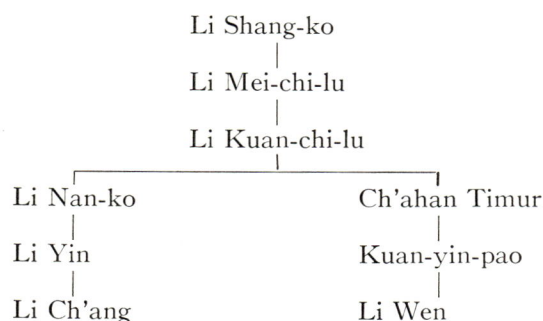

```
              Li Shang-ko
                   |
             Li Mei-chi-lu
                   |
             Li Kuan-chi-lu
         ┌─────────┴─────────┐
   Li Nan-ko             Ch'ahan Timur
      |                        |
    Li Yin               Kuan-yin-pao
      |                        |
   Li Ch'ang                Li Wen
```

HISTORICAL VALUE OF THE DOCUMENTS

Both important documents manifest the confusion existing in the minds of the Li t'u-ssu and their subjects during and at the end of the Ming dynasty. Both Li clans claim (1) their first ancestor to have been Li K'o-yung, (2) who had received the name of Li, and (3) had been created prince of Chin by the Tang emperor. However, on the spirit way stele in the cemetery, erected in 1427, is chiseled that the original name of the Li K'o-yung clan was Topa, while the genealogical chronicle composed by Yueh Nai around 1644 records that the original name of the Shat'o tribe of Li K'o-yung was Chu-hsieh.

The Topa tribe was the leading tribe among one of the two Tibetan Tang-hsiang groups which had fled to Kansu in 627 from Sung P'an-ting (northwest Szechwan), for fear of invading T'u-fan. This group, called P'ing-hsia-p'u, was settled by the Tang emperor in the region of the present Mi Chih Hsien (northwest of Shensi). The group, during the troubles which beset the Tang empire, had founded its own Hsi Hsia kingdom, and from 982 on waged war with the Sung empire.

In 808 Shat'o, belonging to the Chu-hsieh tribe of the western Turks, eluded the pursuit of Tibetans and fled from Kanchow through Huangchung and East Kansu to submit to China. They were settled in Ling Chou (Ninghsia), later in Yen Chou and still later eastward through Shansi. They were faithful warriors, who often saved the Tang dynasty. Later they founded their own ephemeral Shat'o dynasties (923–947), whose first emperor originated from the Chu-hsieh tribe.

Yueh Nai, author of the chronicle, writes that the Li clan originated from the Chu-hsieh tribe of the western Turks. He should have known that Li K'o-yung was a Shat'o Turk, that the Shat'o group differed from the Tibetan Hsi Hsia group, and was settled in its own country granted by the emperor, and had its own history. Nonetheless he makes them move into Hsi Hsia, he records two Hsi Hsia leaders, Li Sse-kung and Li Chi-feng, as being ancestors of the Turk Li Nan-ko, and records the offering of four Hsi Hsia districts to the Sung (982) as being an act of his Shat'o ancestor.

Possibly the fact chiseled on the stele, stating that the Li clan had originated from the Topa Hsi Hsia tribe, induced Yueh Nai, who was not conversant with Chinese history, to find a solution combining two impossible data. However, how could the tradition of the origin of the clan have been obliterated to such an extent if stock were taken of the fact that the grandson of Li Nan-ko, Li Kung, who obtained the literary degree of Chin-shih in 1481 and later was promoted minister of the Shang-pao-ssu, certainly must have known all about the Shat'o and the Hsi Hsia history?

It is interesting to compare the two documents. Both stele and chronicle start with the same ancestor Li Shang-ko, his son Mei-chi-lu, his grandson Kuan-chi-lu, his great-grandson Li Nan-ko whose son was Li Yin and grandson Li Ch'ang.

However, on the stele the brother of Li Nan-ko, Ch'ahan Timur, and his son and grandson Li Wen, are not mentioned. It has to be kept in mind that the stele is erected in Hsiang T'ang, in the cemetery of the Li Nan-ko branch, and so it is normal that the members of the Li Nan-ko branch only should be recorded on the stele in this cemetery. The Li Wen branch has its own cemetery situated ten li north of Hsining, with its own steles, etc. But it is normal that in the genealogical chronicle of the entire Li clan, composed by Yueh Nai in 1644, the Li Wen branch should be recorded next to that of Li Nan-ko.

Who was Li Shang-ko? On the stele he is noted as having been an official of the Prince of Ch'i, during the Yuan dynasty (1280–1367). His son Li Mei-chi-lu and his grandson Li Kuan-chi-lu are recorded as having held the same office.

The Ch'i princes had been appanaged by the emperor in East Kansu in Feng-hsiang-fu. Among them was the Prince T'o-t'o-nu-erh Fu-ma [69] who was the younger brother of Chang Chi to whom, at the beginning of the Yuan dynasty, Huangchung had been assigned as appanage, and who in 1287 had been ordered by the emperor to reside in Huangchung. Chang Chi must have known the Li clan pretty well.

In the biography of Li Wen, son of Li Shang-ko, in the *Annals* of Hsining **27** : 11*b*, it is noted that in the Hsuan Te period (1426–1436), Li Wen held the office of Tu chih-huei chien-shih (secretary High Commandant) at the Hsin-tu-ssu in Shensi province. Does this not seem to point to an incumbency near the same Princes of Ch'i? However this seems impossible, because, in 1429 according to the same *Annals* (**27** : 11), Li Wen and all the t'u-ssu of Huangchung participated in the expedition in Nan Ting and Ch'u Hsien, conducted by Li Yin, and according to the *Annals* of Kansu (**42** : 38*a*) this expedition started in 1425.

However, according to the genealogical register of Yueh Nai, Li Shang-ko was T'ung-chih tu hu-chih (vice-chairman of the protectorate office) in Hsining

---

[69] Hambis, *op. cit.*, 108, 49.

under the Yuan; he therefore lived in Huangchung and not in East Kansu in Feng-Hsiang Fu in the appanage of the Ch'i prince. It was also at that time that the Li clan parted in six branches. But the Li clan never parted in six branches because only two Li clans have existed in Huangchung and not six.

The *Annals* of Kansu (**42**: 38), according to "original" documents, record that Li Wen was the son of the first wife of Li Shang-ko and that the *Annals* of Hsining (**27**: 2b, 10a), which printed that Li Yin was the uncle of Li Wen are to be amended. Li Wen and Li Yin were first cousins, Li Shang-ko and Li Nan-ko were brothers. However, the *Annals* do not tell who was the father of Li Shang-ko and Li Nan-ko.

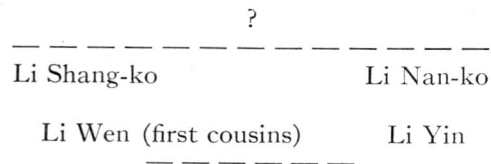

<pre>
                    ?
— — — — — — — — — — — —

Li Shang-ko   Li Nan-ko

   Li Wen (first cousins)   Li Yin
      — — — — — —
</pre>

During the Yuan dynasty, Li Wen discharged the office of Tu chih-huei t'ung-chih (Vice-chairman High Commandant) (*Annals* of Kansu **42**: 38a) and then submitted to the Ming with the officials of Huangchung in a group in 1371. The *Annals* do not note at what time Li Shang-ko died. However the fact, that Li Wen went to submit as chief of the clan means that his father had died before 1371. Because he submitted to the Ming, he and not Li Shang-ko had been granted the office of t'u-ssu. He is considered the founding ancestor of the clan and with him starts the clan cemetery. In this clan cemetery his mound is the principal and highest one. When all the subjects of the clan come yearly to honor him and the later clan ancestors, offerings and libations are first made before his mound and then before the graves of the later ancestors. Li Shang-ko, his father, is not buried in the clan cemetery.

At what time did the Li clan part into two clans? It is certain that before the submission of Li Wen before 1371, the division of the paternal inheritance had long since been accomplished between the two brothers, Li Shang-ko and Li Nan-ko (or between former clan chiefs), because both clans, in the Yuan dynasty, controlled definite territories, were ordered to guard definite passes and keep always ready a definite number of foot and horse (for all the t'u-ssu were in the Yuan times groups of Mongol soldiers or groups of surrendered tribes enrolled as defenders of the country). Because it is said that during the Ming and Ch'ing times they continued to occupy and defend the same territories and passes, it would seem that before the Li Nan-ko and Li Shang-ko time the division of the clan must have been achieved.

Anyway the problem of the exact time at which the partition of the clans had been achieved is not an easy one to solve, and also the problem concerning Li Wen

himself. We know for sure that 1371 was the year of his submission to the Ming, and also the time of his death is historically fixed at 1488. It is hard to explain how this man has been clever enough to be an official during 117 years!

THE SPIRIT WAY STELES

In the first document it is noted that the first spirit way stele was erected in 1427 in honor of Li Nan-ko, the first t'u-ssu and founding ancestor of the clan. According to the *Annals* of Kansu (**42**: 46b), Li Nan-ko died in 1407, his son Li Yin received in 1427 the title of Earl of Huei Ning, and the title granted to the son was posthumously bestowed at the same time upon the father (*Annals* of Hsining **27**: 10a. Annals of Kansu **42**: 47). This distinction which, according to the Chinese mentality, primarily honored the father who had reared so glorious a son, obviously seems to have been the cause of the erection of the spirit way stele at the entrance of the clan cemetery in honor of Li Nan-ko in 1427 by Li Yin himself.

The second spirit way stele was erected in 1475 in honor of Li Yin. Li Yin probably died a few years after 1437. His son, Li Ch'ang, succeeded to his father only in 1457, on account of the discredit weighing upon the clan. Li Ch'ang died in 1493 (*Annals* of Kansu **42**: 46; *Annals* of Hsining **27**: 10). Emperor Hsien Tsung only in 1475 promoted Li Ch'ang, and he honored him in a special way at his death, sending splendid funeral gifts and a funeral oration (*Annals* of Hsining **27**: 2b) written by himself, containing the glorification of the virtues of the deceased. This oration had to be burned before the coffin as a last farewell of the emperor to his faithful subject. The distinguished promotion received from the emperor in 1475 seems to have been the reason for the erection of the spirit way stele by Li Ch'ang to his father Li Yin in 1475, the father upon whom redounded the imperial attention bestowed upon his eminent son.

THE CEMETERY OF HSIANG T'ANG

The cemetery of Hsiang T'ang is definitely the most elaborate cemetery built in the country and it is said to have been erected to glorify the entire Li clan. I trusted this tradition accepted by prominent scholars and officials in the country, who founded their statement on an erroneous text of the *Annals* of Hsining (**27**: 2a) claiming that both Li clans were the descendants of Li Nan-ko (Monguors I: 70, 71). However, not a single stele is encountered in the cemetery pointing to members of the Li Wen clan, which has its own ancestral cemetery at the foot of the Han P'ing mountain, situated ten li north of the city of Hsining, with steles and inscriptions (*Annals* of Hsining **7**: 8a). This cemetery is not as elaborate as the one of the Li Nan-ko branch with its spirit way steles, etc., but its central avenue is also bordered with stone sheep and tigers in a sad state of decay (*Monguors* I: 71, note 57), and every year ceremonies are performed in it by the entire clan, in honor of the founding ancestor Li Wen, Earl of Kao Yang, and all the subsequent t'u-ssu of his clan. The Hsiang T'ang cemetery is definitely the cemetery of the Li Nan-ko clan.

In the Hsiang T'ang cemetery is seen a mound, said to be that of Li Nan-ko, who died in 1407. However, a striking puzzle is the fact that his son, the celebrated Li Yin, Earl of Huei Ning, who died soon after 1437, is buried not in Hsiang T'ang cemetery, but in the forlorn village of Hai Shi Wan, southeast of Nienpei, where a small stele with an inscription is erected, and next to his tomb is the tomb of his son Li Ch'ang, who received promotions in 1475 and the glorifying attention from the emperor at the time of his death in 1493. Still more puzzling is the fact that Li Kung, the eminent great-grandson of Li Nan-ko, the son of Li Ch'ang, who obtained the literary degree of Chin-shih in 1481 and was later promoted minister of the Shang Pao Sse, is buried in the village of Pa-chu-yuan situated southeast of Nienpei (*Annals* of Hsining 7: 17a; 27: 10–11; *Annals* of Kansu 42: 46b, 47a).

The fact that these three most eminent t'u-ssu of the clan were not buried in the ancestral cemetery where two spirit way steles were erected seems to suggest that the present elaborate cemetery might have been built in later times.

No notes are available relating to the ancestors of the other chiefs of the Monguor clans.

HISTORY OF HUANGCHUNG AND THE T'U-SSU DURING THE MING DYNASTY (1368–1644)

This chapter reveals on the one hand the tremendous role played by the Huangchung Monguors in the struggle waged by the Ming dynasty against the Mongols during the nearly three centuries of its existence, which several times shook the foundations of the empire. The help they rendered to the dynasty is unprecedented in history.

On the other hand, the chapter reveals the weakness of the Ming administration in Huangchung and the ordeal the loyal and dependent Monguors had to undergo to remain faithful to it amidst the wicked and ruthless depredations against their country, disastrous forays of brigands, hunger, disease, and poverty.

T'u-ssu Li Nan-ko, after his surrender with the officials of Hsining in a group in 1371 and his summons to court, was ordered to return to Hsining and to assume the administration of Huangchung. He controlled the country, calling on more tribes to surrender; repaired roads and bridges; organized the system of relays and the communications with the central administration; amassed grain in the public graneries, etc. The same year he defeated and took prisoner a rebel-

ling chieftain, Ho Chang-tsa (*Annals* of Hsining 27: 9–10).

The commandery of Hsining was created in 1372 (*Annals* of Hsining 31: 9b). This means that Chinese officials arrived accompanied by some troops to organize the country along the Chinese pattern and to enlist the t'u-ssu in their service.

The Ch'i t'u-ssu, Kung-k'o-hsing-ch'i, who had surrendered in 1368, was sent in 1372 to the country of the salt lake in Kokonor, where the tribal chief I-lin-chen-pen had revolted. He defeated the turbulent chief and pacified and controlled the country. He induced the Mongol chief Ch'i-chih-sun to surrender (*Annals* of Hsining 27: 12b; *Annals* of Kansu 42: 35a).

The heir apparent of the Yuan, Ai-ya-shih-li-ta-la, escaping from Ying Ch'ang in 1370, had arrived at Karakorum and been proclaimed emperor. During 1371 he mustered all available troops in order to recover his lost empire. In 1372 the Ming emperor, informed about the military preparations of the Mongols, dispatched three armies, with the order to deal a decisive blow to the Mongol forces in the very heart of their domain. Troops of three t'u-ssu from Huangchung joined the second army commanded by General Feng Sheng: the troops of the Lu t'u-ssu from Lien Ch'eng, and of the T'u-ssu T'o-erh-chih-shih-chieh and the T'u-ssu Wang Nam-mu-ko, both from Hsining. This army administered a crushing defeat in Liangchow to the forces of the Mongol commander Shih-la-han, and in Yung Ch'ang in Ma Hu Shan, to those of T'o-erh-chih-pa, who had revolted after his surrender and from whom 300 soldiers and 400 horses were captured. Then the troops delivered a severe defeat to the Mongol commander Pu-hua and captured 8,000 families. They went to I-chi-nai-lu (in the Gobi) where they defeated the Mongol Prince Pao Tsang and pursued fleeing Mongols until Kua and Sha Chou. The t'u-ssu troops returned to Huangchung (*Annals* of Kansu 42: 40b–44b; Ming Shih, Biography Fu Yu-te 129: 8; Pokotilov, 7–8).[70]

The expedition of General Feng Sheng in 1372, with his enlisted t'u-ssu troops, was the first attempt by the Ming to conquer the region of the corridor stretching from Liang and Kan Chou to Turkistan. The corridor, bordered on the north by the Gobi desert, the homeland of the nomads, was exposed to recurrent invasions of Mongols from the desert waste, and during three centuries the t'u-ssu of Huangchung would be ordered to repel their forays.

In 1373 the Mongol Prince Pu-yen-pu-hua, endowed with the title of Prince of Ning by the Mongol emperors, had been appointed by them administrator of the region of An-ting (Turkistan). In 1370 he had re-

---

[70] D. Pokotilov, *The history of the Eastern Mongols during the Ming from 1368–1634,* translated from the Russian by Rudolf Loewenthal, Chengtu, China, West China University, 1947.

ceived from the Ming emperor the invitation to surrender. In 1373 he had not yet answered the summons, and the prominent T'u-ssu T'o-erh chih-shih-chieh was ordered to induce him to submit. In 1374 his delegates arrived at court with the submission. The following year the emperor created the two commanderies of An-ting and A-tuan, and to Pu-yen-pu-hua was granted the title of Prince of An-ting (*Annals* of Kansu **42**: 23b; *Annals* of Hsining **31**: 9b).

In 1374 the T'u-ssu T'o-erh-chih-shih-chieh was ordered to induce the barbarians dispersed all over the country of Huangchung to submit to the Ming emperor (*Annals* of Hsining **31**: 9b).

In 1375 T'u-ssu Lu followed the expedition of General Pu Yin against the rebel Mongol T'o-erh-chih-pa in Liangchow, to whose army a severe blow was administered. The rebel managed to escape. The emperor invited T'u-ssu Lu to call at Nanking to receive the imperial congratulations. On account of illness he was prevented from moving to the capital.

In 1376 Hsining T'u-ssu Wang was ordered to participate in another expedition of General Feng Sheng in Liangchow region against the Mongols, plundering the country. Shih-chi-ku, Nan-t'ai and others surrendered with 1,000 men, and also the Mongol T'o-lin, with his 2,200 subjects (*Annals* of Kansu **42**: 40b).

In 1377 T'u-ssu Wang was ordered to join the expedition of General Pu Yin against the Tartar chief Yeh-su-t'o-huo and others who again plundered the Liangchow country. They suffered a severe blow and 1,000 of their brigands were killed. Then T'u-ssu Wang followed the expedition of General Feng Sheng in Kanchow and Suchow where 1,890 families surrendered (*Annals* of Kansu **42**: 40b).

In 1378 T'u-ssu Lu Ah-shih-t'u, oldest son of T'o Huan, fought and took prisoner Ta-kuan-tieh-chih, a chief of plundering Tibetans, living in the mountains between Ku Lang and Liangchow.

General Teng Yu in 1370 had pacified the country of Kui Te situated 220 li south of Hsining, on the southern borders of the Yellow River. In 1376 he had founded the So of Kui Te, leaving a garrison of 500 horse troops and 500 colonists, ordering them to till the soil and provide the subsistence of the garrison (*Annals* of Hsining **25**: 15b; *Annals* of Kansu **57**: 2a). In 1378 Kui Te was attacked and plundered by the Tibetan Ha la kui (*Annals* of Hsining **27**: 9a; *Annals* of Kansu **46**: 25b), who also devastated the Kokonor region. T'u-ssu T'o-erh-chih-shih-chieh was ordered to fight the brigands (Monguors I: 34).

BUREAU FOR EXCHANGE OF TEA AGAINST HORSES

The year 1378 was very important on account of the establishment of the bureau for the exchange of tea against horses. Each year 3,500 horses would be exchanged in the city: first-class horses exchanged for 120 pounds of tea, second-class horses for 70 pounds of tea, and third-class horses for 50 pounds of tea. Every tribe under submission was taxed a definite number of horses to be exchanged at the bureau.[71]

The very first bureau had been established in 1376 in Ch'in Chou in East Kansu, but on account of the distance between Ch'in Chou and An-ting and A-tuan, and the inconvenience of travel through the provinces, a bureau had later been established in Hsining (*Annals* of Hsining **17**: 3b).

The importance of the trading of tea for horses cannot be overrated. On the one hand, it was a means for the nomads to get rid of their horses and secure tea. Tibetans as well as Mongols cannot do without tea, and the stronger the concoction the more delightful it is to them. Even when traveling or indulging in hunting parties where tea could not be prepared, they chewed the tea leaves. The craving for tea among the nomads may be compared with the craving for opium among addicts. On the other hand, the trade was very beneficial to the Chinese. First of all, the cavalry got its badly needed horses in an easy way, and the officials of the bureau also benefitted. They evaluated the quality of the horses according to the gratuity offered by the nomad, cheating in the quality of the tea, and putting the transaction off indefinitely, making the customers wait for weeks on end, or helping them immediately, according to the gratuity presented. Squeeze was the rule in the bureau.

The first benefitters were the traders. The exchange of horses was a boon for the city. Traders from all over Szechwan and Shensi provinces moved into the city with the wares the nomads needed, in addition to the tea they brought with them. The nomads were allowed to bring more horses than the number taxed, and they carried wool, skins, musk, etc., to be exchanged for wares. The exchange of horses for tea was the yearly opportunity for the nomads to make a trip to the city and to provide for the needs of the family.

This institution was also an effective means of attracting the nomads to surrender, for only surrendered tribes were allowed to enter the city and transact business. After two years the institution reached fruition. It was an attraction, especially during the troubled times which were ahead, when the tribes, indulging in plundering each other, had to get rid of the stolen horses. It was an attraction also because the surrendered tribes enjoyed the protection of the empire.

In 1379 both Hsining Wang and Chao t'u-ssu were ordered to participate in the expedition of General Mu Yin, sent to quell the revolt of the turbulent eighteen tribes in T'ao Chou (Tibetans? Uighurs? Shat'o?) where the chief San Fu Shih was taken prisoner. Then T'u-ssu Chao was enjoined to follow the expedition of General Fu Yu-te against rebel Mongols in Yunnan

---

[71] Huang Ming su-i k'ao, Wen tien ko shu-chuang, Peiping, Chiang-fu-ssu chieh, 1937.

province, and T'u-ssu Wang to accompany General Mu Yin to Kan and Su Chou to fight the unfaithful Mongol T'o-erh-chih-pa. Two hundred of his soldiers were taken prisoner. Then the army proceeded to Ch'ih Chin in the Gobi where the Mongol Prince I-lien-cheng, his seal and tribes, were captured (*Annals of Kansu* ?: 42a–b, 40a, 48b).

T'u-ssu T'o-erh-chih-shih-chieh induced the Tibetan chiliarch A-pu to surrender, and in the fourth moon he fought the Tibetan chief I-lin-cheng-pen (*Annals of Hsining* 31: 10b).

At the death of the Mongol emperor in 1378, T'o ku-ssu had succeeded to the throne in Mongolia. He was soon on the warpath, mustering two armies in order to invade China, one in the Gobi at Karakorum, and one in North China at Yin Ch'ang. The army at Karakorum suffered a severe defeat at the hand of General Mu Yin in 1380, but the army of Yin Ch'ang was making inroads in Liaotung province.[72]

In 1380 T'u-ssu T'o-erh-chih-shih-chieh was called to court and ordered to arrive at Peking with his troops to stem the forays of the Ying Ch'ang brigands of the emperor. At the same time he was granted the title of Hsuan-wei general and the hereditary office of Chih Huei ch'ien shih in Hsining. He fought the brigands at Chin Shan Ssu, at Huo Ho, Yung P'ing, Su Chou, etc. His troops were victorious everywhere. He came back to Hsining after the capture of Na ha ch'u in 1387 (*Annals of Hsining* 27: 9b; *Annals of Kansu* 42: 44b).

SURRENDER OF TRIBES IN HUANGCHUNG

Two years after the establishment of the exchange bureau the submission of nine Tibetan tribes is recorded in the *Annals of Hsining*, chapter 16. It is hard to find out which among them were Tibetan, Shat'o, or Uighur tribes. At the time of the surrender of Li Nan-ko with the officials of Hsining in 1371, only thirteen tribes had submitted (*Annals of Hsining* 16: 1b), and the names of the tribes are not recorded. It may be assumed that the reiterated invitations conveyed by the t'u-ssu to the chiefs of tribes by order of the emperor during eight years had reaped small success. Now, however, the fascination of the profits attached to the tea market had stimulated the tribes to surrender.

In the northern part of Hsining the submission of two tribes is noted.

The Pa sha tribe lived in tents on a territory larger than 500 square li, situated more than 100 li north of Hsining on the borders of the Tat'ung River. It controlled the Tsan-tsa tribes, the Ssu-erh-ssu-ko and many small tribes (*Annals of Hsining* 16: 7b).

The Pa Wa tribe were also nomads, living next to the Pa sha tribe on the borders of the Tat'ung River. This tribe must have been smaller than the Pa sha tribe (*Annals of Hsining* 16: 10a).

At that time the expansive country 40 li north of Hsining was inhabited by nomads and had no cities, villages, or farms. Only after the victory of the Manchus over the lamas and Tibetans in 1723 was colonization immediately started on a large scale, and the cities of Tat'ung and Mao Pei Shen were built.

West of Hsining, the *Annals* record in 1380 the submission of three tribes. The Si-na tribe lived 60 li west of Hsining on the northwest borders of the Hsining River. In its territory are tents, houses, and fortified villages. Its people practiced farming and cattle breeding. The tribe had a temple and a lama with the title of Kuo-shih (Master of the Kingdom), a silver seal, and an ivory stamp. The tribe numbered 500 families and was taxed 300 horses every year. It controlled the tribe called little Si-na which lived in Ku Shan, southeast of Nienpei, and it was taxed 30 horses. It also controlled the Ssu-ta-la-ma tribe and the Hsieh-erh-chih-kang temple, which were taxed 50 horses (*Annals of Hsining* 16: 8b).

The Chia-erh-chi tribe inhabited the territory situated north of the Si-na tribe. The part of the tribe living inside the wall lived in houses and fortified villages; the part living outside the wall practiced cattle breeding and lived in tents. At the time of disturbances caused by brigands they moved inside the wall. The chief of the tribe was a lama who had the title of Chih-hui. Every year the tribe was taxed 130 horses. The tribe controlled the Lung-pa tribe numbering 100 families which was taxed 150 horses.

In the region west of Hsining, stretching as far as 40 to 60 li, only farming, combined with cattle breeding, seems to have been practiced in 1380 by Tibetan tribes. After 1723 the region beyond was developed. The title of master of the kingdom was probably granted after the surrender of the tribe ruled by the lama. It was the policy during the Hung-wu and the whole Ming period to grant titles to lamas who induced tribes to surrender (Monguors II: 16). The title of Chih-hui borne by the chief is a title of the Ming time. The walls noted in the references were built only after 1546 (*Annals of Hsining* 13: 15). The author of the *Annals* printed in 1755 seems to have mixed circumstances existing only after 1546 with those of 1380.

Still west of Hsining the nomad Shen-tsang tribe surrendered in 1380. It inhabited a territory situated near Kokonor. At the time of the invasion of the Mongols in 1509 and their occupation of Kokonor, the tribe disappeared (*Annals of Hsining* ?: 5b).

In the region of the southern mountains of Hsining, between Hsining and the Yellow River, stretching in an east-west direction as far as Lao Ya Ch'eng, three more tribes surrendered in 1380, all of them living near the northern borders of the Yellow River.

The Tsan-tsa tribe lived in tents and its territory was situated south of the present subprefecture of Nienpei (*Annals of Hsining* 16: 4a).

---

[72] Pokotilov, *op. cit.,* 10–11.

The Ko-tsa tribe, also a tribe of tent-dwellers, lived east of the Tsan-tsa tribe, and southwest of the city of Ku Shan. The tribe numbered 400 families (*Annals* of Hsining 16: 4a).

The Ssu-kuo-mi tribe, also tent dwellers, lived in a territory situated 150 li south of Hsining, on the borders of the Yellow River. It was divided into two tribes (*Annals* of Hsining 16: 5b).

1386 MARKS A NEW ERA IN HUANGCHUNG

According to the *Annals* of Hsining 25: 1a; 9: 15b, Keng Ping-wen was sent to build the city of Hsining with appropriate circumvallations, using troops from all the commanderies of Shensi. The size of the city had to be reduced to half of its former size, with four watch towers on the corners, nineteen more on the walls, and four gates. The note concerning the use of troops of all the commanderies of the province of Shensi seems to point to the fact that few troops and laborers were available in Huangchung in 1386, and that the former city was too extensive, inconvenient for defense, and probably in bad condition. Keng Ping-wen was ordered to build seven relay stations where official couriers could find horses ready to forward the orders without delay to the upper administration, and also five storehouses for provisions, drill fields for the soldiers, and administrative buildings. Four relay stations were built in an eastern direction covering a distance of 220 li, connecting Hsining with the northeastern part of Kansu. One relay was built in Ku Shan, 160 li south of Nien-Pei in the region of the three tribes which had surrendered in 1380. He also built the fortified city of Nien Pei with a Ch'eng-huang temple (spirit protector of the city) (*Annals* of Hsining 14: 16a). A Wen Miao (temple for Confucius) had been built in Hsining and a temple for the spirit protector of the city, for the emperor had already, in 1370, ordered these temples to be built in all the cities of the empire.

These few data suggest that the Monguors saw the situation changing in Huangchung after they had surrendered in 1371. In 1372 Hsining had been created a commandery and consequently Chinese officials had been appointed very soon. Without indicating the date of the appointments, the annals (*Annals* of Hsining 23: 5b), note that the administration of Huangchung was controlled by two major officials, a civil and a military. The Fen-chou-tao, who resided not in the unimportant Hsining, but in Liangchow, controlled a large area, and the Feng-hsiun-tao who resided in Kanchow controlled the six granaries, the irrigation canals, the finances of the administrative organs and the farming colonies for the whole of Kansu. Only in 1488, a hundred years later, was the civil and military governor of Huangchung Ping-pi-tao appointed with residence in Hsining. Chapter 24, 14a, records without

noting a date that on account of the small population and the extent of the uncultivated land, the Monguors had been ordered to abandon the cultivated land around the cities and fortresses, which would be assigned to artisans and traders and soldiers, and to move to the uncultivated areas they controlled during the Yuan time.

This important note hints at the purpose of the Ming to found Chinese colonies, and suggests that the soldiers had to till the soil and provide for their subsistence. This is the time honored policy of China, practiced since 118 B.C. by Ho Ch'u-ping in Hsining.

Necessarily more civil and military officials had arrived and new administrative organs had to be created, since the establishment in 1378 of the exchange bureau of tea against horses. More troops, traders, and artisans had flooded into the city, and in 1380 more Tibetan tribes had surrendered. Houses and shops had to be built, caravansaries for Tibetans, arsenals and barracks. Taxes had to be collected, disturbances prevented, justice dispensed, and the city defended. It was plain that Hsining had been chosen to become the pivot of the civil and military administration of entire Huangchung.

In 1387 T'u-ssu T'o-erh-chih-shih-chieh, after his return from the expedition in Liaotung, induced the rebel chiliarch A-pu-ti to surrender, and T'u-ssu Ch'i Kung-k'o hsing-ch'i again induced the Tibetan I-lin-cheng-pen (*Annals of Hsining* 31: 10b) and the turbulent Ch'i Chih-hsun to surrender. However, he must not have succeeded in his efforts with Ch'i Chih-hsun because the turbulent Mongol, in 1392, participated in the troubles in Han Tun (Tunhuang) (*Annals* of Kansu 46: 25b).

In 1388 at the time the army of the Mongol Emperor T'o-ku ssu had been defeated by the Ming, 200,000 of his soldiers had surrendered and only 40,000 had fled in various directions with the emperor, whose power was completely discredited in the eyes of his officers. He was strangled by one of them in 1388.[73]

In 1391 T'u-ssu T'o-erh-chih-shih-chieh was sent to the commandery of Kanchow and was soon called back to Hsining to fight the Tibetan A-li-ta-ah-su. T'u-ssu Kan was ordered to join the expedition of General Sung Sheng at Ha mu li (*Annals* of Kansu 46: 2b; 42: 50b).

T'u-ssu T'o erh-chih-shih-chieh died in 1392. He had accumulated thirteen merits during his lifetime and died discharging his office. His son Tuan Chou succeeded his father in 1396 (*Annals* of Hsining 31: 10b; 27: 9b; 24: 7b; 27: 9b; *Annals* of Kansu 46: 35b).

In 1392, t'u-ssu Wang was ordered to follow General Lan Yu, pursuing the turbulent Ch'i Chih-hsun, who at that time was in the region of Han Tun (Tunhuang). On the arrival of Lan Yu most of his tribes fled and were pursued as far as the region of Kokonor. Many were captured with a large number of their cattle.

---

[73] Pokotilov, *op. cit.*, 13.

FIRST LAMASERY BUILT BY EMPEROR— CREATION OF BOARD OF LAMAS

The lama San la of Hsining wrote a letter to the tribes of Han Tun to induce them to surrender and some tribes did so. The Annals of Hsining 15: 12a, note the surrender of the tribes, the tribute of horses offered by them, the appointment of Lama San la as chief of the surrendered tribes, the building of a lamasery south of Nien Pei, the name of Ch'u T'an bestowed upon the lamasery by the emperor, the first creation of the Board of Lamas in Hsining, and the appointment of San la as its director (Monguors II: 16–17). The example set by the emperor encouraged many lamas to act in the way of San la, attracting tribes to move into Huangchung, etc. So nan chi li ssu, the chief of the Han Tun tribes which did not follow the exhortations of San la, surrendered later, in 1397, and their chief was appointed Chih huei ch'ien shih in Han Tun. In the *Annals* of Hsining 15: 1b, is noted an inscription "appeased Tibetans" bestowed by the emperor upon the temple Ta-fu-ssu, built in Hsining during the Yuan by the ancestors of the Shat'o Li Nan-ko (Monguors II: 14), and there is recorded the building of the temple Kung-t'ung ssu in the city (*Annals* of Hsining 15: 2a). At the end of the same year T'u-ssu Wang was ordered to join the expedition of General Lan Yu against the rebel Mongol Yueh Lu Timur in Chien Ch'ang in Szechwan province. The rebel was captured and killed (*Annals* of Kansu 42: 42a; 46: 25b).

DEATH OF EMPEROR T'AI TSUNG (HUNG-WU), 1398

T'ai Tsung, the first emperor of the Ming dynasty, died in 1398.

Since 1371, the date of the submission of the t'u-ssu of Huangchung, the circumstances of the country had changed entirely, the economy had developed, the population had increased, and the influence of lamaism had extended, thanks to the granting of titles and domains to lamas and the founding of peculiar institutions for those among them who induced tribes to submit and to move into the country (Monguors II: 16–18). However, the most important increase of the population was caused by the moving into Huangchung of 7,200 families of Chinese soldiers, numbering 15,854 persons, during the Hung Wu period, to start the first military colonies (*Annals* of Hsining 16: 15a). The civil and military administration of the country had progressively been organized and the conquest of Huangchung stabilized. During the Hung Wu period the Monguor t'u-ssu had proved their faithfulness to the Ming dynasty. They had promoted the stabilization of the country and fought for the empire in the farflung provinces of Liaotung, Yunnan, Szechwan, and Turkistan, and the prominent T'u-ssu T'o-erh-chih-shih-chieh had

discharged his office with distinction until his dying day. The faithfulness of the Monguor t'u-ssu will become more and more manifest during the reigns of the subsequent Ming emperors.

MONGUORS OF HUANGCHUNG DURING THE REIGN OF EMPEROR CH'ENG TSUNG (YUNG LO), 1403–1424

T'ai Tsung, first emperor of the Ming, had appointed as successor his grandson, Huei Ti, an inexperienced young boy. His uncle, the Prince of Yen, youngest son of the emperor, revolted and defeated his nephew in a four year struggle.[74] He ascended the throne in 1403. He was called by the name of the period of his reign, Yung Lo.

Yung Lo, who must have known T'u-ssu T'o-erh-chih-shih-chieh, who during 1380–1387 had fought the brigands of the Mongol Emperor T'o ku ssu in Liaotung, had called the Kansu troops to join his army. T'u-ssu Tuan Chou, who had succeeded his deceased father, went with his troops to rescue Yung Lo in 1399. He died on the field of battle. Yung Lo rewarded the faithful t'u-ssu, granting to his clan the name of Ch'i and giving to the clan chief a mansion in the city of Hsining, and posthumously bestowing upon him the title of Piao-ch'i chiang-chun (*Annals* of Hsining 28: 13a; *Annals* of Kansu 42: 44b).

T'u-ssu Ch'eng Yi also had taken the side of Yung Lo in his revolt against Huei Ti. He was rewarded with the office of Chih-huei t'ung-chih in Lu Chou (*Annals* of Kansu 42: 36b). During this period more troubles occurred in Huangchung. Lu T'u-ssu Kung Pu shih chieh repelled the invasion of the Mongol Pu Yen ta shih in 1402, who looted the region of Liangchow. The t'u-ssu offered to Emperor Yung Lo in 1403 the captured prisoners and a tribute of horses. He was promoted to centurion in Chuang Lang.

The same year, 1402, the turbulent I lin sheng pen revolted again in Kokonor and looted the region of Kui Te and the southern valley of Hsining. T'u-ssu Ch'i Kung-k'o-hsing-ch'i went to fight the rebel and died on the field of battle (*Annals* of Hsining 27: 12b). The troubled conditions in Huangchung at that time seem to have been the reason why no more t'u-ssu participated in the struggle of Yung Lo against Huei Ti.

The new emperor had to contend with the tremendous problem of the Mongols, and this dangerous prospect was not bright. During the reign of his father (1368–1398) nine expeditions had to be launched against them. A constant struggle against the empire and endless dissension of the different tribes among themselves was to be expected. The struggle between

---

[74] In Monguors II: 16, 21, 22, are recorded the history of the foundation of the monastery of Ch'u T'an by San la, and the wonderful legends circulating among the lamas related to the mysterious disappearance of Emperor Huei Ti, who became lama in the monastery of Ch'u T'an, settled there and died.

the eastern and western (Oirat and Kalmuk) Mongols would become especially desperate and obstinate, and Yung Lo would have to launch five campaigns personally into barren Mongolia, and die in that fateful country at the time that the troops from his fifth campaign were on their way back to Peking. During these times of alarming confusion and disorganization in Mongolia, the Monguors of Huangchung had to participate in the expeditions, defend their own country, and die on the fields of battle.[75]

The strangled Mongol Emperor T'o-ku-ssu was succeeded by Elbek, who was murdered in 1399 by Ugetch'i, chief of Kirghiz tribes, who tried to establish his hegemony over the Mongol tribes. He was defeated by A-lu-t'ai, chief of the Asods [76] and Ma-ha-mu, chief of the Oirats. In 1403, the eastern Mongols proclaimed as emperor Pen-chia-shih-li, son of Elbek, who was joined by A-lu-t'ai.

In 1403 T'u-ssu Ch'eng under the command of General Chang Fu, was ordered to fight groups of eastern Mongols, subjects of Pen-chia-shih-li, who came from the Gobi desert into the country of Kan and Liangchow (*Annals* of Kansu **42**: 37*a*). T'u-ssu Chao joined the same expedition and fought in Yung Ch'ang (*Annals* of Kansu **42**: 48*b*); Ch'eng and T'u-ssu Na fought the same groups in Cheng Fan (*Annals* of Kansu **42**: 45*a*; **42**: 39*b*). T'u-ssu Wang was sent to I-chi-nai and Pu-yen-mu, north of Kan and Liangchow, to induce Pa tu Timur to surrender (*Annals* of Kansu **42**: 41*a*). In the same first year of his reign, Yung Lo, in order to stabilize the conquest of Huangchung, organized military colonies, apportioned land to the colonists, and provided them with grain and oxen and farm implements (*Annals* of Hsining **31**: 2*a*).

In 1404 T'u-ssu Lu, Kung pu chih chieh, was ordered to garrison Cheng Fan and Mao Mu Ch'eng.

In 1409 T'u-ssu Lu, Kung pu shih chieh, was sent to I-chi-nai to care for and organize the surrendered Mongol tribes.

In 1410 Pen-chia-shih-li had offended the Chinese emperor by not caring for his subjects invading the frontiers of Liang and Kanchow. He killed the ambassador who conveyed the protest of the emperor. The emperor retaliated forthwith, granting titles to the Oirat chiefs, the foes of Pen-chia-shih-li. A conflict broke out between the two groups, and to Pen-chia-shih-li and A-lu-t'ai was administered a severe blow at the hand of the Oirat Ma-ha-mu. The emperor took advantage of their reverse and equipped an expedition against them, under the command of General Ch'u Fu, who blindly rushed into an ambush where his troops were annihilated. The emperor, in order to avenge the failure and redeem the honor of the empire, himself led an expedition against Pen-chia-shih-li and A-lu-t'ai on March 15, 1410. Pen-chia-shih-li suffered a crushing defeat and escaped with a few soldiers, and a severe blow was then administered to A-lu-t'ai.[77] The emperor was back in Peking September 15, 1410. He had ordered the Monguor t'u-ssu to join the expedition.

T'u-ssu Li Yin, son of the late Li Nan-ko mustered the t'u-ssu and their troops. They participated in the expedition under his command. Among them are noted T'u-ssu A (*Annals* of Kansu **42**: 49*b*), T'u-ssu Chao (*Annals* of Kansu **42**: 48*b*), T'u-ssu Chou (*Annals* of Kansu **42**: 51*a*), T'u-ssu Ch'eng (*Annals* of Kansu **42**: 35*a*), T'u-ssu Na (*Annals* of Kansu **42**: 50*b*), and T'u-ssu Lu. The entire group fought in both battles against Pen-chia-shih-li and A-lu-t'ai. T'u-ssu Lu, Kung pu shih chieh, died on the field of battle fighting A-lu-t'ai. On that occasion to the clan of T'o Huan, prince of An Ting, was granted the name of Lu by the emperor, as reward for its devotion to the dynasty.

In 1411 T'u-ssu Lu Hsien joined the expedition commanded by the eunuch Wang An against Mongol tribes roaming in the region of Hsi Liang (north Kansu). The years 1411 and 1412 were times of intermittent forays by splinter groups of the defeated Pen-chia-shih-li and A-lu-t'ai erupting from Mongolia in the Liangchow and Kanchow regions. In 1412 two Chinese commanders, Sung Hu and Li Lin, had been appointed to repel the invasions and several t'u-ssu lent a hand: Li Yin (*Annals* of Kansu **42**: 46*a–b*), Chou (*Annals* of Kansu **42**: 51*b*), Ch'i (*Annals* of Kansu **42**: 35*a*), Chi (*Annals* of Kansu **42**: 42*a*), Hsin (*Annals* of Kansu **42**: 53*b*), Wang (*Annals* of Kansu **42**: 41*a*), and Na (*Annals* of Kansu **42**: 39*b*). The invading groups were those of Lao ti han,[78] of Ho lo ch'ih, Pa erh ssu and T'olot'ai. A severe blow was administered to them in Sha Chin Ch'eng (region of Liangchow) and they were pursued to T'ao-lai ch'uan (on the Tat'ong River) where 360 of their brigands were captured with their chiefs. The same year T'u-ssu Lu with commander Ch'eng hai took as prisoners Palima, chief of a group of invaders, and Shih T'ai, chief of another group in the region of Sung Shan I.

In the same year the Oirat chief Ma-ha-mu killed Pen-chia-shi-li and proclaimed as emperor of the Mongols, Delbek son of Pen-chia-shih-li. A-lu-t'ai, his foe, immediately tried to befriend the Chinese, and received the title of Prince of Karakorum. The granting of this title was as a red rag before a bull. Thereupon the enraged Oirat chief mustered his troops to invade China. The emperor himself decided to launch an expedition against the Oirat Ma-ha-mu. It was the age-

---

[75] Chinese and Mongol sources are very confusing relating to the history of these times. Pokotilov, *op. cit.,* Wolfgang Franke, Yung Lo's Mongolei-Feldzuge, *Sinologische Arbeiten* **3**: 1–54, Peking, Deutschland Institut, 1914. Louis Hambis, *La Haute Asie,* 58–104, Paris, Presses Universitaires de France, 1953. Henry Serruys, Notes on a few Mongolian rulers of the 15th century, *Jour. Orient. Soc.* **76** (2): 82–89, 1956.

[76] Asod-Alains: originating in the Caucasus, their faithful troops had been enlisted in the imperial guard and had followed the defeated Mongols fleeing toward Mongolia.

---

[77] Pokotilov, *op. cit.,* 28; Franke, *op. cit.,* 5–6.
[78] A descendant of Aoluch'ih. Hambis, *op. cit.* **107**: 122, 7.

old imperial policy to sow strife among the tribes, making them destroy each other. Yung Lo was as frightened of a Mongol power under the leadership of an offspring of the old Chingis Khan family as of one under the leadership of a rising new and tremendous Oirat group. He decided to launch a campaign against the Oirat Ma-ha-mu.

On April 6, 1414, the emperor himself led the campaign and administered a blow to Ma-ha-mu who escaped in the desert. The emperor was back in Peking on August 15. The Monguor troops of Huangchung had again been called to participate in the expedition. In the following years Alut'ai administered a defeat to the weakened Ma-ha-mu, who died in 1416. Then the emperor recognized the succession of Togon to his father Ma-ha-mu, as chief of the Oirats, and bestowed upon him the title of his father. The flames of hatred of A-lu-t'ai were fanned again against the Oirats and China. In the meantime A-lu-t'ai had secured the help of the Urianghai tribes living on the northern borders of China, which had transferred their allegiance from China to him. He had considered himself strong enough to antagonize China openly.

On April 12, 1422, the emperor started on a third campaign in Mongolia, this time against A-lu-t'ai, and called the Monguor troops. On the arrival of the strong Chinese army, A-lu-t'ai escaped in the desert waste, and the frustrated emperor vented his rage upon the unfaithful Urianghai tribes. The Monguors fought on the borders of the Wu-lang River in Liao-tung and in the Toyen district under command of T'u-ssu Li Yin. T'u-ssu Lu, having captured the Mongol chief Alahan on the Han t'an River, was rewarded with titles, silver, and silk clothes (family chronicle).

In 1423 the emperor resolved to finish definitely with A-lu-t'ai and started personally with a fourth expedition, calling the Huangchung troops. T'u-ssu Lu, on his way to the north, passed through the country of Ho-lan-shan and encountered the Mongol Prince Chung T'ung and troops of Yeh-hsien, which he captured. Just at the time the expedition was on the move, the Oirat chief Togon administered a blow to A-lu-t'ai, who escaped in the Gobi. The emperor understood that the expedition was doomed. He returned to Peking on December 9.

In 1424 A-lu-t'ai, despite the defeats he had suffered, was still strong enough to plunder the borders of the empire. The frustrated and enraged emperor decided to equip and lead a fifth expedition. All available troops were mustered and the expedition moved the second of May. A-lu-t'ai again vanished in the desert. The Mongols proved once more not to be easy game. The despondent emperor died on his way back to Peking, in Yu-mu-ch'uan, on August 18.[79]

In 1423 a Tibetan lama, Chang ta lama, was living in Hsining, appointed by Emperor Yung Lo as a translator of Tibetan texts. His morals were dissolute. He

appropriated the tributes brought by chiefs of Tibetan tribes, protected and hid people prosecuted by the courts of justice, and for more than ten years had fostered subversive influences. T'u-ssu Li Yin, discharged at that time the duty of Chi-hui ch'ien-shih in Hsining, conversant with these facts, killed the lama and his family. The country again enjoyed peace (Annals of Hsining 27 : 10a).

During the Yung Lo period (1403–1425) the military colonies of Huangchung did not increase in number. The same 7,200 families are recorded as at the end of the Hung-wu period. However, the number of persons constituting these families had decreased by 3,000 (Annals of Hsining 25 : 15a). During the same period four more temples had been built in Huangchung: Yung-hsing-ssu, situated five li north of the city of Hsining, 1410; Hua-tsang-ssu situated south of the city, 1410; Tsang-chin-ssu situated in the southwestern corner of the city, and Kuang-fu-kuan in the northwestern corner of the city, 1426 (Annals of Kansu 30 : 45b, 46a). Emperor Yung Lo had established in the valley of Sha t'ang, 80 li northeast of Hsining, controlled by the Li t'u-ssu, some pasturage for cavalry horses. In 1378 after the institution of the exchange bureau of tea against horses, 3,500 horses were acquired for the cavalry every year, and had to be fed on pasture.

T'U-SSU LI YIN

In 1426 Li Yin again was ordered to muster the Monguor troops, and to equip an expedition with the Chih-hui K'ang Chou, against the tribes of Anting and Ch'u Hsien (the old Tunhuang region), in which country the Chinese ambassadors Ch'iao Li-sse and Teng Ch'eng had been plundered and murdered on their way to Turkistan. The Monguor t'u-ssu who participated in the expedition under the command of Li Yin were Li Wen (Annals of Kansu 42 : 28a), t'u-ssu Lu, t'u-ssu Kan (Annals of Kansu 42 : 29b), t'u-ssu Ah (Annals of Kansu 42 : 49b), t'u-ssu Ch'i Hsien (Annals of Hsining 27 : 12b), Wang (Annals of Kansu 42 : 41a), Chao (Annals of Kansu 42 : 48b), Chi (Annals of Kansu 42 : 42b), Yeh (Annals of Kansu 42 : 52a), Chou (Annals of Kansu 42 : 52b; Annals of Hsining 28 : 13a). T'u-ssu Chou died on the field of battle during the expedition. Li Yin knew from first-hand information that the commanders of Anting, Ah-san-hsun-san-ho, and San-chi-ssu of Ch'u Hsien were the murderers. He led the army straight to their countries. The murderers fled with their tribes. Li Yin pursued them to the K'unlun mountains, and continued the pursuit several hundred li more, to the Ya-lin pass. There he administered a crushing defeat to them, capturing 1,100 men and 140,000 head of cattle. The brigands of Ch'u Hsien fled further on, but the Prince of Anting, Sang-erh-chia shih-lan, scared to death, went to court to confess his fault.

The emperor praised the military prestation of Li

---

[79] Pokotilov, op. cit., 28–32; Franke, op. cit., 5–12.

Yin and sent delegates from Peking with laudatory letters and with the order to come to Peking, the expenses to be defrayed by the empire. He received the promotion of Yu-fu tso-tu-tu and rich gifts. The next year he was honored with the title of Duke of Hui Ning, and received an emolument every year of 1,100 *tan* of grain. At the same time the emperor, with delicate attention, bestowed upon his deceased father, Li Nan-ko, the same title of Duke of Hui Ning (*Annals* of Kansu **42**: 47a; *Annals* of Hsining **27**: 11a).

Li Yin seemed to have reached the summit of a glorious career. However, a more eminent honor was in store for him. His merits would be chiseled on a stele in a temple built by himself to remind future generations of the imperial dignities bestowed upon him.

In the Kuang-fu-kuan, a temple built in 1426 in the northeast corner of the city of Hsining, the following is chiseled on a stele (*Annals* of Kansu **30**: 45a–b; *Annals* of Hsining **35**: 6a–b):

In 1422 in the eighth moon, Emperor Yung Lo, on his way back from an expedition in the desert took a breath in Yu-lin (Shensi) and called to his tent the officials who had won the most distinguished merits during the expedition. He granted Li Yin the titles of Yung-lu ta-fu, Pillar of the Empire and Duke of Hui Ning. Then the duke asked the emperor for permission to build in Hsining a temple in honor of the god of the war, in order to show gratitude for the blessings bestowed upon the empire and the people, and to secure more blessings in the future. The emperor agreed. Back home, Li Yin ordered, a few days later, the building of the temple. In the tenth moon of 1426 he informed the emperor about the completion of the construction. The emperor granted to the temple the name "Kuang-fu-kuan" (Taoist temple of glory and felicity), and appointed five Taoist priests for the performance of the sacrifices and worship in the temple.

One evening Li Yin was dreaming: he heard a man saying to him, "The God of War will appear." Instantly he dressed and adjusted his hat. Another man arrived carrying a tray with fine dishes. He invited Li Yin to come to his home to enjoy the dishes. Li Yin could not understand the circumstances of such an invitation. He thought it should be a spirit. Then he invited this man to come to his home. They were about to start with the dinner when all of a sudden the man said, "The spirit is there." Li Yin opened the door. He saw a man perfectly dressed, riding a white horse with a beautiful saddle and escorted by a numerous retinue. The man was like a king. The Taoist priest Ho Chao-tsung accompanied him, dressed in Taoist fashion, holding a book in his hands. He asked Li Yin: "The god will go first to the temple of the King Li. Is that correct?" Li Yin answered that he would first call at the Ning-fan Ssu (the temple of the appeased Tibetans). The entire group left. The sky was bright. On the way they passed a beautiful high building, enclosed by a high wall. They said, "The man who is living here does not belong to the lower range of society." They arrived at the gate of the temple. Li Yin dismounted from his horse. He was terrified. This happened on the eighth day of the seventh moon in 1423. In the winter of the same year the Duke was invited to see the emperor in Peking. He received his titles and precious gifts and returned to Hsining. What the Duke saw in his dream was the appearance of the god of war. It was a reward for his devotion to the empire. Emperor Yung Lo whom he had served in the expeditions in the desert had given him a precious sword and a famous horse. In 1425 Li Yin had fought the brigands in Anting and at the head of his soldiers had attacked the brigands and himself had killed many among them. He had captured a booty of 130,000 cattle. The emperor had sent minister Yang Yung to congratulate him. His merits were unusual and therefore he received in his dream a visit from the god of war . . . all these circumstances we have recorded on the stele, etc.

Without doubt the titles received by Li Yin, the building of the temple and the name given to it by the emperor himself, the stele, and the wonderful dreams went straight to the heart of the clan members and strengthened the cohesion of the Li clan. All these circumstances normally seem to have been conducive at that time to the building of an elaborate clan cemetery and to the erection in 1426 of the famous "spirit way stele" in honor of Li Nan-ko, the founder of the clan, father of Li Yin.

However, the behavior of Li Yin, puffed up with pride, had changed after he had been honored so magnificently by the emperor. The Governor of Ninghsia, Shih Chao, who had previously been Governor of Hsining, accused him of fostering subversive intentions. Li Yin could disprove the accusation. In Hsining he had assembled 700 families, fugitives from justice, whom he protected. He had settled them in the country and had given them land to till. But they harmed their neighbors, stealing and upsetting the country. Again complaints were lodged with the board of military justice, and Li Yin was ordered to turn over his tenants to the civil authority. In 1432 Ch'i Ch'eng, descendant of T'u-ssu Ch'i, T'o-erh-chih-shih-chieh, was his father's lawful successor to the office of t'u-ssu. The bold Li Yin, not bothering to offend the prominent Ch'i t'u-ssu clan, supported as successor to the t'u-ssu office Chien Tsang, the nephew of Ch'i Ch'eng, who was the son of his sister. He appointed murderers to kill Ch'i Ch'eng. He was accused again. This time the military judges rolled all the accusations into one, condemned him to prison, to the revocation of his titles and honors and to capital punishment. In 1437 the emperor pardoned him, allowing him a small emolument. Soon thereafter he died (*Annals* of Kansu **42**: 47a; *Annals* of Hsining **27**: 11a).

HUANGCHUNG T'U-SSU UNDER THE SUBSEQUENT EMPERORS

After the death of Yung Lo, (1424) the alarming confusion and struggle continued unabated among the eastern and western Mongols, both groups appointing their own Khans, who were merely nominal supreme chiefs and actually blind tools in the hands of Togon and A-lu-t'ai who controlled the two groups. A-lu-t'ai, weakened after many encounters with the Chinese and Oirat troops; was finally defeated and killed by the Oirat, Togon, in 1434; and the hegemony of the Oirats was achieved. It would reach the summit of its power again under the son of Togon, Esen, who was assassinated in 1455. Then the hegemony would be recovered by the eastern Mongols in 1470, after internal troubles had arisen among the Oirat tribes themselves.

After the death of A-lu-t'ai in 1434 his tribes separated: one group under the leadership of the Khan At'ai settled in I-chi-nai (500 li north of Kanchow), and one group, controlled by T'o-erh-chih-pa, settled in Yeh-k'o-lin-sha-erh-t'an, west of Liangchow. These groups would be the scourge of the countries of northwest Kansu for many years to come. A-lu-t'ai had already made forays in Liangchow in 1428. T'u-ssu Chao (*Annals* of Kansu **42**: 36*b*) and Chi (*Annals* of Kansu **42**: 42*a*) had been ordered to fight his turbulent tribes in I-pu-la-shan. In 1433, on account of the insecurity in the country, the commandery of Hsining had been reorganized in Chun-ming chih-huei-shih, six *so* had been established and the villages grouped in four *li*.

In 1435 T'u-ssu Chou (*Annals* of Kansu **42**: 51*a*), Wang (*Annals* of Kansu **42**: 41*b*), Chao (*Annals* of Kansu **42**: 48*b*), and Lu had been ordered to join the expedition of Commander Wang Kui against the tribes of At'ai and T'o-erh-chih-pa in Chengfan, Tsing-shih-shan, and Ho-shan. In 1436 a new expedition was launched against the same Mongol tribes, in which T'u-ssu Kan (*Annals* of Kansu **42**: 51*b*), Chou (*Annals* of Kansu **42**: 51*b*), and Wang participated (*Annals* of Kansu **42**: 41*b*). Then the tribes of At'ai invaded the country of Chuang-lang (P'ing-fan) but were beaten by T'u-ssu Lu, who pursued them to I-pu-la-shan.

In 1437 the same turbulent Mongol groups invaded Liangchow and Chuang-lang again, they were beaten by T'u-ssu Lu and Chao (*Annals* of Kansu **42**: 48*b*) in Tu-pei-ku and Mi-ho-ch'uan and 1,000 of their horses were captured. In 1438 the same brigands suffered a severe blow in Wei-yun, Pei-ya-wu, and I-pu-la-shan, at the hands of T'u-ssu Lu and Ch'eng (*Annals* of Kansu **42**: 36*b*).

The Monguors during these times were the faithful defenders not only of northwest Kansu but also of the most western Chinese frontiers, in the commanderies of Han Tung, Ch'u Shien, An Ting, and Ah Tuan. After the successful expedition of Li Yin in 1426, in combination with all the Monguor t'u-ssu, the petty tribes living in this area sustained themselves by pillage and robbery.

In 1429 the Governor of Hsining, Shih Chao, was ordered to prepare an expedition against the Chu-shien and Anting tribes whose chiefs still intercepted and plundered envoys bringing tribute to court. T'u-ssu Chou (*Annals* of Kansu **42**: 51*a*), Li Wen (*Annals* of Hsining **27**: 11*b*; *Annals* of Kansu **42**: 38*a*), Wang (*Annals* of Kansu **42**: 41*b*), and Ch'i Hsien (*Annals* of Kansu **42**: 45*a*) joined the expedition. The fleeing tribes were pursued, severely beaten and 340 of their brigands captured. The army returned with a booty of 300,000 camels, horses, sheep, and cows (*Annals* of Kansu **42**: 26*b*, 27*a*).

Se-ngo-ko, chief of a Tibetan tribe, was accustomed to stealing horses of neighboring tribes. The commander of Hsining, Mu Su, could not apprehend him. Later the thief arrived at Hsining to sell horses. The commander seized the horses, convinced they were stolen ones, but they were his own. The tribes were upset and about to start a revolt. Li Wen accused the imprudent commander, and the tribes were pacified. Li Wen was promoted (*Annals* of Hsining **27**: 12*a*; *Annals* of Kansu **42**: 38*a*).

In 1442 T'u-ssu Ch'i Hsien (*Annals* of Hsining **27**: 13*a*) was ordered to garrison the commanderies of Ah-tuan and Ch'u-hsien, to protect Anting, and to induce the scattered tribes to come back to their lands and surrender. In 1445 the Oirat chief Esen, who had succeeded his father Togon, who had died in 1439, attacked and occupied Hami. In 1447 Ch'i Hsien (*Annals* of Kansu **42**: 45*a*; *Annals* of Hsining **31**: 12*b*), t'u-ssu Chao (*Annals* of Kansu **42**: 48*b*), and t'u-ssu Lu followed the expedition of commander Jen I in Sha Chou. In 1448 Wa lo, chief of the Tibetan Pa-sha tribes started plundering Huangchung. T'u-ssu Ch'i Hsien was ordered to fight Wa lo. He succeeded in killing the chief. These tribes had submitted in 1380, their chief controlled 30 or more tribes, which inhabited a country as large as 500 li, starting 60 li north of Hsining and running to the borders of the Ta-t'ung River. Pa Sha was ill-famed for its predatoriness (*Annals* of Hsining **27**: 13*a*; **19**: 7*b*). In 1450 T'u-ssu Chao and T'u-ssu Lu repelled Mongol invaders in Kao-ssu-yuan (*Annals* of Kansu **42**: 48*b*). In 1452 T'u-ssu Ch'eng followed commander Su Chieh, fighting Mongols who were plundering Nan-chuan. They pursued them to Su-wu-shan and captured their chiefs (*Annals* of Kansu **42**: 36*b*).

During the Cheng T'ung period (1436–50) at the time the northwestern part of Kansu was riven by inroads of Mongols and the t'u-ssu were fighting the Mongols in Kansu and in Turkistan, Liu Ch'uan, commander in Kuei Te (situated south of Hsining on the southern borders of the Yellow River), induced 72 tribes of Tibetans to surrender, promoted cultivation and farming among them, established a tea bureau and every year exchanged 1,740 horses for tea, protected the traders and the communications in the country, built a route and relays connecting the important city of Ho Chou with Kuei Te. The country of Kuei Te was at peace and the people enjoyed the trustful and honest commander (*Annals* of Hsining **25**: 16*a*).

The chronicles of the Lu t'u-ssu clan note that during 1450–1464 raids had to be intermittently repelled along the Liangchow and Kanchow borders, perpetrated by the same eastern Mongol groups and some Oirat groups, which ventured to lay waste and devastate even

Chuang-lang, Ch'ing-yang, and East Kansu. The raids furnished to the invaders a considerable amount of loot and fostered their predatory instincts. The example set by the Mongols whetted the appetite for plunder among the Tibetan tribes also. The people lived in desperate conditions, and the t'u-ssu troops had always to be ready to comply with the orders of military commanders.

This note, recorded in the Lu chronicles, is quite acceptable for the reason that during just these years a tremendous confusion reigned in Mongolia, and the Mongol tribes located along the Kanchow and Liang-chow borders had nobody to care for them, for the Oirats, now at the summit of their power, had thought themselves strong enough to challenge the Chinese empire.

HEIGHT OF OIRAT HEGEMONY

To Esen, the powerful Oirat chief, had been promised an imperial princess by the eunuch Wang Chen, the favorite of the emperor. He had not notified the emperor of this promise and when the envoys of Esen arrived at court with the nuptial presents they were refused. In the autumn of 1449 the humiliated Esen began raids on the empire frontiers and approached Ta-t'ung. An army of half a million men was raised in a hurry, and sent against the Oirats. The emperor accompanied the army. His troops were routed, the emperor was taken prisoner, the remnants of the army tumbled back to Peking, and the capital was in jeopardy. Ching Ti, the brother of Emperor Ying Tsung, ascended the throne in 1450. The Oirats were unable to seize the capital. After endless deliberations, the released imperial prisoner reentered Peking in the eighth moon, after an absence of one year.

Esen, swollen with pride after his resounding victory over the empire, his ambition soaring to the throne, proclaimed himself emperor of the Mongols in 1454; but two of his commanders revolted against him in 1455, he fled and was killed the same year. For the time being the balance of political power of the Oirats shifted to the eastern Mongols who struggled again for the hegemony. One of the commanders who had killed Esen was killed by Polai, a tribal chieftain of the Ta-tan Mongols. Po-lai enthroned a new Khan, Markorgis, the son of T'o-to-pu-hua, known under the name of Hsiao-wang-tsu, the little king, and began with raids on the frontiers of the empire.[80]

In 1457 Emperor Ching Ti fell ill, the secluded Yin Tsung ascended the throne for the second time and thereafter his brother died.

T'U-SSU LI WEN

The same year T'u-ssu Li Wen arrived at Peking from Hsining with his army, to congratulate Yin Tsung

on his second ascension to the throne, and to present his offices in these times of troubles which beset the empire. He was promoted Tu-tu ch'ien-shih and somewhat later Yu-tu-tu, Governor of Tat'ung. Two thousand Mongols arrived and plundered the region of Wei-yuan. Li Wen defeated and pursued them. The emperor granted him the title of Duke of Kao Yang. In the autumn of 1460 the Mongol Polai started a raid on a large scale invading Yen-men-kuan and devastating the country. The officials in the capital grew very anxious. Li Wen, however, forbade his troops to move. He was committed to prison and deliberation concerning capital punishment was held. The emperor pardoned him, but he was stripped of his titles except that of tu-tu ch'ien-shih, and an opportunity was granted to redeem his honor by fighting the Mongols in the regions of Yenan and Suei-te (*Annals* of Kansu **42**: 28a; *Annals* of Hsining **27**: 11b).

What was the reason of the unusual behavior of Li Wen?

During the whole reign of Emperor Ching Ti (1450–1457) intrigues went on among the ambitious eunuchs and the most prominent officials, some of them friends and some of them foes of Emperor Ching Ti or of the secluded Emperor Yin Tsung. The factions seethed with hatred, accused and slandered each other, coveting the highest positions, wreaking ruin on their rivals. Many executions of high officials cast a blot in the reigns of Ching Ti and Yin Tsung.

General Shih Heng had defended for Emperor Ching Ti the capital beseiged by Esen in 1449. During the illness of Emperor Ching Ti, he hatched a plot preparing the dethronement of Ching Ti and the enthronement of Yin Tsung. Near Yin Tsung he accused his rivals and seven executions of the most prominent officials followed. He was bestowed with the title of Pilar of the empire. But a comet appeared in the sky. It was an ominous portent, indicating that the seven executions caused by Shih Heng were disapproved by Heaven. Shih Heng was committed to prison. Later during one of the brightest days it thundered terribly for a whole day, and one of the doorgates of the palace was smashed. Then deluging rains caused inundations in many provinces. Yin Tsung, at his wit's end, proclaimed an amnesty in 1458. Shih Heng could leave jail. In 1459 Shih Heng invited an astrologer to read his horoscope. The clever man guessing his client's meaning, predicted that in the Shih family an emperor would arise, founder of a new dynasty, but that he would have to act with the utmost caution. Shih Heng broke the news to his son, Shih Pien, for whom he had previously secured the office of Governor of Ta-t'ung. The young man, not cautious enough in his speech, let the secret leak out in Ta-t'ung. The officials of Ta-t'ung reported at court and judges arrived. Shih Pien poisoned himself. His father was committed to jail and ended his life in the same way. The officials of Ta-

---

80 H. Serruys, *op. cit.,* 85; Pokotilov, *op. cit.,* 58–60.

t'ung were promoted. However, Li Wen was by-passed. Deeming that he had provided the judges with the most important data, he could not stand being ignored and waited for an opportunity to avenge himself on the promoted officials. Consequently he did not fight in 1460, giving them the opportunity to show their gratefulness and abilities to the emperor. Later in Yenan and in Suei-te he succeeded in fighting the Mongols and was promoted to tutu T'ung chih. During the period Ch'eng hua (1465–1488) he was sent to Hami with Commander Liu Wen. The expedition was unsuccessful. He died during the first years of the Hung-chih period (1488–1506) and was rehabilitated with the title of Duke of Kao Yang in the first years of the Cheng-te period (1506–1521) (*Annals* of Kansu **42**: 38*a*; *Annals* of Hsining **27**: 12*a*). In 1468, during the time Li Wen was participating in the unsuccessful expedition in Hami, his young son Li Yung had been promoted to centurion and thereafter Chih-huei ch'ien-shih (*Annals* of Hsining **24**: 8*b*). This seems to suggest that after the punishment of Li Wen, the emperor must have been informed about the way in which he had acted, and have forgotten about it.

In a former chapter have been related the promotion of T'u-ssu Li Yin, as Duke of Huei Ning, his dishonorable behavior, his punishment, his death soon after 1437, and the promotion of his son Li Ch'ang in 1457. For twenty years the clan had been discredited on account of the behavior of Li Yin. But in 1457 Li Wen, the cousin of Li Yin, went to Peking with his army to congratulate Emperor Yin Tsung on being enthroned for the second time. The delighted emperor promoted him twice and Li Wen may have seized this opportunity to recommend Li Ch'ang, the son of his cousin Li Yin, and to remind the emperor of the merits of his grandfather Li Nan-ko, who had induced the t'u-ssu of Huangchung to surrender in 1371. Li Wen and Li Yin were the sons of the brothers of Li Shang-ko and Li Nan-ko. The emperor at that time was in high spirits, enjoying the jubilations of the entire population of the capital. Moreover ascensions to the throne were customarily accompanied by a general amnesty and this seems to explain why the son of Li Yin, just at that time (1457), started receiving distinguished promotions one after another, and after his death in 1493 an imperial funeral oration. In that way the honor of the entire clan was redeemed in Huangchung, and Li Ch'ang erected the spirit way stele for his father Li Yin in 1475.

HEGEMONY OF THE WESTERN MONGOLS

After the death of Esen in 1455, whose empire reached from Lake Balkash to the Great Wall of China, conflicts arose among the eastern and western Mongols and among the eastern groups themselves. The Ta-t'an (Tatars) Po-lai and Mao-li-hai tried to control the eastern Mongols, who grew more and more independ-ent. They secured the help of the Urianghai tribes whose chief was Tolohan. They appointed their Khan (Hsiao-wang-tze) and incessantly made inroads on the borders of the empire, seizing rich booty. Po-lai killed Hsiao-wang-tze and Mao-li-hai killed Po-lai. The Ordos Mongols appointed the Khan Mantulu who defeated Tolohan and Mao-li-hai. The latter died on the battlefield and dissension continued unabated. In 1470 the widow of Mantulu secured the proclamation of Dayan as sovereign of the Mongols and controlled the tribes herself. Dayan, a boy seven years of age, was the only descendant of the house of Kubilai. He married in 1481 and was proclaimed Khan of the Great Yuan (1470–1543). He united and laboriously grouped the tribes in right and left wings and divided and appanaged them among his sons. The eastern Mongols seemed united, but each time at the death of the father, the appanage was divided among the sons and so the power of the appanages and tribes diminished after each division, and sons and cousins were torn with inner conflicts. At the time of the Manchu dynasty (1644) the tribes had become an easy prey for the new rulers of China.

In 1450 the eastern Mongols under the leadership of the chieftain Ah-lo-ch'u had started settling in Ordos and in 1457 were firmly established there.[81] From Ordos they could more easily make inroads into Huangchung, Shansi, Shensi, etc. Desperate times were to be expected for Huangchung. However, the Monguor t'u-ssu and their subjects stood faithful and loyal as a rock, defending the dynasty for two more centuries.

The strong Tibetan Pa Sha tribe of Huangchung, which lived in tents between the Tatung River and the city of Tatung, had surrendered in 1380, and whose chief had been killed by Ch'i Hsien during his raid in 1448, started a raid in 1457 on a large scale, just at the time the Ta-t'an Po-lai, chief of the western Mongols, invaded the frontiers of Ninghsia (*Annals* of Kansu **46**: 28*a*). They raided the countries of Liangchow, Yung Ch'ang and Chuang Lang, and on their way home devastated and plundered the country of Huangchung, killing Chinese officials and capturing a huge number of cattle of the surrendered Tibetan tribes. Finally the Chinese troops from the commanderies of Kansu arrived, and administered a crushing defeat, killing 7,700 Pa Sha brigands (*Annals* of Hsining **19**: 7*a–b*; **31**: 12*b*). The Lu t'u-ssu had defended Chuang Lang and the other t'u-ssu had defended their own villages.

In 1461 Po-lai with an army of more than 10,000 Mongols arrived at Chuang Lang and made forays in Liangchow. The Chinese army was defeated, but more troops arrived and beat Po-lai who sent envoys suing for peace. Every year he sent tribute, but continued his raids. T'u-ssu Lu (*Annals* of Kansu **46**: 28*a*), t'u-ssu Ah (*Annals* of Kansu **42**: 49*b*), and t'u-ssu

---

[81] Pokotilov, *op. cit.*, 72.

Chao (*Annals* of Kansu **42**: 48*a*) had fought with the Chinese army.

In 1463 the Pa Sha tribe made a foray again in the Sa-t'ang Valley but was repelled (*Annals* of Hsining **31**: 12*a; Annals* of Kansu **46**: 28*a*).

In 1464 again the Pa Sha tribe raided Huangchung. This time the Chinese army entered their country and exterminated some of their tribes (*Annals* of Kansu **46**: 28*b*).

T'u-ssu Lu followed the commanders Liu Yu and Shih Hsiang-chung in 1468, repelling the brigand Manssu in Ku Yuan. He fled to his fortress Shih-ch'eng. The army, having lost many soldiers, finally captured the fortress; the brigand was captured, sent to Peking, and killed (*Annals* of Kansu **46**: 29*a*).

In 1470 T'ing Chang built more schools in Hsining. Shih Chao had built the first schools in 1428 (*Annals* of Kansu **31**: 12*b*).

In 1472 T'u-ssu Lu was ordered to help repel the Ordos Mongols making raids in Yenan and Suei-te. At the same time incursive Mongol tribes made forays in the regions of Chin-pien-i (Ku-lang). T'u-ssu Yeh (*Annals* of Kansu **42**: 52*a*), T'u-ssu Ah (*Annals* of Kansu **42**: 49*b*), T'u-ssu Chao (*Annals* of Kansu **42**: 48*b*), followed the Chinese troops, beat the brigands and pursued them as far as Hua-ling-erh.

T'u-ssu Li Wen and Commander Liu Wen were sent to Hami in 1473 to investigate the troubled conditions prevailing in the country. Having secured the promise of help from the Ch'ih-chin and Han Tun tribes, they sent an army to Hami in 1474. Upon the arrival of the army both tribes refused to move. Li Wen, deeming his forces too feeble to fight the enemy, returned to Kansu.

In 1475 Emperor Hsien Tsung ordered the local officials to erect an honorific arch in front of the mansion of the T'u-ssu Lu Chien, granting the inscription *"During his life he confirmed his faithfulness and probity, incessantly he exercised fidelity and zeal."*

It has been noted that the erection of the spirit way stele in honor of Li Yin happened in the very same year, 1475.

In 1480 T'u-ssu Lu Chien was promoted lieutenant colonel in Hsining.

In 1482 the tribes of Ch'ih-chin and Han Tun with the help of Chinese troops and T'u-ssu Yeh (*Annals* of Kansu **42**: 52*a*), Chao (*Annals* of Kansu **42**: 48*b*), attacked and conquered Hami.

In 1488, ninety years after the surrender of the *t'u-ssu* in a group in Huangchung (1371), there was appointed a military and administrative tao t'ai (ping pi tao), a governor, vested with civil and military powers (*Annals* of Hsining **22**: 5*b; 23*: 4*a–b*) with residence in the city of Hsining. There was also established a bureau of customs, and a bureau of colonization. In the city of Nienpei, in the strongholds of Chinghai, Kuei Te was appointed a major, in the fortress in the northern valley, and Ku Shan and San Ch'uan second captains. In the city of Hsining there were appointed a secretary commandant, a high commandant, seven assistant commandants, seven secretary commandants (among them are noted many t'u-ssu) a director of education, and a secretary. In Nienpei was appointed a Chiliarch with seven under-chiliarchs, nine centurions, twenty-nine second centurions. In Hsining a general director was appointed in each of the departments: for graneries, feed for horses, taxes, and exchange bureaus, in each of the seven relays. These regulations seem to suggest that Huangchung was no more a depopulated and uninteresting country. However, the appointment of the overwhelming number of military officials seems to suggest that the authority did not deem the peace prospects to be very bright, and that more troubles had to be expected.

In 1484 the Ordos Mongols made a raid in Yung Ch'ang. T'u-ssu Lu defended the country and was beseiged in the city for several days. He made sallies one after another and succeeded in escaping. More raids were made in Liangchow and P'ing Liang in 1497 and in Kanchow in 1498 by Hsiao Wang-tze. T'u-ssu Lu, T'u-ssu Ch'i (*Annals* of Kansu **42**: 35), and T'u-ssu Li (*Annals* of Kansu **42**: 38) helped the Chinese commander administer a severe blow to the raider.

T'u-ssu Lu participated in an expedition in 1499 against the eighteen tribes (Uighur Shat'o) of Chieh Chou in south Kansu, and sent prisoners to the capital. In the same year T'su-ssu Ch'i (*Annals* of Kansu **42**: 35*b*) and T'u-ssu Li (*Annals* of Kansu **42**: 38) participated in the expedition against Ordos brigands in Pei-ta-ch'uan (Ling Chou).

T'u-ssu Lu was ordered to chase the Mongols who obstructed the communications along the route leading from Yung-ch'ang to Kanchow and Suchow. Ch'i T'u-ssu (*Annals* of Kansu **42**: 35), back from the expedition in Pei-ta-ch'uan in 1499, was ordered to accompany the Governor Yin Ch'ing, investing in Hami the Prince Chung Shun, Shenpa, as chief of the country (*Annals* of Hsining **31**: 12*a; Annals* of Kansu **42**: 35). In 1500 the turbulent Hsiao Wang-tze settled in Ordos, from where he continued his forays. In 1504 he raided Shuei-ts'ao-ku and Hung-ch'eng-tze and was repelled.

In 1507 Mongol brigands, passing through Ming-shuei-ku in the P'ing-liang region, were defeated by General Wu Ch'i and T'u-ssu Ch'i (*Annals* of Kansu **42**: 35; **42**: 44).

RUIN OF HUANGCHUNG

The year 1507 was fateful in the history of Huangchung and all of Kansu. It marked the ruin of the whole country for a century. Until that time Huangchung and Kansu had suffered only from intermittent, transient, but disastrous raids from incursive Mongols whose aim did not reach beyond plunder. Dayan, the ambitious young Hsiao Wang-tze, who was laboriously striving for the unification and the subjection of the tribes under his leadership, had appointed one of his sons commander of tribes. He was killed by his subjects. The rebelling chief I-pu-la, apprehensive of the vengeance of Dayan, seceded and fled with his tribes to Liangchow. He asked the commander of Liangchow to allot a territory to him and promised to live in peace with the empire. The petition was refused. The Mongols, incensed by the refusal, for ten days wreaked their vengeance, devastating and laying waste the country. On their way westward they plundered the tribes of the Prince of Anting and stole his seals and diplomas. They reached Kokonor in 1509 and occupied the territory (*Annals* of Hsining 31 : 13*a–b*; *Annals* of Kansu 46 : 31*a*).

Kokonor at that time was the country of the Tibetans. The behavior of the savage Mongols was unusually ruthless. On their arrival they murdered Tibetans, reduced the young folk to the level of slaves, stole their wives and cattle. Cowed by their truculent manner, some Tibetan tribes fled to Tibet, some to East Kansu and Huangchung. The destitution of the fleeing tribes was tragic. On their way they plundered the country and Kansu was upset. But some tribes returned to Kokonor and submitted to the invaders. Being conversant with Kansu, they accompanied and led the Mongol forays and plundered in combination with them. The Tibetan tribes submitted to China and East Kansu and Huangchung were plundered. Despairing of the help of China, their ingrained predatory nature soon asserted itself and they revolted and went plundering on their own account. Every time Mongol tribes in Mongolia had a score to settle with Dayan, they seceded and fled to Kokonor adding strength to the Kokonor group.

Huangchung and East Kansu, which during the previous centuries had been laid waste and destroyed so many times, had to pass again through the ordeals of war and destruction at the hands of Mongols and rebel Tibetans for a whole century, and to have their economic life disrupted and shattered.

In 1510 T'u-ssu Lu, Li (*Annals* of Kansu 42 : 38*a*), Chao (*Annals* of Kansu 42 : 48*a*), Wang (*Annals* of Kansu 42 : 40*b*), Ah (*Annals* of Kansu 42 : 40*b*), and t'u-ssu Ch'i (*Annals* of Kansu 42 : 35*a*) under command of the Lieutenant Colonel of Chuang-lang administered a blow at Hsiao Wang-tze in Huei-huei-mu and captured a considerable number of his oxen and horses. Hsiao Wang-tze pursued the seceding tribe of I-pu-la. Having met defeat at Huei-huei-mu, he was pursued to Yenan and beaten again in Shih-p'eng-ku, P'o shan-ku and T'ung-ssu-p'u.

In 1511 the Kokonor brigand I-pu-la made a raid in Yung-ch'ang and Cheng-fan, but suffered a defeat. Ch'i (*Annals* of Kansu 42 : 52*b*), Ah (*Annals* of Kansu 42 : 49*b*), Yeh t'u-ssu (*Annals* of Kansu 42 : 52*b*) participated in the punitive expedition. From now

on recurrent raids of Kokonor brigands will be recorded incessantly. The hardships doled out by the Monguors and t'u-ssu during a century will be tremendous.

In the fifth moon the Kokonor brigands invaded the northern valley of Hsining and were repelled. All the *t'u-ssu* of Hsining under command of Wang Yung helped in the action. The son of T'u-ssu Li died on the field of battle (*Annals* of Kansu 42 : 38*a*), in Ta-la-tu-ch'uan. T'u-ssu Ch'i (*Annals* of Kansu 42 : 45), Chi (*Annals* of Kansu 42 : 22) and Kan (*Annals* of Kansu 42 : 50*b*) pursued the retreating raiders and slaughtered many among them in Hung-yang t'an.

In 1514 Tibetan tribes from around Kokonor, in combination with Mongol brigands, invaded the southern valleys of Hsining and Nienpei. All the t'u-ssu of Hsining helped Commander Chin Mao repel the invaders. However, they were severely beaten, and T'u-ssu Ch'eng died in the battle of Pien-tu-ling (*Annals* of Kansu 42 : 36*b*).

The situation drifted to a critical point and then finally a Chinese army of 10,000 men was equipped to chase the brigands from Kokonor. The brigands, informed about the serious military preparations, left Kokonor, passed the Yellow River at Ho Chou, plundered and slaughtered savagely the subject Tibetan tribes, in the commanderies of T'ao and Ming Chou, and invaded Sung P'an and Mao Chou in Szechwan Province. When they were informed that the Chinese army had left Kokonor, they returned to Kokonor.

At that time the Hsiao Wang-tze invited I-pu-la etc., to return to their original country. Complying with the invitation, he moved his tribes to the north, but soon news was broken about the intention of Hsiao Wang-tze to kill him. He returned to Kokonor (*Annals* of Hsining 31 : 13*a–b*).

In 1515 Tibetan tribes living in the mountains between Liangchow and P'ing-fan had plundered envoys from Turkistan bringing tribute to the emperor. T'u-ssu Lu was sent to punish them. He killed many of them in Sha-chin-ku and Ho-shih-ku.

The next year a group of Ordos brigands invaded and devastated Ku-yuen and P'ing-liang. T'u-ssu Wang (*Annals* of Kansu 42 : 40*b*), T'u-ssu Na (*Annals* of Kansu 42 : 39*b*), and T'u-ssu Lu were ordered to help in the punitive expedition.

In 1517 many Tibetan tribes who suffered on account of the brigands felt their old predatory instinct reviving. The conditions in Huangchung grew worse every day. The chief of the Lung-pu and Wu-ssu-pa-erh tribes (*Annals* of Hsining 19 : 13*a–b*), controlling 2,000 families, nomadizing on a territory 200 li wide between Hsining and Kokonor, revolted. The Chinese Chiliarch Li Wen quelled the revolt. Then the tribes revolted on a large scale, defeated and killed the Chiliarch. Finally the lama of the Ta-ming temple succeeded in inducing them to surrender (*Annals* of Kansu 46 : 31; *Annals* of Hsining 31 : 14*a*).

In the same year the Ko-tsa Tibetan tribe which had surrendered in 1380, whose chief controlled 400 families and nomadized southwest of Ku Shan along the northern borders of the Yellow River, plundered the lamasery of Hung-hua. Captains Kao Hsien and Yang Yu with T'u-ssu Lu (*Annals* of Hsining **19**: 4; **31**: 14) pursued and defeated the rebels in the mountains of Pa-yen-jung (*Annals* of Kansu **46**: 31a).

In 1520–1521 T'u-ssu Lu twice repelled Ordos brigands invading Ku Yuan and Chuang Lang.

The very first *Annals* of Hsining composed by the scholar Chang Chih were printed in 1520 (*Annals* of Hsining **27**: 15a).

The Chinese army revolted in Kanchow in 1522. The Tibetan tribes in Huangchung seized the opportunity to plunder the country (*Annals* of Hsining **31**: 14a). Governor Cheng Yang could not control the situation. At the same time 20,000 Ordos brigands invaded Ku Yuan, P'ing Liang, Chin Chou, killed the military officials Yang Hung and Liu Tuan, terribly devastated the country and killed and captured more than 10,000 people (*Annals* of Kansu **46**: 31b).

In 1525 Pu-erh-hai, a Mongol chief, had a score to settle with Dayan. In order to avoid his vengeance he joined the I-pu-la group. On his way to Kokonor he plundered the country. He was defeated by Yang Chung aided by T'u-ssu Li (*Annals* of Kansu **42**: 38a), Chi (*Annals* of Kansu **42**: 42a) and T'u-ssu Kan (*Annals* of Kansu **46**: 32b). The next year T'u-ssu Lu was impeached by the officials of Chengfan and Hsining. He was removed from office (*Annals* of Hsining **31**: 14a–b; **27**: 15).

After the officials had lost control over Huangchung in 1522 they convened to discuss these disastrous circumstances and find a solution. There was complete absence of direction and the officials were at loggerheads with one another. One group among them stubbornly defended the policy of Tuan Ying who, seventeen centuries earlier, had exterminated the Tibetans in order to pacify the country. At present, they said, the conditions are favorable, the Kokonor brigands control only two or three thousand Mongol horse and foot; from the moment the troops are moved the Tibetan tribes will abandon them. The other group obstinately advocated the policy of Chao Ch'ung-kuo who also, seventeen centuries before, won over the Tibetan tribes, granting titles to the chiefs, opening markets, etc. They said, "Because their army at present is in poor shape and money is lacking, this policy is the only one possible." The third group was as stubborn as the other two: Tuan Ying had exterminated the Tibetans and won only a barren worthless country, void of people. Chao Ch'ung-kuo had fooled himself, and after a couple of years the country had been out of control. Both generals had applied their policy to the utmost and failed. The right way is a middle way, the way of wise moderation; whoever

is fighting must be fought, but always at the same time the tribes should be induced to surrender peacefully. The debates lasted for seven years and nothing was done (*Annals* of Hsining **20**: 10b, 11a). Finally in 1530 the Tibetan tribes of T'ao and Ming Chou started plundering the country. The tribes had fled from Kokonor for fear of the Mongols. Their destitution was tragic. Commander Liu Wen-yu, protagonist of the third group, left with his army, but at the same time sent officials to induce the tribes to surrender, promising them help. Among them only twenty-one tribes decided to revolt, the Lung-po (Uighur) tribe being the leader of the group. The commander defeated two tribes, killed 360 rebels and then started peace talks. He succeeded, receiving the surrender of seventy or more tribes. He returned with the army. The regions of T'ao and Ming Chou were at peace.

The same year, while the tribes of T'ao and Ming Chou, situated south of the Yellow River, were pacified, the Tsantsa tribes, living on the northern bank of the Tatung River, plundered the region of Nienpei, but were defeated in the T'u-ku-hung valley. Splinter groups of Mongols raided Chengfan, and small groups of Kokonor brigands invaded Hsining and were pursued.

In 1534, amidst all these troubles, the Ming dynasty was still interested in education and instruction. More schools were built in several small fortresses, and in Hsining the Hall of the Faithful and Meritorious officials was constructed. On the stele erected inside the hall, we read among the names of the celebrated personalities those of four Monguor t'u-ssu: Li Nan-ko, Li Yin, the Duke of Huei-ming, his son, T'u-ssu Ch'eng Chih, and T'u-ssu Li Ch'ang, son of Li Yin (*Annals* of Hsining **35**: 9b, 10a).

The situation grew worse every day and all of Huangchung was upset. Liu T'ien-ho, vice-president of the ministry of war, was sent in 1536 to direct the military operations in Kansu and Shensi. The third son of Dayan, Barsa Bolot, with his son, the Jinong had settled in Ordos. The turbulent Jinong made raids in Ninghsia, Liang and Kanchow. T'u-ssu Wang (*Annals* of Kansu **42**: 40), Na (*Annals* of Kansu **42**: 49), Hsin (*Annals* of Kansu **42**: 54), were ordered to help stem the forays. T'u-ssu Hsin died on the field of battle. The Jinong invaded Hsining and hit a severe blow. T'u-ssu Lu and Ah (*Annals* of Kansu **42**: 52) helped the commander beat the Jinong.

The next year the Kokonor brigands made a raid in Hsining and were severely beaten, twice, at the temple T'ieh-fu, 50 li north of the city.

General Liu T'ien-ho, having studied the situation of the country, ordered first the repair of the walls and towers of the eighteen existing small fortresses and villages and cities, and to start immediately with the building of seventeen new fortified villages. He promoted agriculture around the fortresses, dug irrigation canals, helped the people with grain and oxen, etc. He built the two large cities of Pa-yien-jung and San-ch'uan, south of Nienpei, and established there two strong garrisons, in order to control the whole region north of the Yellow River, reaching from the south of Hsining to Nienpei (*Annals* of Kansu **24**: 18; **23**: 16). At that time the only fortified villages were near the mansions of the t'u-ssu, where in time of troubles the people found shelter with their cattle and helped to defend the fortress, and from which they attacked and pursued brigands. Only near these fortresses were living and farming possible. No wonder that the helpless scattered tribes incessantly revolted, plundered on their own account, or joined the invaders after having been plundered.

In 1537 groups of Ordos brigands raided the fortress of Cheng-ch'iang-I, situated between Liangchow and Lanchow. T'u-ssu Yeh defended the fortress heroically and died in the battle. The people esteemed his brave conduct and erected a stele in commemoration inside the village.

In 1541 the Jinong from Ordos raided Hsia-ch'uan-ku in Huangchung; a crushing defeat was administered to him by General Liu T'ien-ho in Ho-shuei-wan. His son Chin-shao was killed in the battle. T'u-ssu Lu, Li (*Annals* of Kansu **42**: 38), Wang (*Annals* of Kansu **42**: 40), Ch'i (*Annals* of Kansu **42**: 45) participated in the action. Groups belonging to the Tsa tsa tribes of Huangchung plundered San-ch'uan and were chased by T'u-ssu Ch'i (*Annals* of Kansu **42**: 45), and Li (*Annals* of Kansu **42**: 38).

In 1543 the turbulent Jinong, leading a strong army, arrived at Kokonor, where he defeated I-pu-la, and captured half of his followers. I-pu-la fled to Mongolia plundering the Liangchow country on his way back. The Jinong was the grandson of Dayan and had a score to settle with I-pu-la, who, seceding with his tribes, had offended his grandfather Dayan. I-pu-la had raided and plundered Huangchung, had scattered or subdued and ruined the Tibetan tribes of Kokonor during thirty-four years (*Annals* of Hsining **31**: 15*b*; **20**: 12*a*). Pu-erh-hai, a Mongol chieftain who had joined I-pu-la in 1525, had already abandoned I-pu-la, and had hidden in the mountains to avoid the Jinong. Previously he had manifested his intention to submit to China and was better disposed toward the Tibetans. Many tribes returned to Kokonor hoping to enjoy a precarious peace for some years (*Annals* of Hsining **20**: 12*b*). The same year T'u-ssu Lu was ordered to lead his troops to Tatung in Shansi province to help chase the invading Mongols.

In 1546 the emperor ordered the officials to erect an Honorific Arch glorifying the merits of T'u-ssu Lu.

Until 1549 the students in Hsining had been unable to pass the literary examination and acquire titles. This year, on account of the new regulations, diplomas were granted in Hsining.

REVOLT OF TIBETAN TRIBES IN HUANGCHUNG

Really desperate times were still in store for the population of Huangchung, for a half-century to come. This time the troubles were caused by the Tibetan tribes from Huangchung itself. After the restless Pa sha tribes had been defeated in 1516 by the Chinese army, some of their sub-tribes were exterminated or disintegrated. The chief of the Tsan-tsa tribe, one of the sub-tribes of Pa sha, succeeded in gathering some tribes under his leadership and in controlling 1,500 families. Other tribes living in the northwest of Hsining joined the group. Among them was the strong Tibetan Erh-chia-ting tribe. They beseiged the city of Nienpei in 1550 and laid waste the country. Commander T'ang Yung beat the brigands. However, the brigands, using the time-honored ruse of a feigned retreat, killed the commander in an ambuscade.

In 1551 all the tribes northeast of Hsining plundered the Hung-nai valley. They administered to the Chinese army a crushing defeat; three officers and two thousand soldiers died on the field of battle. T'u-ssu Ch'i, Li, Hsin, and Wang participated in the battle (*Annals* of Hsining **31**: 15, 16; *Annals* of Kansu **42**: 34).

The next year small groups of Kokonor brigands made raids in Yen-mei-ch'uan, north of Hsining, but were chased away (*Annals* of Hsining **31**: 16).

In 1553 Tsan-tsa tribes with those of Erh-chia-ting again plundered the villages north of Hsining and Nienpei (*Annals* of Hsining **31**: 16; *Annals* of Kansu **42**: 34).

In 1554 Kokonor brigands plundered Sa-t'ang valley and were beaten. They fled toward the southern valleys of Hsining, where they plundered for five days. On the arrival of the army they fled to the western valley of Hsining, but were put to flight (*Annals* of Kansu **42**: 34; *Annals* of Hsining **31**: 16).

Tsan-tsa and Erh-chia-ting tribes in 1557 again raided the valleys south of Nienpei and plundered the lamasery of Ch'u-t'an-sse. Pursued by the army they plundered the valleys situated north of the Hsining River. More Tibetan tribes had joined the group, the Hung-mao, the La-tsa, the Ko-tsa, etc. The depredation in the country was wicked and ruthless. The t'u-ssu had to defend their own fortresses and villages. In the meantime Altan, the brother of Jinong beseiged the city of Kanchow calling all the Mongol brigands of the country, and went with his new army to Peking, plundering on the way the villages and cities of Shan-tan, Yung-ch'ang and Liangchow (*Annals* of Hsining **31**: 16; **19**: 7*a*; *Annals* of Kansu **42**: 34, 35) in Kansu.

The raids of Kokonor brigands and Tibetans raged unchecked during 1558 in all of Huangchung. The situation was out of control, the plight was desperate. T'u-ssu Li (*Annals* of Kansu **42**: 47), and Yeh (*An-

nals of Kansu **42**: 52) had died in recent actions, and the troops suffered many reverses. Most of the armies, most of the time, did not fight, but liked better to stay at bay behind walls and barricade themselves in the cities. There were very few pitched battles on a large scale. In the meantime, the brigandage grew with the passing of the years, for it proved to be beneficial to the brigands, who at the same time revenged themselves on their former oppressors, murdering anyone who made a stand. The confidence in the empire, among the population beset with starvation and abject poverty, was shaken, and there was nothing to relieve the dreariness of life. The outlook remained gloomy and no new troops arrived in the country.

One can hardly understand why, in such critical circumstances, no more troops should have been sent to Huangchung and Kansu by the emperor, to save the starved and pillaged people and prevent the total ruin of the country. However, the troubles which beset Kansu were not the only ones with which the empire had to cope. During the entire reign of Emperor Cheng Te (1605–1622) the borders of the empire from Kansu up to Peking itself had been exposed to persistent and incessant attacks of Mongols, under the command of Dayan. In 1516 two groups, one of seventy, the other of fifty thousand Mongols, invaded Hsuan-hua-fu in Shansi Province. The conditions were similar during the reign of Chia Ching (1522–1567). In 1532 Hsiao Wang-tze with 100,000 men invaded the empire. In 1536 Chi Nang controlled 100,000 soldiers and raided Ninghsia, Tatung, and Hsuan-hua, and in 1544 the country around the capital was devastated and looted of its wealth. In 1550 the Mongols administered a crushing defeat to the Chinese armies and reached the northern gate of the capital where for eight days they laid waste the country and returned to the desert carrying with them a huge amount of booty. The raids, whetting the appetite for plunder, were resumed every year in the northern country. In 1561 they camped again under the walls of the capital. The raids continued unabated until finally in 1570 peace was granted to Altan (Dayan's grandson), who had sued for peace since 1542. Then markets were opened for his tribes and the title of Shun-i-wang bestowed upon him. The Obedient and Righteous Prince!

These circumstances explain why the brigands in Kansu had been fought in a nearly desultory fashion for half a century. They explain also the danger looming over the Ming dynasty, on account of the still strong savage Mongol forces and the lack of discipline and direction in the army.

The same conditions continued for more than a half century for the same reasons, lack of discipline and direction on the part of the army, and unity among the Mongols, strengthened by the benefits to be expected from the amount of loot furnished by the forays. Even when later the Mongols divided in two groups, each of them remained united and strong because of the benefits derived from brigandage and loot.

Altan, who controlled all the Mongols, was in 1559 making forays and harrassing China. For a long time he had been conversant with the fertile Kokonor country, the El Dorado of peoples engaged in cattle breeding, and also with the weakness of the Chinese forces which defended the country, and the helplessness of the disunited Tibetan tribes. Being eager to occupy Kokonor he sent to the country his two sons Pin-tu and Ping-tu with several thousands of Mongols. In 1561 Pin-tu occupied and looted the country of Sung-shan-i, situated between Chuang Lang and Ordos. Ping-tu went to Kokonor, plundering and looting East Kansu (*Annals* of Hsining **20**: 12). He defeated the Chinese army sent against him. The Li T'u-ssu died in the battle (*Annals* of Kansu **46**: 35a). In 1568, however, he was severely beaten around Kuei Te and lost many of his people (*Annals* of Kansu **46**: 35a). In the meantime the Tibetan Tsan-tsa and Ko-tsa tribes had invaded the Ma-ha-la valley in Hsining but were chased away. Mongol groups of Pin-tu made raids from Sung Shan, in the Pa-yen-jung region (Hsining) and were beaten (*Annals* of Hsining **31**: 17). Again the military authority ordered walls and small fortresses built on the mountain passes and on the routes used by the brigands to invade the country (*Annals* of Hsining **13**: 9, 10).

In Hsining the bureau for the administration of the military colonies was erected in 1567 (*Annals* of Hsining **23**: 5).

In 1568 the emperor ordered the officials of Hsining to build an honorific arch in the city of Hsining for the meritorious T'u-ssu Li Kung, grandson of Li Yin, who in 1481 had passed the literary examination of *chin shih* and fulfilled the office of minister in the Chang-pao-sse. The arch was built on the great street of the eastern gate of the city, and still exists. The emperor granted the honorific inscription chiseled in the arch: Ch'ing Yun (clearing clouds)—meaning bright sky, and thus bright intelligence.

In 1569 the Tibetan Ssu-erh-ko and Hung-mao tribes raided Hsining and were administered a blow. Two chiefs of Ssu-erh-ko were taken prisoner, but a Chinese commander was killed by the Hung-mao tribe (*Annals* of Hsining **31**: 17). The commander succeeded in inducing the Ssu-erh-ko tribes to surrender and titles were bestowed upon the chieftains of their twelve tribes. They aided in inducing the Hung-mao tribes to surrender and both groups agreed to combat the Kokonor and Sung Shan brigands in combination with the Chinese armies (*Annals* of Hsining **25**: 19b). The Mongol brigand Ping-tu raided the Ta-erh-wan valley in Huangchung from Kokonor and was repelled by the army which lost its commander (*Annals* of Kansu **46**: 35b).

Altan surrendered in 1570 and concluded peace with

China; markets were accorded to his tribes and he was created "the Obedient and Righteous Prince"! However, the perspicacious Governor Wang Ch'ung-ku asked for a declaration of submission from other chieftains, such as Chinang and T'uman. T'uman refused boldly.[82] Apparently groups of Mongols, dissatisfied with the peace concluded by Altan, had already decided to gather under the banner of T'uman, liking better their adventurous life of looting and plundering than the submission to China. The group was strong and numerous, and administered, during the following years, many crushing defeats to China. Altan, however, endeavored to make his people desist from raids,[83] but he did not succeed in controlling his sons, nephews, and other relatives in Kansu and Huangchung. Since in 1559 Altan had sent his sons to occupy Kokonor and Sung-shan many Mongol chieftains, mostly nephews and cousins had followed them. They had forced the Tibetans to recognize their lordship, bring tribute and help them in the raids made in Kansu. They wrought tremendous havoc among the Tibetan tribes. The Chinese troops fought many losing battles and lost many officers and soldiers. Pin-tu and Ping-tu groups were the scourge of Kansu province. Altan was succeeded by his son Huang-t'ai-chi in 1583, and by his grandson Ch'ih-li-ko in 1587, who was unable to control his people. The emperor, in 1591, ordered the suspension of trade with his tribes (Pokotilov, *op. cit.*, 141). From the death of Altan on, Huangchung suffered tremendously for years, on account of the savage raids of the relatives of Altan, whose real nature immediately asserted itself in all its crudity and brutality.

In 1572 the Tibetan Erh-chia-ting tribes again plundered Hsining country. Their chief was captured and killed (*Annals* of Hsining **31**: 17).

In 1573 General Ta Yun rebuilt and fortified the city of Nienpei exposed to the recurrent raids from the Tibetan tribes living north of the cities of Hsining and Nienpei (*Annals* of Hsining **31**: 17).

The fortifications of the city of Hsining were again overhauled and improved in 1575, and the city was enlarged in the prospect of troubles on account of the building of the temple in Kokonor, the opening of markets and the incessant arrival of more Mongols (*Annals* of Hsining **31**: 17b).

Altan arrived at Kokonor in 1577 to meet the great lama (*Annals* of Hsining **31**: 17b). The *Annals* of Hsining record (**20**: 14) that a lama of Wu-sse-tsang (on the borders of Szechwan Province) was proclaimed Living Buddha. The shrewd Ping-tu, knowing the religiosity of the Tibetans, proposed to build two temples, one in Kokonor and one in Chia-yu-kuan and to invite the Living Buddha. He intended to secure the support of the Tibetans by pretending to be fond of Buddhism. The question was vividly discussed in Peking, and the emperor agreed. Ping-tu forced the tribes to build a road to Wu-ssu-tsang in order to meet the lama. The entire Szechwan province was upset for fear of invasion by the savage Kokonor brigands. The governor wrote Altan to order his sons to desist from plundering the country. Altan answered that the only reason for the behavior of his sons was the lack of any markets where they could fill their needs. In 1574 markets were opened for Pin-tu and Ping-tu and the emperor granted to the temple of Kokonor the name Yin-hua-sse and the title of vice-commander to Ping-tu. However, the sons and cousins and nephews of Altan plundered as before. Again the officials asked Altan to reprimand them. Altan arrived with his army feigning to meet the lama; however he had an axe to grind with Oirats, his old foes. Coming back, he asked the governor to allow all the Mongol chieftains to attend a meeting with the lama in Kokonor. The Tibetans, taken with panic at the sight of the demonstration of power and magnificence, fled in all directions. Altan returned to the north (1577) but Ho-lo-ch'ih and Yung-chao-pu, his nephew and cousin, and others refused to leave Kokonor, and Ping-tu started plundering the Tibetans again. The officials immediately asked the emperor to close the markets. Altan reprimanded his son and urged him to return the stolen people and cattle. However, Ho-lo-ch'ih continued looting (*Annals* of Hsining **20**: 13, 14).[84]

In 1579 the governor of Hsining was engaged in developing agriculture in Huangchung. He gathered the destitute people who had fled with fear of the Mongol brigands, located them in villages, provided them with grain and oxen, dug irrigation canals, etc. In each village he opened a school. He gathered more than 100,000 families, and more uncultivated land was tilled. When Altan left the country in 1577 he had asked him to leave peacefully and to protect the country against more raids by his people (*Annals* of Hsining **25**: 20).

Ha-tsa, a Tibetan tribe of Kokonor, raided the western valley of Hsining in 1580, but was repelled. Two

---

[82] Pokotilov, 129.
[83] Pokotilov, *op. cit.*, 137–141.

[84] René Grousset, *Empire des Steppes*, 592, Paris, Payot: The Ordos Mongols started professing the lamaism of the Yellow Church from 1566 on. The *jinong* Khutukh Setsen Hung-t'ai-chi of the Uchin banner, coming back from an expedition in Tibet in 1566, had invited lamas to accompany him to Ordos and convert the Mongols to lamaism. The fervent *jinong* succeeded in converting his grand-uncle Altan who at that time was in the heyday of his power (1576). Altan and his grand-nephew invited the chief of the Yellow Church, the great lama bSod-nams rgya-mtso to come to Kokonor. The Mongols met him magnificently and opened with him an official convention at which was laid the foundation of the Yellow Church among the Mongols (1577), and Altan honored the great lama with the title of Dalai Lama, which title is still borne at present by his successors. The Dalai Lama, returning to Lhasa, appointed the Living Buddha Dongkur Manjucri in Kukuhoto the residence of Altan. The Dalai Lama left Lhasa again to travel to Ordos in 1586 for the performance of the cremation ceremonies of Altan who had died in 1583.

centurions pursued them to Kokonor and perished in an ambuscade (*Annals* of Hsining **31**: 15*b*; *Annals* of Kansu **46**: 35*b*).

In the autumn of 1583 Chulit'u, a Mongol chieftain of the group of Pin-tu from Sung Shan, in combination with the chieftain Yung Chao-pu of Kokonor, nephew of Altan, invaded the Sa-t'ang valley in Hsining with 8,000 horses. They killed and wounded more than 1,200 Tibetans, men and women, and drove away with them more than 4,000 cattle (*Annals* of Hsining **33**: 28*b*).

In 1585 the Kotsa tribe invaded the valleys south of Hsining and was repelled (*Annals* of Hsining **33**: 28*b*).

In 1586, in the sixth moon, the Mongol brigand Ho-lo-ch'ih of Kokonor with Tibetans subject to him, numbering 10,000 horses, invaded Hsining, killed 500 surrendered Tibetans and stole 4,000 cattle (*Annals* of Hsining **33**: 28*b*). At the same time Chuang T'u-lai from Kokonor raided Nienpei plundering many villages, while the brigands of Pin-tu and Sung Shan invaded the Yen-meich'uan valley, north of Hsining. They were repelled by the commander Wang Shih-te helped by the *t'u-ssu*. T'u-ssu Na was killed pursuing the brigands to Pien-Tu-Ku (*Annals* of Hsining **31**: 17*b*; **31**: 18).

The next year the Mongol brigand Ho-lo-ch'ih in combination with Hung-mao tribes invaded the western valleys of Hsining, killed few people but stole 3,000 cattle (*Annals* of Hsining **33**, 28*b*).

The Oirat Wa-la-t'a-pu-nmang, who had joined the Kokonor brigands with 5,000 Tibetans, invaded the valleys south of Hsining in 1588. He stole 1,400 cattle and 700 horses from the Chinese army. The Chinese army suffered a crushing defeat. Three t'u-ssu, Li, Ch'eng, and Chao were killed and 800 soldiers, among them 40 centurions (*Annals* of Hsining **31**: 18*a*; **33**: 29*a*).

In 1589 the Tibetan Ha-tsa tribes raided San-ch'uan south of Nienpei. The centurion Liu Ts'ung-jen repelled them and was killed (*Annals* of Hsining **31**: 18*a*). At the same time the Mongol brigand Ho-lo-ch'ih of Kokonor invaded the valleys south of Hsining and Nienpei with 500 horses, joined Chineng, the grand-nephew of Altan, and Tsaisengfu and Mangko-tsu, belonging to the Pin-tu group of Sung Shan with 4,000 horses. They beseiged the monastery of Ch'u-t'an-sse for seven days, killing many people and burning the houses. The monastery offered them some hundreds of oxen and horses and they left. T'u-ssu Yeh and Wang pursued them and were killed (*Annals* of Hsining **31**: 19; **33**: 19*a*).

In 1590 the Tibetan Tsantsa tribes plundered Sa T'ang valley and were repelled but a centurion was killed. Ch'ih-li-ko, who in 1587 had received the title of Obedient and Righteous Prince and was the second successor of Altan, accompanied the Dalai Lama with his army on his way back to Lhasa after the perform-

ance of the ceremonies for Altan. After having lingered for a while in Kokonor, he assisted on his way back home in the plundering of the cities and the regions of T'ao and Ming Chou by the Mongols. The same year the brigands Tsai-Seng-fu and Achihtu of the Pin-tu group of Sung Shan plundered the Lungpu tribes southwest of Hsining (*Annals* of Hsining **25**: 19). Tibetan tribes from Szechwan came to finish the looting of T'ao and Ming Chou and were repelled. Then the turbulent Ho-lo-ch'ih looted Lin-T'ao region (*Annals* of Kansu **46**: 36).

HELP SENT BY THE EMPEROR

The situation in East Kansu and Huangchung in 1590 was completely out of control. The country was entirely laid waste and devastated, the Mongol brigands and the Tibetans had incessantly overrun the country, the Chinese forces could not contravene their strength. Many surrendered Tibetan tribes had disintegrated, had disappeared, had been exterminated; the cattle were stolen; many young women had been abducted and many had fled and hidden in the mountains. The depredation of the country was wicked and ruthless and the destitution of the people was tragic.

A note in the *Annals* of Hsining (**33**: 19*a*) records to what extent and in what way the Mongol brigands of Kokonor had terrorized, and subjected, reduced to the level of slaves the Tibetan tribes of Kokonor, East Kansu and Huangchung. The chieftain Yung-chao-pu, nephew of Altan, controlled at the time of his arrival in the Kokonor only 1,000 subjects: at present he controlled more than 10,000. The chief Sang-ehr-huang t'ai-chi formerly controlled 800 subjects but now 3,000. The chieftains Kosina and Lashala formerly controlled 4,000 people each but now each of them controlled 10,000 and more. The number of the subjects controlled by the other chiefs is not known.

Finally in 1590 the emperor sent Cheng Lo, president of the ministry of war, to cope with the situation (*Annals* of Hsining **31**: 18*b*; *Annals* of Kansu **46**: 36).

On the first moon of the following year Cheng Lo sent Colonel Shih Chia with the t'u-ssu Lieutenant Colonel Ch'i Te, to call the Tibetan tribes to surrender; 165 tribes numbering 74,710 persons surrendered (*Annals* of Hsining **31**: 18*b*; **25**: 20*a–b*; **33**: 16*b*). Among the surrendered tribes in Huangchung are noted the Hung-mao tribes (*Annals* of Hsining **19**: 7*a*), the La-pu-erh tribes (*Annals* of Hsining **19**: 7*a*), the Lung-pu tribes led by their lama Sonanchintso (*Annals* of Hsining **19**: 3*a–b*), the 29 Tsan-tsa tribes (*Annals* of Hsining **19**: 4*b*), and the Sukomi tribes (*Annals* of Hsining **19**: 5*b*).

In the ninth moon he sent the brigade General Wang Shih-te, the t'u-ssu Lieutenant Colonel Lu Kuang-tsu and groups of surrendered Tibetan tribes, seething with hatred against the Mongol brigands and eager to avenge all the sufferings they had endured, to fight the Mongols in Kokonor and burn the temple built by Altan. They returned in a flush of triumph with 1,200 captured families. The number of brigands they killed is not known. The Brigadier General Chiao Chi defeated tribes of Ho-lo-ch'ih with the help of Tibetans and beheaded 120 of his men (*Annals* of Kansu **46**: 36*b; Annals* of Hsining **31**: 18*b*).

The energic Cheng Lo must have commanded at the time of his arrival in Huangchung a fair number of fresh troops. Otherwise the shaken confidence in the empire among the Tibetan tribes would not have been restored so quickly. In two years time the outlook had changed and become bright and full of hope for the people, beset for ten years with starvation, squalor and misery, and anxious uncertainty.

The same year the markets, opened for the Mongols in Kansu, were closed on account of their incessant raids and brigandage. The Obedient and Righteous Prince Ch'ih-li-k'o who had assisted at the looting of T'ao and Ming Chou, sent back the abducted people and stolen cattle and presented excuses to the emperor (*Annals* of Hsining **25**: 20*a–b*).

In 1594 orders were given to repair and improve again the fortifications of the city of Hsining. More villages and military colonies were built. Maybe the officials had seen some new straws in the wind (*Annals* of Hsining **31**: 19*a*). A strong group of Kokonor brigands arrived to plunder the valleys south of Hsining. The Chinese generals Liu Mei-Kuan, Ta Yun, T'ien Yueh had called all the t'u-ssu of Huangchung and captured groups of Tibetans to defend the country. They used flanking movements, skillfully settled ambuscades, and administered a crushing defeat to the raiders, 680 of whom were beheaded. A few months later the brigands came back with all the brigands of Nalu, to loot the valleys west of Hsining. The same generals, t'u-ssu, and Tibetans obtained a resounding victory and killed 700 and more brigands, among them some chieftains (*Annals* of Kansu **46**: 37*b; Annals* of Hsining **31**: 19*a*).

These two victories were the most important ever won in Huangchung. In the report relating the military presentation are encountered the names of the most meritorious military and civil officials who had contributed to the success. We encounter among them the names of T'u-ssu Lu Kuang-tsu, Li Yu-mao, Li Hsien-hua, Ch'eng San-chi, Ch'i Ping-chung and Ch'i Te (*Annals* of Hsining **33**: 23*a–b*). A delegate of the ministry of war was sent with titles and gifts to reward the meritorious officials.

Immediately after the victories, in 1596, orders were sent to the military officials to build more walls especially along the roads used by the invaders of Kokonor and Sung Shan, to build fortresses at strategic points and more villages in the valleys for the farmers. The officials expected that the brigands would not take these blows lying down but would avenge themselves by means of new raids. In Cheng-hai-pu in the western

valley of Hsining, 60 li distant from the city on the way to Kokonor, a strong fortified city was built and a strong garrison appointed. The place controlled the western valley and the raids from Kokonor. In Chung-tsai in the Sa-t'ang valley, which so many times had been looted by invading Tibetans, a strong fortress was also built and a garrison appointed. The same dispositions were taken to improve the strength of the cities of Pa-yen-jung and San Ch'uan against brigands of Sung Shan and Ordos. For the first time troops were available to occupy permanently the strategic points in the country and from the t'u-ssu were required good soldiers to share with the Chinese troops the burden of the defense of the strongholds (*Annals* of Hsining **33**: 29*b*, 30*a*). General Liu Mei-kuan started with the exploitation of iron ore in the mountains north of Hsining, three foundries were built and blacksmiths started preparing weapons to be distributed among the subdued tribes. To the nineteen tribes of Komi numbering 7,000 people, reputed first-rate warriors, were sent military instructors with weapons, to drill them. The director of colonization reported that 80,000 acres of uncultivated land were still available to farmers. To destitute Tibetans of Kokonor and East Kansu, pouring into the country every day, were given land to till and grain and oxen. Orders were sent to promote education, build schools in each village and improve existing ones (*Annals* of Hsining **31**: 19*b*; **25**: 23*b*; **35**: 24).

In a report sent by General T'ien Yueh is encountered an interesting note relating to the education given to the people of north Kansu and Huangchung in these desperate times. In each of the schools of the city of Kanchow, sixty or seventy students attend the lessons of three teachers. In each of the schools of the cities of Kao T'ai, Shantan, Yung Ch'ang, Liangchow, Cheng Fan and Chuang Lang are encountered only thirty or forty students, in the smallest of these cities only twenty or thirty students. In each of the schools are two teachers. Then follows an exhortation to promote education (*Annals* of Hsining **33**: 20*a*).

In the same year, 1596, after the brilliant victories, the country seeming radiant and everywhere walls and fortresses being built, the lamas of T'a-erh-sse (Kumbum) (situated 40 li south of Hsining) decided to build a wall around the hermitages existing at that time. In 1560 some cells had been built for ten monks and, in 1577, a small temple next to a tower whose walls enclosed the celebrated tree, the glory of Kumbum (Monguors II: 25 sq.).

The same year the brigand Ho-lo-ch'ih, feeling insecure in Kokonor, intending to leave the country and to return to Ordos, asked to pass through Huangchung. The request was refused. He passed the Yellow River, looted T'ao and Ho Chou and was pursued in his flight to the Ordos (*Annals* of Hsining **31**: 20*a*).

The La-pu-erh tribe boldly repelled alone an attack of Kokonor brigands, killing fifteen brigands and capturing thirty horses (*Annals* of Hsining **31**: 20*a*). The Wa-la tribes, afraid of the Chinese army, moved to a salt lake deeper into Kokonor.

In 1597, however, Kokonor brigands still raided surrendered Tibetan tribes in the Hsining region. They were vigorously repelled from the Mang-la valley (*Annals* of Hsining **31**: 20; *Annals* of Kansu **46**: 52). Chih-li-ko, Ordos brigand, raided the borders of Huangchung; 60 of his brigands were killed and 3,300 surrendered (*Annals* of Kansu **46**: 38*a*).

The same year Liu Mei-kuan and Lung-yin finished the editing of a set of new *Annals*. However, a note is added, no woodblocks had been carved, only a few texts existed (*Annals* of Hsining **31**: 20*a*; **27**: 14, 15), and most of them were indecipherable.

In 1598 the Ordos Mongol Ch'ih-li-ko intended to reoccupy and to pasture in Sung Shan. He was repelled and suffered a defeat in Liu Ko Chin. In the fifth moon he plundered the Wolanko region and was repelled again. In the fifth moon one of his tribes, the Shao-hai-hai tribe, surrendered (*Annals* of Kansu **46**: 38*a*). In the seventh moon Generals T'ien Yueh and Ta Yun definitely cleared the Sung Shan region of brigands. The chieftains Pin-tu, A-shih-tu, Tsai-cheng, Chih-li-ko had long infested the Huangchung and East Kansu countries. This time the brigands were chased as far as 500 li (*Annals* of Kansu **46**: 38*b*). In the eleventh month the Mongol Hao-erh-ch'i occupied Sung Shan. The Chinese Commander Li Wen and surrendered Tibetan tribes repelled them and administered a severe blow. They built a wall as long as 400 li, indicating that Sung Shan belonged to China proper and was no longer the country of the barbarians (*Annals* of Kansu **46**: 3*b*).

In 1600 Sung Shan, the country from which during many years many raids had been perpetrated, was cleared of brigands and integrated into China. No more raids are recorded of Kokonor and Sung Shan brigands in Huangchung. For some time the Ordos brigands tried to recover Sung Shan and make forays in East Kansu, T'ao and Ming Chou, Liangchow, Chengfan, Ninghsia, but Huangchung enjoyed relative and temporary peace.

Kokonor brigands having lost many tribes previously subject to them, raided T'ao and Ming Chou to subdue Tibetan tribes not yet surrendered to China. They suffered a severe blow and 5,000 Tibetans surrendered to China (*Annals* of Kansu **46**: 38*b*).

The year 1604 is important in the history of lamaism in Huangchung. On the northwest of the so many times devastated Sa-t'ang valley, on the borders of one of the small affluents of the Sa-t'ang River, a Tibetan lama Diasai, belonging to the Saskya sect, started the building of the humble hermitage of Erh-ku-lung. The hermitage developed to the point that it became the first lamasery of Huangchung for many centuries and founded all over the country forty daughter monasteries. Its Living Buddhas, Chang Chia, T'u Kuan

and Sung Pa, were learned men and enjoyed prestige in Peking, Mongolia and Tibet (*Monguors II*: 27, sq.).

In 1607 the Brigadier General, T'u-ssu Ch'i Ping-chai, with his troops, was ordered to help General Ta Yun repel the raids of Kokonor brigands who in combination with Ordos brigands invaded and looted Chengfan and Liangchow. They repelled them, administering a severe blow (*Annals* of Kansu **46**: 39).

In 1612 the emperor ordered an honorific arch built to the meritorious Brigadier General Ch'i Teh, and sent the inscription to be chiseled on it: "Honorably favored by Heavenly Grace." The arch was built on the west street of the city of Hsining and still exists. Ch'i Teh is a descendant of T'u-ssu Ch'i-Kung-ko-hsing-chi, who during the Yuan period fulfilled the duty of myriarch, with golden badge and purple tassel, in the region 90 li south of Hsining. The Ch'i t'u-ssu clan should have been well acquainted with the Tibetan tribes living south of Hsining. No wonder the Ch'i Teh T'u-ssu was called upon by minister of war Cheng Lo in 1591, together with Colonel Shih Chia, to induce the Tibetan tribes to surrender. His successful efforts must have been the reason for the imperial distinction (*Annals* of Hsining **10**: 4*b*; **27**: 28).

In 1616 the t'u-ssu Lieutenant Colonel Ch'i Ping-chung (descendant of T'o-erh-chih-shih-chieh) appointed at Yung Ch'ang, saw the Mongol Yin-ting-ssu-ts'ing arriving with 1,000 horses to besiege the city. He controlled only 300 men but fought for two days and nights, defending the city. He himself killed three Mongol brigands. When auxiliary troops arrived he himself immediately pursued the enemy and saved all the people and cattle captured by the Mongols. The grateful people of Yung-ch'ang erected in the city a stele in commemoration of his heroic behavior. The stele still exists. Commended by his superiors for his leadership and energy, he was ordered, in 1621, to move with his troops to Liaotung Province (north of Peking) to defend the region of the Pu River. When he arrived, Liao Yang was already captured. Ten thousand more soldiers were put under his command. He remained in Liao tung for two more years. Later he encountered at P'ing-yang the Manchu troops invading China. In a pitched battle he was wounded by two sword cuts and three arrow hits. He was helped on his horse by his soldiers but died on the way. On account of his meritorious achievements, the emperor bestowed upon him the title of "T'ai-tze-t'ai-pao" "Junior guardian of the heir apparent," and an imperial oration was granted at his funeral and an order given to build an honorific arch in the city of Hsining with the inscription: "Served the country, manifested loyalty." The arch still exists. It was built in the large south street of the city (*Annals* of Hsining **10**: 4*b*; **27**: 21*a–b*; *Annals* of Kansu **42**: 45*a–b*).

A very important date in the history of Kokonor, Tibet and lamaism is 1636. Ku-Shih-han, chieftain of the Khoshot tribes (Oirats) went to Kokonor with his armies. He conquered Kokonor, Tsaidam and East Tibet, defeated the enemies of the Dalai Lama, occupied Lhasa and proclaimed in 1642 the Dalai Lama Nag-dbang bLo-bzang temporal and spiritual sovereign of Central Tibet.[85]

From 1597 until 1642 no events are recorded in either *Annals* concerning Huangchung. The country enjoyed a relative peace, while its borderlands still suffered raids from the same Mongols.

THE MONGUORS AND THE FALL OF THE MING DYNASTY

Desperate times were still in store for the Monguors and their t'u-ssu, and tremendous sacrifices were still requested from them to save the tottering dynasty, but the Monguors with their t'u-ssu stood loyal as a rock to the end.

The restless Mongol tribes had, during two and a half centuries, harrassed the dynasty, administering many crushing defeats to the armies, devastating the border provinces of the empire, and the neighborhood of the capital, causing the ruin and the revolt of the Tibetans, draining the resources of the empire and weakening the discipline of the armies and administrations. This sword of Damocles was still hanging over the dynasty when another ominous plague threatened the empire, the plague of brigands from inside the empire. The Ming dynasty was so effete her fall was imminent.

During the T'ien-ch'i period (1621–1627) Chinese brigands led by Li Tzu-ch'eng and Chang Hsien-chung ruthlessly murdered the people and savagely devastated the cities and villages, to the point that the exasperated Chinese population hoped for new rulers.[86]

According to the Lu chronicles, in 1628 a severe famine desolated the region of Yenan and Suei-te (Shensi), so many times plundered by Mongols during two and one-half centuries. Wang Chia-yun, a native of Fu-ku, stirred the starving people to band together and go plundering through the country. Li Tzu-ch'eng and Chang Hsien-chung, planning a revolution against the dynasty, seized the opportunity to organize the already plundering groups of brigands and realize their plan.

During 1628–1640 the revolution raged unchecked. The rumors spread like a prairie fire in Huangchung and North Kansu, and the population was frightened out of its wits, when the brigands poured from Hsi-an through the Kuan-chung pass toward Kansu.

In 1641 the old Hsining t'u-ssu Ch'i T'ing-chien (descendant of the Myriarch Kung-k'o-hsin-chi, founder of the Ch'i clan) and his two sons, Hsing-chu and P'ing-chu, invited to a secret convention to discuss

the situation, the official Hu Lien-ch'i, the t'u-ssu Lu Yung-ch'ang from Lien-ch'eng, the t'u-ssu Li T'ien-yu from Nienpei (descendant of Li Nan-ko, founder of the clan), and others, including Wang Chung, chief of the strong Tibetan tribe of Cheng Chung. They decided to defend the country, chose Hu Lien-ch'i their own lieutenant colonel, drank blood, and swore to die for the dynasty (*Annals* of Hsining 28: 1).

In the spring of 1642 the Tibetan tribes of Hsining revolted. The military commander Ma Kuang quelled the revolt, killing more than 700 rebels. Then he accepted the submission of 38 tribes (*Annals* of Hsining 31: 20b; *Annals* of Kansu 46: 42a).

In the autumn Li Tze-ch'eng sent to Huangchung and North Kansu his commander Huo Chin, with a strong army. He attacked the city of Hsining. The Hsining troops administered a crushing blow and he went to North Kansu to conquer the cities of Suchow, Kanchow, Shantan, Yung Ch'ang, and Liangchow. Suchow was taken, devastated and 4,700 people and troops were killed (*Annals* of Kansu 56: 38b); then the other cities surrendered one after another without fighting (*Annals* of Hsining 31: 20b; *Annals* of Kansu 46: 43b).

In the autumn of 1643 Huo Chin returned from Kanchow to avenge the previous defeat suffered in Hsining. He went along with Hsi Ta-tung. He was conversant with the dissensions existing among the subjects of the Lu t'u-ssu clan, part of whom considered the resistance useless, after more than half of China was lost at the hands of the brigands. One of the influential members of the clan, Lu Wen-lin, had sown strife in the clan and even led an army of brigands to occupy Chuang-lang. However, the stubborn T'u-ssu Lu fought back nine attacks of the army of Huo Chin in Hsi-Ta-tung. Both armies suffered many losses, and finally the t'u-ssu retreated with his outnumbered troops into his fortified city of Lien-ch'eng. The city was taken and the t'u-ssu tied in front of the gate of the city. He refused obstinately to surrender, swore and insulted the brigands. He was put to the sword with many of his soldiers. His son, a young boy, and his daughter were abducted. This happened in February, 1644 (Lu Chronicles, *Annals* of Hsining 28: 15, 16).

In 1644 Huo Chin went with his army to conquer Hsining, and met the Hsining army. The defenders of Hsining, conversant with the strength of the enemy army and in order to check the advance of the enemy, had used Tibetans set in ambush on the way the brigands had to pass, stretching ropes and digging holes in the ground. The enemy horse was unaware of the traps laid for them and rushed furiously on the Hsining army which was waiting behind the ambushes in a resolute array. More than a thousand brigands were killed, among them their commander Huo Chin.

The brigand vice-commander, Hsin Wei-chung, mustered the troops and went immediately to attack

[85] Grousset, *op. cit.*, 603.
[86] Erich Hauer, Li Tzu-ch'eng and Chang Hsien-chung, Ein Beitrag zum Ende der Ming Dynasty, *Asia Major,* Vol. secundum fasc. 3/4: 436 sq., 1925.

Hsining city. The city was carried by storm and delivered to sack and slaughter: for the soldiers there was but death. The brigands knew that the t'u-ssu had stirred the people to resist the brigands, and they wreaked ruin on them. The old T'u-ssu Ch'i T'ing-chien (*Annals* of Hsining 28: 1*a–b*), and the T'u-ssu Li T'ien-yu (*Annals* of Hsining 28: 2*a*) were taken prisoner. The T'u-ssu Li Hung-yuen (of the old Li Wen branch) was killed with his wife and 120 members of his family (*Annals* of Hsining 31: 21; 28: 15; *Annals* of Kansu 46: 43*b*). The wife of Li T'ien-yu, the concubine, the two brothers, and 300 persons of his family and servants were killed. The same year the T'u-ssu Yeh kuo-chi, who had been called by the emperor early in 1643 to fight the brigands in Ch'ang p'ing in Liaotung, died on the field of battle in 1643 (*Annals* of Hsining 28: 15). All these t'u-ssu with their families laid down their lives defending the dynasty.

Then the brigands went down into the country devastating, burning villages, murdering anyone who made a stand, abducting women, stealing livestock, etc. A group of them went to Kokonor, where all the chiefs surrendered.

The brigands knew that the old T'u-ssu Ch'i T'ing-chien had been the promoter of the resistance and had killed their chief Huo Chin. They decided to kill him. His son Hsing-chu spent the entire family fortune, buying 100 fine horses. He went to see the chief of the brigands in P'ing-Jung-i, hoping to redeem his father. The chief not only refused to accept the horses, but told him straight to his face that his father was to be killed. Then his brother Ping-chu protested, saying that his father had not killed Huo Chin, but that he himself was the murderer. The chief looked at him a long time and finally said, you are a filial son. He ordered the father to be bound to a car and to leave for Hsi-an. Hsing-chu cried the whole way home. However, his father was not killed (*Annals* of Hsining 28: 19*a*).

His father was sent to Hsi-an, together with Li T'ien-yu. In T'ung Kuan they met the Manchu Prince Ah-Ki-Ko (*Annals* of Kansu 42: 48*a*). Both submitted to the newly established dynasty and were released. The Governor General Meng Ch'iao-fang, sent by the Ch'ing dynasty to pacify Kansu, had already arrived in 1645. He rehabilitated both t'u-ssu in their former office of commander of the clan, enjoining them to pacify the t'u-ssu of Hsining and Ho-hsi, to induce the Tibetans to be submissive, to abstain from revolts and to capture the rebel Tibetan Chao Chin-chung (*Annals* of Hsining 28: 2*a–b;* 31: 21; *Annals* of Kansu 46: 44*b*). To the T'u-ssu Li Hung-yuen who had perished with his wife and 120 members of his family the emperor later ordered built an honorific arch in Hsining with the inscription "Loyal servant and faithful wife, glory of the noble clan" (*Annals* of Hsining 28: 15*b*).

While the t'u-ssu and their subjects were fighting and suffering and dying in Hsining, the despairing Ming emperor, on April 25, 1644, had hanged himself in the Wan Sui Shan in Peking. On June 6, 1644, the troops of the new Ch'ing dynasty entered Peking and started at full speed with destruction of the troops of Li Tze-ch'eng who had already proclaimed himself emperor. On October 7, 1644, he ended his life by hanging himself.[87]

The t'u-ssu and their subjects served the Ch'ing dynasty with the same faithfulness they had served the Ming dynasty.

At the time the Ming dynasty (1368–1644) started with the occupation of Huangchung, this was an insecure colony of China, which during the previous dynasties had been lost several times and recovered. The Ming organized the country, providing a civil and military administration on the Chinese pattern. In Huangchung they started with the founding of military colonies, induced the Tibetan tribes to submit to them, established the exchange bureau of tea for horses, favored and protected the arrival of traders from inside China, and promoted agriculture and commerce. They attracted Chinese to settle in the country, built schools, promoted education, and repelled forays of Tibetans and Mongols from outside the Huangchung borders. Huangchung was at peace.

However, in the fateful year 1509 the first group of Mongols arrived and settled in Kokonor, followed by one after another, which ruined and cowed into submission the Tibetan tribes of Kokonor. At the same time the population of Huangchung and East Kansu, from 1509 to 1597, succumbed to the recurrent onslaught of avid, restless and predatory Mongols. The Tibetan tribes, robbed of their cattle, having seen their women and young folk abducted, beset with starvation and abject poverty, started raiding, devastating, and laying waste Huangchung and East Kansu. The army could not deter the forces of destruction. Raids prevailed over the entire northwestern borders of the empire, and the emperor gave the Huangchung officers insufficient reinforcements. It was only in 1590 that the energetic Minister of War, Cheng Lo, commanding new forces, succeeded in defeating the brigands. In the meantime the administration had incessantly built cities, villages, schools, walls, and fortresses all over the country. The aspect of the country had changed completely, despite the desperate times. The country had been organized and the administration established.

During these times, when raids and destruction raged unchecked, Chinese and Shat'o and Uighurs, Tibetans and Monguors had suffered together, helped and sheltered each other, and blended and fused in the compound called the Huangchung population.

In 1644 when the Ch'ing dynasty occupied Huangchung it was no longer the depopulated unorganized

---

[87] Erich Hauer, *op. cit.*, 488, 494, 497.

colony which the Mongols had handed down to the Ming.

HUANGCHUNG MONGUORS AND THEIR T'U-SSU DURING THE CH'ING DYNASTY (1644–1911)

The establishment of a new dynasty in China used to entail desperate times for a long period. The faithful Monguors with their t'u-ssu, after having defended the Ming dynasty to the end, pledged allegiance to, and cast their lot with the new Ch'ing dynasty, and again would prove their faithfulness. This time they had to fight at the side of the Manchu troops against the rebel Chinese officials of Kansu and all China, even though the power of the new dynasty was still problematical, but all of them remained heroically loyal and dependable to the end, suffering hardship and dying for the dynasty. Their faithfulness in such trying and tragic circumstances cannot but be admired. The history of the Monguors is a shining example of faithfulness seldom recorded in history.

The people in the northern provinces of China had, for many years, had a desperate time on account of the brigands of Li Tzu-ch'eng and the invading groups of Manchus looting the country of its wealth. The despairing Ming emperor had hanged himself on April 25, 1644, and Li Tzu-ch'eng had entered the capital and proclaimed himself emperor. The Ming general Wu San-kuei defended the northern part of the great wall of the empire and the pass of Shanhaikuan against invading Manchu plunderers. Considering that the very existence of the empire was at stake and abhorring and loathing the savage brigands of Li Tzu-ch'eng, Wu San-kuei invited Manchu troops to come over to annihilate the brigands and save the dynasty. However he had little thought that in making this compact he was sealing the fate of the Chinese empire. He opened the pass, and his troops in combination with those of the Manchus rushed to the capital which they entered on June 6, 1644. The brigand emperor Li Tzu-ch'eng had fled, but the Manchus proclaimed their own emperor and inaugurated their Ch'ing dynasty. On October 7 Li Tzu-ch'eng died. Jealousies and dissensions arose among the chiefs of the brigands and their impact was broken. Immediately Wu-San-kuei, leading his troops in concert with the Manchu army, pursued the brigands and achieved the surrender of the Chinese provinces.

At the end of 1645, T'u-ssu Ch'i T'ing-chien and Li T'ien-yu surrendered in T'ung Kuan to the Manchu Prince A-ki-ko, came back to Kansu, and called on General Meng Ch'iao-fang. They were rehabilitated and ordered to induce the surrender of the Monguor t'u-ssu. All the t'u-ssu submitted to the new dynasty (*Annals* of Hsining **31**: 21a). Meng Ch'iao-fang immediately sent to Hsining Commanders Chiang San-chih (*Annals* of Hsining **26**: 3b) and Chang Chi-yao

with troops (*Annals* of Hsining **26**: 6b) who, in concert with the t'u-ssu troops, exterminated the groups of brigands still roaming in the country without chiefs, and they induced the rebel Tibetan tribes to surrender. The commanders started repairing the cities, villages and fortresses in Huangchung.

In 1646 T'u-ssu Ch'eng was appointed commander in Chuang Lang by the Manchu Prince Su and given the title of Piao-ch'i Chiang-chun. At that time groups of brigands plundered the country of Sung Shan I north of Chuang Lang. The son of T'u-ssu Ch'eng pursued and exterminated them and died on the field of battle (*Annals* of Kansu **42**: 36b).

However, the Chinese abhorred and hated the uncouth Manchu barbarians. Many among the governors and commanders could not resist the temptation of espousing the cause of the crumbled dynasty. The opposition would last for eighteen years before the entire empire would be conquered by the Manchus. Several times their empire met precarious circumstances, but party intrigues and jealousies among the Chinese divided them, and never could they offer a permanent united front against the conquerors.

The whereabouts of the heir apparent to the Ming throne being unknown, several princes of the imperial family arose in the provinces and tried to restore the dynasty. Prince Kuei succeeded in the formation in Kiangsi Province of a coalition of governors and military commanders, and the news spread like a prairie fire over the entire empire. Several governors and commanders in north China who had surrendered at the arrival of the Manchu troops, waited for the signal of the general uprising. A storm was brewing even in the remote northern region of Kanchow, Liangchow, etc. Two chiefs of the Mohammedan colony of Kanchow, Ting Kuo-tung and Milayin, started the revolt against the Ch'ing dynasty (*Annals* of Kansu **42**: 48b). They joined the group of Chou Shih-chuan, a scion of the Ming princes, and enrolled as many Tibetans and brigands of Li Tze-ch'eng as possible. The Chinese officials of Kanchow and Liangchow followed in their wake.[88]

At the end of the Ming dynasty in North Kansu, Huangchung, and East Kansu, in nearly all the important cities and villages along the trade routes, colonies of Mohammedans were established, having their mosques and religious leaders who were obeyed and honored by their people. Meng Ch'iao-fang, conversant with this situation, informed the emperor about his apprehensions concerning the participation of the Mohammedans in the revolt. He wrote that an order issued by their religious chiefs would suffice to enroll all the Mohammedans of Kansu in the insurrection, and then he indicated the cities and villages in Kansu where the most important groups of Mohammedans existed (*Annals* of Hsining **26**: 1a–b; **34**: 1b, 2b).

[88] E. H. Parker, Kansu Mussulmans, *China Review* **16**: 335, 1887.

General Meng Ch'iao-fang seems to have trusted the faithfulness of the Monguor t'u-ssu of Huangchung and therefore decided to stabilize his position first in Hsining before attacking Kanchow, Liangchow, etc., notwithstanding that in Hsining a strong Mohammedan colony existed. Therefore, in 1645 he sent two commanders to Hsining, and at the end of 1646 he sent another commander with troops, Ma Ju-shin, probably foreseeing imminent troubles.

In 1647 the rebels of Kanchow aimed to join the already revolting Mohammedan groups in East Kansu. Dissension seems to have existed among the Mohammedan colonies of Hsining and those of Kanchow, Liangchow, etc. Anyway the rebel Mohammedans, Chinese, and Tibetans united, led by the two Mohammedan chiefs Ting Kuo-tung and Milayin, and marched their troops first towards Hsining in order to compel the Mohammedan colony and the whole region of Huangchung to follow in their wake. On the borders of the Tatung River, north of Hsining, a ruthless battle was fought by the Manchu commanders of Hsining, supported by all the Huangchung troops of the t'u-ssu and a resounding victory was obtained (*Annals* of Hsining **31**: 21*a*). The Hsining Mohammedans refused to mix in the revolt, maybe for fear of the overwhelming Manchu and Monguor forces guarding the country. Anyway, the victory secured a temporary peace in the country of Huangchung.

In 1648, after this victory, Meng Ch'iao-fang started attacking the cities of North Kansu. The cities of Liangchow and Yung Ch'ang surrendered, but Major Ma Hu-ya resisted in Kanchow. The city was carried by storm, the commander, eighteen officials, and eighty others were killed. The resistance of the rebels of Suchow was more serious. The city suffered tremendously, the commander and many people were killed (*Annals* of Hsining **26**: 1, 3). T'u-ssu Li fought in Kanchow and Suchow with 500 soldiers (*Annals* of Kansu **42**: 47*a*), helped by Hsin (*Annals* of Kansu **42**: 54), Na (*Annals* of Kansu **42**: 40*a*), and Ch'i t'u-ssu (*Annals* of Kansu **42**: 46*a–b*). Meng Ch'iao-fang, informed that the rebels (*Annals* of Kansu **56**: 40*a*) had proposed to move to East Kansu after the defeat on the Tatung River, had appointed t'u-ssu to guard the passes and the roads leading to East Kansu. T'u-ssu Ch'i Pei-chai (*Annals* of Kansu **42**: 35*b*) fought the rebels in Chin Pien I, T'u-ssu Ch'i Ta-hsun (*Annals* of Kansu **42**: 36*b*) in Ta Tsing, T'u-ssu Ch'eng (*Annals* of Kansu **42**: 36) and T'u-ssu Lu (*Annals* of Kansu **42**: 59*b*) fought them in Wu Chao Lin. T'u-ssu Kan with three hundred of his soldiers guarded the ferry on the Yellow River. However, the rebels managed to reach East Kansu and succeeded in capturing within a few months the cities of Lanchow, Ho Chou, T'ao Chou, Lin T'ao, and Kuei Te, and beseiged the city of Kung Ch'ang.

In 1649 Meng Ch'iao-fang led his army and all the troops of the t'u-ssu to East Kansu, in order to re-capture the cities lost at the hands of the revolting Ming commanders. He recovered all the cities, one after the other, Lanchow, Ho Chou, T'ao Chou, Lin T'ao and Kuei Te, and saved the beseiged city of Kung Ch'ang. The brother of T'u-ssu Lu was killed in the fight at Ho-ya-lung (*Annals* of Kansu **42**: 60). In a little more than three years Meng Ch'iao-fang had recovered one hundred and more cities and fortified villages (*Annals* of Hsining **26**: 1, 2). T'u-ssu Li (*Annals* of Hsining **28**: 2) and T'u-ssu Ch'i (*Annals* of Hsining **28**: 3) fought at Kuei Te. After these arduous campaigns the Monguor troops were released, and could start repairing the tremendous havoc wrought by the Mongol brigands of Kokonor and Sung Shan I, and by the rebel Tibetans, during the last 150 years of the Ming regime. In the meantime the Manchu armies conquered more provinces in the empire and still had intermittent revolts to quell in the very south of East Kansu and on the Szechwan borders.

In 1660 a revolt is recorded of the Mohammedan Ta Erh-han, a member of the Yeh t'u-ssu, who induced Tibetans of Kokonor to help plunder the valley of Milaku, the region situated on the northern borders of the Yellow River south of Nienpei. The guard of the Milaku region had been entrusted to the Yeh t'u-ssu since the Yuan and Ming times. The faithful T'u-ssu Yeh killed the rebel and nine of his men, and captured two others whom he delivered to Hsining. The invaders fled to Kokonor. The Yeh t'u-ssu was a clan of Mohammedans from Turkistan which was settled in Milaku in Yuan times (*Monguors I*: 32; *Annals* of Kansu **42**: 52*b*). Later, at the time of the revolt of Wu San-kuei in 1673, a group of the Yeh clan started following the rebels. The faithful t'u-ssu again succeeded in quelling the revolt, killing many of them. He was promoted to secretary commander as a reward for his faithfulness (*Annals* of Kansu **42**: 52*b*).

In 1665 Huai Erh-lai, a Tibetan from Kokonor, with his two brothers and their tribes, looted the country along the trade road between Kanchow and Liangchow. Wang Chin-pao, the commander of Hsining, repulsed the brigands (*Annals* of Kansu **46**: 46*a*). T'u-ssu Li (*Annals* of Kansu **42**: 47*b*) and T'u-ssu Ch'i (*Annals* of Kansu **42**: 46*b*) helped him.

The tremendous rebellion of Wu San-kuei, the first benefactor of the Ch'ing dynasty, who had put the Manchus in possession of the empire started at the end of the year 1673. The revolt spread through eleven of the eighteen provinces of the empire, and required eight years for its suppression. East Kansu was soon lost to the Manchus and the cities of Lanchow, Ho Chou, T'aochow, Lin T'ao, Kung Ch'ang, etc. were taken by the rebels. The bridge of Lanchow, which secured the communication between East and West Kansu, was broken up. In that way no armies along West Kansu could come to the rescue of East Kansu. However, General Wang Chin-pao of Hsining rushed to Lanchow with his army and all the Monguor troops under command of T'u-ssu Ch'i Pei-chai (*Annals* of Hsining **28**: 3; *Annals* of Kansu **42**: 46*b*). The Monguors, familiar with the customs of the country, prepared fifty or more rafts of sheep and ox skins, and crossed the river at night in the locality of Chang Chia Wan. In the morning they unexpectedly met a large group of rebels in Hsin Ch'eng and administered a crushing defeat to them. They arrived at Lanchow which was unprepared to meet the enemy, and the city was recovered (*Annals* of Kansu **42**: 47*a–b*). T'u-ssu Ch'i was appointed defender of the city (*Annals* of Kansu **42**: 46*b*). Then the Hsining troops of Wang Chin-pao and the Monguor troops helped recover, one after another, all the cities of East Kansu, with other Manchu troops. T'u-ssu Li commanded 1,000 of his Monguor troops (*Annals* of Kansu **42**: 47*b*), and T'u-ssu Kan and Ah 300 (*Annals* of Kansu **42**: 50, 51). Then the t'u-ssu participated in the seige and the recovering of the city of P'ing Liang, and the capture of the rebel governor Wang Fu-ch'eng. The Lu t'u-ssu sent 400 *tan* of wheat to the hungry Monguor soldiers beseiging P'ing Liang, which was recovered in 1678. Wu San-kuei died August 17, 1678. After a campaign of six years the t'u-ssu returned to Huangchung with their troops.

In 1677 groups of Tibetans, in combination with Uighurs, had attacked Salar villages. Probably during the insurrection of Wu San-kuei, Salar brigands had plundered them. The Manchu army had put them to flight (*Annals* of Kansu **46**: 50*a–b*). In 1681 they returned to avenge the previously unsuccessful attack. Under the leadership of the Tibetan Huang La T'aichi they attacked the village of Su Chih and killed many Salars. The Manchu commander at night attacked the camp of the aggressors and killed many of them. They fled toward the Lao Ya pass and occupied it, blocking the communications. Troops had to come from Liangchow to repel and pursue them (*Annals* of Kansu **46**: 51).

In 1689 a tremendous famine desolated East Kansu. It was followed by revolts of hungry people. In 1691 the revolt, led by a Taoist priest, had spread over the entire country. Troops of all the commanderies of Kansu were summoned, the revolt lasted until 1693 (*Annals* of Kansu **56**: 45*b*). The Monguor t'u-ssu did not move into East Kansu. They had to protect their own country against inroads of poor and destitute people and forestall uprisings of the army in Huangchung, which was lacking food and was restless, for the crops in Huangchung had been bad also. In 1702, 50,000 *tan* of rice were sent from Sian to Huangchung for the troops (*Annals* of Hsining **31**: 21*b*).

In 1693 T'u-ssu Li Hsia, assistant commander in Hsining, informed the emperor concerning the situation in the Pe-ta region, in the northern valley of Hsining. In 1647, after the rebel Mohammedans and Chinese of Kanchow had tried to compel the Mohammedans of Hsining to revolt but had hit a severe blow on the border of the Tatung River, the Chinese who had followed them dared not return to Kanchow, for fear of severe punishments. They liked better to settle in the region of Pe-ta, situated 120 li north of Hsining, outside the jurisdiction of the prefecture, and belonging to the Mongols. They tilled the soil and built houses. More people had joined their group which already numbered 10,000 families in 1693. They brought the regulatory *t'ien pa* (land) taxes to the Mongols. T'u-ssu Li, having investigated the circumstances with other commanders, reported that the Pe-ta region had become a favorite thoroughfare along which Mongols and Tibetans traveled, spying on Huangchung. The group of settlers conversant with the Chinese regions where they constantly traveled also supplied them with information. Lamas traveled the whole year long on their way to Tibet without regulatory passes, etc. The t'u-ssu proposed to compel the entire group of settlers to return to their original countries, for the offense of having revolted had long since been forgiven, and to forbid the bringing of the *t'ien pa* taxes to the Mongol princes, according to the regulations issued by the Manchu emperor in 1658. He proposed to forbid lamas to travel to Tibet through the Pe-ta region, but to travel with passports secured on fixed passes. If serious measures were not taken, sooner or later troubles would arise, all the more since Tibet is for the moment seriously troubled and Galdan is disturbing the empire. Nobody knows what would be in store in the future. If the Mongol princes and settlers would not comply with the regulations, the army should be used to compel them to obey (*Annals* of Hsining **34**: 5*a*).

T'u-ssu Ch'i Chung-chai, brother of T'u-ssu Ch'i Pe-chai, having graduated from the military academy and in 1673 fought the rebel Wu San-kuei in combination with all the Monguor t'u-ssu, had been promoted to second captain in Wei Yuan Pu. He had also fought rebels in Chin Chou and Li Hsien in East Kansu, had been promoted to major and transferred with his troops to Chang Chia Ku north of Peking in Chihli Province, to participate in the war the emperor was waging against the Jungar (Oirat) chief Galdan. After the death of the Oirat chief Yeh Hsien, who had captured the Ming emperor and proclaimed himself emperor of all the Mongols and had been killed in 1455, the Oirats had divided into four groups. Galdan, chief of the Choros group and the Jungar tribes, dreamed of building a new Jungar empire and expelling the Manchus from China.

Galdan, having already conquered Kashgaria, Turfan and Hami, and been ruling over Central Asia, had still to win the four Khalkha groups in order to control the united Mongol race. In 1688 he invaded their territory. The Khalkhas fled to Tumet and asked the emperor for protection. In 1690 Galdan had struck a severe blow at Kalgan. In 1696 the emperor, himself leading one of his three armies, went to meet Galdan in the Kerulen region. T'u-ssu Ch'i Chung-chai

(*Annals* of Kansu 42 : 46*a*) with his troops accompanied the emperor. Galdan fled but was met by the army of General Fei Yang-ku who completely annihilated his army at Chao Mu To. The Khalkhas reoccupied their country.

In 1697 the emperor went with his armies to Ninghsia in order to destroy entirely the Jungar forces. Again T'u-ssu Ch'i Chung-chai with his troops followed the imperial army. However Galdan died May 3, 1697, and the emperor returned to Peking. The t'u-ssu was promoted to lieutenant colonel of the Ho Pa division in Shansi, then brigadier general in Chin Hua in Chekiang Province. In 1713, upon his retirement, he fulfilled the duty of assistant commander of his clan. At his death the emperor honored him with a funeral oration.[89]

In 1703 the Khoshot Mongols of Kokonor submitted to the empire. The emperor conferred on the descendants of Ku Shih Khan, bLo-bzang tanchin, and others the titles of Prince, Pei-le, Pei-tse, Kung, T'aichi (*Annals* of Kansu 64 : 52*a; Annals* of Hsining 31 : 22*a*).

This record points to the troubles in Lhasa which had long threatened Huangchung and the Monguors. Ku Shih Khan, chief of a Khoshot group (one of the four Oirat groups), had invaded and conquered Kokonor, Tsaidam, and Kham in 1636, and had been invited by the fifth Dalai Lama, Nag dzang bLo bzang, chief of the Yellow Sect, to help him in the struggle against a Tibetan prince, fanatic adherent of the old Red Sect, who had occupied Lhasa. He defeated the prince, installed the Dalai in Lhasa, proclaimed him Sovereign of Central Tibet and assumed the duty of protector of the Yellow Church.[90] Ku Shih Khan had been under the Manchu suzerainty since 1637. He died in 1656. His son Dayan, his grandson Dalai, and his great-grandson La tsang assumed the same duty. The Dalai entrusted the temporal administration of his kingdom to an official called a *desi*. In 1670 the *desi* revolted. On the request of the Dalai Lama, Dayan quelled the revolt and committed the *desi* to prison. Sangs rgyas rgya mcho was appointed to the *desi* office. The Dalai died in 1680–1681. The *desi*, with the Panchen Lama, appointed as reincarnation of the Dalai Lama a boy born a year after his death, called Chang Yang bLo bzang, the sixth Dalai Lama. The Tibetans and lamas

should have been cognizant of the fact and have considered the boy as the legitimate successor of Nag Dzang. However, the shrewd *desi,* offended by the growing interference of the emperor and of the Khoshot prince in Tibetan affairs, kept secret from the outer world both the death of the Dalai Nag dzang and the appointment of the reincarnation. He himself planned to rule the kingdom politically. Galdan who had been lama in Lhasa had been the friend of the Dalai and the *desi,* who at the time of his struggle with the Khalkhas had imprudently spoken in his favor near the emperor. In 1689 the distrusting emperor started inquiring into the matter and knew that the old Dalai had died in 1680–1681. He suspected connivance between the *desi* and the Jungars. After the crushing defeat administered to Galdan in 1696, the emperor learned that Galdan would fly to Tibet to build a new army. The emperor back in Peking immediately sent to the Khoshot princes of Kokonor the order to apprehend Galdan, his family and followers in order to check their faithfulness to the empire. However, Galdan had fled to the west and died in 1697. The princes of Kokonor, in order to dispel the suspicion of the emperor concerning their faithfulness, gathered in a group of thirty-one presided over by an eminent lama and swore allegiance to the empire. It seems that on account of the unanimous testimony of faithfulness sent to the emperor, the princes, being all descendants of Ku Shih Khan, were awarded titles.[91]

However, the *Annals* of Hsining present another version: the emperor, preoccupied with the troubled situation in Tibet and Kokonor, ordered the lama Chang Nan to *erh chih* (induce to submission) the princes of Kokonor. Having obeyed, the emperor granted titles to the descendants of Ku Shih Khan: to Blo bzang tan chin, the title of prince, to the others the titles of *Pei-le, Pei-tse, Kung, T'aichi.* A yearly allowance in silver was also granted. They were requested to bring tribute to the capital. As long as the lama was in Hsining the princes were loyal and dependable. Later Chinese officials were appointed to care for them (*Annals* of Hsining 20 : 16*b*).

In the *Annals* of Kansu 46 : 52, is recorded in 1708 a serious revolt of Hsi Ku Tibetans, in the region of Wen Hsien in the farthest southern corner of East Kansu. The Hsi Ku tribes are the Hsi La Ku tribes, the Shera Uighurs, the Yellow Tibetans, already noted (pp. 17, 18). They were still autonomous in 1708 and had their own chiefs, and joined in the revolt. They depended upon the Yang t'u-ssu, and their chiefs were granted titles after the revolt by the emperor, thanks to the intercession of the Yang t'u-ssu.

In 1718 the Board of Agriculture of Hsining announced that 14,678 acres of uncultivated land were

[89] *Annals* of Hsining 28 : 4a. *Annals* of Kansu 42 : 45b. Réné Grousset, *L'Empire des Steppes,* 607, 610, Paris, Payot, 1935.

[90] Tucci, *Tibetan painted scrolls* 1 : 59–70, Roma, La Liberia della Stato., 1949. The Dalai Lama who died in 1680–1681 had built up a mighty kingdom and the supremacy of the Yellow Sect over all Tibet, leaning on the power of the Mongols, who were foreigners, arousing the suspicions of the Tibetans and the jealousy of the other sects and the old nobility. At the same time he had laid the foundation of the ruin of his kingdom, having recognized the right of some Mongol tribes to act as patrons over his lands, being bound in that way to the vicissitudes of political events. He had to take side with his protectors, later the Jungars, in their struggle with the Chinese empire.

[91] Maurice Courant, *L'Asie centrale au XVII et XVIII siècles. Empire Kalmouk ou Empire Mantchou,* 62, 72, 73, Paris, Picard, 1912.

still available for culture. More troops had arrived in Hsining on account of the troubles in Tibet and those in Turkistan caused by the Jungars. Troops had to be fed and more grain was required (*Annals* of Hsining 31: 21a).

The period of troubles and calamities originating from Kokonor and already long present in Huangchung started in 1723.

Tsewang Rabdan, nephew of the late Galdan, had succeeded his uncle as chief of the Jungars (1697). He was as hostile to the emperor as his uncle, and was as good a friend of the *desi* Sangs rgyas as his uncle. The sixth Dalai Lama, appointed by the *desi* and the Panchen Lama and enthroned in 1697, had proved to be a debauched man. In 1701 the Kokonor Prince La Tsang, protector of the Yellow Church, the Jungar chief Tsewang Rabdan and a delegate of the emperor compelled him to resign. He obeyed but, backed by the *desi,* he reserved for himself the temporal rights of his kingdom. Prince La Tsang confined the *desi* to prison and killed him. The emperor appointed La Tsang to the office of *desi* and ordered him to bring to Peking the dethroned Dalai Lama. However, many lamas and Tibetans still favored him and objected strongly. Finally the unpopular La Tsang succeeded in 1706 in moving the escort to Peking. The caravan was attacked on the way by lamas and Tibetans, and the Dalai was killed. La Tsang, in concert with the Panchen lama, appointed as sixth reincarnation, the lama Yeches, but he was taken in ill grace by lamas and Tibetans. All the more rumors were spread that in Li T'ang the genuine reincarnation was born. The emperor, to nip in the bud all these rumors, confined the Li T'ang reincarnation and his parents in the lamasery of Kumbum in Hsining. Despite the protestations of lamas, and even of many of the princes of Kokonor, the enthroning of the sixth Dalai Lama Yeches was ordered by the emperor and performed in 1710.

The Jungar chief Tsewang Rabdan was incensed by the repeated intrusions of the emperor in the affairs of Tibet, conversant with the animosity instilled in the hearts of the lamas of the entire Yellow Church and of the Tibetan tribes against the Chinese empire, conscious of the hatred fostered in the whole nation against the Khoshot La Tsang, who had dethroned their Dalai Lama and was told to have him murdered on the way to Peking. Well informed about the anti-Chinese dispositions of even the princes of Kokonor, Rabdan considered the time ripe to take possession of Tibet and Kokonor, and to rule the Yellow Church. He resolved to pose as the savior of the religion, leading his armies to Hsining to bring to Lhasa the Dalai Lama, the idol of the nation, together with lamas and the princes of Kokonor. His first army marching on Hsining was defeated, but the second, commanded by his brother Tsereng Dondoub, reached Lhasa in 1717, defended by Prince La Tsang. Treacherously, a city gate was

opened and for three days the wild Jungars destroyed and looted the temples and the city, killing many people. La Tsang was killed.

The emperor could not take this affront lying down. However, his first punitive expedition to Lhasa was defeated in 1718. The second in 1720 parted in two columns, one leaving Szechwan Province, the other starting from Hsining. On the way both encountered Jungar troops which were defeated, fled and left Tibet. T'u-ssu Lu T'i-sin was taken ill at that time and sent his son Lu Hua-lin, commanding his troops, to participate in the expedition. Back in Huangchung he was promoted to lieutenant-colonel in the Hsining army, and later colonel in Liangchow and brigadier general in Kanchow (*Annals* of Kansu **42**: 57a). The emperor, cognizant of the growing animosity of the lamas and the people against his appointed Dalai Lama Yeches, and of the aversion aroused in the hearts of the lamas and the Tibetans against the savage Jungars who had looted their temples and carried away the riches of the nation and killed many people, conversant with their eagerness to see enthroned in Lhasa the Dalai Lama secluded in Kumbum, resolved to send the lama to Lhasa with the Hsining army and to enthrone him as a new sixth Dalai Lama. The decision seemed to him apt to reconquer the sympathy of the Tibetans and the lamas, and to plant in their hearts aversion for the Jungars, who were waging war with him in Central Asia with an eye on Tibet.

The emperor, averred politician, in order to assure the success of his plan, ordered the Monguor Living Buddha, T'u Kuan, chief of the renowned Monguor monastery of Erh Ku Lung in Hsining, a learned man of high repute in Tibet and Mongolia, to convey the Kumbum Lama to Lhasa in the capacity of imperial envoy. He bestowed him with the title of Huthukhtu, the highest imperial distinction for lamas, in order to dignify his position. He gave him letters and unusual gifts to bring to the Panchen Lama and to the heads of the most important monasteries in Tibet, his former teachers and friends. The Kumbum Dalai Lama, brought to Lhasa with a display of pomp and magnificence and enthroned in 1720, was enthusiastically congratulated by the lamas and the Tibetans. This act put an end to the autonomy of Tibet and of the Yellow Church. The Monguors were proud of their Huthukhtu (Monguors II: 31). The sixth Dalai Lama Yeches was dethroned and called to Peking in order to prevent possible complications.[92]

[92] Maurice Courant, *op. cit.,* 76–77. W. W. Rockhill, The Dalai Lamas of Lhasa and their relations with the Manchu emperors of China 1644–1908, *T'oung-pao,* 1–92, 1910. E. Haenich, Bruchstücke aus der Geschichte Chinas unter der Gegenwärtigen Dynastie, *T'oung-pao,* 197–235, 375–424, 1911. Réné Grousset, *op. cit.* Arthur W. Hummel, *Eminent Chinese of the Ching Period,* Washington, 1943. L. Petech, *China and Tibet in the Early 18th Century,* Lieden, Brill, 1950. H. H. Howorth, *History of the Mongols,* I, *passim.*

REVOLT OF 1723–1724

After the successful enthronement of the Dalai Lama in Lhasa in 1720, it seems that a period of peace was to be expected. However Huangchung had to go through a new tremendous ordeal of destruction, ruin, and ruthless murder, caused by the revolt of the Khoshot Prince of Kokonor, bLo-bzang tan-chin, a grandson of Ku Shih Khan.

All the princes of Kokonor had participated in the Lhasa expedition in 1720 and had seen their wishes fulfilled by the enthronement of their beloved Dalai Lama. On account of the troubles in Lhasa which had lasted for so many years, related to the enthronements and the depositions of Dalai Lamas and the interference of the Chinese emperor in Tibetan affairs, the princes must have shared for a long time the grudge and the hatred of the lamas and the Tibetans against the Chinese empire.

Back in Kokonor the ambitious Prince bLo-bzang tan-chin had started dreaming about the unification under his command of all the Kokonor tribes, and at the rebuilding of the nation of his ancestor Ku Shih Khan. He enticed the Kokonor princes and the chiefs at a convention in Ch'a han t'o lo hai to swear to renounce the titles previously granted to them by the emperor. He started calling himself Dalai hun t'aichi in order to induce them to follow his example. It was an act of rebellion against the empire. However two princes Ch'a han tan-chin and Ah-erh-te-mi refused to follow his injunctions; they compelled their troops to abandon him. A fight was about to start between them but, deeming their forces too inferior to those of bLo bzang, Ch'a han tan-chin, first sent his wife and 140 of his people to the pass of Lao Ya Kuan outside the great wall of the city of Ho Chou. Ch'ang Chou vice-president of the administrative organ of Hsining invited him to move his people into the city of Ho Chou, and ordered him to leave the defense of the pass to his troops. bLo bzang prepared to cross the Yellow River to fight. This happened in the eighth moon of 1723 (*Annals* of Kansu **46**: 52*a–b*).

But Nien Keng-yao, Governor General of Szechwan and Shensi provinces, and Yueh Chung-ch'i, commander in chief of the troops of Szechwan, had already arrived from Szechwan Province with their troops to quell the revolt. The Chinese had long since had firsthand information concerning the unrest brewing in Kokonor. They knew that Ch'a-han nomenhan, appointed by Lhasa as chief of the lamasery of Kumbum, had pledged allegiance to bLo-bzang, that princes of Kokonor in combination with all the Tibetan tribes of Kokonor depending upon bLo-bzang, and those of Hsining, subjects of the monasteries, and others were ready to revolt with the lamas of Huangchung.

In the tenth moon the revolt burst forth like a pent-up stream; 200,000 rebels invaded Hsining, stealing cattle, burning villages, and fighting with the troops.

The situation was very serious, because the revolt spread over the whole country of Huangchung and was general. In the northern part of Huangchung, the monastery of Erh Ku Lung alone controlled forty daughter monasteries. Each monastery was a center of revolt, situated in a tortuous valley, guarded by towering mountains, for Huangchung is a mountainous country with poor means of communication, with almost impassable trails, and passes hard to overcome and control.

However, Nien Keng-yao was equal to the situation and extensive powers had been granted to him. He had called from Szechwan, Shensi, and Kansu provinces combat troops inured to hardships, and had chosen capable officers whom he appointed to jobs that gave them full scope for their abilities. He called the Monguor t'u-ssu and ordered 2,000 of their troops, conversant with the intricate geography of the country and conversant with the chiefs of the tribes who lived in their neighborhood. He called all available resources into play.

Everywhere the lamas, the Kokonor Mongols and the Tibetans were the most furious fighters. This seems to point to the fact that they seethed with the greatest hatred against the empire, despite all the favors the lamas had received from the emperors. Nien Keng-yao understood that he had to fight savage and enraged enemies. He went about the job with draconian severity and acted without let-up and with incredible speed.

In the tenth moon the northern, western, and southern valleys of Hsining were cleared by three armies and the besieged fortresses saved. Many, many rebels were slaughtered. In the eleventh moon one army cleared the region of Chuang Lang and defeated Tibetan tribes. Another had to return to the Tatung valley, north of Hsining, to finish drastically the new rebellion.

bLo-bzang, considering the overwhelming forces marshalled against him and their ruthless behavior, asked to surrender. This was refused. More troops arrived at the rebelling monastery of Ch'i Chia Sse where 500 lamas and 1,000 Tibetans were mercilessly killed in the fight.

In the twelfth moon, Mongol Khoshot princes surrendered with more than 100,000 of their followers, while the army still defeated the rebelling Tibetans in the region of Kuei Te, where the monasteries were burned down.

In the first moon of 1724 the armies had to fight the monasteries of Erh Ku Lung, Kuo Mang (Seerkok), and Ch'ieh bzang, the most important centers of resistance. The lamas of Erh Ku Lung had called to arms all their subjects, who awaited the army in resolute array; 13,000 of their subjects were killed in the action. The number of lamas killed is not noted, but it is recorded that they fought furiously, that 700 lamas were killed in Seerkok alone (Monguors II: 34–37).

The three biggest monasteries in the country were burned to the ground, also 7,000 houses and 17 villages of the subjects of the monastery of Erh Ku Lung. The whole country was a ruin.

In the second moon a crushing defeat was administered to bLo-bzang in Kokonor by General Yueh Chung-ch'i; 8,000 of his troops were killed in several encounters, and 10,000 surrendered. bLo-bzang fled riding a white camel. Another army led by Nien Keng-yao, consisting mostly of Monguor soldiers, burned the monastery of Shih Men Sse, where 600 lamas and Tibetans were killed and a huge quantity of weapons was found hidden.

In the third moon Yueh Chung-ch'i went again to Kokonor in pursuit of bLo-bzang, clearing the country of the scattered rebels. Arriving at their central camp unawares, he captured the mother of bLo-bzang, his sister-in-law, and a large number of people and horses. Eight princes submitted. The Kokonor troops had been dashed into rout and ruin.

In the fourth moon the T'ieh Pu tribes from the region of Ho Chou, depending upon bLo-bzang, had started plundering while the troops were fighting in Kokonor. General Nien destroyed 41 of their villages and received the surrender of 37. Two thousand Tibetans had been killed and many had been captured with a number of cattle.

In the fifth moon General Yueh cleared the region between Chuang Lang and Liangchow from where the troops had incessantly been attacked. The Tibetan tribes and the lamas were defeated, several thousands of Tibetans captured, and the monasteries Chu Kung, Chiarto, Hoki, Nan Ch'ung, Simi and T'ien T'ang destroyed or burned. Then the army cleared the region of Cho Tze Shan. Most of the Monguor troops had participated in the punitive expedition.

In the tenth moon bLo-bzang was still not captured. An army was sent again to find him. Only one of his important officers and his wife were captured, but 33 princes submitted.[93]

It is hard to understand the reticence concerning the destruction of the entire monastery of Kumbum and the killing of eight of their most prominent lamas, for whom eight stupas were later erected. Now the Chinese call Kumbum the "monastery of the eight stupas." Nothing is said either, in the *Annals* of Kansu, concerning the beheading of two Living Buddhas (Monguors I: 34–37; II: 25, 26).

THE T'U-SSU HAD PARTICIPATED IN QUELLING THE REVOLT

T'u-ssu Ch'i Tsai-hsuan in 1723 had guarded the Ta Hsia rapids with his troops, in order to impede fleeing lamas and Tibetans from spreading the revolt in the eastern countries. In 1724 he had participated in the destruction of the monastery of Erh Ku Lung, and the defeat of the savage lamas and their subjects. With General Yueh Chung-ch'i he fought in Cho Tze Shan (*Annals* of Kansu **42**: 46a) and escorted the food transport for the troops, which was incessantly attacked by the rebels in the mountains.

T'u-ssu Li Shen-ch'eng in 1723, with 300 of his troops, guarded the passes in the Shih Ta mountains, and defeated several groups of Tibetans. In 1724 he administered several blows to the Tibetans in the Cho Tze Shan region, who attacked the food transport escort (*Annals* of Kansu **42**: 47a). The Chiliarch Li Hung-tsung, uncle of T'u-ssu Li Shen-ch'eng, and Li Wen-p'eng, uncle of T'u-ssu Li Yao-ch'eng, fought the rebels in the southern valleys of Hsining, in 1723 in the eleventh moon, and died in action with 14 of their Monguor soldiers (*Annals* of Hsining **28**: 18b).

T'u-ssu Chao in 1724 fought in Cho Tze Shan (*Annals* of Kansu **42**: 49a).

T'u-ssu Kan Kuo-cheng guarded the ferry on the Yellow River in 1723 (*Annals* of Kansu **42**: 51a).

T'u-ssu Yeh Yao-ch'eng guarded the passes in the Shih Ta mountains in 1723 and fought the Tibetans in Pa P'an Shan and in Cho Tze Shan. He escorted the food transport as far as T'ien T'ang Ssu along impassable trails. He helped in the destruction of the T'ien T'ang monastery (*Annals* of Kansu **42**: 53).

In 1723 T'u-ssu Li Yao-ch'eng guarded the passes in Shih Ta Shan and fought in Cho Tze Shan and at the T'ien T'ang monastery (*Annals* of Kansu **42**: 53a).

The participation of T'u-ssu Lu Hua-lin in the Lhasa expedition has been noted.

T'u-ssu Lu Chan, in 1723, guarded the Lao Ya Hsia with T'u-ssu Ch'i Tsai-hsuan. In 1724 he fought with his nephew Lu Wei-fan in Cho Tze Shan (*Annals* of Kansu **42**: 58b).

The Salar T'u-ssu Han Ta-yung quelled the revolt of Tibetans in the Hsun Hua region in 1723. In 1724 he followed General Yueh Chung-ch'i in the expedition to Cho Tze Shan, participated in the destruction of the Monastery of Simi, and fought the Tibetan tribe Hsieh Erh Ssu (*Annals* of Kansu **42**: 28b).

The revolt, quelled with draconian severity in less than a year, had been the ruin of Huangchung. Not a single valley in the country was encountered through which the troops did not pass, fighting or pursuing the enemy. The number of villages destroyed and burned, and the number of stolen cattle were countless. The number of Tibetans, Mongols and lamas killed rates terribly high. The war was one of the bloodiest. All who made a stand were killed. All the provisions and properties of the people had disappeared. All the lama-series were destroyed or burned down. The depredation of the country was wicked and ruthless, the destitution of the people tragic. Huangchung, which during the previous centuries had so many times suffered

---

[93] *Annals* of Kansu **46**: 52–58; **42**: 24a. *Annals* of Hsining 16a–b. bLo-bzang had fled to the Jungars, where his friend Tsewang Rabdan protected him.

from wars and revolts, never had suffered as much as in 1723–1724.

PERSECUTION OF CHRISTIANS

After relating the successful repression by General Nien Keng-yao of the terrible revolt of the Mongols, Tibetans, and Lamas in 1723–1724 in Huangchung, something should be said concerning two Manchu princes, accused by the general before Emperor Yung Cheng, of having contributed of their own money to the building of a Catholic church in Hsining in 1723–1724.

This is the first document concerning the existence of a Catholic church in Hsining and consequently of a Catholic community. It seems unusual to see a general make such an accusation directly to the emperor, at a time when the conjunctures of war absorbed all his forces and energies (July 1, 1724).

Emperor K'ang Hsi died on December 20, 1722. His fourth son, Yung Cheng, ascended the throne in 1723. According to the time-honored custom, some of the brothers of the new emperor assumed an attitude of menacing hostility toward him. The Emperor Yung Cheng suspected his ninth brother, Sessaka, of being the chief of the discontented faction and sent him (April 15, 1723) far away to Hsining to fight the Mongols, Tibetans, and Lamas under the command of General Nien Keng-yao. Together with Sessaka two sons of the Manchu Prince Surniana were also sent, the sixth, Lessihin, and the twelfth.[94]

Surniana, a brother of the late Emperor K'ang Hsi, member of the oldest branch of the Manchu dynasty, had been a notorious governor in Liaotung province and was the chief of one of the eight Manchu banners. He was suspected by Emperor Yung Cheng of being a sympathizer and supporter of the Sessaka group. He and his entire family were banished to Yu Wei, on the northern outskirts of the empire. His properties were confiscated, his three hundred servants and slaves taken away, all his dignities removed, and he and his family reduced to the state of subjects. The wealthy Surniana had thirteen sons and sixteen daughters. Most of the these princes and princesses were Catholics. The sixth son, Lessihin, was baptized before he left for Hsining and the twelfth son when he arrived at Hsining. They were confined in separate houses and guarded by soldiers.

The reason for these troubles were the accusations sent September 7, 1723, by the Viceroy of Chekiang and Fukien provinces to the tribunal of rites, concerning the building of Catholic churches in the provinces, the customs observed by the Catholics, the large number of priests in the country, etc. The viceroy favored a

prompt prosecution and quick forwarding of the accusations to the emperor. The emperor sanctioned the accusations January 1, 1724. An edict was sent throughout the provinces on February 11, 1724. Probably on account of this edict and the connections of the Surniana family with the Sessaka faction, General Nien Keng-Yao accused both sons of Surniana on July 1, 1724. In February, 1725, both sons were ordered to join their family, already banished to Yu Wei. In June, 1725, both were carried from Yu Wei to Peking, bound in chains, and condemned to die in prison. The twelfth son died in prison after two years of suffering, and the sixth son died in prison a couple of years later. These are the conjunctures of the accusations against the sons of the Surniana in 1724 by General Nien Keng-yao. They reveal the existence of a Catholic community and the building of a church in Hsining.[94a]

Recently in Volume 18 (1959) of *Monumenta Serica,* I encountered the very interesting article, "The Description and Map of Kansu by Giovanni Battista Maoletti De Serravalle," by Professor B. Szczeniak, Notre Dame University, dealing with the same subject.

Maoletti was born in Serravalle, near Milan, in 1669. He entered the order of the Franciscans in 1689. In 1705 he arrived in Canton and went from Sian (Shensi) to Lanchow (Kansu) in 1710. He was chased from there by bonzes in 1713, and moved to Liangchow and Hsining (Kansu) where he worked until 1716. He had been appointed Administrator of the vicariate of Hukwang, but left China during the persecution in 1724. He died on the way to Canton on January 14, 1725. The report had been written by Maoletti in Hsining, where he lived from 1713 to 1716. Maoletti's map was made four to five years before the *K'ang Hsi* or Jesuit Atlas was printed in 1719. It is not a studied piece of cartography, but a sketch-map to illustrate a mission report.

The map and the description of Kansu and Kokonor at this date is the more significant, for only a short time later great changes were brought about by the Jungar invasion of Tibet (1717), and again by the terrible revolt in 1723–1724 of Mongols and Tibetans of Kokonor and Huangchung, and Lamas. The report is interesting for it deals with many details about places and people and the products of the country,—rhubarb, musk, and coal, silver and gold mines. (*Monumenta Serica* 18: 294–298, 1959.)

Professor B. Szczesniak, in his very interesting article, also notes the work of F. Dehergne, S.J., "Les Missions du Nord de la Chine vers 1700," Archivum Historicum Societatis Jesu **24**, 1955. Both sources help to give a view of the mission work in remote Kansu during the period of revolts.

The Maoletti report, following the map, is alive with interest in the Tartars (Mongols) who figure so prominently on the map, with the eagerness to further mission work among them, and with details about places and people. Maoletti's interest for the conversion of the Mongols is manifest in many places of the report. He is pleased to note that north of Topa sits a prince who is lord of Topa—

[94] The charge seems to have been based on slander. Lettres Edifiantes et Curieuses 3: 366–465, Paris, Paul Daffis, 7 rue Guenegaud, 1877. Histoire Generale de la Chine, De Mailla. 11: 373–408, Paris, Clousier, rue Saint Jacques, 1880.

[94a] *Lettres edifiantes et curieuses* **2**: 366–465, Paris, Paul Daffis, 7 rue Guenegaud, 1877. De Mailla, *Histoire Generale de la Chine* **11**: 373–408, Paris, Clousier, Rue Saint Jacques, 1880.

"an acquaintance of mine." East of Lake Kokonor, on the west side of the Yellow River, is a prince who "wants to become a Christian." West of where the great wall protrudes around Chengfan (Liangchow) is a Christian outpost conducted by the governor of Yung-ning-p'u. Here "I preached at the tents of the Mongols." Today there are Christians there. North of this settlement is a prince of 20,000 families. In the extreme north sits a Mongol prince whose wife is the daughter of the Emperor of China. He rules over 40,000 families. (This text points to the Prince of Alashan.)

The Khan, bKrasis Batur, second son of Gushri, the Khoshot, who conquered Kokonor and Tibet (1635) died in 1714. The Queen Mother of the successor accompanied the bier. The cremated bones of the Khan were carried for burial to the tomb of the Mongol kings situated on the borders of his kingdom between Chuang Lang and Hsining [94b] in steep mountains. I have sent an Armenian and one of my catechists to present the Queen Mother with a handkerchief and a snuff box filled with European tobacco. She has sent one of her major domos to thank me and to hear about the holy law.

Maoletti awaited the return of the Queen in the Church of the Armenians in Topa.

Maoletti worked for about fifteen years in Shensi, Kansu and Ili (Turkistan) and mentions nine places with churches or oratories (three of them with two) and fifteen or sixteen other Christian communities, some larger, some consisting of only a handful of converts; some of the congregations had been founded by the Jesuits, others by zealous laymen, but the bulk of the achievement was doubtless due to the pioneering effort of Maoletti. One may speculate that to some extent the ground had been prepared for the work of the Catholic missionaries by the Nestorians who were strong in these regions. (*Monum. Serica,* 298–303.)

In Hsining, which at that time was an emporium of China with a garrison of six thousand soldiers, seven or eight adults had been baptized in 1706 by the Jesuit, Father Dehergne. The city had been visited several times in 1708–1709 by the Jesuits Jartoux and Regis, preparing the map of Kansu and Tibet on the order of the Emperor K'ang Hsi. In 1713 Maoletti bought a small church in Hsining which he dedicated to St. Gregory, the Armenian, and entrusted to the care of a fervent Armenian Catholic living in Topa. Later, the community having developed, Hsining had two churches, one of Our Lady of Angels for the men, and the other for the women. Later both had come under litigation [probably after the accusation by General Nien Keng-yao of the sons of Surniana].

At that time Topa, 60 li north of Hsining, was a stronghold, subject to a Mongol prince who was tributary to the Mongol Khan. Topa was the trading place of the foreigners, Mongols, Tibetans, Lamas, Indians, Persians, Turks, Armenians, and Muscovites. Fifteen different languages were spoken here. In this Babylon is an oratory or small church built by Armenians at my insistence.

Cheng-hai-p'u, with a garrison of one thousand soldiers, a village near Topa, and at the great Gate of the Foreigners, had a very large church, which had a literate merchant as head of the congregation of the Chinese as well as the neighboring Tibetans.

94b Between Chuang Lang and Hsining are the tombs of the Li and the Lu t'ussu in Siangt'ang and Lien ch'eng, but I suppose no connections exist between these three cemeteries and both t'ussu and Khoshots.

Two days east of Hsining, at the junction of the Hsining and Tatung Rivers, in Chang Ch'uan Ku, was a Catholic community. These seem to have been the four communities existing in the region of Hsining in 1715.

In most of the important cities in the northern part of Kansu Catholic communities existed in 1716, with churches or oratories. Lanchow had two churches since 1699, depending on the Tung t'ang of Peking (Dehergne p. 287). Kanchow had its church since 1660. In Suchow was a group of worshippers of the Cross. Maoletti, before 1713, during his stay in Liangchow, founded fifteen communities (two churches in Liangchow and one in Yung Ning P'u).

In the eastern part of Kansu, in many of the important cities, Christian communities were also encountered, with or without churches, in 1716.

Dehergne, p. 282, notes that in the middle of the seventeenth century the Jesuit missions flourished in Shensi and numbered 12,000 Christians. In 1683 Christians were in twenty-three cities of the province.

In the five prefectures of Shensi there were Christians in 1700. In 1699 there were five residences of fathers and sixteen Jesuit churches (Dehergne, p. 275).

In Turkistan in 1708, there were some Christians in Ili and Hami (Dehergne, p. 287, No. 89). During the Ch'ien Lung period, 1776–1796, many Catholics were relegated to Ili for the sake of religion (Dehergne, p. 287, 288) and also to Hsi Tatung, four days distant from Hsining (Dehergne, 289, 293).

This is a sketch of the conjectures in Shensi, Shansi, Huangchung, and Kansu concerning the mission work around 1700, according to the report of Maoletti and Dehergne.

HUANGCHUNG REORGANIZED

Nien Keng-yao, the pacification of the country having come to a successful close, presented to the throne a memorandum in thirteen articles, on the methods of pacifying the Mongols, Tibetans, and the lamas. The first article was radical. All the revolts originated on account of the too extensive power of the chiefs. The Tibetan tribes, depending upon the authority of the Supreme Khoshot Chief, have to be withdrawn from him and organized in independent units, living in their own territories allotted by the emperor, ruled by their own chiefs appointed by and responsible only to the Chinese administration. The Khoshot and other Mongol tribes, who at present depend upon the authority of one single supreme chief, have to be divided into single independent units. Titles have to be granted to each of the chieftains, and territories have to be allotted to them by the Chinese administration. Each tribal chief is to be responsible for the administration of his tribe under the supervision of the Chinese authority. The entire administrative physiognomy of Kokonor changed at once, and Kokonor was annexed to the empire.

The power of the lamas consisted in the number of their subject tribes and their expansive territorial possessions. Their properties were confiscated, and their subjects became subjects of the Chinese officials, liable to their corvees, and subject to their land taxes. The revolt had ruined forever the power of the lamas. Then followed a lot more regulations (Monguors II: 34, 49).

However, nothing was changed in the regime of the Monguor institution. Their extensive properties remained intact, and their subjects continued under the administration of their t'u-ssu, because they had been faithful for centuries to the empire, and because this time their support had been of untold value to the army. Even T'u-ssu Lu was especially rewarded for his services, and received more new subjects: the 8 Tibetan villages in the Cho Tzu Shan region, which had belonged to the Khoshot princes of Kokonor, numbering 453 families, totaling 2,365 persons (Monguors I: 33).

This terrible revolt, which had threatened the very existence of Huangchung as part of Kansu Province and the empire, ended with the annexation of Kokonor to the empire, the ruin of the lama institution in Huangchung, and the stabilization of the regime of the t'u-ssu and Monguors in Huangchung. Thanks to the connivance of the Huangchung lamas and Tibetans with the Kokonor Khoshots, all of them seethed with hatred against the empire.

In 1725, the revolt having been quelled, the commandery of Hsining became a prefecture and the So of Nienpei a subprefecture. According to one of the thirteen articles in the memorandum, presented to the throne by the Governor General, Nien Keng-yao, the building was started of three cities in the northern valley of Hsining, in Tatung, in Pe-ta, and in Yung Nan, which countries formerly belonged to the Kokonor Khoshots. Garrisons were appointed in order to forestall inroads of nomads and Jungars, and to provide easy communications between the two cities of Kanchow and Hsining. Tatung became a commandery (Annals of Hsining 1: 21b).

It had been noted that in 1647 after the defeat of the Mohammedans of Kanchow on the Tatung River, trying to compel the Mohammedans of Hsining to follow them in the revolt, Chinese of Kanchow who had participated in the expedition dared not return to their original countries, but settled in the extensive pastures of Tatung and Pe-ta, recognized the lordship of the Mongol proprietors and started farming and building houses. It has been noted also that in 1693, after fifty years, the assistant commander of Hsining, T'u-ssu Li Hsia, had reported that already more than 10,000 families were living there. The census of 1730 noted that the population of these settlements, started in 1647, was composed of Chinese, Monguors, Mohammedans, and Tibetans, living in twenty-two villages. The population of two villages was entirely composed of Chinese,

one entirely of Tibetans, four completely of Monguors, one entirely of Mohammedans originating from Liangchow, one entirely of Mohammedans from Ho Chou, three occupied by Chinese and Mohammedans together, two by Chinese and Tibetans together, four by Chinese and Monguors, and four by Chinese, Mohammedans and Tibetans (Annals of Hsining 22: 15a–b).

During these ninety years all these people had abandoned their original homes hoping to enjoy more peace in this lonely country. They had developed the country and made possible the building of the two cities of Tatung and Pe-ta. Before that time the northern valley of Hsining was cultivated only as far as the fortress of Hsin Ch'eng, situated 70 li north of Hsining, where a great wall marked the boundaries between Hsining and Kokonor.

In 1726 the newly appointed Governor of Kokonor, Ta Ting, started with a big retinue of officials and soldiers to visit all the Tibetan tribes of Huangchung, East Kansu, and Kokonor, depending upon the Khoshot princes and the lamas, taking the census of the people and the herds of each tribe, appointing in each tribe the chief they desired, notifying them that they depended from now on upon the Chinese officials. He fixed the tribute each tribe was to pay yearly, and informed them that all the taxes formerly paid to the princes and lamas, the t'ien pa tax, and the incense offering required yearly by the Dalai Lama in Lhasa were abolished. He allotted to each tribe a territory clearly defined, and handed it the deed officially sealed.

Now an idea can be had about the power of the princes of Kokonor. The governor had to travel as far at Tatung, Kuei Te, Ho Chou, and T'ao Chou in East Kansu, and to Chuang Lang and Liangchow where Tibetan tribes lived, depending upon the princes. The Khoshot Ku Shih-han in 1636 had conquered Kokonor and all the Tibetan tribes of that country, and those formerly dependent upon the Mongols, which later had fled far away from them. They pursued them as far as T'ao Chou and Ho Chou and so they became their subjects again. This had happened at the end of the Ming dynasty and during the beginning of the Ch'ing dynasty when China could not care for these countries on account of the troubled conditions. However, Ku Shih-han had been recognized by the Manchu dynasty as chief of Kokonor. In 1642–1644 Ku Shih-han conquered Tibet and offered it to the Dalai Lama who immediately sent lamas to collect t'ien pa and incense offerings from the tribes, which normally had to pay a tax to the princes also. During these times the Khoshots had even been able to receive the submission of Tibetan tribes living as far as Cho Tze Shan, situated inside the prefecture of Chuang Lang, and of the tribes living in the mountains south of Ku Lang, Liangchow, and Yung Ch'ang. This gives an idea about the number of people and warriors they had been able to call to arms in 1723–1724 (Annals of Hsining 31: 21b).

Then the governor notified the lamas about the confiscation of their territories and subjects, and informed them about the revocation of the titles of Kuo-shih and Ch'an-shih granted to the most prominent among them by the Ming emperors, and an order was given to hand to the Chinese officials the diploma of the promotion granted to them by the emperor.

Most of these titles had been granted to lamas who had induced tribes to submit, and to move into the depopulated Huangchung, especially in the first century and a half of the Ming. At that time these lamas belonged to the Red sect, were married, and lived among the tribes they had induced to submit, but not in monasteries. They had received personally large proprietaries from the emperor, with a document written in their name, and a title. This had been the origin of the Karwas and Nang so (Monguors II: 18, 19). The son of the lama succeeding to the father, inherited the property and the title and was considered to be a lama. This institution lasted until 1723–1724. The entire lama family during all these years had earned a wealthy living, free from taxes and corvees, and received some taxes from the tribesmen. The *Annals* of Hsining noting this fact, and the confiscation of the territories and subjects of the lamas, adds jubilantly, "and so in one day these unjust conditions, existing for centuries, were abolished" (*Annals* of Hsining 31: 22b).

In the same year, for the very first time in history, officials were appointed by the Szechwan and Kansu provinces to fix the boundaries of both provinces in the Kokonor region, and to designate which among the Tibetan tribes should depend upon each of the provinces (*Annals* of Hsining 16: 13a).

During the years 1733–1745 orders were repeatedly issued for the building of more graneries in the cities and most important strongholds all over the country, for the amount of grain formerly collected by the lamas and the Khoshot princes was now collected by the officials and had to be stored (*Annals* of Hsining 31: 23b, 25a).

In 1745 the Hsining *Annals* were printed by Yang Yin-ch'u. The first *Annals*, only two small volumes, contained many errors which were amended.

In 1759 there was famine in the prefecture of Chuang Lang. Grain was loaned to T'u-ssu Lu of Lien Ch'eng to help his subjects. The next year also was one of bad crops. Again grain was loaned for distribution to each of the Monguor families of the t'u-ssu for which restitution was to be made after three years (*Annals* of Kansu 2: 29b).

The commanderies of Tatung and Kuei Te became subprefectures in 1761 with complete civil and military administrations (*Annals* of Hsining 18: 4, 11b, 14). In Pe-ta and Yung nan a brigadier general and a lieutenant colonel with strong garrisons had already been appointed in 1725, after the revolt of bLo-bzang tan-chin (*Annals* of Hsining 18: 71a).

Huangchung and the Monguors, after the troubles of 1723–1724, enjoyed peace for sixty years. All that time they assisted in the complete change of the administration and of the country, caused by the confiscation of the large properties and Tibetan tribes which belonged to the lamas. They assisted in the rebuilding of cities, villages and fortifications, schools and graneries, and rebuilt and overhauled their own properties. Every day new regulations were issued to which everybody had to comply, and everywhere Chinese officials and bureaus were encountered. The Chinese officials played the capital role in the country. A large army occupied the country. The influence the t'u-ssu had enjoyed during centuries was waning rapidly.

FIRST MOHAMMEDAN REVOLT— WAHHABISM

All of a sudden in 1781 the terrible revolt broke out among the Mohammedans in Kansu. It portended ominous events.

The Salars, Turks, originating from Turkistan (Samarkand, according to the traditions) inhabited during the Yuan time both borders of the Yellow River, in the region of Hsun Hua T'ing in East Kansu, and in the regions of Pa Yen Jung in southern Huangchung. The time of their arrival in Kansu is unknown, but certainly they lived in that region at the end of the Yuan because two of their chiefs had already surrendered to the Ming in 1370, and received the office of t'u-ssu. The Salars live in thirteen groups called *kong*. The four upper and the four lower groups are called the eight inside Salar *kong* and are controlled by their t'u-ssu. The remaining five groups, called the outside Salar *kong,* are controlled by the subprefecture of Pa Yen Jung (Monguors I: 22, 23). Han Pao-yuan, t'u-ssu of the four upper Salar groups, lives with his subjects in the region of Hsun Hua. His subjects adopted the surname of Han. Han Sha-pa, t'u-ssu of the four lower Salar groups, inhabits the region east of Hsun Hua. His subjects adopted the surname of Ma (*Annals* of Kansu 42: 43b). Both t'u-ssu are the founders of the two Salar groups. The Salars profess Islam, but all over the country among their neighbors are many Chinese Mohammedans.

Wahhabism, a sect founded by Ibn Abd-al-Wahhab who died in 1787, aimed at the revival of the primitive orthodoxy of Islam and the abolition of the innovations contrary to the Sunni. He reacted violently against, at that time, the more and more popular cult of the Saints, Prophets, and the Graves.[95]

It happened that in 1762 a Mohammedan from Anting in Kansu, called Ma Ming-hsin, arrived back in Hsun Hua from a pilgrimage (to Mecca?). On his way he had been captivated by the violent discussions, at that time in full swing, relating to the new sect of the

---

[95] Henri Masse, *L'Islam,* 208–209, Paris, Armand Colin, 1930.

Wahhabits, and had witnessed the fanaticism and the successes reaped by its promoters. He was enthusiastic about the idea of a return to the original orthodoxy. On his arrival, he posed in the Hsun Hua community as the possessor of the genuine doctrine and the champion of the religion founded by Mohammed and his companions. In the services in the mosques he urged the recitation of prayers with a loud voice, for it was the rite practiced in the new sect. It tremendously shocked the other Mohammedan communities, used to reciting the texts in a low voice, so that they accused the disturbers of the religion to the officials. The Salar, Su Forty-three, with other Salars, invited Ma Ming-hsin as teacher and head of all the Mohammedan communities of Hsun Hua. Bitter discussions arose between the two groups, and forty adherents of the old religion were killed. An accusation was dispatched to the governor in Lanchow, who immediately sent two military officials with their troops to Hsun Hua to quell the revolt. However, the new religious group had already grown so fast and become so numerous, that Su Forty-three was able to beat the troops, kill the officials, and occupy the city of Ho Chou. New troops which arrived did not dare go to Ho Chou and they garrisoned in Ti-tao. Then the new religious rebels ran to Lanchow. They defeated the 800 poor troops of Lanchow, besieged the city, occupied the western corner of the city, and broke up the bridge over the Yellow River. New troops came from Kanchow and Szechwan. In the meantime, the officials of Anting had captured Ma Ming-hsin, the fomenter of the revolt in the city and sent him to the prison of Lanchow. The rebels requested their leader. From upon the city wall, the official made him exhort the rebels to keep quiet and return home. It did not work. Then Ma Ming-hsin was killed with his son.

Just at that time T'u-ssu Lu Fan, from Lien Ch'eng, had arrived with 300 Monguor troops and was attacked by the rebels. His troops were nearly all killed and the t'u-ssu was wounded. Then the rebels retired to the nearby Hua Lin mountains and prepared entrenchments. General A Kuei was called from Szechwan to quell the revolt. The army dared not attack the fanatic rebels in the mountains. The Salar T'u-ssu Han Yu, leading his Salar Mohammedan troops of the old religion, was first to attack and enter the mountains. He was very successful. Later he recovered the city of Ho Chou. More troops arrived from Szechwan and Mongol troops from Alashan. In the mountainous country they administered a crushing defeat to the rebels who fled to the Hua Lin temple. It was burned down with the rebels inside. Few escaped, among them Su Forty-three, who was captured and killed. The revolt was quelled. Then followed the murdering of the entire families of hundreds of the adherents to the sect, forbidden to pray with a loud voice, to collect money and alms, etc.

Where were the Monguor t'u-ssu during the revolt?

The defeat of the troops of T'u-ssu Lu Fan has been related. He was rewarded later by the honor of wearing the double peacock feather (*Annals* of Kansu 42: 57).

The five outer Salar groups, adherents of the new religion, inhabited Pa Yen Jung situated south of Nienpei. The danger of inroads on and the plundering of these groups had to be forestalled. Lu Chen-hsien, member of the t'u-ssu clan, guarded with the troops the region of Hsiang T'ang and Huei Ho Tung (*Annals* of Kansu 42: 60).

T'u-ssu Kan San Yuen-pao guarded the city of Pa Yen Jung (*Annals* of Kansu 42: 51).

T'u-ssu Chou Lin guarded the passes of Ch'i Shih near Pa Yen Jung and Feng T'ai Shan (*Annals* of Kansu 42: 51). T'u-ssu Ch'i T'iao-yuan guarded the city of Nienpei and was later called to Pa Yen Jung (*Annals* of Kansu 42: 46a–b).

T'u-ssu Li Shih-t'ai helped guard the city of Ti-tao in East Kansu with 200 Monguor troops (*Annals* of Kansu 42: 48a). T'u-ssu Ch'eng Yu-fan guarded the Hsiao Hsia pass near Hsining (*Annals* of Kansu 42: 37). Salar T'u-ssu Han Yu who had fought in Lanchow and recovered Ho Chou, was rewarded by the honor to wear the Blue Plume or Crow feather, and received the button of the second degree, worn on the cap (*Annals* of Kansu 42: 43b).

The Salar T'u-ssu Han Kuang-tsu fought in Lanchow and was rewarded with the same honor as the former Salar t'u-ssu (*Annals* of Kansu 42: 44a).

Huangchung had been spared from inroads and devastation.

YEN CH'A HUI REVOLT

After the death of Ma Ming-hsin in Lanchow in 1781, T'ien Wu, a fanatic *ahong,* leader of the new sect in Fu Ch'iang in East Kansu, was proclaimed chief of the new sect. At that time the Chinese officials were brutally murdering the entire families of the rebels, and rumors were spread that all the Mohammedans of the old and new sects were to be killed. Already in 1782, in Shih Feng Pao, in the T'ung Wei district, T'ien Wu had started digging entrenchments and moving the wives and children to strongholds in the mountains, weapons had been prepared and flags, etc. Around Ku Yuen and Fu Ch'iang encounters continued unabated between the army and the rebels, who grew stronger and stronger by the accrual of countless adherents of the old sect. In 1784 T'ien Wu was wounded in a fight in Fu Ch'iang and died. The rebels, beaten in many encounters, fled to the Shin Feng Pao mountains where they finally were exterminated, and 3,000 wives and children brutally murdered. The revolt was quelled.

During the revolt T'u-ssu Lu Fan had helped guard the city of Lanchow (*Annals* of Kansu 42: 57a) and

T'u-ssu Lu yin, member of the Lu clan, guarded the Yang-chia temple region (*Annals* of Kansu 42: 58).

T'u-ssu Ch'i T'iao-yuan guarded the Ping Ku pass near Lien Ch'eng (*Annals* of Kansu 42: 51).

T'u-ssu Ch'i T'iao-yuen guarded the Lu P'an Shan region and was later called to guard Lanchow (*Annals* of Kansu 42: 46a–b).

T'u-ssu Li Shih-t'ai with 300 Monguors guarded the Kuan Miao T'an in Lanchow (*Annals* of Kansu 42: 48a). T'u-ssu Chao Huai-peh guarded the Ping Ku pass with Kan T'u-ssu (*Annals* of Kansu 42: 49a). T'u-ssu Ch'eng Yu-fan guarded the bridge in Lanchow (*Annals* of Kansu 42: 37). Salar T'u-ssu Han Yu fought in Fu Ch'iang and was rewarded with the title of lieutenant colonel (*Annals* of Kansu 42: 43b). Salar T'u-ssu Han Kuang-tsu fought in Fu Ch'iang (*Annals* of Kansu 42: 43b).

Huangchung again had escaped devastation, but East Kansu for the second time had to bear the brunt of the revolt. The country and the people suffered tremendously for the officials were determined to annihilate completely the adherents of the sect and their families.[96]

NEW SECT IN HSINING

However, the sect of the new religion was already rooted too deep in the minds of the Kansu Mohammedans to get rid of it by crushing two revolts and killing many people. In 1789 a small group of adherents to the sect were discovered among the Mohammedans in Hsining by the officials. They held meetings and created disturbances in the Mohammedan colony. They were captured, a number of them killed with their families, the rest exiled to Ho Lun Chiang by order of the emperor.[97]

The sect of the White Lotus religion had already spread in five provinces in 1796. It would still last seven years before it would be quelled. In 1798 a strong group of 12,000 rebels invaded East Kansu in the third moon, parted in two groups and started devastating and plundering the country. All available troops were ordered to come to the rescue of the Shensi and Kansu troops. T'u-ssu Lu Chi-hsun went with 300 Monguor soldiers (*Annals* of Kansu 42: 57a). The Salar T'u-ssu Han Yu went with his soldiers of the old religion (*Annals* of Kansu 42: 43b). Salar T'u-ssu Han Kuang-tsu also went to the rescue and died on the field of battle (*Annals* of Kansu 42: 44a). The remaining t'u-ssu protected the borders of Huangchung along the Yellow River.

In the seventh moon of 1800 the country was at peace (*Annals* of Kansu 46: 59–61). Huangchung

again had escaped devastation, but East Kansu had borne for the third time the brunt of the revolt.[98]

In 1806 tremendous rains ruined the districts of Chang Hsien, Ming Chou, and Leang Tang. Inundations of the Yellow River followed in the southern part of East Kansu. Cattle were drowned, many villages no longer existed, and the poor and destitute Tibetan tribes started plundering the country. T'u-ssu Ch'i Ping-ming was sent in 1807 to Ch'i Chia Chai to guard the banks of the Yellow River where the people were used to crossing it, in order to prevent inroads of starving, pillaging people into Huangchung (*Annals* of Kansu 42: 46a–b).

TIBETAN REVENGE UPON THE MONGOLS OF KOKONOR

In 1822 a revolt of twenty-three Tibetan tribes broke out in the regions of Hsun Hua and Kuei Te. The Mongols in 1509 had invaded Kokonor, the pasture grounds of the Tibetans. They had occupied the best pastures and relegated the Tibetans to poor and small pastures, or annihilated them entirely. This situation had lasted until 1726 when each tribe became the proprietor of the grounds it occupied, but the Khoshots were favored by the fact that they remained the proprietors of the large and best pastures stolen from the Tibetans in 1509. The glorious period of the Khoshots was at a very low ebb and the Tibetans deemed the opportunity at hand to recover their old pastures, to chase the hated, enfeebled Mongols and to occupy the pastures on the northern borders of the Yellow River which were in the hands of the Khoshots.

A long period of devastation and murder succeeded. The Tibetan lama Chaghan Nom-un Khan was one of the leaders of the revolt. Many Khoshots left the country. The revolt spread rapidly. Many Tibetan tribes of the Kanchow and Yung Ch'ang and Liangchow regions joined the revolt and plundered the lands of the Mongols. Those of Liangchow attacked Mongol tribes in Sung Shan and stole 4,000 cattle, those of Kanchow plundered the Uighur tribes in the vicinity of the city, etc. The whole country was upset; the army was in a hurry. Except for an inroad in Tatung and one in Hsiao Hsia, Huangchung was not devastated. The officials removed from the lama the tribes he controlled. The revolt was not quelled until 1854, after thirty years. No notes are recorded concerning the movement of Monguor troops against the revolting Tibetans (*Annals* of Kansu 46: 62a–b).

The empire had a bad time, for in the meantime revolts raged unchecked in the provinces of middle and north China. A new uprising of the White Lotus sect had started in 1831. The sect continued its ravages and destruction under new names. The revolt was followed in 1850 by the insurrection of the Taiping, which

---

[96] Both revolts are summarized according to *Annals* of Kansu 47: 1–3. J. J. M. De Groot, *Sectarianism and religious persecution in China*, 311–327, sq., Amsterdam, Muller, 1903. Commandant d'Ollone, *Recherches sur les Musulmans Chinois*, 229, sq., Paris, Leroux, 1911.

[97] J. J. M. De Groot, *op. cit.*, 327.

[98] J. J. De Groot, *op. cit.*, 363, sq.

lasted until 1864, during which 20 million people of Kiangsu province were killed. Simultaneously the Nien Fei sect (mounted brigands) started its ravages in 1850. This revolt ended in 1868, having devastated the same provinces of the empire.

In Turkistan the Mohammedan Chang Ko Erh revolted in 1826. He conquered Turkistan and in 1828 the city of Suchow in North Kansu, situated along the well-known trade road to Central Asia. The regular troops of Liangchow, Kanchow, and Hsining were moved in a hurry to cope with the invasion which threatened to overrun Kansu. The Monguor troops had not been called to come to the rescue of the army. However, T'u-ssu Lu had sent grain to Suchow to feed the hungry troops. He was rewarded with the button of the second degree worn on the cap (*Annals* of Kansu **42**: 57a). The long exhausting war of China with the Jungars ended in 1857 and a new Mohammedan uprising broke out in Turkistan in 1864. It lasted until 1876 and conquered the entire region of the Tarim basin.

REVOLT OF THE EAST KANSU AND HUANGCHUNG MOHAMMEDANS, 1860–1873

The revolt is summarized according to the *Annals* of Kansu **47**: 4 sq.

In 1859 the Mohammedan Ma-ha-pu-tu revolted in the eastern suburb of the city of Ho Chou in East Kansu. The revolt was soon quelled. The reason for the revolt is not noted.

In 1860 the Salars of Hsun Hua in East Kansu and those of Pa Yen Jung in Huangchung revolted in combination with the Mohammedans of the Shensi province, far more numerous than the Salars. A group started plundering in the Ho Chou region, and a group (that of the Salars of Pa Yen Jung who lived in Huangchung south of the subprefecture of Nienpei, north of the Yellow River) invaded the southern valleys of Hsining.

In 1861 these groups, drawing near Hsining, were put to flight by the commander Chao Erh-hsun, but they popped up in the eastern valley of Hsining, burning, destroying villages, and killing many people. The local militia could not withstand their fierce attacks.

In 1862 the rebels having no aim beyond plunder and the satisfaction of seeing their hatred against the Chinese fulfilled, roamed in strong groups all over Huangchung and East Kansu. Every day more Mohammedans of Kansu joined their groups. The lamas, Nangso, and Tibetans fought with the army. Some groups were victorious; some suffered hard reverses. The Salar t'u-ssu of the four upper and lower groups submitted with the Shensi Mohammedans in Tsa Pa Ch'eng. The suspicious officials nonetheless accepted their surrender, because the Nien Fei and Fa Fei brigands roamed in the vicinity of T'ungkuan, and they

were afraid these brigands would join the rebel Mohammedans.

T'u-ssu Ch'eng Hsing-nan was ordered to join the troops of General Fan Pei-lin and guard the passes of Cha Ssu Kuan and Ch'ing Ling nao (*Annals* of Kansu **42**: 37). T'u-ssu Ch'i Ch'eng-kao joined the army, fighting the rebels on the passes (*Annals* of Kansu **42**: 46a). T'u-ssu Chao Yung-li guarded the passes in Pa Yen Jung country, and was rewarded with the two-eyed peacock feather (*Annals* of Kansu **42**: 49a).

T'u-ssu Lu Chi-hsun, having the title of brigadier general, fought with 500 of his troops around Hsining. He was helped by his nephew Lu Su-chou (*Annals* of Kansu **42**: 57, 60).

In 1863 the revolt was growing more intensive every day. East Kansu suffered tremendously.

In the tenth moon rebels of the district of Ninghsia, led by Ma Hua-lung [99] took the important city of Ninghsia by storm. The city was devastated. Many fires were set and tens of thousands of Chinese were killed. Thereafter Ma Hua-lung besieged and captured the city of Ling Chou where he killed 20,000 Chinese.

In the tenth moon Mohammedans besieged the city of Hsining. For a long time dissension concerning the old and the new religion divided the Hsining Mohammedans into two camps. Governor Yu T'ung invited the Mohammedan chief Ma Wen-i to patch up the trouble and to make them desist from plundering the country. Both parties consented but a strong group of Salars and Shensi Mohammedans arrived, besieged the city, and then plundered the country. During the year 1863 T'u-ssu Lu was ordered to garrison in Sheng T'ang and Ch'i-li-pu, and guard the western highway *Annals* of Kansu **42**: 57b).

In 1864 the revolt raged unchecked in East Kansu, and the city of Hsun Hua was taken by storm, followed by a tremendous massacre of the Chinese population. Another Mohammedan group attacked the city of Donkir west of Hsining, but was beaten. It invaded the Sina valley and was put to flight. Long before the attack of the city, dissension among the Mohammedans concerning the two religions had divided them into two groups. The old group was called the great group (*ta huei*), the adherents of the new religion, the group of the flowered temple (*hua sse*). The first group disapproved of the attack on the city and called into the city 1,000 of its members from outside. The Chinese population of

---

[99] The Moslem Ma Hua-lung, back from Turkistan, had founded a new sect in Chin Chi Pu in the prefecture of Ninghsia. He claimed to have received revelations from Allah. The people honored him as an equal of Mohammed. He was to be succeeded by his descendant after his death as chief of the sect. However, after his death, his son-in-law and his grandson struggled for the succession, and the sect parted in two groups. He did not proscribe attendance at the mosques, but he recommended praying at home, two or three families together, praying in a loud voice, with the palms of the hands turned upward. The sect spread even as far as Szechwan and Yunnan provinces (d'Ollone, *op. cit.*, 374).

the city was grateful and ready to help them. The second group called three thousand outsiders. However, the attackers were beaten by the old group, the local militia of the Chinese population.

In 1865 the depredation of the cities of Ku Lang, Yung Ch'ang, Shan Tan, and Kanchow, situated on the trade road to Turkistan, was wicked and ruthless. The rebels carried by storm the city of Suchow, and a terrible massacre of the population took place; 10,000 Chinese were killed. The pass of Chia Yu Kuan was captured by the rebels. At the time the rebels passed Liangchow, many Mohammedans from the vicinity fled into the city for shelter. The official, unable to put reliance on them and suspecting their connivance with the rebels, massacred them all in the city.

In the third moon the city of Hsining was besieged for a second time. The rebels were put to flight. Then they attacked the city of Donkir again. They were chased and looted several villages. At that time the dissension among the two groups had subsided. Mohammedans of Hsining attacked the city of Lao Ya Ch'eng but were beaten.

T'u-ssu Ah helped defend the city (*Annals* of Kansu 42: 49a). T'u-ssu Chou Hsieh-chi died on the field of battle defending the city (*Annals* of Kansu 42: 51a). T'u-ssu Hsin, after the defense of the city, disappeared in the mountains and returned only in 1886 (*Annals* of Kansu 42: 53b). During the whole year the Mohammedans had devastated East Kansu and Huangchung.

During 1866–1867 the attacks continued, and the army resisted in the same desultory fashion. The power of the Mohammedans was too strong and that of the army too feeble and uncoordinated. All these expeditions were in the nature of pillaging parties, which were murdering and kidnapping people, and carrying away all the valuables they could find. They stirred the bitter hatred which burned in the hearts of the Chinese against the Mohammedans, and that of the Mohammedans against the Chinese.

In 1868 the Mohammedans of Hsining again looted the Donkir region and were defeated in Shen Chung. Their chief Ah Wu was captured and killed with 1,300 of his brigands.

In the tenth moon, the new governor general of Shensi-Kansu, Tso Tsung-t'ang, appointed in 1866, arrived with his troops to quell the revolt.

In 1869–1870 the general first attacked the most important center of the uprising. He quelled the revolt of Ma Hua-lung and cleared the Ninghsia district of rebels. He acted as ruthlessly with the Mohammedans as they had behaved with the Chinese. The massacre of the Mohammedans was tremendous. The stronghold of Chin Chi Pu, the center of the revolt, was burned to the ground with the defenders of the city who fought with the courage of despair. Nothing was heard of them any more. Ling Wu was taken in the same way and few defenders escaped.

The Mohammedan population of Ninghsia was very dense. It inhabited many important villages. One village after another was destroyed but a few Mohammedans managed to escape toward Shensi or Huangchung. The army commanders of Ninghsia and the local militia, which had suffered so many reverses and lost many soldiers at the hands of the Mohammedans, were in high spirits and revenged themselves against their former oppressors. In the meantime the revolt went on in the other prefectures of Kansu-Shensi.

In 1871 Ma Hua-lung, who had surrendered the previous year, was killed with his father, his son, brothers, and the commander of his troops. The revolt was quelled in the prefecture of Ninghsia.

In the third moon the city of Lien Ch'eng, the stronghold of the Lu t'u-ssu, was attacked by the rebels. The attack failed and the rebels were put to flight (*Annals* of Kansu 42: 57b).

In 1872, in the third moon, Tso Tsung-t'ang, leading his army, went to Hsining. The Mohammedans of Hsining, in combination with Salars and Shensi rebels, were at that time plundering the country, killing people, and converting their villages into fortresses, in expectation of attacks from the Chinese army. Tso Tsung-t'ang followed the tactics he had successfully used in Ninghsia, and before long he had the situation in hand. In combination with the Hsining troops he cleared the country, destroying the villages of Mohammedans one after another, and killing all the Mohammedans he could lay hand on. The figure of those killed ran into the ten thousands. More than 100 villages had been destroyed. The Mohammedan population of the Hsining country was very dense. This fact gives an insight into the power of the Mohammedans in the country, and the difficulty for small armies assigned to defend definite countries, and, without coordination among them to cope with the situation.

In the seventh moon the general moved to Lanchow to recommence the same tactics, annihilating the strongholds, killing and demoralizing the rebels.

In the eleventh moon several thousand Mohammedans besieged the city of Hsining again. Among them were Salars of the two Salar t'u-ssu from Hsun Hua, the four upper and lower kungs, Mohammedans from Shensi province and from the suburbs of Hsining. The situation in Hsining seems to have been critical, for troops were sent by General Tso Tsung-t'ang from Lanchow. The troops could not cross the Tat'ung River, the boats having been burned by the rebels. The T'u-ssu Lu of Lien Ch'eng, living on the borders of the river, immediately called his people to prepare a floating bridge, and the troops arrived on time in Hsining. The army administered a crushing defeat to the rebels, destroyed the Mohammedan suburb of Hsining, and the massacre followed. Then the local Mohammedans sued for peace and surrender in concert with the Salars. The officials suspected their faithfulness. They retired and started plundering again. They were pursued, and 3,000 among them were killed. The remaining Salars fled to Pa Yien Jung and the surrender of the Hsining Mohammedans was accepted. The Hsining revolt was quelled. The Mohammedans had suffered tremendous losses.

In 1873, in the first moon, the troops recovered the subprefecture of Tat'ung and cleared the country in the same ruthless way. For many months the army had tried to recover the city of Suchow, situated on the trade road to Turkistan. In the Suchow area the Mohammedan population was very dense. Troops were sent from Lanchow and Hsining, but did not succeed in the action. Finally, in October, Tso Tsung-t'ang himself arrived with more troops from Lanchow. In November the city was recovered, the country cleared, and the Mohammedan population of the whole country massacred.

The same year the cities of Hsun Hua and Ho Chou were recovered and the country cleared. The number of the slaughtered Mohammedans in the cities and the surrounding villages was tremendous. Huangchung and East Kansu were pacified. Both Chinese and Mohammedans had borne the brunt of the revolt, and suffered equally.

During this last revolt, 1860–1873, a relatively few number of notes are encountered concerning the role played by the t'u-ssu and their troops. The fact is quite understandable. Mohammedan groups were running all over the whole country, and the forces of the regular army were insufficient to cope with the situation on a large scale. The t'u-ssu had to protect their own strongholds and fortified villages which sheltered their subjects, in the way the officials had to protect the cities with their population. Huangchung had suffered terribly and the destroyed villages and cities told the tale. The Monguors had had a bad time, but comparatively few had lost their lives, having hid and resisted the rebels in the strongholds of their t'u-ssu. The loss of cattle, houses, etc., was tremendous.

For the second time dissension concerning the old and new religion had caused a terrible revolt. The fanatic Salars, as well as the Chinese Mohammedans, had been responsible for all the harm suffered in Kansu and Shensi. However, every time their revolt had been on the brink of disaster, both groups forgot their dissension about religion and together fought fanatically their common enemy, the army of the hated Chinese.

REVOLT OF MOHAMMEDANS IN 1895–1896

During the revolt of the Mohammedans in 1860–1873, many cities and villages of Huangchung had been devastated and many, many thousands of Chinese and Mohammedans killed. During the following twenty-two years, the country had more or less recovered from the disaster, when a new revolt of the Mohammedans broke out, as terrible as the preceding, and forecasting anew many days and nights of black despair. The news of a revolt of the Mohammedans was enough to cause a feeling of awe all over the country.

This time the revolt started in Hsun Hua in East Kansu where, in 1762, Ma Ming-hsin, coming back from a pilgrimage, had founded his new religion. It was caused by dissension among the Mohammedans of Hsun Hua concerning the old and new religions. Han Mu-li was the leader of the old religion group, and Han Ssu the leader of the new religion group. Fifty thousand Salars prepared to join the revolt. In Hsun Hua, at that time, there was a garrison of only five to six thousand soldiers.

The viceroy of the provinces of Shen Kan Yang, Ch'ang-chun, was informed. Immediately he ordered the commanders of Kanchow, Hsining, and Turkistan to move their troops around the Hsun Hua region, in order to encircle the revolt (*Annals* of Kansu **47**: 63b, 64a). The troops arrived too late, the city of Hsun Hua was already besieged by Han Mu-li and the Salars, the Mohammedans of Ho Chou, Hai Ch'eng, and Pa Yen Jung, Nienpei had already joined the revolt (*Annals* of Kansu **5**: 49, 58a–b).

But there is another version of the cause of the revolt. The troubles arose in Hsun Hua from the dissensions related to the old and new religions, in the first moon of 1895. Then the viceroy sent Commander Lei Cheng-kuan immediately to garrison with his troops in the city of Ho Chou, in order to prevent the spread of the revolt. However, the whole region was upset on account of the misconduct of the troops of Ho Chou. Two Mohammedan leaders of Hsun Hua went to see the commander in Ho Chou, asking to put his troops in order. He killed the two leaders and then the revolt started and spread like a prairie fire. Hsun Hua was besieged by Salars, Ho Chou and Hai Ch'eng joined the revolt.

Later, the investigations of the conduct of Commander Lei Cheng-kuan disclosed that the reason for the misconduct of the soldiers of his troops had been the overdue payment of his soldiers (*Annals* of Kansu **5**: 42a–b, 43a).

Then followed many reverses and small successes of the Chinese troops, the flight of the besiegers of Hsun Hua in the fifth moon, and the spread of the revolt in Huangchung. In the sixth moon the Mohammedans of Hsining revolted, and with them all the Mohammedans of the whole country: Tatung and Pe-ta were besieged and captured. The Chinese troops were unable to cope with the revolt.

General Teng Tsen of Hsining asked for permission to order the enrollment of 200 soldiers of each of the tribes in the country (*Annals* of Kansu **47**: 64).[100]

This note seems to point to the enrollment of the Monguor troops and their t'u-ssu, besides that of the

---

[100] d'Ollone, *op. cit.* **21**: 299.

Tibetan tribes. However, nowhere is recorded in this section the name of a t'u-ssu. Records about the t'u-ssu do not reach as far as 1895.

Here we must close the chapter of the history of the Monguors during the Ch'ing dynasty, but a few words more will help one to understand the terrible devastation wrought in Huangchung during this revolt.

In the tenth moon, when the situation was completely out of hand, General Tung Fu-hsiang arrived with a strong army from Turkistan. He first went to Ho Chou and Hsun Hua, the centers of the revolt, ruthlessly murdering the Mohammedans in the way they had behaved with the Chinese. Then he pacified the Salars of Pa Yen Jung and the entire region south of Nienpei, along the northern borders of the Yellow River, all in the same bloody way. He went to Tat'ung and Pe-ta, and reached all the strongholds and fortified villages of the Mohammedans north, south, and east of Hsining, one after another, devastating the country and slaughtering the people.

In the second moon of 1896 the revolt was quelled. The remaining Mohammedans, having no way to live, fled toward Kokonor. The Tibetans and Mongols in Kokonor had been prevented from keeping in readiness to exterminate the rebels, pursued by the army. Small groups of them fled to Turkistan across the southern mountain range and submitted to the officials of Turkistan; most of them died from starvation and cold in the middle of the winter.

In 1920, traveling in the country, one encountered ruined villages and cities which told the story of both terrible Mohammedan revolts and this made it easy to understand the hatred which today still smolders in the hearts of Chinese and Mohammedans against each other in Kansu province.

This first part of the book sheds light on the hopeless situation on the frontier regions during the Ming time.

On the one hand, the uncouth Mongols were unable to organize a united front for the recovery of their lost empire; they were divided and subdivided in groups, fighting each other under the leadership of chieftains, seething with hatred and killing one another. They tumbled back into barbarism, invading the frontier regions, plundering, ravaging the country, abducting and killing the people. In Huangchung, East Kansu, and Kokonor they ruined and scattered the Tibetan tribes, reducing them to the level of slaves.

On the other hand, the few demoralized Chinese troops, unable to cope with the situation, tried only to defend the few cities and strongholds, barricading themselves behind the walls, looking at the destruction wrought around them. Their forces were too feeble to pursue mighty bands of invaders. They were afraid to enter into the barren unknown Mongolian and Tibetan countries, exposed to ambushes of enemies, to lack of food and provisions, and to extermination. The defenders of the cities had little or no communications between them as the country was too extensive. They did not muster their scattered forces to fight in pitched battles and liked better to take it easy behind the fortified walls.

All the imperial orders issued to the officers during the Ming time, as will also be read in the second section of the Chronicles, enjoined them to obey their superior officers and not to act independently; to send messengers to keep contact with each other; to muster troops and fight in pitched battles; not to be lazy, sitting with a wait-and-see attitude behind fortified walls; and always with threats of severe punishment for high as well as for low officers, who did not comply with the orders.

Very seldom was a new strong army sent to save a critical situation. When this happened the invaders fled, but they returned after the departure of the troops.

In these circumstances it is easy to understand that a lot of abuses must have existed among the troops garrisoned for long times in the frontier regions.

The imperial orders constantly enjoined the officers not to mix with the affairs of the civil administration, not to oppress the people, or impose taxes, exactions, etc. The people during the Ming dynasty suffered during two centuries from the inroads of barbarians, the oppression of the troops, and the maladministration of a dynasty becoming more and more effete.

In the Ch'ing dynasty the invasions of Mongols subsided a little until 1723, when bLo-bzang tan-chin launched his terrible revolt which might have caused the loss of Huangchung. Fortunately it was quelled with troops of Szechwan commanded by chiefs equal to the situation.

Then the revolts of the Mohammedans, more ruthless than those of the Mongols wrought terrible havoc, and a tremendous number of Chinese, as well as Mohammedans, lost their lives.

The Monguors had a hard time during these centuries, but remained faithful defenders of the empire.

II. THE CHRONICLES OF THE LU CLAN

GENERAL INTRODUCTION

Chronicles of families are important historical documents, for they record trustworthy facts not included in the official histories.

In the present chronicle of the Lu clan are recorded the origin of the clan, its relations with the empire, the military art of the time, the civil and military administration, the laws of succession in the t'u-ssu family, the history of the inroads of barbarians and brigands in the country, etc.

I was happy to come into possession of these Chronicles in 1916, thanks to the kindness of General Ma K'och'eng of Hsining. At that time rumors were persistently spread about the abolition of the t'u-ssu institution by the new Republic (1911). The widow of T'u-ssu Lu, a Mongol Khoshot lady, daughter of the Prince of Alashan, administered the tribe, keeping the seal, and caring for her young son. In order to ensure the succession of her son to the office of his father, she had traveled to Hsining to solicit the help of the powerful general by inviting him to be so kind as to become the boy's adoptive father, and at the same time offering him precious gifts. The general accepted the offer, and a few days later the boy arrived at Hsining to recognize the general as his father and to prostrate himself three times before him. Knowing this fact, I asked my friend the general to obtain the Chronicles for me, and so they came into my possession.

NATURE OF THE CHRONICLES

The Chronicles, written in Chinese, consist of two small xylographic volumes. The first one consists of two sections. The first section, only 2 pages, contains a preface and the lists of the genealogies of the chiefs of the tribe to the fifteenth generation. The second section, 52 pages, starts with a preface followed by the records concerning the imperial orders sent to the clan chiefs, the titles and promotions received by them, the inroads of barbarians and brigands into their country, and the wars in which they participated until 1850.

The second volume, 20 pages, the third section of the Chronicles, starts with a preface and presents the biographies of the fifteen t'u-ssu who successively controlled the clan until 1850.

Both volumes start with the accession of the Ming dynasty in 1368 and end in 1850 on the death of the fifteenth ancestor of the clan. To each of the two volumes are added two pages, written in Chinese with a pencil, relating facts from 1851 to 1896 and adding the biographies of the sixteenth and seventeenth ancestors. The Chronicles of the Lu Clan given on page 74 seq. are a translation from the Chinese of the two xylographic volumes referred to above.

AUTHORS OF THE CHRONICLES AND THE TIME OF THEIR COMPOSITION

The preface of the first section of the first volume starts: (this is) "the genealogical register RECOMPOSED by Lu Chi-hsun, descendant of the fifteenth generation fulfilling the hereditary office of commandant, with the possession of the seal, commanding the Monguor officers and the soldiers in the commandery of Chuang Lang."

Lu Chi-hsun succeeded his father in 1792, at the age of fifteen (Vol. I, section 2, 48) and died in 1850 (Vol. I, section 2, 52). Consequently the present genealogical register must have been recomposed between 1792 and 1850.

But an earlier Chronicle had been composed. Who was its author and at what time was it composed?

In the biography of the eighth ancestor, Lu Kuang-tsu, it is said that he returned to Lien Ch'eng in 1602, retiring on account of illness from the office he held in Nanking, that he composed in Lien Ch'eng the Chronicle of the family, in three sections: he started with the imperial orders, then he continued with the biographies of the ancestors, the correspondence with the court, and then he added some things of interest, particularly about the family. He died in 1607 in his mansion of Lien Ch'eng (Vol. I, sect. 2, 42; Vol. II, sect. 3, 10). Consequently the first Chronicles were composed between 1602 and 1607 in Lien Ch'eng, by Lu Kuang-tsu, and the second, by Lu Chi-hsun, were a continuation and perhaps a revision of the former ones.

In 1644 T'u-ssu Lu Yung-ch'ang, ancestor of the ninth generation and successor of Lu Kuang-tsu, was killed in Lien Ch'eng by brigands. Lien Ch'eng was destroyed, the palace burned down, and the wooden blocks used for the printing of the Chronicles disappeared in the flames (Vol. II, sect. 3, 52). After the recomposition of the Chronicles by Lu Chi-hsun wooden blocks must have been carved, if not during his lifetime, certainly during and before the end of the incumbency of his successor Ju Kao (1852–1893), because the biography of Ju Kao is not printed in the Chronicle, but is added, written in pencil, after 1850.

NOTE ABOUT THE AUTHORS OF THE CHRONICLES

Who was Lu Kuang-tsu? He succeeded to the office of t'u-ssu after the death of his brother Lu Kuang-hsien, who died without issue. Before that time, having no hope of becoming t'u-ssu, he devoted himself passionately to the study of the Chinese classics and nurtured this passion through his later lifetime. People of an inferior civilization admire the higher civilizations and endeavor to assimilate them. Nomads who conquered

China tried to become Chinese, and the process of sinization was always started by the chiefs. In the t'u-ssu clans of Huangchung eminent scholars are noted. Lu Kuang-tsu was of Mongol origin and adored the Chinese civilization, becoming more Confucian than the Chinese scholars themselves. In the seven biographies composed by him, an abnormal stress is laid upon the examples of filial piety, faithfulness toward the empire, and the austerity and nobility of the ladies displayed in the family of his ancestors. The examples are noted with great care and love. He was enthusiastic about the cult of the ancestors, built an ancestral hall in 1602 in Lien Ch'eng according to the principles of the Chinese scholars and fixed the rites which should be observed in the hall at the sacrifices for the ancestors. He fervently promoted the cult of ancestors among the subjects.

No wonder that he composed a family Chronicle as a means to promote his ideal, hoping it would be read by the subjects and stimulate them to become more civilized according to the Chinese pattern. In his Chronicle nothing is noted concerning shamanism or lamaism, which were ardently practiced by the subjects. Reading the Chronicle it is useful to be conversant with the mentality of the author.

Who was Lu Chi-hsun, the author of the recomposed Chronicle? He also was a scholar, a thorough Confucianist, eager promoter and admirer of filial piety and faithfulness toward the emperor. In the biography of his father written by him, his mentality is displayed candidly and typically. He was not only a Confucianist, he was at the same time a fervent frequenter of high society. He made day and night trips to Peking to see the emperor and the splendor of the palaces. He made friendships with high officials, and was a lover of luxury, fine clothing, dinners, and songs. He had inherited these qualities from his father.

In the prefaces of the second and third sections of the Chronicles he develops the principles he recognized for their recomposition: to inform future generations about their ancestors, their glorious achievements and Confucianist virtues, in order that they might honor them and offer sacrifices to them according to the right principles; to check all the facts in order to provide posterity with authentic and genuine data; and to help the future historians with data not noted in the official history, but worth being noted.

What was the religion of Lu Chi-hsun? Was he Confucianist as well as shamanist and lamaist? Anyway he must have believed in the Living Buddhahood of his second son who controlled the monastery of Tung Erh Ku Lung which belonged to the t'u-ssu of Lien Ch'eng, and was inhabited by 500 lamas. Two other monasteries also belonged to the t'u-ssu, the Si Erh Ku Lung with 200 lamas and the Pao Nan Sse (*Annals* of P'ing fan 25a). In the city of Lien Ch'eng was a very renowned Buddhist temple belonging to the t'u-

ssu, to which was attached a lama chaplain, who every day offered incense in the temple and also in the ancestor hall to the ancestors of the Lu family.

T'O HUAN, FOUNDING ANCESTOR OF THE CLAN

According to the Chronicles of the clan, T'o Huan is its founding ancestor. He was a member of the imperial family of the Yuan dynasty, with the title of Prince of An Ting, since 1313 (Section 1, Preface. Section 3, Biography of T'o Huan, *Yuan Shih,* Chapter 108, 3rd section 24, *27a–b*).

In 1368 the Ming emperor entered the capital of the Yuan, whose emperor had fled to Ying Ch'ang with the imperial family. T'o Huan, prevented from accompanying the emperor, arrived in Kansu in 1369. At the end of 1369 or the beginning of 1370, General Teng Yu was sent to invite him to see the emperor. He submitted to the Ming, and was ordered to muster his troops, and he followed General Su Ta in the war against K'uo-k'uo Timur, the last general of the Yuan. In 1375 he helped General Pu Yin to beat the rebel Mongol T'o-erh-chih-pa (Dorjibal). He was invited to court to receive the congratulations of the emperor, but on account of illness he could not obey the order. He died in 1376 (Section 3, biography of T'o Huan, Section 2 and beginning of Section 3, biography of Lu Yung ch'ang and letter of concubine Yang to the emperor).

His oldest son Ah-shih-t'u succeeded him, became blind, and died in 1377. His second son, Kung-pu shih-tieh succeeded in 1378, and is recorded as the ancestor of the second generation. He fought brigands in 1403 and followed the expedition of the emperor against Ah lu t'ai in 1410, and died on the field of battle.

His oldest son Shih-chia succeeded him in 1412 and is recorded as the ancestor of the third generation, with the name Hsien. In 1414 he received from the emperor the name Lu. From that time on, the clan was called Lu clan (T'o Huan was a Mongol belonging to the Borjigin clan of Chingis, he had no family name).

The Chronicle records the history of T'o Huan, the founding ancestor of the clan, and that of the ancestors who succeeded him as chiefs of the clans. It does not pay attention to the other t'u-ssu of the clan, or to groups which branched off, even by sons of T'o Huan, or by members of the principal or lateral branches.

T'o Huan is recorded as having been appointed by the emperor chief of his tribes and controller of the territory he occupied during the Yuan time.

The *Annals* of P'ing Fan (1739) record only the title of P'ing-chang cheng-shih of T'o Huan, without noting the title, Prince of An Ting, granted to him by the emperor, although this important fact should have been known among the Lu Monguors. Lu Kuang-tsu, renowned scholar, had already composed his Chronicles between 1602 and 1607 in Lien Ch'eng. The *Annals* bypass Ah-shih-t'u who had succeeded T'o Huan in 1377 and died in the same year, and record Kung-

ANCESTORS OF T'O HUAN

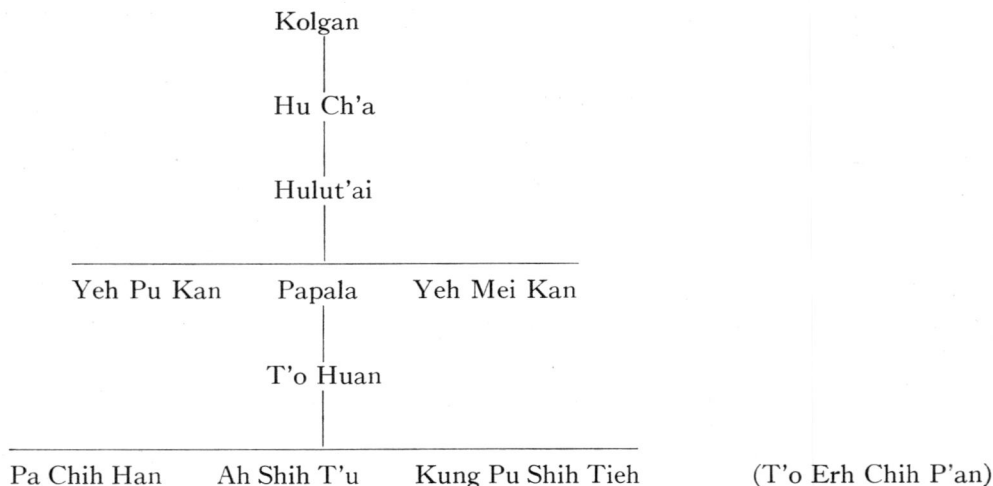

Kolgan

Hu Ch'a

Hulut'ai

Yeh Pu Kan	Papala	Yeh Mei Kan

T'o Huan

Pa Chih Han	Ah Shih T'u	Kung Pu Shih Tieh	(T'o Erh Chih P'an)

pu-shih-tieh, his younger brother, as the ancestor of the second generation without noting that he had died in 1410 on the field of battle, accompanying the emperor on an expedition in Mongolia. The *Annals* note Shih Chia as the ancestor of the third generation without recording his name Hsien, and without noting that he was given the name of Lu on account of the death of his father on the field of battle, but seem to suggest that he had been granted the name of Lu on account of his own merits. Anyway Kung-pu-shih-tieh is the ancestor of the second generation and T'o Huan is the founding ancestor of the clan.

The *Annals* of Kansu **42** : 55, start with Kung-pu-shih-tieh, a member of the imperial family who led his sons and tribes to submit in 1371, and received the title of Pei fu-chang from the emperor and was ordered to settle in Lien Ch'eng. He received the title of centurion and died in 1410 on the battlefield. However, the *Annals* record that his father was T'o Huan bearing the titles of P'ing-chang Cheng-shih and the dignity of Prince of Wu Ting. In the official *Annals* of the Yuan, Pen chi 24, 27, T'o Huan is not noted on the list of princes of Wu Ting but on those of the princes of An Ting. Not Kung-pu-shih-tieh but T'o Huan according to the Chronicles of the Lu clan, submitted with his sons and tribes, at the end of 1369 or beginning of 1370. T'o Huan fought with the Ming armies in 1370 and 1375 and died in 1376. He acted as chief of the submitted clan. Kung-pu-shih-tieh succeeded only in 1378 and could not have led the tribes to submit in 1371. In the *Annals* it is not noted either that Kung-pu-shih-tieh was the ancestor of the second generation nor the founding ancestor of the clan. In the Kansu *Annals* in the articles concerning the Monguor clan is never noted the number of the ancestors who succeeded each other. Anyway Kung-pu-shih-tieh was

a member of the imperial family of the Yuan and the son of T'o Huan.

KOLGAN

T'o Huan, Prince of An Ting, is a descendant of Chingis Khan (who died in 1227), by his sixth son Kolgan, according to the Chinese sources.[1]

Kolgan was the sixth son of Chingis, by his fourth wife Kulan, a Merkit beauty offered by the Merkit chief after Chingis had attacked and crushed the tribe.[2] She bore a son Kolgan. He participated in the conquest of Kipchack (Central Russia) with the Mongol princes of all the branches, under the command of Batu, and besieged the city of Ban (Riazan?) in the autumn of 1237. They stormed the city of Iga (?) where Kolgan was mortally wounded.[3]

K'o Chao-Ming in *Hsin Yuan Shih* 110, 8a, writes: Kulan was the favorite of Chingis, who loved her son Kolgan as much as those of the Empress Borte. Kolgan is recorded as the sixth among the sons of Chingis immediately after the five sons of Empress Borte (*Yuan Shih* 107, 6a). Chingis, in fixing the maintenance of his sons, fixed Kolgan's share nearly equal to those of the five sons of Borte (*Yuan Shih* 95, 5). However,

[1] For the study of the study of the descendants of Kolgan, we follow the Magisterial Study of Louis Hambis, *Le Chapitre CVIII du Yüan che* (64–70) avec notes supplementaires par Paul Pelliot. Supplement au Volume 38 du *T'oung Pao*, Leiden, Brill, 1945. And also *Chapitre CVII du Yüan che* par L. Hambis. Monographies du *T'oung Pao*, 3, Tome I, Leiden, Brill, 1954. There the texts recorded in the official history of the Yuan (1369) concerning the ancestors are discussed relating to Meng wu erh shih chi by Tu Chi (1911), the Cho Keng Lu (1366), the two recent sources composed during the Republic, and the Mohammedan histories by Rashid-ed-Din and Khondemir.

[2] George Vernadski, *The Mongols and Russia*, 26, 1953.

[3] E. Bretschneider, *Médieval Recherches* **1** : 315, London, 1910.

nothing is recorded in the *Yuan Shih* relating to the appanage of Kolgan. Kolgan accompanied Chingis on the expedition in Central Asia and probably died in 1237.

HU CH'A

The son of Kolgan was Hu Ch'a, according to the unanimous testimony of all Chinese and Mohammedan sources.

On the panel recording the princes of Ho Chien, the name of Hu Ch'a is encountered (*Yuan Shih* 107, 6a). However, his name is not written on the list of the appanaged princes, but there the name of his son Hulut'ai is written. The date of his promotion as Prince of Ho Chien is not given either, but it is noted on the list of the sustenances and subjects allotted to the Prince of Ho Chien.

Hu Ch'a probably died in 1264.

HULUT'AI

All the Chinese sources unanimously call Hulut'ai the son of Hu Ch'a. Hulut'ai was Prince of Ho Chien, but the Mohammedan sources do not mention it. The history of the Yuan calls him "great prince" (107, 6b), and also Prince of Ho Chien and notes the date of his promotion (108, 4). Consequently, he was really Prince of Ho Chien, as his father Hu Ch'a had been. The name of Hulut'ai is written in Chinese in different ways and the same name is encountered among many offspring of the second son of Chingis, Chagatai (Hambis, note 60, 3).

When Kubilai was proclaimed emperor in 1260, his brother Arikboga opposed him, was proclaimed emperor also, and was followed by nearly all the princes of the East and the West. The revolt lasted for more than fifty years.

Hulut'ai received from Emperor Kubilai in 1265 the seal of Prince of Ho Chien and a gift of a thousand *tan* of grain for his destitute subjects, probably to keep him from mixing in the revolt. However, in 1277, at the time Haitu fought Kubilai, Hulut'ai, living among rebel princes, followed Haitu, but in the eighth month he left the rebels and clung again to the faction of Kubilai (*Yuan Shih* 9, 20b).

In the history of the Yuan neither the death nor the date of the death of Hulut'ai is noted, but he died before 1287.

THE SONS OF HULUT'AI

All the sources concerning the three first generations of the ancestors of T'o Huan, agree that Kolgan was the primordial ancestor, succeeded by his son Hu Ch'a, and grandson Hulut'ai, who was the son of Hu Ch'a. The confusion in the list of succession starts with the sons of Hulut'ai.

The oldest lists, corroborated by the Mohammedan lists and that of 1911, mention three sons: Yeh Pu Kan,

Papala, and Yeh Mei Kan. The lists in both recent histories mention four sons: Yeh Pu Kan, Papa, Pei Ta Han, and Yeh Mei Kan. The old lists note Papa to be the son of Yeh Pu Kan. The recent lists note Papa as the brother of Yeh Pu Kan and Papala the son of Yeh Mei Kan and not his brother.

T'o Huan in the three old lists belongs to the fifth generation, in the recent lists to the sixth generation, but in all these lists T'o Huan is recorded as the son of Papala. Anyway T'o Huan is noted as a descendant of Kolgan, whether his father was the son or the grandson of Hulut'ai.

YEH PU KAN

Yeh Pu Kan succeeded to his father Hulut'ai. On all lists he is noted as the son of Hulut'ai.

To Yeh Pu Kan seems to have been granted the dignity of Prince of Ho Chien which had been bestowed upon his grandfather Hu Ch'a and his father Hulut'ai and the reason is that in the history of the Yuan (14, 17b) is recorded that his appanage of Ho Chien and his title of Ta lu hua ch'ih had been removed from him in 1287. It thus seems that he had inherited the title from his father and that his father had died before 1287. However, his name is not recorded in the lists of the princes with title (108, 4a) but only in those called "great princes" (107, 6b).

Also, his grandfather Hu Ch'a (107, 5a) is recorded Prince of Ho Chien in the official history and also in the list of the sustenance given to the princes (95, 5a). However, his name is not mentioned in the list of Princes of Ho Chien (108, 4a). Also, his father Hulut'ai is noted only as "great prince" in 107, 6b, but in the principal *Annals* he is recorded as Prince of Ho Chien (6, 2), with the date of the granting of the title and the seal, and also in 108, 4a, he is noted as Prince of Ho Chien. Does this fact suggest that only the grandfather and the father had enjoyed the title of Prince of Ho Chien and that after the death of Hulut'ai, the title had no longer been granted to Yeh Pu Kan and later successors? Or is it possible that it had already been removed from Hulut'ai after his revolt in 1277?

Anyway, Yeh Pu Kan's appanage and title were removed from him in 1287 after he had participated in the revolt against Kubilai, in which Hai Tu had lured Na Yen, descendant of Hasar, the fourth brother of Chingis, appanaged in Manchuria.

Marco Polo, at that time at the court of Kubilai, tells that Na Yen was a baptized Nestorian Christian, who in the battle against Kubilai bore a cross, but that this did not avail, because he had revolted against his lord.[4]

Before his revolt Yeh Pu Kan in 1284 had accompanied the imperial Prince Namuhan in the region of Kobdo, to inquire about the line of action of the rebellious and turbulent Mongol princes.

Many hypotheses have been suggested related to the

---

[4] de Mailla, *Histoire générale de la Chine* 9: 432.

place the appanage of Yeh Pu Kan was really situated. It seems to have been north of the Altai Mountains, and north of the appanage of the descendants of Chagatai, the second son of Chingis.

Yeh Pu Kan died in 1288.

YEH MEI KAN, PAPALA, PEITAHAN, AND PAPA

In all the lists of the descendants of Kolgan, Yeh Mei Kan is recorded as the son of Hulut'ai, except in the list of the Cho Keng Lu where he is entirely obliterated. In the history of the Yuan are encountered many Yeh Pu Kan and Yeh Mei Kan and it is not always easy to distinguish them.

In the history of the Yuan (20, 7a) Yeh Mei Kan the son of Hulut'ai, having simply the title of prince, is recorded as having received a silver gilded seal in 1300 and having died in 1301, and his son Papala as having succeeded him (20, 13). Hambis encounters in the same history two texts concerning Papala: one of 1286 related to an imperial gift for his destitute people, another recorded the granting of the title of "great prince" in 1314 (108, 6b). On p. 66 Hambis explains the discrepancies between these texts and those related to Yeh Mei Kan, and concludes peremptorily that Papala must have been the brother of Yeh Mei Kan, and not his son, but the son of Hulut'ai. In the Mohammedan lists and in *Yuan Shih hsin pien* he is also noted to be the brother.

The Cho keng lu not only notes Papala as the son of Yeh Mei Kan, but substitutes for him Peitahan, as brother of Yeh Mei Kan. However Peitahan does not belong to the group of the descendants of Hulut'ai, but to that of Chagatai, the second son of Chingis (Hambis, p. 66).

It has been noted that all the old lists of the descendants of Hulut'ai record only three sons. However, the two most recent histories printed after 1911 note four sons: Yeh Pu Kan, Papa, Peitahan, Yeh Mei Kan. Papa noted as the son of Yeh Pu Kan in all the other lists, is noted in both recent works as the brother of Yeh Pu Kan. In all the lists of the descendants of Hulut'ai, Papa is noted as having two sons: Hapin Timur and Wu T'u-sse Timur. Hambis, in his magisterial study, proves conclusively that Papa belongs to the group of the descendants of Chagatai, in which lists he is consigned with his two sons, bearing names entirely the same as those recorded in the Kolgan lists.

The Cho keng lu, in order to make the question more intricate, records the two sons of Papa not to be the sons of Papa, but of T'o Huan! In the family Chronicles, however, these names are not encountered.

T'O HUAN

All the sources, together with the family Chronicles of the Lu clan, unanimously attest T'o Huan to be the son of Papala and descendant of Kolgan in the fifth generation. The two most recent studies, however, claim him to be the descendant in the sixth generation, Papala being the son of Yeh Mei Kan and grandson of Hulut'ai. Anyway, T'o Huan is a member of the imperial family of the Yuan by the Kolgan branch.

It is interesting to conclude with the note that Papala had lived and died in Lien Ch'eng. In the *Annals* of Kansu and P'ing Fan, and in the Chronicles of the Lu clan, it is noted that T'o Huan, after his submission, was ordered to reoccupy the old country he had occupied during the Yuan dynasty. In the biography of T'o Huan (3rd section) it is recorded that he and his wife were buried in the ancestral cemetery of Hsi Tatung. Because it is called the ancestral cemetery, ancestors must have been buried there.

THE SONS OF T'O HUAN

The Chronicles of the Lu family note only two sons, Ah-shih-t'u the oldest, and Kung-pu-shih-tieh the second. The *Annals* of P'in Fan and those of Kansu, however, claim Pa chih han to be the first son of T'o Huan. In the study are noted the disastrous consequences of the submissions by T'o Huan, his first son, at the moment of the appointment of his successor as chief of the clan. In the history are noted three more sons: Hapin Timur, Wu T'u-ssu Timur and T'o-erh-chih-pa. Hapin Timur and Wu T'u-ssu Timur are proved by Hambis to belong to the line of Chagatai. T'o-erh-chih-pa (Dorjibal) is noted in Cho Kung lu as son of Pei Ta Han, in the Mohammedan sources. However, in the official history of the Yuan and the two recent historical works, he is claimed to be the son of T'o Huan. In the official history he is recorded as Prince of An Ting, without notice of the date of appointment. It is impossible that a son could have borne the title of his father during the lifetime of the father. T'o Huan died in 1376 and was still Prince of An Ting at the time he submitted to the Ming in 1368–1369. In the family Chronicle, however, are only noted the sons who succeeded to the office of supreme chiefs of the clan. It is not impossible that T'o Huan had had more sons, but that Dorjibal should have been one among them is not proved. In the family Chronicle it is noted that in 1375 T'o Huan helped General Pu Yin to beat the rebel Mongol Dorjibal, who can therefore hardly have been his son. Anyway, he did not succeed T'o Huan.

GENEALOGICAL REGISTER OF THE FAMILY LU

PREFACE

The genealogical register was composed by Lu Chi-hsun, descendant of the fifteenth generation, who filled the hereditary office of commander, with the possession of the seal, controlling the Monguor officials and troops of Chuang Lang.

Families have genealogical registers as kingdoms have histories. In olden times during the Chou and Ch'in dynasties, the one hundred-twenty kingdoms each had precious books. When Ssu-Ma Ch'ien composed the Shih-chi (history) he took these books as models. The coordination of the work seemed to be so clear that future genealogical registers were built according to that model.

Ssu Ma-ch'ien composed the genealogical registers of the San Tai period (Hsia, Shang, and Chou dynasties, 2205–250 B.C.). However, from Huang Ti on, the number of generations is hard to determine, and because of this and of the length of time elapsed the registers are contradictory and not entirely reliable. The same problem exists with the genealogical list of Ou-Yang Hsiu and of Su Shih, which were highly esteemed at that time. From Hsun on, Ou-Yang records only five generations for a period of 300 years, and from Tsung on, he records eighteen generations for a period of only 140 years. Checking the list of Su, one notes the omission of Chang Shih from Chou, but we see him go as far upward as Lu-Chung and Kun-wu, and we feel once more its vagueness. It is difficult to rely entirely upon them.

The Lu family originates from the imperial family of the Yuan. However, their genealogical register does not go back that far. It reads: "(Reverentially) we dare not to look at the emperor as our ancestor. Our family name Lu started with Lu Hsien, the ancestor of the third generation. However, our first ancestor was Prince of An Ting during the Yuan. This is recorded in the genealogical lists of the Yuan dynasty, and so there is no need to investigate it again. Those who recorded the original name would not have noted it without having proof." [5]

We start with the first section of the genealogical register.

GENEALOGICAL REGISTER

Primordial Ancestor	T'o Huan
Second generation	Kung-pu-shih-tieh

Two sons: Ah-shih-tu succeeded, died soon, Kung-pu-shih-tieh succeeded

Third generation	Hsien
Fourth generation	Chien
Fifth generation	Lin
Sixth generation	Chin
Seventh generation	Tung

Two sons: Tan succeeded, died soon, Tung succeeded

Eighth generation	Kuang-tsu

Cheng-wu son of Tan succeeded, died soon. Tung three more sons: Kuang-tsu, Kuang-hsien, Kuang-kuo; Kuang-tsu succeeded

[5] Yuan Shih, 107, 3b, 6a–b, 24, 27b, 113.

Ninth generation	Yung Ch'ang
Tenth generation	Hung
Eleventh generation	Ti Hsin

Two sons: Ti Ch'eng succeeded, died soon, Ti Hsin succeeded

Twelfth generation	Hua Lin
Thirteenth generation	Feng Chu
Fourteenth generation	Fan
Fifteenth generation	Chi Hsun
Sixteenth generation	Cho
Seventeenth generation	Ju Kao

CHRONOLOGICAL BIOGRAPHIES

PREFACE

In former times Huang Li-chou (Huang Tsung-hsi) always said that the science of the composition of chronological biographies is a distinctive branch (of history).

Li Wen-chien composed the chronological biographies of Sires Fan, Han, Fu, Wu Yang, Ssu Ma, and the three Su's. The later generations admired their completeness and correctness. These men had been renowned ministers and eminent scholars.

Kingdoms have official histories. Families have chronological biographies in which men are the warp and years the woof. If the biographies cover only a few years, the collection of the material is easy. In 1643 our family met with the insurrection of Huo Chin during which (our) archives, books, law registers, and official deeds, were consumed by fires set by the brigands. A dynasty is only a fraction of the history, a single man a fraction of a generation, and an event only a fraction of the life of a single man. Weaving with the warp of men and the woof of years, collected over periods of hundreds of years, and then trying to put the events of several hundred years in a one-foot roll is difficult.

Now I summarily coordinate all the events, I record our submission (to the empire) in order to conform with the will of Heaven, I record our military successes, in order to recall the glorious achievements of the ancestors, I note the dates of the birth and the death of the ancestors, the place of their interment, in order that the ulterior generations will remember to make sacrifices to them. I eliminate all doubtful events and avoid writing unchecked facts, in order not to mislead posterity. Facts which have to be believed and are important have to be recorded and insignificant ones omitted. This is the rule of the Ch'un-ch'iu. The dates of the period of the reigns of the emperors are noted with the first day of the moon.

Now we proceed to the second section, the chronological biographies.

CHRONOLOGICAL BIOGRAPHIES

PRIMORDIAL CLAN ANCESTOR: T'O HUAN

1368. First year of the period Hung Wu. Emperor T'ai Tsung on the eighth moon enters the capital of the Yuan.

1369. The Ming captured K'ai P'ing. The Yuan emperor fled northward.

1370. In the fifth moon Su Ta captures Hsing Yuan. Teng Yu was sent to inform the tribes in the western countries about the new conditions in the empire, and to call them to submit. The ancestor T'o Huan submitted, accompanied Su Ta, conquering the northern countries and fighting K'uo-k'uo Timur in Cheng Erh Yu.

1371. Sire T'o Huan followed Su Ta, Li Wen-cheng, Feng Chen and others to fight K'uo k'uo Timur.

1375. Sire T'o Huan followed Pu Yin to fight T'o-erh-chih-pa,[6] a chief in Ho Hsi (Liangchow) and defeated him. He was invited to court. On account of illness he could not go.

1376. Sire T'o Huan died. His oldest son Ah-shih-t'u succeeded him.

SECOND GENERATION: LU KUNG-PU-SHIH-TIEH

1377. Sire Ah-shih-t'u was transferred from the commandery of Lanchow to that of Chuang Lang, with the title of centurion.

1378. Sire Ah-shih-t'u captured the rebel Tibetan chief Ta-kuan-tieh-chih and killed him. He became blind and soon died. The ancestor of the second generation Kung-pu-shih-tieh succeeded him. The imperial order he received read:

I govern the empire, to talented men who love justice I give official duties. Kung-pu-shih-tieh, for a long time you have lived in the western country, you are able to devote yourself to the submission of the people. I appreciate your intention, I give you the title of Chao-hsin Chiao-wei and the title of centurion in charge of the troops of the commandery of Chi Ning. You will devote yourself to obeying the law and controlling the people with kindness. I hope you will respond to my desire in the office I entrust to you. Devote yourself to it.

1390. By imperial order was granted to him the use of the Ma-fu-yen (the half of a tablet having the form of a horse, the other half being deposed in the bureau of the administration; the presentation of the tablet permitted free entrance and right to call on the superior).

1402. Kung-pu-shih-tieh fought Ta-ming-pu-yen-to-shih on the territory of Liangchow. He defeated him and captured many of his followers. He went to the capital to offer captives. Emperor Ch'eng Tsung (Yung

Lo) ascended to the throne. He was promoted centurion in the commandery of Chuang Lang.

1404. Kung-pu-shih-tieh was transferred and promoted to the defense of Cheng Fan and other places.

1405. He was entrusted with the defense of Mo mo ch'eng and other places.

1409. He was ordered to move to I-chi-nai to induce the Mongols to submission.

1410. He followed the emperor on the expedition in the northern countries. He died on the battlefield in Ho-la-ho.

1411. He was buried in Ch'ing Shih Shan.

THE THIRD GENERATION: LU HSIEN

1412. Sire Hsien with the high commandant Ch'eng Huai fought the rebel Mongols Yang-ku-erh and others and captured many at Pa-li-ma. In winter he fought with commandant Liu Mu the rebel Mongol Shih T'ai in Sung Shan and killed the chief.

1414. Sire Hsien was transferred to defend Hsuan Fu and was promoted secretary commandant. On the second of the twelfth moon an imperial order arrived for the commandant of Chuang Lang to choose from the tribe 200 soldiers inured to war, to be commanded by the Lu chiliarch.

When the imperial order arrives they must leave for Hsuan Fu and await orders there. You must care for the provisions of the soldiers and the animals yourself and act according to the order.

1419. On the seventh of the third moon we received the imperial order:

I govern the empire making no distinction between subjects living inside or outside the empire. It is the old rule of the empire. You, Sire Lu, since long ago, have lived in the western country. You serve the emperor reverentially. How old are your faithfulness and sincerity, and how reliable and strong! Since I ascended the throne you have received many promotions. At present I promote you Ming Wei general and secretary commandant in the commandery of Chuang Lang. Try always to be good and to care for your subjects with more zeal. Instill in yourself the feeling of a great love in order to improve your faithfulness and zeal and to enjoy peace eternally. Pay respect to this order.

1421. Sire Hsien was transferred to the defense of Ho Chou. The twenty-ninth of the eighth moon the imperial order was received with respect.

Commander of Chuang Lang, choose in your circumscription the soldiers of the tribes, the people of the tribes and the Chinese capable of fighting as many as possible, and entrust them to the commandant Lu Hsien. Each of them must carry his weapons. On the passes along the way provisions must be delivered for the men and the animals. The first of the second moon they must reach Peking. Obey and act according to the order.

1422. Sire Lu Hsien followed the emperor on the expedition against the northern rebels. On the seventh moon he arrived at the river Han T'an and captured

---

[6] D. Pokotilof, *History of the eastern Mongols during the Ming dynasty from 1368 to 1634, 7,* translation by Rudolf Loewenthal, Chengtu, China, West China Union University, 1947.

the rebel chief Ao la han. He was granted money and flowered silk. In the tenth moon he fought in T'ien Ch'eng and was again granted money.

1423. The thirtieth of the seventh moon the imperial order was received:

High commander of Chuang Lang chose instantly 300 men among the soldiers, the Monguor subjects and the Chinese, to be commanded by Lu Hsien. They first have to march to Ninghsia, and there they have to accompany Duke Ning Yang, Brigadier General Ch'eng Yao, and the eunuch Wang Nan on a hunting party. Obey and act according to the order.

Sire Hsien entered the Alashan country and entrapped the Chung Yung prince, Yeh Hsien t'u-ch'ien and captured many prisoners.

In the twelfth moon the imperial order was received:

Lu Hsien, Monguor official in the commandery of Chuang Lang; immediately upon the arrival of the order you must command soldiers of the regular army; each of them must carry his weapons and ride his horse; provisions must be delivered to men and animals on the passes on the way; and on the third moon in 1424 they must arrive at Peking. Obey and act according to the order.

1424. Sire Hsien followed the emperor on the expedition against the rebels. In the seventh moon the army camped at T'u Mu Ch'uan. The emperor died. Jen Tsung ascended the throne.

1425. The fifth of the second moon Lu Hsien personally received the imperial order:

Monguor official commandant Lu Hsien, of the commandery of Chuang Lang, on the arrival of the order take immediately 260 officers and soldiers chosen from among those you formerly commanded. First go to Hsining and then together with the High Commandant Li Yin, the commandant K'ang Shu and others, go to the three wei of Han Tung, Chu Hsien, An Ting (Turkistan) and inquire about the case of the audacious brigands who plundered and killed the ambassadors on the road to Wu Sse Tsang (on the Szechwan and Tibetan borders). Inquire to what tribes they belong and order their chiefs to capture and conduct them to the capital. Be careful not to be deceived when they incriminate each other. This is the aim of the order.

In the fifth moon the emperor Jen Tsung died, and Hsuan Tsung ascended the throne.

In the seventh moon Lu Hsien participated in the expedition in Chu Hsien and other places. He killed and captured many brigands. He induced Prince Wu Ting, Sang-erh shih-chia to submit. He was promoted high secretary commandant with the promise that three generations would enjoy the favor of this title.

On the fourth of the eighth moon an imperial order arrived informing Lu Hsien, Monguor commandant in the commandery of Chuang lang:

You served reverentially my ancestor T'ai Tsung, displayed faithfulness, exercised your sincerity, zealously and intelligently expended your forces. Many times you became illustrious by glorious achievements. Successively, dignities and gifts were bestowed upon you. You received from my late father Jen Tsung, whose tablet is honored in the ancestral temple on the place Chao and whose succession I received, an imperial order relating to the affair of the brigands of An Ting and other places who had plundered and killed the imperial ambassadors, to lead your troops to exterminate them, to bring peace in that country, and put an end to the miseries of the people. You have capably complied with the order of the emperor. Acting with zeal and courage, you led your strong troops into the den of the brigands, killing and capturing more than 1,000 men and capturing booty of 130,000 camels, horses, cows, and sheep, suppressing even the vestiges of the brigands, rendering peace to the people, so that the communications (with central Asia) might start again and no more troubles occur (on the highway). I praise your faithfulness and zeal. When I ascended the throne I appointed generals to keep peace in the frontier regions. If all of them will expend their forces in that way, peace can easily be enjoyed and great success achieved. Who among the generals of former times are equal to you?

Now by special favor I send Yang Yun, chief of the ministry of civil appointments, to congratulate you.

The captives, camels, and horses have to be sent to the capital, cows and sheep have to be distributed among the officers and troops who participated in the expedition. You will soon come to court, the expenses defrayed by the empire, in order to comply with my sentiments.

On the eleventh moon he obeyed and went to the capital. He received silver, flowered silk, precious trinkets, and paper money.

1426. On the eleventh of the first moon the imperial order arrived at the quarters of the commandant of Chuang Lang, to choose 260 officers and soldiers who formerly served in the cavalry and put them under the command of high secretary Commandant Lu Hsien to receive training in the defense of the frontiers. They may expect to be transferred soon. Obey and act according to the order.

1427. The chief of the Tibetan Erh-chia tribe revolted but the revolt was quelled by Lu Hsien.

On the twentieth of the twelfth moon the imperial order was received:

We informed the Prince of An Ting, I p'an tan, of the An Ting commandery, the secretary commandant Ah la ch'i pa and others, concerning the mission of the eunuch Hu Hsien and others to Wu-sse-tsang. Order your 3,000 officers and soldiers to protect the ambassadors, under command of high secretary-commandant Lu Hsien and the chiliarch Li Pao-tung. They have to wait for the ambassadors on Sse ha erh ma yang. They have to encounter the ambassadors in a group. Do not disobey the order or commit errors. It is the aim of the order.

1428. The ambassadors, protected on the way, arrived at Ao Chieh Ch'uan. The Lama Cheng nan ho pa of the Erh-chia tribe had moved far away. Lu Hsien treated his troops well on the way.

The imperial order of the twentieth of the eleventh moon informed the high commandant Lu Hsien and the quarters of the commandery of Chuang Lang, to call immediately the troops which have received training.

Each of them must carry his weapons and ride his horse, provisions will be delivered at the passes. Lu Hsien will command them. These troops and others will obey the orders of Duke Hui Ning, Li Yin of Hsining, and be at Peking for the fifteenth of the second moon (1429). On the way the behavior of the troops must be strict. Those who disobey will be punished severely. Obey and act according to the order.

1429. Lu Hsien, obeying the orders went to Peking.

1430. Lu Hsien led an expedition and quelled the revolt of Ho-sse-san Chi-sse.

1434. In the ninth moon Lu Hsien fought and defeated the Mongol Wan Chih Timur. The eighteenth of the twelfth moon an imperial order is received:

Lu Hsien, first captain commandant of Shensi province, you are becoming old. During long years you expended your forces with zeal. Your name is engraved in the heart of the emperor. Now I promote you, by especial favor, assistant Tu-tu at the headquarters of the Tu-tu. You will obey the orders of the brigadier general defender of the country. You will practice more faithfulness and sincerity in order to manifest your gratefulness. Try to respond to the affectionate solicitude of the emperor. Receive this order with reverence.

1435. Emperor Hsuan Tsung died in the first moon. Emperor Yin Tsung ascended the throne.

Lu Hsien fought and defeated the rebel Pai pe ta li ma.

In the eleventh moon Lu Hsien fought Ho Shan-erh in Kanchow, beheaded the chief and captured his baggage.

1436. Lu Hsien participated in the expedition of the brigadier general Jen Li, in I-pu-la-shan. He pursued and defeated the brigands. In concert with the brigadier general Chao Nan he participated in the expedition in Ho Yun Sse. In the tenth moon the Mongol Ah t'ai t'o erh chih-pa invaded Chuang Lang. He was pursued by Lu Hsien. Nai lai-wa, one of the chiefs of the brigands was killed.

1437. Lu Hsien put to flight Tu so lo in Mi la ch'uan, captured the chiefs Pa tu so lo and Mi li ku, and more than 1,000 brigands.

1438. Lu Hsien put to flight and beat Pe ya wu in I-pu-la-shan. He was promoted to high commandment.

1445. On the second moon Lu Hsien was promoted to Piao ch'i general, and secretary commandant at the headquarters of the left army. He sent his son Chien to offer a tribute of horses at the capital. His son was promoted to Centurion.

1447. In the twelfth moon Lu Hsien, the Piao ch'i general, died. Chien, the ancestor of the fourth generation succeeded the father.

THE FOURTH GENERATION: LU CHIEN

1448. Chien defeated the Mongol brigands at Ch'a nan wu la, and was promoted to commandant.

1449. Emperor Ying Tsung was captured by the Mongols in T'u mu. Chin Ti ascended the throne.

1450. Imperial order of the twenty-sixth of the seventh moon:

Lu Chien commandant in the commandery of Chuang Lang, I order you to have strict discipline among the Monguor officers and soldiers and to defend the country with the 400 soldiers in combination with the commandant Kao and others. Train the troops continually and be kind toward them. Where troubles arise move the troops to the danger spots. Do not consider your troops as being your own, imposing on them corvées on your personal behalf, and so provoke trouble among the subjects by taxes and exactions, exciting their antipathy and neglecting the defense of the country. If you disobey you will be accused. I hope you will obey the order, be careful.

(Did a reason exist for this order and had accusations been made against him?)

1457. Emperor Chin Ti died. Emperor Ying (the liberated emperor) ascended the throne again. Lu Chien pursued and beat Mongol brigands in Chuang Lang. He was promoted to secretary high commandant.

1458. Imperial order of the twenty-fourth of the third moon, informing Lu Chien the secretary commandant:

I, emperor, consider that Hung Ch'eng situated between Lanchow and Chuang Lang, is an important place on account of the passing ambassadors, travelers and traders, and the transportation of grains. You, commandant of Monguor troops, used to defeat and kill brigands and extend your faithfulness, you enjoy the sympathy of your subjects. I order you to choose two groups of soldiers from among the Monguor troops you command or from among the Chinese troops of Chuang Lang, and to move them to Hung Ch'eng, to exercise the cavalry and defend the country. If alarmist rumors are spread, take council with the other commandants. Combine your plans and act accordingly. You will obey the orders of the brigadier general, defender of the country and of other commandants. Try by all means to be honest and just and to become more and more perfect in order to be able to control the subjects better. It is not allowed to bother the inferiors or to use the troops in your personal behalf, be provident in defending the country. If you disobey you will be punished severely. I hope you will obey the order with reverence. This is the purpose of this order.

1459. Lu Chien attacked the Mongol brigands at Wu Chao Lin, killed and captured many. He was promoted to assistant commandant. Imperial order of the twenty-fourth of the fourth moon:

Lu Chien, secretary commandant defender of Hung Ch'eng, Mongol brigands incessantly invade the country. You are capable of combining plans and killing them, your faithfulness and zeal are worth praises and admiration. By special favor I promote you to assistant commandant. As before, you will defend the country with zeal, in order to display your gratefulness and make the country peaceful. This is the aim of this order.

1461. Wang Pai made an inroad in the country of Liangchow. Lu Chien with his troops beat him and put him to flight.

1463. The Tibetan Huang-tu-erh tribe revolted. Lu Chien quelled the revolt and pacified the country.

Imperial order of the fifth of the twelfth moon:

Lu Chien assistant commandant and defender of Hung Ch'eng, as before Tibetans incessantly make inroads and plunder. The eunuch Meng T'ai, General Wei yin, Wu Cheng, and others assembled to devise means either to induce them to submission or to exterminate them. I received the report of Meng T'ai. You will inquire which among the tribes causes troubles, and how many horse troops will be required for an expedition against it. You will submit your plan with the minutest details. At the arrival of the imperial order you will immediately choose and move the troops in full number, prepare the weapons and provisions. Each of the commandants will have to assume his responsibilities. Have council with them, related to the date to start the expedition, the way to follow, and the place where they will fight. You will wait until the arrival of the fixed date and move according to orders you will receive from Meng T'ai, Wei yin, Wu Cheng, and others. Expend your forces unanimously, pursuing the Tibetan brigands either to exterminate them or to induce them to submission and pacify the country. It is strictly forbidden to have discordances among you, and to let slip away favorable opportunities. I hope you will endeavor to obey the order. This is the aim of the order.

Emperor Ying Tsung died. Hsien Tsung ascended the throne.

Imperial order of the twenty-eighth of the second moon to Lu Chien, assistant commandant and second captain in Hung Ch'eng:

At the beginning of my accession I consider your zeal and fulfillment of your office. I have to be generous according favors. I hope you will respond to my grand sentiments, exercising more and more your faithfulness and sincerity in the office I entrust to you. This is the aim of the order.

The emperor sent a gift of 200 taels and the lining and facing of silk gowns.

In the winter the Tibetan Huang-tu-erh tribe revolted again. Lu Chien quelled the revolt and pacified the country.

1465. Lu Chien on account of his merits was promoted to high commandant, piao-ch'i general, Shu-tu-tu Ch'ien-shih with the function of lieutenant colonel of the left, defender of Chuang Lang.

Imperial order of the twenty-eighth of the fifth moon:

Lu Chien, high commandant, according to the decision of my councilors you are capable of combining plans and you are courageous and you have already defended Chuang Lang. Immediately at the arrival of the order, with 400 officers and soldiers you commanded before, foot and horse, Monguors and Chinese, move to Chuang Lang to defend the country, exercise the troops, repair the city walls to prevent attacks of the brigands. If alarms are reported, act according to the conditions. As formerly you will have to obey the orders of the commandant in chief of Kansu. Each time you will have to discuss the circumstances and together with the high commandant Chao Yin arrive at a decision before moving. Do not obstinately cling to your own ideas, resisting stubbornly and harming the country. Be honest and just, amend your shortcomings in order to control better your inferiors. It is not allowed to use officers and troops by imposing corvées in your own interest, and so neglect their military training and the defense of the country. It is not permitted to indulge in your whims toward your inferiors and disturb the people by taxes and exactions. If you disobey these rules you will not be forgiven. I hope you will obey reverentially. This is the aim of the imperial order.

In the eighth moon, three moons later, the imperial order was sent:

Lu Chien, high commandant and defender of Chuang Lang, today reports have been sent by official defenders of Shensi province, informing that the brigand Liu Ming-hai mustering his troops invaded the country to a large extent, plundering and ravaging Ku Yuan and P'ing Liang districts. This brigand formerly has been the scourge of the country, intermittently making inroads starting from Ho T'ao. I ordered the eunuch P'ai Tang and the officials Yang Sui and Kung Chung and others to exterminate his group. Now he has become more and more audacious. Troops have to be mobilized to attack him in combination and exterminate him. Already orders are issued to the defenders of the frontiers in Yenan, Sui Te and Ninghsia to have ready horse and foot troops, to inquire about the way the brigand will take to return to his den, to organize among the commanders a communication service by means of flying couriers and to devise plans to intercept his escape route and kill him.

Receiving the imperial order, you must instantly mobilize foot and horse troops. Some among you must guard the borders of the Yellow River, separated in groups, in order to impede his crossing the river. The others have to set ambushes at strategic points obstructing his course and kill him. If you can devise other strategems it is permitted to discuss them together and put them in operation. I have been informed that the brigand disposes of 10,000 reserve troops, which in Ho T'ao block the way to the Oirats. Because elders and children follow the troops, their movements could be hampered and you may seize this opportunity to act. Care for my orders and obey. This is the aim of the order.

One moon later on the sixth of the ninth moon was received the order:

Lu Chien, high commandant and defender of Chuang Lang: the autumn is quickly passing, grass and bushes are dry, it is the suitable time to burn them and lay naked the country in order to observe better from afar the movements of the enemy.

When you receive the order, immediately dispatch groups of intelligent officers and soldiers, who according to the old customs set on fire the country outside the frontiers, when the wind blows suitably. Burn entirely naked the country along which the invasions are usually made in order to hamper the hiding of the enemy in the bushes and the setting of ambushes. Send intelligent scouts to the four corners of the country to spy on the movements of the enemy. If some rumors are heard, move instantly and act according to the conditions. Be extremely careful to avoid errors, note the burned areas, and the number of officers and soldiers entrusted with the task and send a report. I hope my order will be executed with the utmost care. This is the aim of the imperial order.

1468. Lu Chien put to flight and exterminated the brigands of Man Ssu in Ku Yuan. Imperial order of the sixth of the eighth moon:

Lu Chien, assistant chairman at the military headquarters, I order you to defend the country of Chuang Lang as before, to train the Monguor and Chinese foot and horse officers and soldiers, repair the walls of the city, to be kind to the officers and soldiers, to prevent invasion. If alarms are reported, act after deliberation with the commanders. You will continue to obey the orders of the commandant in chief and other defenders of the country. In commanding soldiers do not indulge in whims, impose corvées, taxes, and exactions and provoke their antipathy. If you do not obey, the fault will not easily be forgiven. I hope you will receive the order with reverence and not be remiss. This is the aim of the order.

Imperial order of the twenty-first of the eighth moon:

Lu Chien, commandant in chief and defender of Chuang Lang: the burning of dry grass and bushes is of the utmost importance to defend the country. Recently it was reported that my orders had not been executed carefully. The Mongol brigands are able to approach the frontiers, feigning to graze their herds. They may easily make inroads and ruin the people. At present I will not press for more investigations. However, the autumn is progressing, the grass and bushes are dry. It is the suitable time to burn them to have a wide view. On arrival of the order correct your remission, think of the security of the country and the invasions of the brigands. Choose some armed troops, send them outside the frontiers, conducted by centurions, chiliarchs, and commandants. Use scouts to inquire about the movements of the cavalry of the brigands, and their invasion routes. Along the routes burn naked the country when the wind blows suitably, as far as three to five days distant. Carefully burn the country at the passes and around the garrisons. When this has been executed report the name of the officers and soldiers who were charged with the duty. It is not permitted to disobey and to be remiss.

1472. Po Lu Hu and Pei Chia Sse Lan invaded the country. Lu Chien defended Yenan and Sui Te, and beat and pursued the brigands on the way to An Ting. On the way back he put to flight brigands at Huan Hsien and Ch'ing Yang Fu.

Imperial order of the fourteenth of the second moon:

Lu Chien, defender of Chuang Lang: Recently the Mongols Po Lu Hu and Pei Chia Sse Lan, who live in Ho T'ao and who made several inroads in the frontier regions, plundered the region again. In order to end this calamity and save the lives of the people, troops must be mobilized and the brigands exterminated. Immediately, deliberate with the commandant-in-chief and chairman of the military headquarters and other officials. In Chuang Lang choose 1,500 horsemen of the imperial army and 2,000 among those who are not in service at present. You yourself must command them, to control their number and weapons, to train them according to the military art and follow the orders of Wang Yueh, supreme commandant of the expedition. Move to the fixed place in groups or all together, and, uniting your forces, try to be victorious. It is not permitted to hesitate, to disobey orders, to be remiss. It is not permitted to not dare to advance, to draw back and let slip suitable opportunities. I hope you will endeavor to obey.

1474. Imperial order of the sixteenth of the first moon:

Lu Chien, commandant-in-chief and defender of Chuang Lang, the high commandant Hsuan Yü reports: According to the saying of the people who came back from the Mongols, Man Tu Lu and Po Lu Hu cross the river in the east, Pei Chia Sse Lan will cross in the north. Pei Chia Sse Lan is a shrewd brigand of the northwest. In case he crosses and goes northward, be sure he will ravage your country.

At the moment you receive the order, organize and muster your cavalry instantly, watch the strategic points, block the roads of the brigands, and kill them. Do not hesitate a moment or let slip a favorable opportunity. If you disobey you will be punished. I hope you will look at the order with reverence. This is the reason for the order.

Imperial order of the fifteenth of the eleventh moon:

Lu Chien, assistant chairman at the military headquarters (a title) and defender of Chuang Lang: the high commandant Hsuan Yu reports news of the commanders of the six commanderies of Tat'ung: the ninth of the eleventh moon, seven Mongol horsemen destroyed the great wall and crossed the frontier, shot arrows and wounded soldiers. From Pien Ti Ku it is announced that since the sixth of the tenth moon, much smoke and many tents are seen in the far distance in the northwestern direction. It seems that Pei Chia Sse Lan mustered his troops and is camping near the frontiers in order to invade and plunder the country. We have to be ready to resist the brigands. The New Year is not far away. I fear that some commandants might be remiss in their duty on account of the New Year festivities, that some might impose corvées on the soldiers, send them outside the frontiers to collect fuel, and have hunting parties to provide meat for New Year's, thereby tempting the brigands to make a sudden inroad. The losses suffered would be heavy.

I order you to control strictly the troops, to enforce the day and night watches, to keep the troops in full strength, to sharpen the weapons just as if the enemy were in front of you. When the enemy starts the invasion, inform the commandants and act according to the circumstances, attack the enemy, or consolidate the city walls, or burn the surrounding country to dispel amongst the enemy the temptation to make inroads. Try to resist the enemy and to insure the peace. I hope you will carry out your duty, remembering that peace cannot be enjoyed by taking it easy. To be entrapped in the snares of the enemy will not be forgiven. Use prudence. This is the reason for the order.

1475. An imperial order enjoins the local officials to build an honorific arch in front of the mansion of Lu Chien. The emperor sent the inscription to manifest his affection toward him. It reads: "During his life he confirmed his faithfulness and sincerity, incessantly he exercised devotedness and zeal."

1480. Lu Chien was promoted to lieutenant colonel and defender of Hsining. Imperial order of the thirteenth of the fifth moon:

Lu Chien, assistant chairman at the military headquarters (a title not a function), I order you to fulfill the function of lieutenant colonel. You will still care for the defense of Chuang Lang and assume at the same time the defense of the country of Hsining.

You will train Chinese and Monguor foot and horse, repair the city walls, deal with officers and soldiers with kindness, prevent inroads of brigands. In time of alarm act according to the circumstances. You will still obey the orders of the commandant in chief and the Governor of Kansu. You will be honest and just, amend your shortcomings in order to command more effectively your inferiors. Do not use troops for your own interests, imposing corvées for your private use, impeding the military training and the defense of the country. Do not indulge in whims in commanding inferiors, imposing taxes and exactions in order to avoid complaints. In case you disobey, the fault will not easily be forgiven. I hope you will receive the order with reverence and be attentive. This is the aim of the order.

1481. To Lu Chien was granted a piece of red silk woven with red colored silk thread, also a piece of satin with dragon designs to make a gown, facing and lining included. He was promoted to vice-commander in chief of the left.

1483. An imperial order informed Lu Chien:

Today I, by special favor, promote you to be vice-commandant in chief of the left in Kansu. I received reports of the defenders, officials of Yenan and Sui Te. On the tenth moon they had spied on the Yu Yang valley at the foot of the Ching mountains and the vicinity. On the northern borders of the river numerous rows of tents and smoke were seen. To be sure, Mongol brigands are camping there. Now the river is frozen and may be crossed everywhere; it is difficult to believe that they will not invade the T'ao (Ordos) country. The report was sent to the ministry of war which, after deliberation, ordered him to notify the officials residing along the river, and especially those near the Ho T'ao regions, to mobilize the troops for the defense of the country.

After receiving the order of the ministry of war, send a report concerning your proposed execution of the order and then act according to the next order. Organize the troops under your command, train foot and horse, defend vigorously the cities and passes and the watchtowers situated along the roads from which dangers are signaled. The troops, day and night, must keep watch intensively. If brigands cross the river then the commandants will inform each other by means of flying couriers. According to the circumstances, take the offensive or stay on the defense and send a report by couriers. It is allowed to move troops according to the circumstances which develop. It is not permitted to sit, wait and see, and let favorable opportunities slip away. Offensive or defensive actions depend upon the officers of the frontiers, but plans have to be discussed before the invasion of the brigands in order to be ready to put to flight and kill the enemy and pacify the country. I know you are capable of doing that. This is my desire. I hope you will receive with reverence the order.

On the first of the seventh moon was received the order:

Centurion Lu Lin, by special favor I order you to command the officers and soldiers in Chuang Lang, in the way of your ancestors. Your ancestors controlled the country and enjoyed the sympathy of the people. Deal with the people with kindness, train the troops, repress the brigands. At the time of alarm you must obey the orders of the defenders of Kansu province and then move the troops. Later, when you have merited it, I will promote you according to the rules. You must not consider the troops as belonging to you personally (and not to the empire), impose corvées and trouble the people, indulge in whims, retain the salary of the troops, be unjust, alienate the sympathy of the people, or neglect the defense of the country. If you disobey, it will be easy to know who is responsible. Receive with reverence my order. Be not remiss. This is the aim.

1484. Imperial order of the third of the second moon:

Lu Chien, vice-lieutenant colonel, assistant chairman of the military headquarters of Kansu, I ordered Fan Chin to act as lieutenant colonel and defender of the country. Always act in concert with him, devise plans together, and act after they have been fixed. Never be stubborn as to your own ideas or waste opportunities. I inform you in a special way to keep the seals for the time being, and the tablets (which allow free entrance at court) which Wang Yu has received before. On the arrival of Fan Chin deliver them to him. This is the reason for the order. Your son, the centurion Lu Lin, has received promotion as commandant of the Monguor troops.

1486. Lu Chien was promoted Pacificator General of the Mongols and vice-chairman at the military headquarters of the left army.

Imperial order of the seventh of the third moon:

Information for the vice-chairman at the military headquarters of the left army, Lu Chien. Today I deliver to you the seal of general pacificator of the Mongols (a mere title) and the function of commandant in chief for the defense of the country of Yenan and Sui Te. Defend vigorously the cities, train the troops. In case of alarm, according to the circumstances, exterminate the brigands. The vice-lieutenant colonel, the lieutenant colonel, and others will obey you. Defend the country and the officers and soldiers will obey your orders.

Imperial order received the nineteenth of the fifth moon:

Lu Chien commandant in chief of Yenan, and Sui Te, vice-chairman at the military headquarters. I received from the defending officials of Tat'ung the report: two divisions of Mongol brigands numbering probably 10,000 men have been seen in the region of Wei-Ning and Hai Hsi. South of T'o La Ch'eng the brigands advance, plundering, forming a line as long as 70 li. They probably passed as far as 10 li from the garrisons on both sides of the Ta Ho River. I sent the report to the ministry of war and received the answer that already orders have been delivered to all the officials to mobilize the troops and to be ready strongly to resist the invaders. When we consider that these brigands had decided in T'o Yen San Wei, to make an invasion at the time the new grass is growing, and that now they are camping near the frontiers, we may more or less guess their intention. However, it is hard to see through their duplicity. They claim they will invade the east and plunder the west, so we have to order each frontier region to keep ready.

When the order arrives, transmit instantly to your inferiors, the instructions received, prepare sufficient provisions in each village and city, instruct the vice-commandant in chief, the lieutenant-colonel and other commandants to choose troops inured to war, to feed the horses so they will be fat and strong, and examine the quality and number of the weapons. Strictly order the soldiers caring for the watchtowers to send the signals on time. Use intelligent scouts, teaching them to inquire day and night about the conditions of the country, and if they really see the brigands move their tents and approach the frontiers and seeming to prepare for an invasion, according to the news, immediately deliberate with the commandants, devise plans, dispose the troops, intercept the route of the invaders and kill them. At that time the commandants must be with their troops directing the operations and disposing the battle. The plans and the orders must be kept strictly secret. Make the victory sweeping and complete. Press the preparations. Such tremendous responsibility is entrusted to you by the court. Receive the imperial order with reverence. This is the aim.

Imperial order of the seventeenth of the seventh moon: the same textually as those of 1466 and 1470 concerning the burning of grass and bushes.

Imperial order of the eigtheenth of the tenth moon:

Lu Chien: Today it is reported from Hsuan Fu that in the region of Yu Wei the brigands plunder the people, that six divisions of horsemen of T'o-lao-han-chih-t'o, marching in the western direction, move to the Chin Shan regions to camp. It is also reported that the troops of Hsiao Wang-tse have left the sand dunes moving toward Hsing Ho in a western direction. From Kansu it is reported that Wa la ha prepared a big army, and that Prince Ti ha li ku to wu and their scouts spy on the frontier regions. The five Tat'ung armies, according to the orders, will have to defend vigorously the passes in Ninghsia, Yenan, and Sui Te. Now the weather is cold, the ground frozen, the horses fat and strong. It is time for the brigands to make inroads. Our troops have to be vigilant, all the more because the New Year's festivities are not far off. Some among them like the New Year's festivities. Some use the troops for hunting parties and for collecting fuel, and in that way tempt the brigands to make inroads. Then the suffering of the people will be tremendous. At this time troops have to be commanded with severity, day and night they have to watch just as if the brigands were in front of them. They have to receive training and sharpen the weapons. As long as the brigands are few in number, try to put them to flight and beat them. When the group is important immediately send couriers with the news to each other, block their roads and kill them, or set ambushes and attack them. You are allowed to send troops where the danger is imminent to help each other. I hope you will fulfill your duty carefully and will not hope to gain victories barricading the city gates, sitting at ease protected by the city wall. If the country is ravaged then we will find out the culprits. This is the aim of the order.

Imperial order of the thirteenth of the eleventh moon:

Lu Chien, today I received the report of several commandants of Kansu that several groups of brigands commanded by Wa-la are camping around Hami and plan an invasion in the frontiers, and also that Uighurs (Yellow Mongols) have stolen cattle and killed people in Ch'ih Chin region and are moving eastwards. The Mongol brigands deceived us many times and their inroads are intermittent. Every year when the river is frozen they invade the country of the three commanderies. Several times they made unexpected invasions in Ho T'ao, parted into several groups, and plundered. All our precautions to defend the country have been useless most of the time. When you receive the imperial order, act according to the orders issued in former times, discuss together plans and attack together and beat the brigands. Lu Chien, send your orders to the vice-commandant in chief, the lieutenant colonel, and the commandants who share the defense of the country to muster the troops, and to prepare the weapons. Use scouts to spy in the country day and night and send to each other news about the movements of the brigands. According to the circumstances prepare to combat them in concert, to resist and kill them. If beating their vanguard you obtain a small victory, do not permit your troops to come home and let slip the opportunity to obtain a complete victory. I hope you will endeavor to the utmost to comply with the orders.

Your son has been promoted to be secretary high-commandant on account of his merits.

1487. Imperial order of the sixteenth of the first moon:

Lu Chien, I received today the report of the eunuch Ao Hsien and other defenders of Shensi announcing that Mongols from Kokonor invaded the country of Ho Chou and Lanchow and are still camping in the Chuang Lang region. I ordered Brigadier General Peh Wang to intercept their route and kill them. Ao Hsien is on the way to clear the situation. Yenan and Sui Te are very near to the invaded countries. According to the imperial orders enjoin the vice-brigadier general, the lieutenant colonel, and other commandants to muster their troops and proceed in full haste where the brigands are plundering, to help Peh Wang and other commandants. Discuss the plan of concentrating the forces. Frighten the brigands, inflict on them a crushing defeat and make them flee back to their country. You are capable of doing that. In case you hesitate and let slip the suitable opportunity, the law is there (to punish you). Receive the imperial order with reverence. This is the aim of the order.

1488. Lu Chien begged permission to retire. The retirement was accorded. The favor was granted to honor posthumously his ancestors of three preceding generations with titles bestowed upon him.

FIFTH GENERATION: LU LIN

1489. Imperial order of the sixth of the fourth moon:

Secretary high commandant Lu Lin, by special favor I granted this promotion, more important than the previous one. You will control all the Monguor families in Chuang Lang. Since your ancestors successively have controlled the country the people have been happy. Try to deal with the people with more kindness and make them happier. Try to acquire more perfectly the military arts in order to stem better the inroads of the brigands and make the people suffer less. When alarms are reported, you have to obey the orders of the official defenders of Kansu and accordingly mobilize your troops and kill the brigands. Do not indulge in stubbornness and laziness. Consider that the troops belong to the empire. Do not impose upon them corvées and taxes in your behalf, avoid exactions, do not indulge in whims or retain the salary of the troops. Avoid injustices. Do not provoke the antipathy of the people and neglect the defense of the country. If you disobey, the culprit will easily be detected. I hope you will receive the order with reverence. This is the aim.

1490. Imperial order of the twelfth of the second moon informing Lu Lin about his transfer to Hung Ch'eng: the same text as that of 1458.

1491. Lu Lin was promoted to assistant commandant in Hung Ch'eng Tze.

1494. Lu Lin was promoted to Yu Chi general, to put to flight the brigands in Yung Ch'ang. Imperial order of the eleventh of the second moon:

Lu Lin, I order you to become Yu Chi General in Kansu, command the officers, choose 2,000 soldiers, examine their number, horses and weapons, camp in Yung ch'ang on the western highway (to Turkistan), train the troops and stimulate their morale. When the brigands invade the country confer with the vice-commandant in chief, Lieutenant Colonel Yen Yu about intercepting the brigands and killing them, and the pacification of the country. It is forbidden to flee with fear, causing calamities in the frontiers. Since you received this promotion by special favor, you have to be more honest than before and perfect yourself in order to deal with your inferiors with humanity, to be more courageous fighting the brigands, and to be equal to the duty entrusted to you. For all questions related to fighting and defense of the country obey as before the orders of the governor. In case you are obstinate in your ideas and do not command the troops according to the rules, and lack severity and neglect the condition of the frontiers, the fault will be ascribed to you. I hope you will endeavor to obey. This is the aim of the order.

1496. Lu Lin loaned his troops to Liangchow officials to put to flight and defeat the Mongols at the foot of the Chin mountains.

1499. In combination with Liu Sheng, Lu Lin made the expedition in Chieh Chou. He captured prisoners and sent them to the capital. He received the reward of the official Man p'ao dress (with dragon designs).

1500. Lu Lin was promoted to be lieutenant colonel and defender of Chuang Lang. Imperial order of the eighth of the fifth moon:

Lu Lin, assistant high commandant, I order you to fulfill the duty of lieutenant colonel of the left and to defend Chuang Lang and other places, train Chinese and Monguor foot soldiers and cavalry, repair the city walls and prevent the inroads of brigands. At the time of alarms, according to the circumstances, take the offense or stay on the defense and pacify the country, in order that the people might attend to their duties. You are capable to do that. In all military matters obey as before the orders of the commandant in chief, the governor and defenders of Kansu, and after that mobilize your troops, avoid being obstinate in your ideas and resisting your superiors. Do not be lazy and provoke calamities in the country. Be honest and just; perfect your shortcomings in order to be more capable of commanding inferiors. Do not use the troops in your own interests and hinder their training and the defense of the country.

In case of disobedience your fault will not easily be forgiven. Receive the order with reverence. This is the aim of the order.

I promote you to be vice-commandant in chief of the left, and order you to defend Chuang Lang.

Imperial order of the twenty-sixth of the twelfth moon:

By a special favor I promote you to be vice-commandant in chief of the left and defender of the country of Kansu. Especially you will protect the highway between Kanchow, Suchow, Shan Tan, and Yung Ch'ang. In case of alarm go to the rescue, order the troops to repair the cities, the walls, and the passes, prevent and resist invasions, control Tibetans and barbarians with kindness. All military affairs concerning barbarians have to be discussed with the commandant in chief, the governor, and other commandants of the country, and then executed. Do not be obstinate, quarrel among yourselves, and act contrary to the decisions.

Be honest, just, considerate, and accommodating in dealing with the affairs of the frontiers. I hope you will fulfill the assignment correctly. Avoid the imposition of taxes and exactions, and the complaints of the people. Receive the imperial order with reverence. This is the aim of the order.

1501. Lu Lin put brigands to flight and defeated them in Wei Chou. His son Lu Chin was promoted to be centurion.

1502. Sire Lu Chien died. When his death was announced he was awarded posthumously the title of Yung-lu Ta-fu, pillar of the empire, and chairman of the left at the military headquarters. By special favor Li Shih, the treasurer of the province of Shensi, was dispatched. The funeral oration at the sacrifice, sent by the emperor, reads:

You received from your ancestors the favor to fulfill military duties; several times you gained merits on the battlefields; incessantly you pacified the frontier regions, and eventually obtained the office of chairman of the military headquarters. By special favor, on account of illness, you were permitted to retire and care for your health.

It is normal to enjoy the happiness of an old age. How did you leave us all of a sudden? This announcement coming from so far grieves us cruelly. On account of your merits we accord you official burial and sacrifices. In case your spirit is still conscious and able to breathe the fragrance of the sacrifices, accept and enjoy them.

Imperial order of the eighth of the fourth moon: he was granted the official burial. The imperial oration at the sacrifice reads:

You have fulfilled the duty of commandant in chief and have been a first rank officer. The luster of your heroic achievements has long glittered. How is it possible that after a short illness you died so fast? The time is fleeting, the time of the burial already has arrived. By special favor we dispatch an official to preside at the sacrifices, as ever our solicitude is beneficial. If your spirits are still conscious, they may enjoy the sacrifices.

On the thirteenth of the sixth moon the hundred mourning days were completed.

1503. The thirtieth of the third moon was the anniversary of the death.

Imperial order of the tenth of the tenth moon:

Lu Lin, assistant high commandant, vice-commandant in chief of the left army, engrossed in the defense of Kansu. I examined your report, reading that your father Lu Chien, dying from illness, had left a great number of troops he commanded and families he controlled. I am fearful that the troops and the families will disperse. You report that your son Lu Chin has received an office very recently, that he is an inexperienced man and incapable of controlling the troops and the families effectively and peacefully. You implore permission to stay temporarily in Chuang Lang to control and pacify the tribes. Your solicitation is urgent. I grant you the request. I order you to stay temporarily in Chuang Lang, to command the officers and soldiers and control the families. Deal with them with kindness and provide them with what they need. Train the troops zealously, resist the brigands. In case of alarm you are permitted to mobilize the troops and kill the brigands as before. Take care of the education of your son so that he may become capable to succeed to the office, acquire some more experience, and become a capable man enjoying the sympathy of the people. I order you to take his place. For long your reputation has been unimpeachable, your achievements on the frontiers are numerous. Later I will promote you to another function. I hope you will receive this order with reverence. This is the aim of the order.

1504. The thirteenth of the fifth moon is the third anniversary of the death of Lu Chien. The mourning is finished. A sacrifice is offered.

The sixth of the tenth moon the imperial order was received:

Lu Chin, having the function of vice-chiliarch, by special favor I order you to command the Monguor officers and soldiers of Chuang Lang as before, and to control the tribes. Your ancestors have administered the country and enjoyed the sympathy of the people. Endeavor to deal with the people with kindness, resist and suppress the brigands. When alarms are reported always obey the orders of the defenders of Kansu and then mobilize the troops. Later, according to your merits and to rules, I will promote you. It is not permitted to consider the troops as being your own. . . . [Then follow the usual recommendations.]

1505. On the fifth moon Emperor Hsiao Tsung died and Emperor Wu Tsung ascended the throne. Imperial order of the fourth of the ninth moon:

Lu Lin, assistant high commandant, and vice-commandant in chief of the left army, I have received information concerning the intermittent inroads of Mongol brigands in Chuang Lang country. The appointed defender, Lieutenant Colonel Su T'ai, is not sympathetic with the people and many affairs are neglected. I appoint the vice-commandant in chief, Pa Tsung, to the function of defender. Your whole life long, since the time of your ancestors, you have considered the defense of the frontiers as the most important duty. The capacities of your son Lu Chin have increased with the years, his education is achieved, it is time for him to gain merits, defend the empire, and continue the traditions of the family. Every time you meet incursion of the brigands, feeling in the same way as Pa Tsung, join your forces and combine together the plans. Order your son and the reliable chiefs of the tribes to command and mobilize the troops and to attack the brigands in combination with Pa Tsung, or to stay on the defense according to the circumstances, and make the people enjoy peace. The day he will have gained merits, promotions will be granted generously. Let him not sit and wait and see, avoid moving and neglect the duty entrusted to him. This is the aim of the order.

1506. When the death of Lu Lin was announced, the posthumous title of secretary chairman of the military headquarters of the left army was granted to him. The provincial treasurer of Shensi, Lieutenant Colonel Chu Tsai, was delegated with the favor of three sacrifices, according to the rites.

SIXTH GENERATION: LU CHIN

Lu Chin succeeded. He repelled the brigands in Hung Ch'eng Tse.

1507. Lu Chin was promoted to be secretary chairman of the military headquarters and received the seal of Chao Yung Chiang-chun.

Imperial order of the twelfth of the fourth moon:

Lu Chin, secretary high commandant, after the death of your grandfather Lu Chien, you commanded the Monguor troops of Chuang Lang and controlled the tribes. The people were sympathetic to you during the lifetime of your father, you replaced him to command the troops with the title of vice-chiliarch. Now you succeed to the duty of your father with the title of high commandant. Because your title is of the same degree as that of the officers of the tribe, and because you accompanied your father in the expeditions in Ninghsia and other places, killed many brigands and accumulated many merits on the battlefields, I promote you. You will, as before, command the same officers, soldiers, and tribes. Endeavor to console and help the people, incessantly repel the brigands, and train the soldiers. For important affairs and mobilization of troops, obey the orders of Chang Hsun and other commandants of Kansu. Later I will be generous, rewarding your merits. Respond to the special favors granted to you, and increase the luster of faithfulness and zeal specific to your family. Be honest and just and devoted to the empire. Do not consider the troops as belonging to you, do not impose corvées and taxes, urge discipline among the officers. Do not be exacting with the people and alienate them from you. Do not neglect the defense of the empire. If you disobey, the fault will be punished. I hope you will comply with the orders with reverence. This is the aim of this order.

In the seventh moon in concert with Lieutenant Colonel Wu Yun, Lu Chin defeated the brigands in Ming Shui Hu and was promoted to be assistant high commandant.

1508. Imperial order of the twenty-ninth of the twelfth moon:

Lu Chin, assistant high commandant, succeeding to your grandfather, you commanded in his place the Monguor troops of Chuang Lang, and controlled the tribes. You received promotions on account of your merits. Now on account of your merit in Ming Shui-hu, attested by the military inspector, I confirm your previous promotion. [Then follow textually the same recommendation as in 1507.]

1509. Imperial order of the nineteenth of the fourth moon: Lu Chin reports that Mongol brigands plundered and ravaged Hui Hui Mu, that he attacked and repelled them and captured a huge booty of cows, horses and weapons.

1510. Imperial order:

Lu Chin, I received your report together with that of the eunuch Sung Lin and the defenders of Kansu, informing me that on the twelfth and the following days of the first moon, Mongol brigands invaded P'o Shan Ku, that together you attacked and beat them, beheaded 158, captured a booty of 160 camels and horses, flags and many weapons. For many years we have not met such a big victory. It proves that you have been courageous and that the Monguors obeyed the orders of their chiefs. Inquire about the merits of the officers and soldiers, about the wounded and the dead, and according to the rules reward them. I give an imperial order, praising and stimulating your zeal. I hope you will endeavor to. . . . This is the aim of the order.

In the sixth moon he repelled the brigands at T'ung Yuen P'u.

1511. Lu Chin was promoted to be lieutenant colonel of the left army, and entrusted with the defense of Chuang Lang.

Imperial order of the twelfth of the third moon:

I promote you lieutenant colonel of the left army and defender of Chuang Lang. Train the soldiers, etc. [Textually the same recommendations concerning the behavior of the commandants follow.]

1512. The Mongols (I pu la of Kokonor) invaded the Hsining region again. Lu Chin defeated them in Ma Ch'ang Ku. He received the title of secretary chairman at the military headquarters, the official dress adorned with dragon designs, the jade cincture.

In the ninth moon he defeated the brigands in Pei Shih Ch'uan.

1514. He defeated brigands at Shih erh Miao.

1515. Tibetans in Ch'a K'u I plundered the imperial ambassadors. Lu Chin pursued and defeated them at Sha Chin Ku, and recovered the tribute stolen from the ambassadors. He received the title of assistant chairman of the military headquarters and defender of Chuang Lang and Hsining.

In the winter the Tibetans of the Huang-t'u-erh tribes plundered the tribute brought to the emperor. Lu Chin beheaded their chief at Hua Shih Ku, captured horses and came back.

1517. Lu Chin repelled Mongol brigands at Ma T'u Ho and was granted silver and pieces of silk.

1519. The emperor sent the eunuch Chao Lin with gifts, among them the Ta Ming Hui Tien and Ming Lien Ta Tien, also a gown adorned with dragon designs, jade cincture, the equipment of a horse, and a golden box containing precious stones.

1520. Mongol brigands invaded La Shan Shui Ku. Lu Chin repelled them and captured a great number of camels and horses.

1521. Mongols invaded the Chuang Lang region. Lu Chin's son Tan repelled them. In the fourth moon Emperor Wu Tsung died and Shih Tsung ascended the throne. Lu Chin because of illness implored for permission to retire. The court refused and ordered him to defend, as before, Chuang Lang and Hsining, with the titles of assistant chairman of the military headquarters and vice-commandant in chief.

1522. Imperial order of the twenty-first of the first moon:

Lu Chin, by special favor, I order you to fulfill the duty of vice-commandant in chief and defender of Chuang Lang and other places. The second captains of Hsining and Hung Ch'eng Tse must obey our orders. In time of peace train the Chinese and Monguor soldiers, repair cities, etc. Then follow the same injunctions concerning the conduct of the chief. At the end of the order we read: taxes,

revenue affairs, and lawsuits are to be dealt with by the civil officials and not by you. [This phrase seems to open a whole horizon upon the abuses existing in the country at that time.]

He received the title of Yung-lu Ta-fu, assistant chairman of the military headquarters of the vanguard troops. His son Tan was promoted to be vice-centurion.

1524. Imperial order of the fourteenth of the tenth moon:

Lu Chin, assistant chairman of the military headquarters and vice-commandant in chief, defender of Chuang Lang and Hsining, and other places, at present the Mohammedan brigands revolt at Suchow. By special order I sent an eminent official to defeat and exterminate them. I ordered you to choose and mobilize troops and designate the officer commandants of the vanguard. Now I have received your report imploring permission to retire, on account of a petty illness. Considering that during your whole life you practiced faithfulness and justice, that you are renowned for courage and the combination of stratagems, I must use you in these troubled times. How do you dare to seek retirement for a petty illness? I order you to fight the brigands with all your energy, to gain merits and make the country enjoy peace and happiness. This means, comply with the important duty I entrusted to you. An imperial order has been sent to the governor to use Li Yi whom you recommended before. Liu Chia and Chang Wu approved his enrollment in the army. Having merits, he will receive his former duty. I hope you will comply with the orders with reverence. This is the aim of the order.

1525. Imperial order of the seventeenth of the third moon:

Lu Chin, today I received your report that your illness is incurable, that you are unable to command troops, and that you wish retirement. You implore the favor of the appointment of your son as chief of the clan tribes, and of a courageous and capable official to take his place for the defense of the country. All this is a proof that during your whole life you have been devoted to the defense of the country. However, considering your merits and the sympathy of the people toward you, considering that in the Chuang Lang mountains the Mongol brigands of the T'ao, feigning to graze their herds, incessantly make inroads, and that the troops have intermittently to be mobilized to protect the country, how is it possible to want retirement? By special order I praise, stimulate, and honor your devotedness. You must double your energy, faithfulness and zeal, to pacify the country and make the people happy. I hope that, considering the importance of the duty which is entrusted to you, you will comply with the order with reverence. This is the aim of the order.

Lu Chin asked to retire again and to be relieved of the defense of the country.

1527. His son Tan was ordered to control the country with the function of vice-chiliarch.

Imperial order of the twenty-sixth of the tenth moon:

Lu Tan, by special favor I permit you to command the Monguor officers and troops and administer the clan tribes. Your ancestors have, one after another, controlled the country, enjoying the sympathy of the people. Now you will fulfill this duty. Try to console and help the people in such a way that all of them may engage in their businesses. Train the troops incessantly; endeavor to study the military arts; prevent and repel brigandage; do not allow the people to suffer. At the time of alarms obey the order of the commandant-defenders of Kansu; mobilize the troops and kill the brigands; be obedient and do not indulge in laziness. The troops are not yours; do not impose taxes and oppress the people; urge strict discipline among the officers and soldiers; do not neglect the defense of the frontiers. If you disobey you will be punished. I hope you will comply with the order with reverence. This is the aim of the order.

Imperial order of the eleventh of the twelfth moon (Lu Chin, despite the fact he had been permitted to retire, was called again to defend the country):

Lu Chin, assistant chairman of the military headquarters, I order you to defend the country of Shensi, together with the eunuch Yen Yun; to train the troops, console and help the people enjoy peace, repair the city walls, prevent and repel the brigands. For all kinds of military questions combine the plans with the eunuch Yen Yun, the intendant of the circuit, and the military inspector; and execute them after deliberation. Each of the participants at the council has to share his responsibility. At the moment of the execution it is not permitted to cling obstinately to personal views. Lu Chin, I entrust you with the duty to be honest, just, amend your shortcomings, and stabilize peace in the country. Do not indulge in greed for riches and behave unrestrainedly. I hope you will comply with the order. This is the aim of the order.

1529. Mongols invaded Chuang Lang. Lu Tan beat and put them to flight. He was promoted to be secretary chairman at the military headquarters.

1532. Imperial order of the twenty-sixth of the seventh moon:

Lu Tan, assistant commandant: I allow you by special favor to command the Monguor officers and soldiers and to control the tribes. [Then follow the typical injunctions to chief commandants.]

1533. Mongols invaded Ta La T'u Ch'uan and were defeated by Lu Tan.

1535. Lu Tan was promoted to be second captain in Shan Tan. At that time the Mongols moved southward. He asked to move to Chuang Lang.

1536. Imperial order of the thirteenth of the first moon:

To Lu Tan is granted the permission to move to Chuang Lang, command his troops and control the tribes. [Then follow textually the same injunctions given to chief commandants.]

1542. Lu Tan died. He was succeeded by Chang Wu.

1543. Imperial order of the twenty-ninth of the third moon:

Lu Chin, assistant chairman of the military headquarters in Shansi province; I ordered the vice-director and inspector of the ministry of war to cope with the problem. However nobody is able to understand the mentality of the

Mongols and their stratagems. The conditions bode ill. You are an old general of the western frontiers and are conversant with the customs of the barbarians. Your reputation is well known among them, they fear you, you are respected on account of your faithfulness and justice. The troops of Chuang Lang are known for their courage and vigor. I order you to appeal to the governor and obey his orders. Mobilize 3,000 experienced Monguor and Chinese troops of Chuang Lang. The governor general will inspect and care for their helmets, armor, horses and weapons, salaries and provisions. Comply with this order with faithfulness. I will be generous with promotions. Do not pretend illness and miss the opportunity to gain merit. I hope you will comply with the order with respect.

1544. Lu Chin received the order to control the Monguor troops as before. Imperial order of the seventeenth of the tenth moon:

Lu Chin, I have examined your request to retire on account of illness. Already I have ordered your son Tan to command the troops. You beg again to retire. The favor I accorded to your grandfather Lu Chien to command the Monguor troops and control the tribes, I accord to you. Try to console and make happy your subjects, incessantly train the troops, make them understand the military arts, to be capable to resist, capture and kill brigands. In case of alerts you are allowed to mobilize the troops. Do not impose taxes, oppress the people, alienate their sympathy. Care for the education of your son and grandsons, make them understand what is faithfulness, in order that they may succeed you and command the tribes. Your merits on the frontiers are highly celebrated. Care for your health. Later I hope to promote you to another office.

1546. An order was sent to the local authorities to build an honorific arch in order to glorify his merits.

1556. Lu Chin died. His son Tung succeeded him.

SEVENTH GENERATION: LU TUNG

1556. On the third moon, Wang Kuang-tsu, member of the provincial treasury administration of Hsining, was sent with the imperial oration to be read at the sacrifice of Lu Chin.

Lu Chin, you inherited the office of your ancestors and succeeded them. Your talents as general of the troops were well known, and frightened the enemies. You were promoted to be lieutenant colonel. Your zeal and merits were highly celebrated. You were promoted to be first captain in the Chinese army. You begged permission to retire on account of illness. Thereafter I called you to return to defend the country. Your incessant merits caused the country to be at peace. Just at the time I was about to entrust to you important duties, your death was announced. In order to manifest my beneficent affection I grant you sacrifices and official burial. I hope your spirits in the outer world will still be able to enjoy this benefit.

On the twenty-sixth of the third moon, on the return after the burial, a sacrifice was offered.

On the fifteenth of the sixth moon, 100 days after the burial, another sacrifice was offered.

1557. On the fifth of the third moon, a year after the death, a sacrifice was offered again.

1558. On the fifth of the third moon, at the end of the mourning period, a sacrifice was offered.

The treasury administration of Hsining sent Wang Kuang-tsu, with the formula of the imperial oration.

During your life you practiced faithfulness and zeal. You have been promoted to high offices. Your achievements have long been celebrated. How did you die all of a sudden? The time is fleeting, already the time of the interment had arrived. We celebrate your glorious achievements. To the former orations is added a new one and a sacrifice. I hope your spirit is still conscious and able to enjoy them and be consoled.

1560. Imperial order of the second of the eleventh moon:

Lu Tung, assistant high commandant, since your ancestors received the duty to command the troops and administer the clan tribes, the entire country has received the benefit of their protection. You succeeded your father. I order you, according to the rule used by your father, to command the Monguor troops and administer the tribes. [Then follows the same injunctions given to chiefs for the fulfillment of their duties.]

1561. The Mongols made an inroad in the west, and were repelled by Lu Tung.

1563. Mongols invaded the K'ai Ch'eng country. Lu Tung went to the rescue and beat and repelled them.

1564. In the twelfth moon Emperor Shih Tsung died and Mu Tsung ascended the throne.

1568. Imperial order of the seventeenth of the eighth moon:

Lu Tung is promoted to be high commandant. The governor, reporting about the *t'u-ssu* official of Chuang Lang, asked to apply the rules used for the ancestors and to issue an imperial order granting permission to administer the clan tribes, and to help defend the Chuang Lang country with the lieutenant colonel. Each of you must have his administrative bureau for the control of his troops. You will command the Monguor foot and horse troops, and train them unceasingly. In case of alerts, you will, according to the conditions, repel and kill the brigands. According to your merits and to the rules, you will receive promotions and rewards. Relating to the problems involving the lieutenant colonel, you will deliberate with him and make the decision, without clinging obstinately to your views and resisting stubbornly. You will obey the orders of the governor general. Relating to your subjects, provide them with what they need. Relating to the troops, remember they are not yours. Urge discipline among them. Do not impose taxes. Relating to the Tibetan problems, try to solve them yourself. Relating to major Tibetan problems, deliberate with the military administrator and act according to the law. In case of alerts do not sit down with a wait-and-see attitude and let the brigands ravage the country. If you disobey, according to the reports received from your superiors, you will be punished. Receive this order with reverence.

1569. Lu Tung in combination with Lieutenant Colonel Li Shih-wei defeated the brigands at Ho Shih Ku, and a second time at Sse Yen Chin, killing and capturing many.

1572. Emperor Mu Tsung died. Chen Tsung ascended the throne.

1578. Lu Tung, because of illness, asked for retirement. The emperor ordered Kuang Hsien to succeed him. Kuang Hsien soon died.

Imperial order of the second of the seventh moon:

Lu Kuang Hsien, commandant in Chuang Lang, from the time your ancestor administered the troops and the tribes, the entire country enjoyed the benefit of his protection. [Here again follow the injunctions given to chiefs.]

EIGHTH GENERATION: LU KUANG-TSU

Kuang-tsu pacified the Kokonor and was promoted to be secretary chairman at the military headquarters.

1583. Lu Tung died.

1584. Imperial order:

Lu Kuang-tsu, commandant of Chuang Lang, you succeeded your ancestor according to the rules applied to Lu Chin. Command the troops, administer the tribes, make the subjects happy. Our last deliberation orders you to choose among the troops 1,000 Monguor soldiers. Deliberate always with the lieutenant colonel of Chuang Lang. Train the troops. Affairs of marriage, and lawsuits related to land, among the Monguors, may be coped with by you. The appointments of officers of your troops are to be discussed by the military superiors. [Then follows again the usual injunctions given to chiefs.]

1586. Kuang-tsu was promoted to be high commandant and vice-defender of Chuang Lang. Imperial order of the thirteenth of the eighth moon:

Lu Kuang-tsu, from the time you took office the people enjoyed the benefits of your protection. After his inspection of the frontier regions, the inspector recommended that you be given the title of "assistant protector of the Chuang Lang region," in order to insure better the repression of the brigands. The ministry of war approved. By special favor, command your troops as high commandant, care for your 1,000 soldiers. The lieutenant colonel and you will have your own administrative bureau. [Then follows again the usual injunctions to chiefs.]

1587. Imperial order of the nineteenth of the seventh moon: repetition of the order of 1586.

1590. Lu Kuang-tsu was promoted to be lieutenant colonel, and cared for Hsining.

Imperial order of the twenty-sixth of the seventh moon:

Lu Kuang-tsu, vice-secretary high commandant, by special favor you will fulfill the duty of lieutenant colonel, in the capacity of major general, defender of Hsining. Repair the city walls, train the troops, be kind to the Tibetans and Mongols of Kokonor, but watch for the inroads of the northern Mongols whom, according to the circumstances, you must repel. Always cooperate with your superiors and execute their decisions.

Take with you 600 Monguor troops, go to Hsining, and in cooperation with the local troops participate in punitive expeditions and exterminate the brigands. You will be rewarded according to the reports received from your superiors. Be grateful for the distinction received, exercise your faithfulness.

1591. Lu Kuang-tsu was promoted to vice-commandant in chief, and defender of Chuang Lang.

Imperial order of the eighth of the seventh moon:

Lu Kuang-tsu, secretary high commandant, I order you to the office of vice-commandant in chief and defender of Chuang Lang. The questions relating to finances, taxes, lawsuits, and administration of the army belong to the superior officers and the officials directly appointed to collect the taxes and revenues. Do not mix in their sphere of action. [Then follow the same injunctions given to chiefs.]

1592. Lu Kuang-tsu was promoted to vice-commandant in chief of the right, and defender of Liangchow.

Imperial order of the twenty-fifth of the tenth moon:

Lu Kuang-tsu, by special favor, you are promoted to be vice-commandant of the right, and defender of Liangchow. [Then follow the typical injunctions given to the chiefs.]

Peh Pai and Peh Ch'eng-nan, father and son, invaded Ninghsia. Lu Kuang-tsu repelled them. Then in co-operation with Governor Li Yu-jen he participated in the expedition against Peh Pai. The rebels were entrapped in ambushes and killed.

1596. Lu Kuang-tsu received the office of assistant defender of Liangchow.

Imperial order of the twenty-sixth of the third moon:

Lu Kuang-tsu, secretary chairman of the military headquarters, by special favor, I order you, having the title of vice-commandant in chief of the right, to the office of lieutenant colonel and assistant defender of Liangchow. In time of peace, repair the city walls and train the troops, stimulate their ardor, cope with the affairs of the Tibetans and barbarians. In time of alerts, combine plans, fight vigorously and kill the brigands. Do not fear them. Obey the orders of the general-in-chief and the governor, do not mix with the affairs of civil officials relating to finances, taxes, lawsuits and administration of the country. Be honest, just, observe the laws, perfect yourself in order to be better able to command your inferiors. Do not be greedy about riches, impose taxes or corvées, oppress the people, or provoke their complaints. If you disobey, you will be severely punished. Be careful and attentive to the order.

1598. Lu Kuang-tsu, having the title of vice-commandant in chief, I order you to defend T'ao and Ming Chou in Shensi province.

Imperial order of the twenty-sixth of the eighth moon:

Lu Kuang-tsu, secretary chairman of the military headquarters, by special favor, fulfill the duty of vice-commandant in chief and defender of T'ao and Ming Chou, and garrison in T'ao Chou. You are allowed to transfer from one place to another the second captains of T'ao and Ming Chou, train the troops, repair the city walls and the passes. In time of alerts, according to the circumstances, fight and exterminate the brigands. If Mongols of Kokonor invade the country, call to the rescue the troops of Ming Chou and Kung Ch'ang Fu, order the second captains to unite their troops and to fight in cooperation, attacking and exterminating the brigands. After the invaders have been beaten and put to flight, send the troops

back to their garrisons. Do not allow them to stay inactive, waste the salaries and the provisions. Deliberate with the chief commandant of the frontiers of Shensi. The lieutenant colonel and the second captains of Chieh and Wen Chou will obey your orders, and you obey the orders of the commandant in chief of Lin T'ao. At the time of alerts, you are allowed to mobilize the troops on your own account, and repel the brigands. If precautions are required for the defense of the river and the autumn conditions, help the officials of Ho Chou, Hui Hsien and An Ting. Lawsuits between the troops and the people are to be dealt with by the civil authorities. Be honest, just, observe the law, stimulate the ardor of the troops, do not be greedy and unrestrained. Your faults will be severely punished.

1600. Lu Kuang-tsu was promoted to provincial commandant in chief, for the military preparations against Japan, and the training fields of the military headquarters in Nanking.

Imperial order of the seventeenth of the third moon:

Lu Kuang-tsu, secretary chairman of the military headquarters, today by special favor, I order you to be zealous in controlling the military headquarters of the left, and to fulfill the office of commandant in chief of the training fields. You will control conditions in behalf of that ministry and obey its orders. You will command the land and sea forces of the left and control the preparations against Japan. In peace time you will command the officers, stimulate the ardor of officers and soldiers, teach the military arts, make them conversant with battles on the sea, and keep the discipline strict. In time of war, you will command and mobilize according to the circumstances, the troops of Hsi Kiang and the two newly prepared land and sea divisions. According to the rules you will have deliberations with chiefs, and make known the orders to your inferiors. In cooperation with them you will fight the enemy and defend the empire. The army has to be dealt with according to the old rules. Be honest, just, faithful, and courageous in the fulfillment of the office. If you refuse the office, or are remiss, the fault will not be forgiven.

1602. Lu Kuang-tsu begged for permission to retire. It was accorded. Secretary commandant Lu Yung-ch'ang succeeded him and commanded the troops.

NINTH GENERATION: LU YUNG-CH'ANG

1607. Lu Kuang-tsu died on the fourth moon. When his death was announced he received posthumously the title of Kuang-lu-ta-fu and was granted official sacrifices and burial.

1620. Emperor Cheng Tsung died on the eighth moon. Kuang Tsung ascended the throne.

1627. Emperor Hsi Tsung died. Emperor Ch'ung Tsung ascended the throne.

1636. Lu Yung-ch'ang was promoted to lieutenant colonel and assistant defender of Chuang Lang.

1637. Lu Yung-ch'ang was promoted to commandant in chief and defender of Hsining.

1640. Lu Yung-ch'ang defended Hsining acting as vice-commandant in chief. According to his merits, he was promoted assistant chairman at the military headquarters, and received the official dress with dragon designs, and the jade cincture.

1644. The brigand Huo Chin invaded Ho Hsi. Lu Yung Ch'ang fought the brigands, but was defeated. He retreated to Lien Ch'eng and was killed, offering his life for the empire. His son was captured and abducted.

1645. Prince Yin called to submission the people of the two rivers. On account of the faithfulness of Lu Yung Ch'ang, his nephew An was ordered to control the tribes and to command the troops ad interim.

TENTH GENERATION: LU HUNG

1645. On the sixth moon Yang, the concubine of Lu Yung Ch'ang, sent to the emperor the report:

According to the genealogical register the name of our first ancestor is not recorded, by reverence for the emperor. Our first ancestor, T'o Huan, originated from the imperial family of the Yuan dynasty. It is noted that he was Prince of An Ting, and fulfilled the duty of P'ing-chang cheng-shih. On account of the victorious armies of the great Ming dynasty, the ancestor leading his tribe retreated in Ho Hsi. He submitted and received the name of Lu and was appointed hereditary defender of Chuang Lang. This blessing, which has lasted 300 years, thanks to the protection of the ancestors, has been passed on to their descendants. Our desires to be grateful to them have not yet had the opportunity to materialize.

Unexpectedly the brigand Li Tse-ch'eng revolted, occupied the pass of T'ungkuan in Shensi and plundered and ravaged Ho Hsi for the second time. My husband Lu Yung-ch'ang, devoted to the defense of the empire, had resisted the savage brigands valiantly, and had secretly deliberated with the Monguor commandants Ch'i T'ing-chien, Li T'ien-yu and others, to unite their troops and fight the rebels. Who could have guessed that traitors, belonging to eminent families of our tribe, had joined the brigands to steal our patrimony? Cooperating with the brigands, they led them to the country and the country was ravaged. My husband died, killed by the brigands. The son of his first wife was captured and led to Sian as prisoner. To this day we do not know whether he is still living or dead. The subjects of our tribe have been divided among the traitors (just as a melon, sliced in pieces) and our properties usurped. Considering the circumstances in which the brigands have been led here, the people of the city slaughtered, my husband killed, my son abducted, I understand that they aimed at the suppression of the sacrifices for the ancestors, the seizure of our patrimony, and the usurpation of the hereditary lordship over the tribes, which they have appropriated until today.

Fortunately we have met the victorious armies of the emperor, who saves the poor and the destitute people. My husband is killed, my son abducted and the sacrifices to the ancestors completely lack incense. Humbly I dare to think of Lu An, the nephew of the first lady. On account of his youth, nobody among the lamas and laymen of the tribe is sympathetic to him.

I implore the emperor to have sympathy for the faithfulness displayed by my husband, killed by the brigands, to think of the hopelessness of the spirits of the ancestors without support, to permit Lu An to administer effectively the tribe ad interim, to restore the prosperity of our old patrimony, and to offer incense to the ancestors. After Lu Hung has been discovered and comes home, I shall humbly dare to send another supplication. I hope this will be beneficial to the living and provide peace to the dead. The frontier regions again will have faithful defenders, the sacrifices to the ancestors will not be offered by unauthorized men, and will not be rescinded. The genealogical register of the Lu family will not be disturbed.

1648. Imperial order of the twenty-seventh of the fourth moon:

Lu An, commandant of the commandery of Chuang Lang, when the t'u-ssu submitted to the empire during the former dynasties they were promoted to be officials, commanded their Monguor troops and administered their tribes. Lu Yung-ch'ang has been killed by the brigands. It has been proven that you, Lu An, are the nephew of the first lady of Yung Ch'ang; you have implored the court to succeed. By special favor, according to the former rules, I order you to succeed to the hereditary office, to command the Monguor officers and troops, lamas, and the families of the tribes. Receive with reverence the special favor of the new dynasty. Try to comfort and bring peace to the people, to provide them with what they need. Bring concord into the tribe, repel and capture the brigands. When alerts are reported, you are allowed to mobilize your troops and kill the brigands. In major military actions, obey the orders of the governor and general of Kansu. I will promote and reward you according to the rules applied to the Chinese. Try to expend your energy with faithfulness and zeal and be grateful for the favor. Do not consider the troops as belonging to you, do not impose taxes, urge strict discipline among the troops, do not oppress the people and alienate their sympathy. Disobedience will be punished severely. This is the purpose of the order.

1650. Lu Hung returned from Wu Ch'ang.

1659. On the ninth moon Lu Hung succeeded.

1673. Lu Hung died on the eleventh of the third moon. His son Ti Ch'eng succeeded.

ELEVENTH GENERATION: LU TI-HSIN

1674. The revolt of the three ministers shook the country of the two rivers. It was the time of the revolt of Wu San-Kuei. The city of Lanchow was recovered by Chang Yun. The widow of Lu Hung, originating from the Wang family, carried grain to the troops and offered horses. She sent troops to the general in chief of the Hsining troops engaged in quelling the revolt of Hsieh-erh-so. The fact having been reported, the widow received a laudatory imperial order.

1688. Ti Ch'eng, still young and without issue, died on the twenty-first of the first moon. The nephew of Hung, Ti Hsin, succeeded.

1699. Ti Hsin, commanding his troops, beat and put to flight the Jungar brigands.

1718. Ti Hsin asked for retirement. On the ninth moon his son Hua Lin succeeded.

TWELFTH GENERATION: LU HUA-LIN

1719. Revolt in Kokonor of the Tibetan Ta-wa-chien shan pa, Hua Lin participated in the expedition and was promoted lieutenant colonel.

1721. Hua Lin participated in the expedition against the Kuo Mi tribes and saved the garrison of Je Yueh Shan.

1723. Hua Lin, under command of General Nien Keng-yao, quelled the revolt of the Hsieh-erh-so tribes in the region of Chuang Lang. He captured the chief, Ho Mu Shan, and six others, attacked and captured their city of Shih Pao Ch'eng, killed hundreds of brigands and captured sixty. He attacked the Ao Lo tribes and others and accepted their surrender.

1724. In the spring, Hua Lin garrisoned with his troops in Ta Ying Wan; the country was at peace. In the fourth moon under command of General Yueh Chung-ch'i, he captured the remnants of the Tibetan rebels and killed many. In the fifth moon, the revolt of Tibetans was quelled. In the fifth moon by imperial order, the eight Tibetan Hsieh-erh-so tribes were granted to him as his subjects.

In the seventh moon he participated in the expedition with General Yueh Chung-ch'i, against bLo-bzang tan-chin, and was granted silver and pieces of silk.

1730. By imperial order, Hua Lin sent half of his troops to colonize the region of Ch'ih Chin.

1731. On the first moon Hua Lin, on account of his merits, received the emoluments of lieutenant colonel, the peacock plume, the *man p'ao* (dress with dragon designs) and the office of major of the right division of the regular troops in Hsining.

1732. Feng Chu, son of Hua Lin, received the title of lieutenant colonel and colonized the country of Pu Lung Chi and others.

1736. Hua Lin went to the capital. He received the imperial order to fulfill the duty of lieutenant colonel of the cannonier division at Sian. Then he was transferred to Kanchow, with the function of lieutenant colonel of the division for the defense of the city.

1739. Hua Lin received the office of general in chief in Yung Ch'ang, and commandant in chief in Liang-chow.

1742. Hua Lin finished the question of the tributes, offered by the barbarians of the Suchow regions.

THIRTEENTH GENERATION: LU FENG CHU

1744. In the twelfth moon his son Feng Chu succeeded.

1764. The permission to succeed his father was renewed.

FOURTEENTH GENERATION: LU FAN

1765. Fan received with reverence the official diploma of his succession.

1781. On the fourth moon, the Mohammedans of Ho Chou revolted and besieged Lanchow. Fan, commanding his troops, fought in Luan Ku Tung P'ing and was severely wounded. However, he was able to move his troops to Sha Mi Shan, and to block the retreat of the rebels. After the revolt was quelled, he received a laudatory imperial order, the peacock plume with coral button on the cap, pieces of silk and satin, and silver.

1784. On the fourth moon revolt of the Yen Ch'a Hui (Mohammedans) Fan again defended Lanchow, the capital of the province. After the revolt was quelled he received gifts from the emperor, and money to be distributed among the soldiers.

1785. Fan asked for permission to call on the emperor at the capital. The permission was granted. On account of illness he could not move. Again he received silk and satin.

1786. On the tenth of the eleventh moon he called on the emperor. On the twenty-first of the twelfth moon he saw the emperor at the Ying Hua Tien, and was granted the peacock plume and coral button, dresses, and precious trinkets.

1787. On the fifteenth of the eleventh moon, Fan died. His son Chi Hsun being too young to succeed, his mother the noble dame Sun kept the seals (administered the tribes).

1791. The Chinese army fought the Kokonor rebel K'uo Erh K'o. The widow sent a million pounds of fuel for the troops in Donkir.

1792. On the seventh of the first moon an imperial order was received, which reported a letter written by the widow to the emperor.

The Lady Lu Sun, caring for the seals of the t'u-ssu of Chuang Lang, reports: Learning that the army was quelling the revolt of K'uo Erh K'o, I was happy to send a million pounds of fuel for the army. The young t'u-ssu carried the fuel to Donkir. T'u-ssu Lu Fan of Chuang Lang during his life expended his forces participating in punitive expeditions. After the revolt of the Mohammedans was quelled, I rewarded him with the peacock plume. Now the lady Lu Sun, his wife, learning that the troops were fighting the rebel K'uo Erh K'o, prepared and sent a million pounds of fuel to the army. The t'u-ssu lady of the frontiers, understood faithfulness and justice. She is to be praised. I reward her with two pieces of satin. To her son, Chi Hsun, though he is only fifteen years of age, I give permission to succeed to the hereditary office of t'u-ssu, with the title of commandant, and reward him with the peacock plume in order to manifest my beneficial commendation toward you. Receive with reverence this imperial order.

FIFTEENTH GENERATION: LU CHI-HSUN

1797. On the seventh of the eleventh moon, my father was buried in Shang Hsiang T'ang.

1799. On the twentieth of the second moon the noble dame Sun died. She was buried next to her husband in Shang Hsiang T'ang, on the fifteenth of the tenth moon.

1801. On the nineteenth of the first moon was born Chou, the oldest son of the first lady.

1809. Chi Hsun asked through his superior, permission to go and congratulate the emperor at the capital, on the anniversary of his fiftieth birthday. He received

FORT HAYS KANSAS STATE COLLEGE

the report of Huo Tu-t'ung, Governor of Shensi and Kansu provinces.

I received the imperial order, reading "for anniversaries of the fiftieth birthday, the rule of felicitating is not used." No need for him to come to the capital to display his solicitude. Later when the rules of felicitating will be performed, the t'u-ssu may send his supplication to come to the capital, through your hands. Then you will report again, and after deliberation the permission will be accorded. Receive the order with respect.

1819. Imperial order of the seventeenth of the first moon:

Lu Chi Hsun, t'u-ssu of Chuang Lang, asks for permission to come to the capital to present his congratulations, for my anniversary of sixty years of age. It is the proper time and the t'u-ssu desires to come. I agree. According to the rules in former times, the trip of the t'u-ssu to the capital was defrayed by the empire. He will come along the way of the couriers, but notice that I do not order the t'u-ssu and others to come to the capital. I order the t'u-ssu to travel with the T'u-lu-fan, Mohammedan prince of the second degree, and with the Mohammedan prince of the second degree of Hami. They will arrive at Je Ho Erh, on the first of the eighth moon. After having called the emperor, having done the prostrations and presented the congratulations, they will return to Kansu. Receive this order with reverence.

On the nineteenth of the fifth moon Chi Hsun left.

On the tenth of the eighth moon he arrived in Je Ho Erh. On the twelfth he met the emperor in the lion garden. He was granted slices of dry deer meat, spiced with pepper and ginger. On the thirteenth, the emperor was so kind as to accept his two beautiful horses and the products of the country. He accepted them all. Chi Hsun was rewarded with the peacock plume and coral button, the official straw hat, the collar (worn by officials of the fifth degree), the long coat adorned with embroidered breast plates, the dress adorned with dragon designs, silk cinctures, an embroidered purse, a dagger worn at the cincture, a small coat, a long brocade dress, carpets, a horse saddle, and other things.

On the fourteenth he was invited to dinner and to the comedy. He received again a collar made with silk from Ch'ang Chou in Fukien, a purse, a dagger, fringes fixed on the hats, tea, and dry fruit.

On the sixteenth he was again invited to dinner and the comedy, and received a clock and snuff box. On the seventeenth, dinner again and attendance at the comedy, and at the fireworks at night. On the nineteenth he thanked the emperor, and received two pieces of brocade, two pieces of silk from Ch'ang Chou, and six pieces of satin and a piece of dry deer meat. On the twentieth he bade farewell to the emperor. The next day he left for Kansu, with permits from the ministry of war to travel at the expense of the empire, permits for the soldiers of his retinue, and another for the passage of his cars free of toll and taxes. He was back in Lien Ch'eng on the fourth of the eleventh moon.

1824. The Mongol Khoshot, daughter of the Prince of Alashan, arrived to marry, as first lady, Chou, the son of Chi Hsun. Chou was born in 1801.

1826. The Mohammedan Chang Ko Erh revolted in Turkistan and captured four cities. The rebel was captured and brought to the capital.

1828. Imperial order:

Lu Chi Hsun, t'u-ssu of Chuang Lang, enobled with the third degree and peacock plume, our troops have been victorious and you fulfilled many duties imposed by the army. You went to the country of Chung Wei to buy camels for the army, you acted carefully and very quickly, the order was executed with accuracy. This means devotedness to the empire. Lu Chi Hsun, I reward you with the button of the second degree, to manifest my praise and appreciation. Receive the order with reverence.

1829. A revolt broke out in Turkistan again. Lu Chi Hsun was ordered by the viceroy of Shensi and Kansu provinces, and by the bureau of provisions for the army, to buy camels and lead them as fast as possible to the troops fighting in Turkistan. On the ninth moon the revolt was quelled. Lu Chi Hsun asked for permission to go to the capital to thank the emperor. The viceroy requested the permission for him. The emperor agreed. On the twenty-sixth of the tenth moon he started on the trip. On the nineteenth of the twelfth moon he arrived at Peking. On the twenty-third he called on the emperor. From the twenty-fourth until the twenty-ninth he enjoyed dinners with the emperor and attended the comedies. He received food from the emperor.

1830. On New Year's he congratulated the emperor in the T'ai Ho Tien, had dinner, assisted at the ceremonies, and at night enjoyed the comedy on the ice in Ying T'ai. On the fifteenth he enjoyed the illumination at the Yuan Ming Yuan, and was rewarded with the peacock plume, clothes, porcelains, and foodstuffs.

On the nineteenth he thanked the emperor and bade farewell.

On the twenty-eighth he moved back home, with permits from the ministry of war to travel at the expense of the empire, free from taxes and tolls for him and his retinue. On the fifth of the fourth moon he arrived at Lien Ch'eng.

On the twenty-third of the twelfth moon a grandson, Ju Kao, was born to the first lady.

1835. On the twenty-eighth of the ninth moon his oldest son, Chou, died.

SIXTEENTH GENERATION: LU K'UNG-CHAO (CHO)

Cho never succeeded his father and was never a t'u-ssu. There is no reason to call him ancestor of the sixteenth generation. He was born in 1801, married a Khoshot princess from Alashan in 1824, and died in 1835, leaving a son Ju Kao, born in 1830. At that time his father Chi Hsun controlled the troops and administered the tribes, and remained t'u-ssu until his death in 1850.

Then the son of Cho succeeded in 1852. Nothing needing to be said about Cho's achievements, an elegy in high literary style, written by his father, laments his unusual talents and virtues, which had not had the opportunity to be displayed and unfolded.

The style name of Cho was K'ung-chao. He was innately considerate and generous, his hands and face were beautiful, his eyes and eyelashes were as those painted in pictures, he was a blossom of an orchid, a bud of a cinnamon tree. He was a son of a family in which every generation had enjoyed dignities, but did not have the bad habits of sons of rich families. His parents loved him affectionately and severely watched his studies and education. They desired that he should perfect himself by means of literary studies. His desires were not limited by being a pious son only. Growing up he was strict with himself, mortifying himself. He endeavored as Shen Sheng [7] to guard his repute untarnished.

Alas he did not reach maturity, he was a flower not producing fruit (died without having produced achievements).

He was as the flower of the Canna Indica, which all of a sudden appears (and vanishes). Is it not the very nature of the jade tree (tree of science) of his former existence, which forboded that?

Alas, among the weeds (medicinal herbs), which grow all over the world, it is difficult to find (one) which makes you live again.

In some places there are cries of cuckoos (who cry upon the death of their young), but none (among these) are equal to the cries of our grieved heart.

The outer world is confusing, life is uncertain.

It is a pity that my child, as the child Wu of Tse Yun (a precocious child that died at a tender age, lamented by his father Tse Yun), had been a child which lived unhappily until the age of six, but if he had lived, he would have carried on the family lineage and would have carried on great weighty achievements (and have been happy).

He possessed, between his eyes, the horn of Rhinoceros (protuberant bone between the eyes is a token of a bright intelligence, so the child was intelligent). The plumes of the phoenix, who lives near the pool, grow slowly (is said of a child whose literary talents surpass those of his father, so he should have been more intelligent than his father). The rain wanted for the flowers makes them grow in the spring, the shadow of the trees is heavy in the summer, those who have no shelter do not worry on the way (and can sit in the shadow). Creeping plants are capable of protecting their roots. (When we have a son, he may grow (spring), the parents in the middle of their lives (summer) take advantage (of the son), even those who have no shelter (who have no sustenance) do not trouble, for they have a son who will work for them, for the son protects the parents as the creeping plants protect their roots).

This child was an unusual one. At the moment of its birth, men wondered that the color of its afterbirth was purple (token of bright intelligence). When an honorable family has a son, everbody admires the yellowness of his eye brows. Now if we put together all the military and literary dignities of today, and put them all on this child, and think that (such) a child would have continued the line of the family, in which every generation had enjoyed

[7] Shen Sheng, son of Prince Hsien Kung of Chin, was falsely accused by the beloved concubine of his father of having poisoned him. He committed suicide, avoiding having to accuse the concubine and hurt his father, protecting his reputation. Couvreur-Ch'un ch'u and Tso chuan 1: 267–268.

honors, how could it be possible to console such a limitless sorrow?

You, Ju Kao, his son, exert yourself and make great efforts.

1844. Ju Kao married a Khoshot princess of Alashan.

1848. During three generations, the Lu t'u-ssu family married princesses of the Prince of Alashan, prince of the first degree. The wife of Ju Kao was the niece of his mother. After a short time she died during childbirth and her younger sister succeeded as wife to Ju Kao. Both sisters were as flowers blossoming on the parterre of the mirror of Jade.

1850. On the second of the sixth moon Lu Chi Hsun died. He was buried in Hsia Hsiang T'ang on the twelfth of the tenth moon, four months after his death.

1851. On the seventh of the second moon, the wife of Lu Chi Hsun died. She was buried in Hsia Hsiang T'ang.

Here end the printed chronological biographies. Two pages in handwriting have been added, written by the son of Ju Kao, Shu, born to one of his concubines.

SEVENTEENTH GENERATION: LU WAN-CH'ING

1852. Ju Kao ancestor of the seventeenth generation, succeeded on the third of the eleventh moon.

1857. In Lanchow the capital of the province was started with the building of the mint. Ju Kao offered the wood for the construction, and contributed to the building expenses for one year. The viceroy of the province informed the emperor about his generosity. Ju Kao received a laudatory imperial order and the peacock plume of the second degree. On the eighteenth of the eighth moon, the mother of Ju Kao died (the wife of Cho).

1862. The Salar Mohammedans of Pa Yen Jung revolted. Ju Kao was ordered to choose 500 Monguor and Tibetan soldiers and officers, to join the regular army in quelling the revolt of the rebels.

On the eleventh moon the revolt was quelled. An imperial order was sent to the judicial commissioner Yang, to make known to the t'u-ssu officers and soldiers the praises manifested by the emperor for their successful achievement.

1863. Ju Kao was ordered to protect the safety on the routes to the west, and to exterminate the brigands. He was ordered to choose 500 Monguor and Tibetan officers and soldiers and to garrison them in Shan T'an Ch'i Li Ho. Ju Kao was delighted to hear the praises of the military inspectors concerning the high spirits of his troops, their good behavior and regularity, the care for the tents, kettles, weapons, salt, tea, and provisions.

1873. The rebel Mohammedans of Ho Chou and Hsining besieged the city of Hsining. The circumstances were critical. The governor of the province Liu Chin-ch'ing went to the rescue of the city. The river of Tatung was so swollen that boats and rafts could not cross. Ju Kao spent more than 1,000 taels, calling artisans to build a floating bridge with his own wood. The army could reach Hsining in time to save the city.

1874. When the revolt was quelled he was favored by a report sent to the emperor by the viceroy, explaining the circumstances of the rescue of Hsining and the recovering of the subprefecture of Tatung. Ju Kao received a laudatory imperial order and the titles of provincial commandant-in-chief, and of Courageous Patulu.

1876. On the twenty-second of the fifth moon Shu was born to a concubine of Ju Kao. Shu later succeeded as *t'u-ssu,* the first lady having no issue.

1883. Imperial order of the twelfth moon:

Lu Ju Kao, high commandant of Chuang Lang, since the t'u-ssu submitted to the empire, they have unceasingly received official duties, have commanded their troops and administered their tribes. You are the grandson of Lu Chi Hsun. According to the former rules, I order you to succeed to the hereditary office, to command the troops and administer the tribes. (Lu Chi Hsun, his father, had died in 1851. It had been said that Ju Kao succeeded in 1852, but now he received in 1883 the official nomination.) Receive with reverence this unusual favor. Try to comfort your subjects, make them happy, provide for their needs, control your subjects, prevent inroads of brigands. [Then the injunctions continue the same as the previous ones.]

1893. On the twenty-first of the third moon Ju Kao died. My father's style name was Wan Ch'ing, his posthumous title Chen Wei. He is buried in the cemetery of Shang Hsiang T'ang. (Thanks to this text we know that the writer of the additional two pages was Shu, the son of the concubine of Ju Kao who later fulfilled the t'u-ssu office.)

The wife of Ju Kao kept the seals.

1895. The twentieth of the fourth moon Shu succeeded. The wife of Ju Kao died on the eighteenth of the ninth moon.

1897. The eighteenth of the twelfth moon the noble lady was buried at Shang Hsiang T'ang (after two years).

BIOGRAPHIES (LIEH CHUAN)

PREFACE

The name Lieh Chuan started (to be used) with Ssu-Ma Ch'ien. Biographies constitute historical material. Authors in the past did not write biographies for private individuals.

During the Tang dynasty, Han (Yu) Ch'ang-li composed the biographies of Lu Chih and Yang Ch'eng, which were incorporated in the Hsun-tsung-shih-lu. Liu Tsung-yuan composed the biography of Tuan T'ai-wei. He did not call it "chuan" but "chuang" (memoir). Li Ao composed the Chuan of Lu T'an, but Fang Pao scorned him.

Since the historians had lost their original profession, those appointed in the bureau of the archives became the disciples of T'an Pai-lu (and no longer composed biographies). From that time on the people were compelled to compose their family biographies themselves, to fill this want. Then, among the vulgar were people who liked to spend money to glorify their ancestors (by means of biographies). Those, among those scholars, who liked to profit from their wealth, tucked up their sleeves to write. They filled pages with falsities and errors, so that their writings were untrustworthy.

In our family, from the Ming time on, each generation took up arms to defend the frontiers, our women and girls ardently practiced love for the country and justice in order to glorify (the country). However, the official history of the Ming did not record their deeds.

In what was recorded in our family history some events were confusing. Again we added (new facts) and eliminated (others). We followed the rules of the biographies in order to provide secure material to the official historians in the future. We dared not add (falsities), embellish (the facts), or deceive (the people), in order not to defile the glory of the anterior generations, and provide the descendants a text whose veracity may be checked.

We start with the third section which contains biographies.

SIRE T'O HUAN, THE ORIGINAL ANCESTOR

Sire T'o Huan was a member of the imperial family of the Yuan.

In 1313 Emperor Jen Tsung bestowed upon him the dignity of Prince of An Ting. Successively, he served several emperors and was renowned for his faithfulness and zeal. During the Chih-yuan period (1335–1341) brigands arose (as numerous) as insects. At the time of the Ming Emperor T'ai Tsung, the brigands of Kansu entered the valley of the Huai. After a few years their bands were exterminated and pacified.

In 1368 Emperor T'ai Tsung sent Su Ta, Ch'ang Yu-chuan, and other commanders, to pacify the north with the army. Wherever they arrived the people met them and surrendered. Sire T'o Huan was grieved, cried and said, "The empire is lost." At that time, orders of the empire were not obeyed beyond some hundred li of both capitals. The army was inferior in number (to that of the enemy) and enfeebled, incapable of taking the offensive or of staying on the defensive. Sire T'o Huan, in cooperation with officers of the imperial guard commanding exhausted troops, day and night fortified and guarded the capital. Besides the famine and lack of food in the city, there was no hope of getting provisions or rescue. The officers stimulated the courage (of the troops) by means of the example of their faithfulness and fidelity. Everybody was happy to expend his forces.

However, the armies of the enemy more and more distressed the troops. They pressed around the capital. Emperor Shun, the heir apparent, and the imperial grandsons fled at midnight, giving up the empire. Sire T'o Huan with some ten cavaliers, unable to follow the imperial group, roamed the country and finally arrived in Ho Hsi (Kansu). Every time he told about the former empire he cried bitterly, striking his breast.

The Ming Emperor T'ai Tsung having heard about it, thought he was a faithful man, and sent a messenger to invite him to come to the place where he sojourned. When T'o Huan entered, the emperor informed him about his intentions. He consoled him several times, and said he would grant him an official office. Our ancestor bowed his head and answered: a servant of a lost empire is unworthy to receive the favors of your dynasty. The emperor (hearing that) appraised him more and ordered him to muster his tribes and control the country (he previously administered).

In 1370 K'uo-k'uo-t'ieh-mu-erh attacked Cheng-erh-yu. The ancestor followed Su Ta and defeated him. K'uo-k'uo-t'ieh-mu-erh fled to Karakorum.

In 1375 T'o-erh-chih-pa, chieftain of Ho Hsi, revolted. The ancestor, with General Pu Yin, fought and defeated his army. Only Chih Pa escaped with his life. The army returned and rewards were distributed. The ancestor was ordered to come to court. On account of illness the ancestor could not obey the order. At the end of the year he died.

His wife, the noble Lady Ma, was earnest, intelligent, and strong minded. The Tibetan Ta-kuan tieh-chih was a clever and courageous man, who could catch a galloping horse with his hands and throw arrows, hitting the target, as well with his right hand as with his left. With his younger brother he induced the Tibetans to occupy Lo Pe mountains, for robbing purposes. He killed imperial ambassadors, robbed travelers and traders. The highway was closed. The noble lady insidiously made him come over to her mansion. When he arrived a tent was pitched, red felt rugs were spread on the ground, and several maid servants clad in gauze dresses, wearing golden bracelets, playing p'i p'a and singing songs of the country, entertained the guests. When they were drunk, copper kettles were beaten and some strong hidden troops jumped out and with iron chains tied the chief, his servant, and seven more men. Awakening a little, they started moving arms and legs. The soldiers beat them half to death, cut off their heads, stuck them on poles and planted them along the Wu Chao Lin highway to make examples of them to the country. The Tibetans were frightened. The young brother of the brigand cut his throat. The lady sent troops (of the clan) to exterminate the tribes and accept the surrender of those who submitted. The country of Liangchow was at peace.

The emperor, having been informed, sent to the lady one thousand ounces of silver, precious golden trinkets, complete sets of hairpins and earrings, four pieces of flowered silk, and ordered a mansion to be built in Lien Ch'eng, and a house of seven rooms. An inscription was sent: "she displayed fidelity." In the country of Chung-ku-erh 305 hectares of land were granted to provide for her toilette expenses.

The lady died at ninety years of age and was buried in the ancestral cemetery of Hsi Ta-t'ung, next to the ancestor T'o Huan.

KUNG-PU-SHIH-TIEH, OF THE SECOND GENERATION

Kung-pu-shih-tieh was the second son of Sire T'o Huan. At the death of Sire T'o Huan, his oldest son Ah-shih-tu succeeded to the office. Having killed the brigand Ta-kuan tieh-chih, he was promoted to be first chiliarch. Soon he lost his sight and died. Sire Shih-tieh took over the office. He was a strong-minded and severe man, endowed with the qualities of his father.

In 1403 the Mongol Pu-yen Ta-shih revolted and was about to invade the country of Chuang Lang. The indignant Shih Tieh said, "This wicked wretch who inhabits the country surrendered a long time ago, and he is about to become the scourge of the country. He prepares his own ruin." The ancestor, leading more than one hundred of his tribesmen, went to the territory of Wu Wei to attack him. He beat him severely and captured seventy-two of his brigands.

At that time Emperor Ch'eng Tsung ascended the throne. It was the first year of the Yung Lo period (1403). The ancestor went to the capital to offer a tribute of horses and the captured brigands. In the eighth moon he was promoted to be centurion in the commandery of Chuang Lang, commander of his troops and administrator of his subjects. Then he was charged with the defense of Cheng Fan and Mo Mo Ch'eng, and with inducement to submission of the I Chi Nai people. Everywhere, the rewards he granted and the punishments he inflicted were severe but just. The people were afraid of him but were sympathetic toward him.

In 1410 Emperor Ch'eng Tsung himself made an expedition in the northern Gobi and ordered the ancestor to accompany him. At that time the noble Lady Ma, his mother, was old, and had also been taken ill. The ancestor could not resolve to abandon her and to leave. The lady said: "You are an official in the frontier regions. Each (of our) generation has received important favors from the emperor. How will you, preferring a private interest, harm the public interest? What is more, death and life are fixed beforehand. Shall I live because you stay with me? Shall I die because you leave me? Go! Son, you may be successful in this important affair. If I die I shall close my eyes in peace. The ancestor wiped his tears and accepted the lesson."

On the fourth moon the army camped in Wei Lu

Cheng. The weather was hot and the camels carried water for the soldiers to drink. Pen Ya Shih Li fled. In the fifth moon he returned and camped at Yin Ma Ho. The emperor commanded the army to move to another place to fight A-lu-ti. Then it rained tremendously, the noses of the horses disappeared in the mud, and the troops were exhausted. A-lu-tai feigned to submit. The emperor commanded the ancestor to dispose the army in strict battle array and to wait. Then A-lu-tai attacked with his whole army. The ancestor courageously fought a bloody battle. His arrows killed ten or more men. The enemy encircled him, and the arrows came down on him as the rain. The ancestor, from the time he had followed the expedition until his death, during months, had not removed his cuirass and helmet. Rust was seen on the visor of the helmet, grains had germinated to grass in it. It was unusual. In the sand dunes the soldiers found the left arm of the ancestor on a finger of which adhered a jade sheath, and so it was possible to identify the ancestor.

His wife was the noble Lady Li, daughter of the Hui Ning Pe, Li Yin. She arranged the burial of the noble Lady Ma. The obsequies were performed according to the rites. She remained a widow to care for the education of the orphan son. All the time she stimulated him to practice faithfulness and filial piety. Thanks to her, Sire Hsien, the ancestor, having the title of governor, could make the family illustrious.

PIAO-CH'I CHIANG-CHUN, SIRE HSIEN OF THE THIRD GENERATION

Piao-ch'i chiang-chun, Sire Hsien, was the oldest son of Shih Tieh. First he was called Shih Chia. Later, the family name having been granted (by the emperor), he changed his first name Shih Chia to Shih Tieh. At a tender age he was remarkable, fostering high aspirations. Faithfulness and sincerity were inborn in him. Not having studied military arts, his science, his combination of plans and stratagems accorded with those of this art.

In 1411, following the eunuch Wang Nan, he fought the rebel Mongols in Hsi Liang, capturing and killing many of them. On account of his merits he was promoted to be second chiliarch. In succession, he served meritoriously four emperors, Ch'eng, Jen, Hsuan, and Ying Tsung, and was promoted from secretary commandant, to assistant commandant, to secretary high commandant, to assistant high commandant, and to high commandant. He received the titles of Piao-ch'i chiang-chün, and secretary of the military headquarters of the left army. He participated in ten battles and never suffered a defeat. He was conversant with the frontier regions, his troops obeyed him and, therefore, he was successful in his actions.

In 1414 he followed the emperor in his expedition against A-lu-tai. His troops, on the river Kan-t'an, captured the rebel chieftain Ah-la-han.

The emperor's esteem and affection for him increasing, the emperor said:

In former times Tan, Duke of Chou, had made distant expeditions in the Yen Hsi countries. Prince Ch'eng appanaged him with the country of Lu. Your family submitted to the empire a long time ago. In expeditions in remote countries it gathered merits. Your brilliant achievements may be compared with those of the Duke of Chou. For these reasons I grant you the name of Lu, so that your descendants in each generation may be protectors of the frontiers and consolidate my empire.

The ancestor prostrated himself twice and obeyed.

In olden times the family names were determined by the sounds of musical tubes, in order to make them correspond with the five tones of the gamut. An appanage was granted and a name. The emperor presided at the ceremony. Later, the names of the clans became so confused that the people forgot their origin. At present some of the names are identical with those of the kingdoms. The people say that the names of the families originated from those of the kingdoms, and they do not know that they are wrong.

The name of Hsia originated from Chao Hsi of the Ch'eng kingdom, and not from the name of the Duke of Hsia. The name of Ch'i originated from Ch'i no of the Wei kingdom, and not from the name Ch'i of the Ch'i kingdom. Ch'in Chin-fu does not originate from the name of the Ch'in kingdom. The name Ti does not originate from the name Ti of Ti Ssu mi. The names in olden times originated from posthumous names, or from style names, or from names of cities, or from fulfilled incumbencies. To be sure, when people fled to another kingdom, the name of the kingdom of their origin became their name. This happened with Ch'en Ching-chung of the kingdom of Ch'i, and with Sung Ch'ao of the kingdom of Wei.

I write with the minutest details the way in which our family received its name. I will prevent later generations from misinterpreting the meaning and circumstances in which it was granted and I hope that they will be grateful for the favor bestowed by the emperor and increase the luster of the merits of the ancestors. How should we not be attentive for all eternity (not to tarnish such a glorious past) and endeavor (to be worthy of it).

During the reign of T'ai Tsung of the Ming, the Mongol academician Huo-mi-ch'ih was gratified with the name of Huo Chuang, Pa-tu-t'ieh-mu-erh with the name of Wu, Lun-tu-erh-hui with the name Ts'ai, and Pa chou with that of Yang. They had submitted at the same time and had received varied favors. This proves the love nurtured by the emperor toward his subjects living in the remote countries, and proves that our ancestors had acquired merits for our family.

The ancestor was a nice tall man. Every time he fought the enemies his beard and mustache bristled fiercely.

His wife, the noble dame Li, was the daughter of the

Hui-ming-pe, Li Yin. She was intelligent and her needle work and cooking showed her skill. She was proficient in weaving baskets and cups, in which were poured the grains offered to the spirits. The baskets and cups were elegant and gracious and can still be seen. They are conserved and admired as benefits from her hands.

The ancestor died in 1447 in the twelfth moon. When the death was announced, the court was troubled and mourned. Lang Kai was sent and ordered by the emperor to make the sacrifice. He was buried in the ancestral cemetery. To the widow was granted a fine dress, sent by the emperor.

CHIEN, SIRE CHING LU, OF THE FOURTH GENERATION

The style name of Chien, Sire Ching Lu, was K'o Ming. He was the oldest son of Hsien. In 1445 he offered a tribute of horses to the capital, and received the title of chiliarch. In 1447 he succeeded to the office (of his father who had died in 1447) with the title of assistant commandant. At the end of the year, bands of Mongol brigands gathered outside the pass of Chia Yu, in the regions of Kua and Sha Chou, and seized the opportunity (the country was poorly defended) to make inroads. Sire Ching Lu said to the eunuch Liu Yung-chou, guardian and defender of the country: "The brigands just arrived from far away. I seize the opportunity to beat them when they are tired, and shall gain a complete victory. If I wait until they have spied the conditions of our army, it would be difficult to be sure either of the victory or the defeat." The eunuch agreed. Then our troops, 1,500 in number, arrived at Ch'a-han wu-la and administered a crushing defeat. Prisoners and killed were numerous. On account of his merits, Sire Ching Lu was promoted commandant. Sire was courageous, valiant, fearless, and enterprising.

During the periods Chin T'ai and T'ien Shun (1450–1464), the signals (fires) in the watchtowers on the great wall many times announced alarm. Brigadier General Su Ching and Wei Yin, Duke of Hsuan Cheng, and others, received orders to have the troops ready. Wherever the drums were beaten the ancestor with his troops constituted the vanguard. In every battle they preceded the troops and attacked fiercely, flourishing their swords and howling ferociously. Wherever the ancestor fought he was victorious. When in the enemy army there were violent savage types, he jumped on his horse and rushed to kill them in the midst of their troops. The troops called him the fleeing general. With few troops he could beat large bands of brigands, and every time he managed to be victorious. The brigands who opposed him flew away as birds, or escaped in groves as wild animals. They were frightened of him as of a spirit.

In that way he defeated Wang Pe in Liangchow, Man Sse in Ku Yuen, and fought Pe-lo-hu and Pe-chia sse-lu in Ho T'ao. All these victories were gained, thanks to the ancestor. The emperor relied on him as on the Great Wall.

In 1475 an order was given to build an honorific arch in front of his mansion, in commemoration of his merits. In 1486 he received the seal of General Pacifier of the Mongols. He had inborn kindness and considerateness toward the people, and did not pride himself on his merits. Upon receiving gifts he instantly shared them with his officers and his soldiers. He was especially devoted to stimulating and promoting education, and to honoring and revering scholars. He glorified our family. Starting by fulfilling humble duties, he accumulated merits to the point of being promoted General Defender of Chuang Lang, mandarin-at-large, in Huan Ch'ing, and Military Governor of Yen Chou and Sui Te. His fame lasted for more than forty years, until his death. Though this might have happened because of good fortune, his faithfulness and sincerity however have also been its cause.

In 1488, at the accession of Emperor Hsiao Tsung, he asked for retirement. In 1494 his son Chin was appointed major in Kanchow and Suchow. Because nobody was able to command the Monguor troops except the ancestor, the emperor especially ordered him (to emerge from retirement) to command them. The ancestor presented at court a memoir of several thousand words, in four articles, concerning the problems of the frontier regions relating to defense and the organization. Many times the memoir was discussed and used.

He died in 1502 from an old sore which had opened again. When his death was announced, the titles of Yung-lu Ta-fu, of pillar of the empire, and of chief of the military headquarters of the left troops were granted to him posthumously. Li Shih, councilor (of the supreme council), was sent to offer three sacrifices.

His wife was the daughter of Li Wen, Duke of Kao Yang. She was chaste and peaceful; she knew the art of educating children; she died five years before the ancestor. She received titles according to the customs (in accordance with those bestowed upon the husband). She had a daughter married to Wang Hsu, second captain in Kanchow. During the Cheng Te period (1506–1521) the almighty eunuch, who knew that she was nice and attractive, praised her beauty within hearing of Emperor Wu Tsung, who sent a special order to the eunuch Chao Lun to prepare the ritual gifts and to escort her to court. The girl refused, and said, "An unsightly girl from the frontier regions is unworthy to receive orders from the emperor. All the more the decision of a wife of the common people is not to change the husband she married. I desire you will inform the emperor that I cannot avoid the capital punishment (I prefer to die)." The eunuch answered, "The order of the emperor is strict and cannot be eluded." The girl surreptitiously took a knife and cut her throat. She was grieved not to be dead. The eunuch ordered the family to guard her closely day and night. One day she seized the opportunity to burn her face with absinthe and died after many days.

Alas, the father was a distinguished officer, the daughter a chaste wife. This event is significant in that it is a lesson related to the three Kang (observance of the three relations between prince and subjects, father and sons, husband and wife), and related to the five Ch'ang (the five virtues of charity, justice, urbanity, prudence, and sincerity). In that way this event is not only painful for our family (but also glorious because our family provided a model of the three Kang and five Ch'ang). I record this fact because it has to be inserted in the chapter of the glorious wives in the official history of the Ming dynasty.[8]

LIN, SIRE THE GOVERNOR, OF THE FIFTH GENERATION

The style name of Lin, sire the governor, was Shih Hsiang. He was the oldest son of Chien. He was brave, strong and had the qualities of his father.

In 1484, the ancestor Ching Lu was military governor of Yen Chou and Sui Te. The troops of his clan had no chief (to care for them, Yen Chou and Sui Te were too far from Chuang Lang). Lin was promoted centurion with golden badge, chief of the troops of the clan. At that time the Mongol brigands from Liangchow, Yung Ch'ang, Kanchow, and Suchow intermittently made inroads. The ancestor moved his troops to rescue the countries where the danger arose. Always he was victorious and his fame was well known in distant countries.

After a year there was great famine in Kuan Chung (Shensi). Along the roads the people sat looking at each other (not knowing what to do). The ancestor Lin carried 600 *tan* of grain to relieve the miseries of the people east of the Yellow River. He saved the lives of some thousands of people. The court was appraised

---

[8] In Huangchung are encountered two Li clans. Li Nan-ko is the founding ancestor of the first clan and Li Wen, Duke of Kao Yang, the founding ancestor of the second clan. Both clans have their own cemetery, in which the cult of the ancestors starts with their respective founding ancestor.

Li Nan-ko had a brother Li Chang-ko, who died during the Yüan dynasty. In that way he is not recognized as the founding ancestor of the clan, but his son Li Wen who submitted to the Ming dynasty together with his uncle Li Nan-ko, is considered the founding ancestor of the second clan.

Li Nan-ko had a son Li Yin, Duke of Hui Ning, who was the cousin of Li Wen, son of Li Chang-ko.

The ancestor of the second generation of the Lu clan was the father of the ancestor of the third generation of the Lu clan. Both father and son married daughters of Li Yin, Duke of Hui Ning. According to the Chinese rules of marriage, such marriage is highly unbecoming, especially among eminent people.

The ancestor of the fifth generation of the Lu clan married the daughter of Li Wen, Duke of Kao Yang, who was a cousin of the daughters of Li Yin, Duke of Hui Ning. Again this marriage was very shocking for the Chinese, who used to call the Monguors barbarians.

of the fact and he was promoted to be commandant. After one year more, together with Lieutenant Colonel T'ien Kuang, he put to flight the brigands in Ch'ing Shih Hsia. In the autumn in the ninth moon, he put to flight and defeated them again on the river Fu Tung Erh. He was promoted to be high secretary commandant.

In 1488 his father Chien asked for his retirement. The emperor agreed and in 1489 the ancestor Lin succeeded his father. In 1494 Mongol brigands invaded the Yung Ch'ang region. The ancestor leading his troops rescued the country and fought in Liu Yuan. The brigands retreated a little, but soon they besieged Yung Ch'ang with more bands. Because his troops were inferior in number, he fortified the city and did not fight. The siege and attacks became more impetuous, arrows fell as rain; officers and soldiers used saddles to protect themselves. In three days they were reduced to the utmost point. T'ao Cheng, the lieutenant colonel of Liangchow, without coming to the rescue, waited for the issue of the battle. The ancestor implored the aid of Heaven, stimulating the courage of his troops. Ten times or more they had already fought bloody battles when Heaven made a tremendous wind blow and sand and pebbles flew in the air. He made a vigorous sally and fled out of the city. The court, learning of the defeat, inflicted on the ancestor the punishment of defending the frontiers, and did not allow him to leave them. The ancestor wrote a report of the battle accusing T'ao Cheng. The imperial censor was ordered to investigate the case. T'ao Cheng was punished, and the ancestor condoned. However his title was lowered one degree. Having captured brigands in the twelfth moon of the same year, 1499, he was promoted to be lieutenant colonel and defender of Chuang Lang, and after a few days more, was promoted to be second brigadier general and military governor of Kanchow.

In 1501 Mongols invaded the Hsi Hsia region. The ancestor went to rescue the country. When he arrived at Wei Chou, the brigands had already entered deeply into the country. He sent the high commandant Yang Lun, who encountered the Mongols at Kung-pa-ku, and could not dispose his troops in battle array. His frightened soldiers and officers took to their heels and fled, pursued by the enemy. It was a disastrous defeat. The ancestor was terribly indignant. With his son Chin, he led some hundreds of wounded soldiers to fight the brigands. His vanguard again retreated. Then Chin himself killed some among them, and went to fight in the first rank, ahead of the soldiers, followed by his father, ancestor Lin. All the soldiers followed him with fierceness. Each of them was worth a hundred soldiers and their savage battle cries shook heaven and earth. The Mongols fled in disorder. The high commanders affixed their seals to an accusation against the ancestor Lin, for having spoiled the battle. The ancestor wrote a defense, Yang Lun was punished, the ancestor was condoned, but his salary was withheld for two months.

At that time the father of Lin, sire Chin Lu, was old, and his son Chin was young and unable to command the army. The ancestor asked to resume his office. Liu Ta-hsia told the emperor, who agreed. Emperor Wu Tsung ascended the throne (1506). Su t'ai, lieutenant colonel of Chuang Lang was not sympathetic to the people and caused many troubles. The court ordered the sub-lieutenant to take over the duty ad interim. The ancestor Chien, of good repute in the frontier region, implored the emperor to grant to Lin help in the military and civil administration. Pi Heng told the emperor, who agreed.

Lin died in the third moon of 1506, receiving posthumously the title of secretary general of the left army. The emperor sent Chou Tsai councillor (of the supreme council) with the favor of official sacrifices and burial according to the rites.

His first wife was the noble Lady Wang, daughter of Wang Yin, high commandant of Yu Lin. She died early without issue. The second wife was the noble Lady Wang, daughter of Wang Chang, *tu tien* of Yu Lin. The ancestor Chin was her son.

CHIN, SIRE PACIFIER OF THE MONGOLS, OF THE SIXTH GENERATION

Chin, Sire pacifier of the Mongols, had the style name of Yuan Ch'ang, and the literary name Hsi K'un. He was the oldest son of Lin.

In 1501, following the general, his father, he defeated the brigands in Wei Chou and was promoted to be centurion. In 1504 he defeated brigands in Shui Ts'ao Ku, and was promoted to be secretary commandant with golden badge. In 1506 his father Lin died and he succeeded him. The court, considering that he had accumulated many merits on the battle front, by especial favor granted him the title of secretary commandant, defender of Chuang Lang, with the seal of Chao Yung general. His gratitude and zeal increased. In 1508 he defeated the brigands at the lake Ming Shui and was promoted to high assistant commandant. In 1510 the Mongols invaded Chuang Lang territory. He pursued and defeated them at Shih P'en Ku, killing and capturing many of them. In 1512 the Mongols invaded Chuang Lang again. He pursued and defeated them at T'ung Wei P'u, killing and capturing many. In the same year the Mongols invaded Hsining. He pursued and defeated them at Ma Ch'ang Ku killing and capturing many.

Then the most important officials affixed their seal to a report to the emperor, praising and exalting his merits. The emperor granted him the *mang p'ao* (official dress adorned with dragons) and the jade cincture and especially promoted him to be secretary governor, lieutenant colonel of the left wing, and defender of Chuang Lang. In 1515 the tribes of Ch'a K'u I stole the tribute brought to the emperor, and the tribes of Huang T'u Erh stole the tribute of horses. The court ordered the ancestor to punish and capture the robbers. The ancestor succeeding in capturing the stolen tribute and offered it to the emperor. He was promoted to be assistant governor and defender of Chuang Lang and Hsining. Emperor Wu Tsung died and Shih Tsung ascended the throne (1522). Chin asked to retire. Su Feng-hsiang, governor of the province, said to the emperor, "Chin has been officer during his whole life, he is courageous in war time, his fame is known among the barbarians. At present the circumstances of the empire are critical and it is not the time to permit him to retire." The emperor himself wrote a letter in order to console him and keep him in charge. He sent an official to manifest his sympathy, sent him precious gifts, promoted him to be second brigadier general, and enjoined him to help in the administration as before.

In 1525 he was promoted to be brigadier general in Yen Chou and Sui Te and received the seal of general pacifier of the Mongols. The scholar Yang I-ch'ing said to the emperor, "Chin has administered Chuang Lang twenty or more years and accumulated many merits. He alone is capable of controlling the Monguor troops. Chang Feng his whole life long has been brigadier general in Yen Chou and Sui Te. If you would remove Chang Feng from Yen Chou and Sui Te and appoint Chin, then we could be assured of keeping the country at peace by means of the army, and the western regions would no longer cause anxiety." The emperor agreed, and immediately ordered Chin to move to Yen Chou.

In 1542 the Mongols invaded Yung Ch'ang at Shang Ku. Repeated reports claimed the circumstances to be alarming. The court ordered the chief of the ministry of war to appoint an official to rescue the region. Just at midnight the emperor sent a eunuch with a decree to the ministry of war.

I consider that Lu Chin of Chuang Lang is a courageous general who controls troops inured to war. I think him equal to meeting the alarming situation, and demand that the decree written by my hand be brought instantly, by the chiliarch Liu Kang ordering him to move.

Just at that time the ancestor suffered an attack of rheumatism, and he limped. Upon receiving the order, doing himself violence, he chose 3,000 of his best soldiers. Obeying the order they arrived at Suchow. The Mongols, conversant with the fame of the ancestor, retreated. The court praised his faithfulness and sincerity and congratulated him again and again. After delivering a gift of silver the messenger returned.

Three years later the governor of the province Ch'eng Chiu-ch'ou was ordered to build two honorific arches with the inscriptions "unceasingly he practiced faithfulness and justice for a long time, and was known for his dignity and fame."

Tan, the oldest son of Sire Chin, died some time ago. He ordered his second son Tung to take over the office. He retired to one of his properties in Hsi Tat'ung. After more than ten years he died in 1556 in the third moon. He received the posthumous titles of Yung-lu Ta-fu, pillar of the empire, governor of the military government of the right wing. He was honored with three sacrifices.

His wife, the noble Lady Wang, was the daughter of Duke Ch'ing Yuan from Hsining. She was a serious and model lady. In 1517 the court, in consideration of the merits of her husband, sent a eunuch with the robe adorned with dragons, the cincture of jade, precious stones, golden bracelets, pieces of very thin silk and satin, and other objects. The gifts were unusually rich and numerous. She died in 1526, in the tenth moon before Sire Chin.

TUNG, SIRE CHAO I, OF THE SEVENTH GENERATION

Tung, Sire Chao I, with the style name Tsung Chou, and the literary name Shih Feng, was the second son of Chin. His oldest brother Tan had gained merits accompanying his father, sire Chin Lu, on expeditions, and had received the promotion of second chiliarch. In 1527 his father had obtained the decree permitting him to retire. The court ordered Tan to control the country and to succeed to his father. Having gained merits he was promoted secretary commandant and second captain in Shan Tan.

In 1535 his father, Sire Chin Lu, presented a memorial to the emperor: "Always the ancestors of your subject have controlled this country (Chuang Lang). At present I am retired and my son Tan is moved to another commandery of the frontiers. The troops of the clan are upset and are not willing to obey another. If, on account of this fact, troubles arise they will cause the ruin of the patrimony of the ancestors, and we will be ungrateful for the blessings received from the ancestors. Your subject implores you to permit my son to control the old patrimony." The court agreed and ordered Tan to move to Chuang Lang. In 1543 Tan died, his son Cheng Wu succeeded him and died also.

At that time Sire Chin Lu was old. Considering that the empire had to cope with many difficulties and that his troops had nobody to control them, he implored permission for his second son Chao I to succeed him.

Tung, Sire Chao I, was endowed with the appearance and distinction of a scholar, and with inborn faithfulness and filial piety. When his father, Sire Chin Lu, was sick, he burned incense and begged to die in his place. He cut a piece of his thigh to heal the disease. Ch'en Pi, governor of the province, asked the court to glorify this gesture of filial piety. Every time he went to fight brigands, he knelt down before his father, asking him for instructions related to the art of war.

In 1561 big bands of Mongols invaded the country.

The frontier regions were upset. Sire Chao I led his troops against them. The brigands dared not invade Chuang Lang. He defeated them in K'ai Ch'eng and in Shih T'u Ku and Pe Shih Ch'uan. Everywhere he was victorious.

In 1568 he was promoted to be high commandant and prefect in Chuang Lang. He helped the lieutenant colonel Li Shih-wei in military affairs. Chuang Lang enjoyed peace.

The disease of his father became more and more deep rooted, his legs and arms were crippled, and for ten years he could not move. In 1578 Sire Chao I implored the emperor for permission to retire. The court ordered Kuang Hsien his oldest son to take over the office, but soon Kuang Hsien died. Sire Tung asked permission for his second son Kuang Tsu to succeed to the hereditary office. In 1584 Sire Chao I died, and received posthumously the title of Chao Yu chiang-chun.

His first wife belonged to the Li family, the second to the Ts'ao family. Both received the title of honorable Lady (title accorded to wives of officers of the third degree). Sires Kuang Lu and Kuang Tsu were sons of the honorable Lady Li.

KUANG TSU, SIRE KUANG LU OF THE EIGHTH GENERATION

Kuang Tsu, Sire Kuang Lu, whose style name was Pe Hsien, was the second son of Tung, Sire Chao I. He was born and grew up in a family in every generation of which were officials. He was diligent in the study of the classics and calligraphy. In his youth he was registered on the roster of the students of the military school of the commandery of his country. He decided to glorify the family by obtaining literary degrees. Soon his oldest brother Kuang Hsien died. Sire Kuang Lu, being the next in age, succeeded. However, until his death he did not enjoy the office. In his disorderly room, next to long guns and spears, were disposed maps, books, and sacrificial vases. Having some spare time, he burned incense and sat motionless studying old books, relaxing his spirit, and enjoying quietness. Those who saw him did not think he was a military officer.

From commandant in Chuang Lang he was promoted colonel in Hsining. On account of his expeditions in Kokonor, he was promoted to be brigadier general in Liangchow. Having defeated P'u Pai, he was promoted to be brigadier general in T'ao and Ming Chou.

In 1600 he was promoted to be commandant-in-chief, in Nan Ching at the military headquarters of the right, and director of the training fields, in preparation against Japan.

Sire Kuang Lu was unassuming, loyal, mild, intelligent, and helpful toward the underlings. Those who inhabited the capital, a noisy city, indulged in pleasures and dissoluteness, rearing dogs and horses. The prominent people pursued the satisfaction of their desires. It was easy to incriminate them. Sire Kuang Lu used his salary only to buy books. The hundreds of books he bought were all pencil marked and filled with notes. When the administrative affairs allowed him some spare time, he invited eminent scholars, composed poems, and drank wine. He visited the ford at T'ao Yeh and the barrow of Sian and he inquired about the old lanes and green brooks and the long bridge in Wu I. He very much enjoyed the strolls he made when he was a public official.

After a short time, on account of illness, he asked for retirement. It was accorded and the costs of the journey were defrayed by the empire.

Back home he delighted in strolling in the woods and on the banks of the rivers. He composed the family chronicles in three sections. He started with the imperial decrees. He wrote the biographies and the correspondence with the empire, and finally the things interesting the family from the first ancestor on. According to the Chia Li composed by Chu Hsi (Chu Hsi, 1130–1200) he built a temple east of his mansion for the ancestors, with five niches inside. In the center niche sacrifices were offered to the first ancestor, in the other four sacrifices to the great-great-grandfather, the great-grandfather, the grandfather, and to the father according to the rite Chao Mu. Sacrifices at the time of the four seasons were fixed on the first day of each of them. The tablet of the first ancestor was never allowed to be moved, the other four, however, had to be removed according to the rites (to allow a seat for the recently deceased). He emphasized the importance of the sacrifices and the rites.

In former times the morals and customs in our village were rough and savage, today the people start knowing the prime ancestor and honor him. That is what the ancestor taught us to do. Now from the time I was a small boy I felt with my hands, the gifts made by the hands of the ancestors. I felt deeply impressed. I feel gratitude for having received this tradition (of honoring the ancestors in the family).

Sire Kuang Tsu died in his mansion in the village in 1607. The death being announced at court, he received posthumously the title of Kuang Lu-ta-fu and sacrifices and burial according to the rites.

His wife, the noble Lady Chang, was intelligent, and quick to understand. She had much erudition and a noble character. She controlled her home with severity and regularity. She had a son, Yung Ch'ang, who died in the service for the empire during the Ming dynasty. This is quite sufficient for her to illustrate our glorious family.

YUNG CH'ANG, SIRE CHUNG TI OF THE NINTH GENERATION

Yung Ch'ang, Sire Chung Ti, whose style name was Ch'eng Pu, his literary name Chung T'ai. He was the son of Kuang Tsu, Sire Kuang Lu. In 1602 Sire Kuang Lu retired. Sire Chung Ti inherited the office of secretary-commandant and the control of the Monguor troops. Chung Ti was an eminent man with high aspirations. He would not be limited by the offices and titles his ancestors had received (he aspired for more). He was fully devoted to the affairs of the frontiers, was self-sacrificing and loved the empire. In 1628 there was famine in Yen Chou and Sui Te. Wang Chia-yun, in Fu Ku, called the people to organize and plunder. The followers of Chang Hsien-chung and Li Tzu-ch'eng waited for the opportunity to revolt. Sire Chung Ti knew that the situation was changing. He used his troops with foresight to defend Ho Hsi.

In 1636 he was promoted to be lieutenant colonel and prefect in Chuang Lang. After a year he was promoted to be brigadier general and guardian of Hsining. Then on account of his merits he was promoted assistant in the military government of the left army. The *mang pao* was granted (robe with dragons) and the jade cincture. In 1643 the rebels broke through the T'ung Kuan pass; Ch'ing Yang and Kung Ch'ang were imperiled. Sire Chung Ti knew that Lanchow was an isolated city in danger, whose defense was problematical. Several times he reported asking to send Su Fan past the river to protect the cities of Ninghsia, Liangchow, Kanchow, and Su Chou in order to combine plans for the recovering of the country. He did not receive an answer.

In 1644, in the spring, the brigand general Huo Chin invaded Ho Hsi. Liangchow and Chuang Lang looked at what other cities did, and surrendered. Sire Chung Ti was raging. He distributed his wealth to the officers and the soldiers and led his troops to attack and fight the brigands in Hsi Tatung. The fame of the Monguor troops frightened the brigands, and they retreated a little. Among the tribesmen of the ancestor, some submitted to the brigands claiming that the troops were outnumbered, that no rescue was to be expected. The courage of the brigands grew. Sire Chung Ti, because his troops were outnumbered, retreated and defended his city of Lien Ch'eng. The brigands attacked the city and it was captured. Sire Chung Ti was tied before the gate of the city. He was called to surrender. He refused. They summoned him to give his wealth. He refused again. They threatened to kill him with the sword. He mocked and cursed them. While he was dying he did not desist from cursing them.

It was the sixteenth day of the first moon of 1644. The brigands abducted his son and his daughter, stole all his wealth, and went westward. Hung, the son of Chung Ti was only a few years old when he fell into the hands of the brigands. The brigands divided the tribes of Chung Ti among the members of the family who had submitted to them. The noble lady Kan, the first wife, overwhelmed with grief wished to kill herself. Among those who consoled her, some said: your son is abducted, your wealth is stolen, to commit suicide is useless. Then the noble lady dressed and took her meals as before.

In 1645 Prince Yin of the Ch'ing dynasty called the people of the two rivers to submit and ordered the concubine of Sire Chung Ti, the noble Lady Yang, to write with her blood a report to the emperor expounding the facts from the beginning to the end, with the minutest details. The emperor ordered the ministers to deliberate and send him their advice. He ordered the nephew of Chung Ti, An, to succeed ad interim, to command the troops and control the subjects.

For two hundred years the descendants have conserved the patrimony of the ancestors, thanks to the endeavor of both noble ladies, and thanks to the loyal spirit of Sire Chung Ti, who from the outer world has been able to arrange events.

COMMANDANT SIRE HUNG OF THE TENTH GENERATION

The Commandant Sire Hung had the style name of Yu Hu. He was the son of Yung Ch'ang, Sire Chung Ti. During the troubles of Huo Chin he had been captured, brought to Chung Chou (Honan Fu) and later to Wuch'ang. In 1645 the court, having been informed about the circumstances of the death of Sire Chung Ti, ordered An to succeed in the interim. In 1648 he received the decree of his appointment and the seal to fulfill his office. At that time the revolt had subsided a little. The noble Lady Kan had sent men in all directions in search of information (about the captive). Every night she burned incense and implored Heaven. In 1650 she obtained certain news from traders, and sent men with money to bring back the captive. Back home son and mother embraced each other and cried with joy. The subjects also cried with joy and skipped at having met their true tribe chief. However, those among the family who had submitted to the brigands had already submitted to the newly established Ch'ing dynasty, and their chief had received the office of lieutenant colonel. He intended to occupy the grounds of the tribes, to control the subjects, and to seize the patrimony of Hung.

What is more, at the time Sire Chung Ti had been killed, the chief of the surrendered clan men had effectively beheaded Chung Ti with the sword. Now he feared that the recovery of the chieftainship of the tribe by Sire Hung would be ominous to him. Astutely using the revelation made by the shaman Wan Lang, whom he had invited, he confused the mind of the subjects (while in trances, the shaman must have said that the returned captive was not the son of Chung Ti). Even using money he tried to make Hung change his decision (to succeed to Chung Ti) but the decision of Hung to buttress his position grew all the stronger. From then on, the most malevolent rumors were spread. The most intelligent among the subjects were paid to testify

to the veracity (of the revelation of the shaman). Sire Hung was brought before the tribunal of the governor of the province. Inhumanly treated he did not die. Put in jail, suffering ruthlessly, he still did not die. After ten years, the truth became evident and the abuse was cleared up.

He succeeded in 1659 at the time the empire was at peace inside and outside. Tibetans and barbarians offered tribute. Sire Hung did not obtain merits in war. He consolidated the patrimony of the ancestors, controlled his subjects and troops with kindness, and the subversive intentions of the traitors dissolved.

The ulterior generations are beholden to Sire Hung for the blessings of the peace they enjoyed. Heaven has been merciful to him. He succeeded for fifteen years and died in 1673 on the twelfth of the third moon at the age of forty.

His wife, the noble Lady Wang, was upright, severe, and determined. After the death of her husband she remained a widow caring for the education of the orphan son.

In 1674 Chang, Kung, and Keng (Ministers of the Ming dynasty who had submitted to the Ch'ing) revolted. The people of the two rivers were upset. Chang Yung captured Lanchow. The widow sent grain and horses to the soldiers and sent the Monguor troops to be commanded by the brigadier general of Hsining. After the revolt of Hsi Erh Su was quelled, she received a laudatory decree. She died in 1707 on the fourteenth of the third moon. She received posthumously the title of Shu jen and was buried in the ancestral cemetery of Ch'ing Yang Shan next to her husband, Sire the commandant.

TI HSIN, KAO-TSU CHAO YUNG, THE GREAT-GREAT-GRANDFATHER [9] OF THE ELEVENTH GENERATION

Ti Hsin, the Sire Chao Yung Kao-tsu had as his style name Chien Tsai. He was the adopted son of Sire the Commandant Hung. Before the troubles for the succession of Sire Commandant arose, the noble Lady

[9] Lu Chi-hsun, ancestor of the fifteenth generation, author of the Chronicles, starts calling the ancestor of the eleventh generation the (his) great-great grandfather, the ancestor of the twelfth generation, the (his) great grandfather, and so down till the ancestor of the fourteenth generation who is called the (his) father.

I suppose the reason for the process is that, according to the rules fixed by Chu Hsi, in the Hall of the ancestors, only five tablets of ancestors are to be honored.

The tablet of the founding ancestor occupies the center and is never to be removed. On both its sides are seen two tablets, one the tablet of the great-great grandfather of the actual living t'u-ssu, the second that of his great grandfather, the third that of his grandfather, the fourth that of his father.

Every time a t'u-ssu dies his tablet occupies the lowest place, and that of the great-great grandfather is removed. Only five ancestors are supposed to be honored and to be capable of enjoying the fragrance of the offerings, and also to be capable of protecting their descendants.

Wang cared for Ti Hsin, still in swaddling clothes and loved him as her own son. Later she bore Shu Kao-tsu whose name was Ti Ch'eng. At the death of Sire the Commandant Hung, Sire Chao-yung, Ti Hsin, and his brother Shu (Ti Ch'eng) were still young. The noble lady kept care of the seal (controlled the tribe). In 1685 there was announced by decree the succession of Ti Ch'eng (the genuine son of Lady Wang). He received with reverence the decree and fulfilled the duty. His name was inscribed on the roster of the students of the director of the school of the commandery (Chuang Lang). After three years he died without issue. Sire Ti Hsin (the adopted) succeeded in the capacity of second son. He was intelligent and capable, he understood the core of the problems. Despite the fact that he was not born of the noble Lady Wang, his filial piety and care for her never decreased. After the death of the commandant the orphan and the lady endured vexations at the hands of powerful and audacious people, as well as in private and in administrative affairs. Sire Ti Hsin succeeded before the age of twenty-one. He examined thoroughly all the questions with intelligence. His mildness and sincerity were on a par. The non-brilliant conditions of the family improved, thanks to Sire Ti Hsin.

In 1699 the Jungar group tried to hinder the submission of the tribes (to the empire). Sire Ti Hsin prepared at his own expense the provisions for his troops and left for the expedition in the western regions. The brigand fled. The Kokonor Mongols invaded the frontiers. The emperor sent troops to fight them, but the river of Tatung was swollen to the point that boats and rafts could not cross. Sire Ti Hsin spent thousands of taels, used his own wood, hired carpenters and built a floating bridge. The troops arrived at the destination on time, and Hsining was saved.

Sire Ti Hsin was engrossed in military affairs outside, but every time he had spare moments he went to sit down with the noble Lady Wang, to tell wonderful stories and enjoy and relax her. The noble lady took ill. He prepared medicines himself and during months did not take rest. At the time of the interment she had grown so lean that the bones protruded on the body. Troops and subjects were compassionately impressed. Her sincerity at home and in public were on a par.

At fifty years of age Ti Hsin asked for retirement (1718). The deceased mother of Ti Hsin, the noble Dame Yueh, was the niece of Yueh Cheng-lung, Duke Ming Su, Governor of Szechwan province. She was the sister of the father of Yueh Chung-ch'i, Duke Wei Hsin. The lady was reared in a family of officials. She liked calmness, studied painting, music, and books in her spare time. She dressed in the way of the common people. People who saw her never thought she was reared in a family of officials.

Ti Hsin died in 1735. He was posthumously granted the title of Chao Yung-chiang-chun. The wife of Ti Hsin died in 1702. The title of Fu-jen was granted to her. She was buried with her husband in Hsi Hsiang T'ang.

HUA LIN, SIRE WU KUNG, THE GREAT-GRAND-FATHER (TSENG-TSU), OF THE TWELFTH GENERATION

Hua Lin, Sire Wu Kung, great grandfather, had the style name Chiu Ju. He was the oldest son of Ti Hsin, Sire Chao-yung. He was remarkable and surpassed common people. In 1718 retirement was granted to Sire Chao-yung. Sire Hua Lin received the decree in the ninth moon and succeeded his father.

In 1719 Ta wa chien shanpa revolted in Kokonor and the imperial army went to fight him. At that time Yueh Chung-ch'i Duke Wei Hsin's troops fought as vanguard. Knowing that he could use the Sire Hua Lin, he ordered him to lead his troops and protect the provisions of their troops. San Pa Ch'iao was the first dangerous pass on the way to Kokonor. It was guarded by Tibetans and impossible to go through. The troops of the Sire, all speaking Tibetan, running as fast as the wind (around the pass), reached the place of Lo Lung Tsung and captured some tens of Tibetans. The Tibetans fled pursued by the army and the pass was open. In the eighth moon Kokonor was pacified. Sire Hua Lin was promoted lieutenant colonel on account of his merits. In 1721 the Tibetan Kuo-mi tribes impelled to revolt by bLo-bzang tan-chin, made inroads and plundered. Sire Hua Lin leading some hundreds of troops went to garrison in Je Yueh Shan to protect the provisions of the army. The brigands failed to enter the place. In 1723 bLo-bzang tan-chin invaded the Hsining region and the countries east and west of the Chuang Lang mountains. The tribes of Hsieh-erh-su, Sa-Ma-chien shan-pa, Chao Ma-chien, and others revolted at the same time. General Nien Keng-yao ordered Duke Wei Hsin to pacify Kokonor and ordered the Sire Hua Lin to quell the revolt of Chuang Lang. Sire Hua Lin setting ambushes captured the chief of the revolt, Ho Mu-shan, and six others, and seized the opportunity to attack the Cho Tse Shan region. The ferocious howling of his troops made heaven and earth shake. The defeated brigands fled to Shih Pao Ch'eng. From the T'o-na valley he besieged the city five days and nights without success. Then Hua Lin ordered some courageous soldiers to cross the Tatung River on rafts, to climb to the source of a small river in order to reach the brigands from the rear. Hua Lin himself conducted a full attack with his whole army. The battle started. Cannons bombarded the city, the army attacked from the front and from the rear, the brigands were defeated, the number killed and captured was great, and the rebels of the Ah Lo tribe were exterminated or captured. The mountainous eastern country was pacified. The rebels in the western part, appraised of the defeat, lost courage. Sire Hua Lin went to fight them. After destroying the monastery of Shih Men, he attacked the den of the brigands and captured the chiefs. The others fled.

In 1724 Hua Lin, presuming that the rebels would plunder again in the spring, garrisoned troops in Ta Ying Wan. The people were no longer anxious (and the revolt was forestalled).

Kokonor was pacified in the fourth moon, and Duke Yueh Wei-hsin came with his troops, clearing the remaining groups of rebels in the region of both mountains. Hua Lin called 1,000 of his soldiers and ordered a chiliarch to clear the country of Hsin Shan with 500 soldiers. He himself went with 500 soldiers into the P'ai Lu valley. He killed 500 brigands and captured 100. He also captured a tremendous number of cows, horses, and weapons.

At that time the commandery of Chuang Lang was converted in the subprefecture of P'ing Fan. Then a report was sent to the emperor imploring him to assign as subjects to the Lu family, the eight tribes of Hsieh Erh Su.

bLo-bzang tan-chin, clad in the dress of a Tibetan woman, had fled to Ko Erh Shun. In the seventh moon Hua Lin pursued him with 200 soldiers to Hua Hai Tse, following General Yueh. Then looking at the red earth reaching to heaven, and the sand dunes seeming to be as waves of the sea, and deeming it impossible to continue the pursuit, they gave up.

In 1730 he loaned half of his troops to colonize the Ch'ih Chin region.

In 1731 he received the salary of lieutenant colonel, was granted the peacock plume, the official robe adorned with dragons, and many pieces of satin. He was promoted to be major in Hsining.

In 1736 at the time of the celebration of the victory, he went to call on the emperor. He received the title of lieutenant colonel of the Huo Ch'i Ying in Sian. Successively he was transferred to Kanchow as defender of the city and as assistant general to Yung Ch'ang, both charges depending on the brigadier general of Liangchow.

The empire was at peace, the armies at rest. Sire Hua Lin, wherever he went, praised the favors and virtues of the emperor and taught the necessity of faithfulness and filial piety. He developed education. Officers had confidence in him, as in a tender mother. He delighted in the rites and the schools. In his spare time he liked to sing songs with scholars and eminent people. When he was transferred to a place and left the country, the elders, leaning on their sticks, pulled his sleeves to keep him, and presented a cup of wine honoring him. They accompanied him as far as several li. The picture representing the people hanging on the pole of his coach, impeding it from moving, portrays a genuine reality.

The noble Lady Wang, the wife of the Tseng Tsu (great-grandfather), was the daughter of Wang Ch'eng,

the brigadier general in Wu Lu Cheng in Yunan province. She was zealous, mild, and considerate. Her virtues were on a par with those of her husband.

Sire Hua Lin died in 1736, the nineteenth of the second moon, at the age of sixty-eight. Posthumously he received the title of Wu-kung. The Lady Wang died in 1768, the fifteenth of the eleventh moon, at the age of seventy-eight. She was granted the title of Fu-jen. She was buried in the Hsi Hsiang T'ang cemetery.

FENG CHU, SIRE WU I, THE GRANDFATHER OF THE THIRTEENTH GENERATION

Grandfather Feng Chu, Sire Wu I, style name Hsiu Lin, was the oldest son of the great-grandfather Chiu Ju. The great-grandfather, for ten years, fulfilled official duties outside. He ordered Sire Wu I to care for the private and public affairs at home. Sire was well talented and dealt easily with affairs, just as he would place things in the right place. All things were done as they should be done. Every time he considered the kernel of the matter and did not waste his time examining minute details. For that reason those who worked with him feared him and loved him.

In 1732, having the title of lieutenant, he went through the pass with 600 soldiers to carry on the job of the colonization of Ch'ih Chin, Pu Lung Ku, and other places. He himself worked hard, examining the quality of the ground for cereals. The crops he gathered were always double that of others. After three years the work was done and he returned to his garrison (Lien Ch'eng). The high officials praised his capacities.

In 1744 the great-grandfather Chiu Ju asked to retire. Sire Wu I received the official decree and succeeded. The great-grandfather had a peaceful and quiet temperament. He liked to sit in a lonely room, boil his tea, burn incense, and did not inquire about outside things. Sire Wu I inquired about the health of the elder, cared for his food, and asked for orders in every circumstance. He never neglected the precepts of filial piety.

In 1756 the great grandfather died. Sire Wu I mourned him and buried him according to the rites. At that time the great-grandmother Wang was old. Sire Wu I afraid to grieve her, took his meals with her and behaved as always, but when he was alone he cried as a child. He succeeded in making the great-grandmother happy. Thanks to him the elders, for more than ten years, had been able to walk in the woods and at the sources of the rivers, and the great-grandmother had reached the age of seventy-eight. This had been possible because the filial piety of Sire Wu I had reached such a point of perfection.

The empire was at peace. On the frontiers no more fires were lit in the watch towers of the great wall announcing alarm, the troops and the people enjoyed happiness, and the virtue of humanity was practiced.

The people lived until an old age. Our grandfather Sire Wu I fulfilled his official office and controlled his subjects. According to the seasons he stimulated and taught agriculture and the culture of mulberry trees. In his spare time he planted flowers and trees, but first of all he was engrossed in calligraphy, writing according to the principles of the eminent scholars of the Chin and T'ang dynasties. He was able to write big characters by holding the pencil in such a way that a hollow could be seen between his thumb and index finger. Symmetrical sentences and inscriptions in our mansions, summer houses and at the waterpool were mostly written by him. They are remainders originating from his pencil and are admired as benefits of his hand and his artistic virtuosity.

Sire Wu I died in 1762, the tenth of the eleventh moon, at the age of fifty-one. He was granted the title of Wu I Ta-fu.

His wife, the noble Lady Wang, was the niece of our great-grandmother. She died before our grandfather in 1759, the fifth of the ninth moon, at the age of forty-seven. She received posthumously the title of Shu-jen. Both were buried in the cemetery of Hsi Hsiang T'ang.

FAN, SIRE WU-KUNG, THE FATHER OF THE FOURTEENTH GENERATION

When I was young I met with piteous misfortunes. I lost my father at seven years of age and my mother at twenty-two. Not being on a par with my parents I nonetheless inherited their patrimony. When looking upward I am grateful for the benefits received from the emperor for having fed and educated me, when looking down I think of what my parents expect from me, and I am afraid. Therefore, I chastise my body and amend my behavior, hoping the blessings received from my parents might endure. This, my intention, is beholden to the inspiration received from my parents' spirits, living in the outer world.

I dipped my pencil in blood and wrote summarily (the facts), to instruct the descendants and to provide material for the use of the historians of the future.

My late father's name was Fan, his style name Yung Ch'i. He was the oldest son of my grandfather Wu I. In his youth he was regal, he did not care much for the wealth of the family. He was a tall strong man, intelligent and perspicaceous.

In 1762 my grandfather Wu I died and my father received the decree for the succession. At that time the empire enjoyed peace. Eminent people liked the companionship of my father. He liked to invite people to dinner and sing songs. Wherever he went the guests were always in full number. He treated his officers and troops cordially. At every meal there was plenty of wine and food, noise and drinking. To people who suffered from the cold he offered clothes, not caring for the cost. This was the reason why the people were devoted to him until his death.

In 1781 the Mohammedans of Ho Chou revolted and approached the city of Lanchow, which was in critical circumstances. Father was ordered to rescue the city. Having crossed the river he fought in Luan Ku Tu P'ing. The rebels were beaten and scattered, the city was saved. However, many of his soldiers had been wounded and killed. Father also had been badly wounded. When the fact was known at court, he received congratulations, the coral button on the cap, the peacock plume, money, and several pieces of satin.

In 1784 the Mohammedan revolt, the Yen Ch'a Hui, broke out. The ancestor was ordered to move again to Lanchow. Day and night he guarded the capital of the province. After three months the revolt was quelled and he was given money to be distributed among his troops.

In 1785, having been recommended to the emperor by high officials, he was invited to call at Peking. On account of illness he could not move. He thanked the emperor and received some pieces of satin.

In 1786 he again received the call. The twenty-first of the twelfth moon (1788) he called on the emperor at the Hsi Hua Men, and later saw him at Ying T'ai. He assisted in the archery exercises in Cheng Yien Kung, and was invited to dinner in Ch'ung Hua Hung and to another dinner in Pao Hua Tien. On New Year's he congratulated the emperor in T'ai Hua Tien and was invited to dinner in T'sai Kuang Ko. He assisted at a literary convention in Ying Hua Tien, at the fireworks in Yuan Ming Yuan, and at the illumination and the fireworks again in Yuan Ming Yuan. On the nineteenth of the first moon while walking with the emperor in the T'ing Lo Yuan, he asked the emperor's permission to leave. The forty gifts he received from the emperor consisted mostly of food, clothes, satin, table services, dishes, etc. He was back in Chuang Lang on the eleventh of the third moon. The next year he died.

My mother originated from the Suan family of Liangchow, a noble family honored for generations by eminent scholars and officials. When she was nubile she entered our family. She was dutiful, zealous, intelligent, considerate, and the sound of her voice had never been heard outside our home. My father was very regal. He used money just as if it were earth. My mother tried to make him spend less money and to act more orderly. At the death of father, bad members of the family vexed the widow and the orphan and aimed at our wealth. The noble lady controlled the military and administrative affairs outside, and directed the family affairs inside. In her spare time she cared for my education. Those who intended our ruin did not succeed "in making us be blown away by wind," thanks to the merits of my mother.

In 1792 the imperial armies fought the Kokonor chieftain K'uo-erh-k'o. The winter was very cold, and the troops suffered. My mother carried to Donkir one million pounds of fuel for the troops. The emperor congratulated her, sent several pieces of satin, and the peacock plume for her son Chi Hsun. In the fourth moon he received the decree for the succession of the office. Then I hoped that mother, being free from cares, would enjoy a happy old age in harmony with the decisions of Heaven, and that I would have the opportunity to manifest my filial piety. Alas, after a few years she died. It is a punishment for my faults against filial piety. The punishment came fast.

Our family has defended the frontiers since the Ming dynasty. It is easy to become conversant with the faithfulness and justice with which our family has become illustrious. During the Ch'ing dynasty we have inhabited its territory and have been nourished during two hundred years. Tibetans and barbarians have been induced to submission. Although the blessings received are enormous, we did not show the smallest gratitude (big as a grain of sand or a small river). Our men fulfilled petty duties on the frontiers, and our ladies at home, but all of them received praises and honors from the emperor. The gifts granted by him are piled up in our homes. We have even been allowed to have dinner with the emperor.

Now I am a small man, one of those who, rubbing his body is ashamed to see he is growing fat (without having been grateful to the emperor), who is ashamed to see that he is becoming old and growing long teeth (as the horses), and that to all the benefits received from the emperor is added the blessing of old age (without still having been grateful to the emperor).

My father died in 1788, the fifteenth of the eleventh moon, at the age of forty-six. He was granted the posthumous title of Wu-kung Ta-fu. My mother died in 1799 on the twentieth of the second moon. They were buried in the cemetery of Ho Tung Hsiang T'ang.

CHI HSUN OF THE FIFTEENTH GENERATION

Sire Chi Hsun's style name was Tan Jen. He was the son of the first wife of Yung Ch'i originating from the Suan family. At the death of Yung Ch'i, Tan Jen was twelve years of age. His mother guarded the seal (acted as chief of the clan).

In 1791 the imperial army fought the rebel K'uo-erh-k'o and the widow sent one million pounds of fuel for the army. The emperor congratulated her and sent several pieces of satin, and to her son the peacock plume, and the decree to succeed his father the next year. It was an unusual benefit. Sire Chi Hsun was intelligent and perspicacious, tall and straight as jade; in trading he was zealous and economical. He was a model man. He liked nice clothes and horses, was gracious and talkative. He adhered strictly to the customs of a family which had reared officials for generations.

In 1796 the crops in Kansu were bad. According to the law, the Monguors in Kansu could not get help from the empire. Sire Chi Hsun sent a report through the hands of high officials. The emperor loaned seeds and food and later excused him from returning the loan. This proves that the emperor loves his subjects without making distinction between Chinese and non-Chinese. However, without the earnest supplication of Sire Chi Hsun the benefit would not have been granted.

At that time the Pe Lien Chiao brigands had spread in Hu Kuang, Nan Hui, and Szechwan provinces. Sire Chi Hsun asked to be permitted to help quell the revolt. He sent 300 of his troops to be enrolled in the expedition army of Kansu. The wounded and killed among his troops received the same compensations as the Manchu and Chinese troops. The very sensitive Heliotrope (subject) turns toward the sun (the emperor) and in that way is able to see its splendor (the virtue of the emperor).

In 1819, at the time of the celebration of the sixtieth anniversary of the emperor, Chi Hsun asked the favor of presenting his felicitations. It was accorded and the journey was defrayed by the empire. He went to call at Jehol. When dinners and ceremonies had taken place, he received the favor of precious clothes and food. In 1826 during the revolt in Turkistan, he was ordered to buy camels and to lead them to Suchow. After the revolt was quelled, he received with reverence the title of the second degree, the coral button on the cap, and the peacock plume. The next year he asked to be permitted to thank the emperor for the favor received. It was accorded and the costs were defrayed by the empire.

In 1830 on New Year's he congratulated the emperor at the T'ai Ho Tien, assisted at the illumination and fireworks, and the comedies on the ice. After dinners and ceremonies were over he received more gifts than on the former visit. During the reign of the emperor the empire was at peace. Drums were no longer beaten, no more alarm signals in the watchtowers on the Great Wall. Sire Chi Hsun had been favored to see the emperor many times, to admire the splendor of the palaces, and to enjoy the varied delights of the capital. He had cultivated friendships with ministers and high officials, and listened to fine singers. He delighted in the association with distinguished people, elegance in dress, beautiful furs, etc.

He was innately intelligent and courageous. Past sixty, every day after washing, rinsing his mouth, and putting his beard in a sack, he covered his hat and adjusted his dress. Leaning on cushions he sat erect, and his intelligence was more alert. All his movements were regulated like those of Chou Ke-liang. It is said that Ma Fu-po, when he was old, descended from his horse and stood straight, along side of it. When he had to ride the horse he grabbed the saddle and jumped on quickly. He looked straight ahead with open eyes, in order to show that he could still serve the emperor. The emperor enjoyed his vigor. Sire Chi Hsun resembled these people. He died in 1850 at the age of seventy-three.

His wife was a Khoshot Mongol, the daughter of Duke Wang of Alashan, prince of the first degree, imperial son-in-law. She arrived at our mansion at the age of twenty. She studied the classics and was conversant with the rites. She was considerate and strong minded, and understood the core of problems. She was kind toward the people, subjects and troops feared and loved her, nobody dared to disregard her. She controlled her household for fifty years, cutting what was superfluous and adding what was needed. She was a big support to Sire Chi Hsun. She died in 1851 at the age of seventy, in the seventh of the second moon. She bore two sons: Cho, the oldest, died prematurely in the middle of his life. The lady was very grieved. The second son, K'anpu-mei-erh-kung-pu-chih-k'ao, was a Living Buddha. He administered the monastery of Tung Erh Ku Lung. He was strict and severe. She had a grandson, Ju Kao, who succeeded to his father Chi Hsun with the title of secretary commandant. She had a granddaughter not yet married on account of her tender age. There were two more sons from a concubine.

[This section of the biographies ended with the fifteenth. Later a sixteenth and seventeenth were added, written with pencil. The sixteenth biography is the only one in the series of biographies of Lu clan chiefs, of a man who did not succeed as chief of the clan. It is irregular to call this biography the sixteenth.

In the fifteenth and seventeenth biographies it is said that the grandson Ju Kao succeeded to his grandfather Chi Hsun. However, in the same seventeenth biography it is said that Chi Hsun was the great-grandfather of Ju Kao and his mother the great-grandmother Fu-jen!]

K'UNG-CHAO OF THE SIXTEENTH GENERATION

Sire Cho's style name was K'ung Chao. He was the son of the wife of Tan Jen (Chi Hsun) born to the Mongol Khoshot lady. He was naturally faithful and kind, had a nice face, fine hands, and his eyelashes and eyes were like those seen in pictures. He was loved very much by his parents who severely watched his education and studies. He hoped to become a model of filial piety and aspired to obtain literary degrees. However, his career was ended before he had reached the goal (he was a grain that did not mature). He died in 1835.

His wife was a nice charming Khoshot girl who joined him at the age she became nubile. She was kind, amiable, and possessed all the required qualities of a good wife. At the time of the death of her husband she remained a widow to care for the education of her son. She was quiet and strongminded. The son Ju Kao, born in 1830, succeeded his grandfather Chi Hsun as chief of the clan. In 1857 she died and was buried in the cemetery of Shang Hsiang T'ang.

WAN CH'ING, THE CHENG-WEI CHIANG-CHUN OF THE SEVENTEENTH GENERATION

Sire Ju Kao's style name was Wan Ch'ing. He was the (great) grandson of Tan Jen (Chi Hsun) born of the wife of Cho. At the death of his father K'ung Chao (1835) his age was only six years. His grandfather Chi Hsun (who lived until 1850) cared for his education. He devotedly served his (great) grandfather, always praising the wine and food he presented to him (in order to make him better enjoy the food). He tried to make the old man happy. The grandfather lived until seventy years of age and his spiritual forces remained bright and strong, thanks to the filial piety and the care of Ju Kao. In 1850 Chi Hsun died and Ju Kao received the decree to the succession.

He was a strong, tall, distinguished man having high aspirations. He liked to ride horses and exercise with the bow. He honored the tradition of a military family. He was intelligent, went straight to the core of affairs and did not spend his time in minute details.

In 1857 the mint was to be built in Lanchow. Ju Kao offered wood and paid the building expenses for one year. He received from the emperor the button of the second degree, and the peacock plume.

In 1864 the Mohammedans of Ho Chou and Hsining revolted. One village after another was captured and destroyed. Sire Ju Kao protected the destitute people.

In 1871 the Shensi Mohammedans attacked Lien Ch'eng at night (the stronghold of the clan). Sire Ju Kao, day and night, defended the lonely city which resisted the attacks of the rebels, thanks to the exertion of the Sire.

In 1872 the Mohammedans of Hsining and Ho Chou attacked the city of Hsining. The governor of the province, Liu Chin-ch'ing, went with the army to the rescue of the city. At Lien Ch'eng the Tatung River was so swollen that no boats or rafts could cross. Ju Kao spent more than a thousand dollars and used his own wood to build a floating bridge. The troops crossed the river and arrived in time to save the city. Although the city had been saved by the army, Ju Kao had helped to save it by building the bridge.

In 1874 the revolt was quelled, and a report at court noted the circumstances of the salvation of Hsining, the recovery of the subprefecture of Tatung, and the help of Ju Kao by building the bridge. He received the title of Pa-tu-lu.

The governor general of the provinces of Shensi and Kansu, Tso Tsung-t'ang, was ordered to build a school in Lanchow for candidates to literary degrees. The institution having a bearing on the formation of eminent scholars and administrative officials, Ju Kao was happy to contribute. He liked to spend his own money and to collect money among his subjects. He offered 2,000 taels and a great number of trees to the officials who arrived to buy trees. The construction being achieved, the governor went to Suchow and stopped on his way in

Chuang Lang. Ju Kao went to call on him. He was invited to dinner, and highly praised by the governor.

The empire was at peace, the troops at rest. Ju Kao executed the orders of his superiors, and controlled his subjects according to the law. According to the seasons he examined farming and the culture of mulberry trees. In his spare time he planted flowers and bamboos and studied calligraphy, in the clerical style, according to the principles of the scholars of the Chin and T'ang dynasties. He was able to write letters as big as the elbow. Most of the inscriptions in our mansions, temples, monasteries, and shops are products of his pencil and admired as gifts of his hand and his artistic talent.

He died in 1891 at the age of sixty-four and received posthumously the title of Cheng-wei-chiang-chun. His wife, the noble Khoshot lady, guarded the seals. She cared for the orphan and controlled the clan. She was intelligent and strong minded.

In 1896 the Mohammedans of Ho Chou and Hsining revolted again. Destitute people fled to Lien Ch'eng. The lady provided them with board and lodging and distributed alms and repaired the city walls. She was clever and was feared and loved by the subjects. Nobody dared to vex her.

She had no children. However, there were three boys of concubines. The first one, Tan Tseng, became a lama, the second one, Yang, died at the time he was adult, the third, Shu, succeeded to the hereditary duty. The lady died at forty-six years of age and received the title of tseng (great-grandmother) Fujen. She was buried at Shang Hsiang T'ang.[10]

FOUNDATION OF A SECOND CLAN WITHIN THE LU CLAN

To the study of the Genealogical Register, the biographies and history of the Lu clan, is to be added a note about the founding of a second clan within the Lu clan.

T'o Huan, at the time of his submission to the Ming dynasty, was ordered to settle with his subjects in the country of Chuang Lang, which he had occupied during the Yuan dynasty. Accordingly, he was the recognized

proprietor of the country and the chief of his subjects, who were not allowed to abandon him. The same principle prevailed among the t'u-ssu in Huangchung, and the first appointed t'u-ssu was considered the founding ancestor of the clan, proprietor of the territory, and chief of the subjects. Regularly he was succeeded by his oldest son. Among the Monguors the founding ancestor distributed among his sons a part of the territory with some villages, to provide their sustenance, but he remained the supreme chief of the territory and the subjects. He was always free to dispense some territories to meritorious members of the clan. The sons of the founding ancestor and their descendants constitute the group of the nobles of the clan, forming as many branches as there were sons. Each branch was free to divide among its members the villages, and the land taxes, furnished by the commoners who tilled the soil of their properties and villages. In Huangchung, in time of war, each branch of the nobles was ordered to send a fixed number of soldiers to the t'u-ssu chief of the clan (Monguors I: 41, 42).

In the Genealogical Register and the Biographies of the Lu clan are noted only two sons of T'o Huan: Ah-shih-tu, the oldest, who succeeded and died after a year, and Kung-pu-shih-tieh, the second son, who succeeded from 1378 until 1410, and is recorded as the chief of the clan of the second generation.

In the genealogical records are noted only the t'u-ssu who succeeded to each other, and nothing is recorded about their brothers and sons who were not affiliated with the government of the clan.

Incidentally, there are encountered in the *Annals* of Kansu 42: 55, and in the *Annals* of Chuang Lang 36, some more interesting details related to the Lu clan and its history.

In both *Annals* it is recorded that the oldest son of T'o Huan was not Ah-shih-t'u, but Pa-chih-han. The text reads:

Pa-chih-han, the oldest son of the Prince of Wu Ting, member of the imperial family of the Yuan, fulfilling the duty of P'ing-chang-cheng-shih, submitted with his father to the Ming dynasty in 1371 and was promoted secretary commandant. Later the name of Lu was granted to the clan by the emperor. The successive chiefs of the branch of Pa-chih-han fulfilled the hereditary duty of t'u-ssu.

What could have been the reason for the creation of a second t'u-ssu clan at the very beginning, when the Lu clan submitted to the Ming dynasty? By analogy with what happened in the Li clan in 1655, as described in Monguors I: 42, we may suppose that it was due to a quarrel within the ruling family of the clan and that similar troubles between Pa-chih-han and his father T'o Huan or his brothers caused the establishment of a second clan in the Lu clan from the very beginning.

No hints are encountered of troubles in the Lu family

---

[10] According to the Chronicles of the Lu clan Ju Kao, born in 1830, succeeded as t'u-ssu in 1850 or 1852 and received the diploma of his incumbency only in 1883. He died in 1891 or in 1893.

His wife, a Khoshot lady, died without issue in 1895.

Ju Kao had three sons born by concubines. The third son, Shu, born in 1876 succeeded his father in 1897. Here end the Chronicles.

In 1916 the widow of Shu, also a Khoshot lady, arrived at Hsining imploring General Ma K'o-ch'eng to accept the "dry fatherhood" of her son. A few days later the boy arrived at Hsining to acknowledge his "dry father," his protector. Certainly Shu had died before 1916, leaving a son. The wife of Shu, the Khoshot lady, hoping to see the son succeed her late husband as t'u-ssu, made a trip to Hsining to secure the protection of General Ma K'o-ch'eng, and the realization of her desire.

at that time, either in the Lu chronicles or in the *Annals* of Kansu **42**: 56, and Chuang Lang 36, but both *Annals* record that, at the time Pa-chih-han was appointed t'u-ssu by the emperor with the title of "secretary commandant with seal," T'o Huan offered him some territories and fourteen villages. Nothing is noted about the number of families they contained. T'o Huan at that time controlled ten tribes of Monguors, numbering 3,245 families with 21,686 persons, and the most extensive territories allotted by the emperor to any t'u-ssu in Huangchung.

T'u-ssu T'o Huan was entitled "Commandant with Seal" and controlled 300 regular Monguor soldiers, 500 irregular soldiers, and 200 regular Tibetan soldiers. He obeyed the orders of the Chinese General of Hsining in time of war but had himself to provide the equipment (horses, weapons) and sustenance to his soldiers, who were not paid for their military services. He did not pay taxes to the Chinese officials. He received a salary of 76.6 taels.

As "secretary commandant with seal," Pa-chih-han also controlled territories offered "by the clan" but only fifty regular Monguor soldiers. He also obeyed the order of the Chinese general of Hsining in time of war, provided the equipment and sustenance to his soldiers, and paid no taxes to the Chinese officials, but he received an annual salary of only 48.96 taels.[11]

The enormous difference between the poor territories and fourteen villages offered to Pa-chih-han by his father and the extensive territories and cities and villages his father controlled must have opened his eyes to the fact that his right of succession as an eldest son had been by-passed by his father, and he must have felt this as an open insult which could never be forgotten and which sooner or later must be revenged.

Even though we encounter no hints in the family chronicles and in the *Annals* concerning troubles in the Lu family, these circumstances lead us to surmise that something must have been wrong between Pa-chih-han and his father, which might well have caused the formation of a second clan within the Lu clan.

THE PA-CHIH-HAN CLAN

During the Ming dynasty (1368–1644) the successors of T'u-ssu Pa-chih-han, endowed with the office of "T'u-ssu secretary commandant with seal," defended the country against the recurrent forays and invasions of Mongols and Tibetans, according to the orders of the general of Hsining. In 1644, at the end of the dynasty, the incumbent T'u-ssu of the Pa-chih-han clan was the secretary commandant Lu Tien, who fought the brigand Li Tze-ch'eng in Huangchung and Kansu. He fought the brigands with his Monguor troops in the same way T'u-ssu Lu Yung-ch'ang, "commandant with seal" of the T'o Huan clan, fought them with his Monguors. However, neither t'u-ssu helped the other during the entire expedition.

In 1646 T'u-ssu Lu Tien's army, in combination with the troops of the Ch'ing dynasty, fought the brigands Huo and Wu in the Hsiang Shan mountains of Ninghsia and the seventeen rebel tribes of Tibetans from the Chuang Lang region, thus accumulating merit.

In 1648 the Mohammedan Milayin revolted in Kanchow. Lu Tien helped the Manchu troops and those of the other t'u-ssu to recover the cities of Kanchow and Liangchow. He was promoted to "major of the Cheng-hai division." Some of the members of eminent families of the T'o Huan clan had mustered troops, on their own account, and lent a hand in the recovering of the cities. From then on their troops participated in all the subsequent fights against brigands.

In 1661 Lu Tien received officially the "hereditary incumbency of secretary commandant with seal" with the offices of "assistant chairman of the military headquarters" and of "vice-commandant in chief of the commandery of Ching Yuan." He died in 1667.[12]

During the Ch'ing dynasty the successors of the t'u-ssu of the Pa-chih-han clan were always at war (one of them, T'u-ssu Su Chou died on the battle field) with the other t'u-ssu of Huangchung and the seceders of the T'o Huan clan. They had helped quell all revolts of Chinese, Mongols, Tibetans, and Mohammedans in Huangchung.

All the successors of T'u-ssu Lu Tien were endowed with the incumbency of "secretary commandant with seal." They received annually a salary of 48.96 taels. They controlled fourteen villages and some territories and subjects granted to them by the founding ancestor T'o Huan. They did not pay taxes to the Chinese government. They commanded fifty regular Monguor soldiers.

THE T'O HUAN CLAN ON THE BRINK OF DISASTER

In the second moon of 1644, T'u-ssu Lu Yung-ch'ang of the T'o Huan clan, after several defeats suffered at the hands of the brigands of Li Tze-ch'eng, retreated with his troops into the city of Lien Ch'eng. The city was taken, T'u-ssu Lu Yung-ch'ang was killed and his only son, his legitimate successor, abducted by the brigands. The t'u-ssu had been betrayed by eminent members of the clan who had refused to fight. For three or four years news had been spread across the country that the dynasty was effete and its fall imminent. Long since at the clan meetings, chiefs and members of the most eminent families of the clan had had heated discussions among themselves and with the t'u-ssu, claiming that already three-fourths of China had been lost to the brigands and the Manchus, that fighting and dying for the Ming were useless, and that

---

[11] *Annals* of Chuang Lang 36a–b.

[12] *Annals* of Kansu **42**: 58–59; *Annals* of Chuang Lang 36a–b.

the surrender to the Ch'ing dynasty was the only solution.

The clan was convulsed by internal discord and on the brink of dislocation. The confusion and discord had grown after the death of T'u-ssu Lu Yung-ch'ang, the abduction of his legitimate successor, and the arrival in the country of the appointed governor of Shensi and Kansu provinces, Meng Ch'iao-fang, sent by the new Manchu dynasty.

Throughout 1644 vehement debates aggravated the confusion, and in 1645 members of the eminent families of the T'o Huan clan, advised by T'u-ssu Lu Tien, decided to follow his example, and to be introduced by him to the newly arrived governor Meng Ch'iao-fang.

The governor appraised the behavior of Lu Tien and appointed him "major of the Cheng-hai division," with orders to fight the brigands in combination with the Manchu army.

The whole country was upset. The Lu clan, the most important among the t'u-ssu clans, was without chief, and rent by internal discords. The governor was in a hurry to pacify the country and to use everyone who was able to give some help with troops. He was happy to meet the t'u-ssu in Huangchung who controlled troops and were ready to lend a hand. He was not averse even to accepting the help of members of eminent families of the T'o Huan clan who during the Ming dynasty had gained distinctions for military achievements and were able to muster troops on their own account from among their groups of relatives. He needed troops badly to cope with the situation.

However, the policy of the governor was destructive to the t'u-ssu clans. The power of the authority of a t'u-ssu is based on his ability to keep the subjects, nobles and commoners, submissive. During the Ming dynasty, when the use of the t'u-ssu troops was very urgent and the t'u-ssu accused at court subjects intending to secede from the clan, the Chinese officials were ready to protect the t'u-ssu and punish the seceders. Secession of groups of clan members caused the ruin of many clans among the nomads.

FIRST GROUP OF SECEDERS FROM THE T'O HUAN CLAN IN 1645

Who were the members of eminent families of the T'o Huan Clan who caused disunion in the clan?

The chief of the first group of seceders from the Lu clan was Lu P'ei-tso who, in 1645, was led by T'u-ssu Lu Tien to surrender to the new Ch'ing dynasty.

Lu P'ei-tso was a descendant of Lu Fu, the second son of Lu Chien, who had been one of the most famous t'u-ssu of the clan. During forty years (1444–1488) he had successfully fought Mongol and Tibetan invaders. In 1475 the emperor had honored him with an Honorific Arch with the inscription: "During his life he confirmed his faithfulness and sincerity; incessantly he exercised devotedness and zeal." Lu Fu, the second son of Lu Chien, had accompanied his father on the expeditions and had been named by the emperor "secretary commandant" of the city of Chuang Lang in 1519. The son of Lu Fu, Nen, died on the battlefield fighting Tibetans. His grandson was made "assistant commandant." His great-grandson died with the rank of second captain of the garrison of Hung Ch'eng. The group of the descendants of Lu Fu was one of the most prominent defenders of the Ming dynasty.

In 1648 the Mohammedan Milayin revolted in Kanchow. Lu P'ei-tso with his own army accompanied Lu Tien and other t'u-ssu to quell the revolt and recover the cities of Kanchow and Liangchow. He was given the original title of the family, that of "Assistant Commandant."

His descendants fought in 1723–1724 in Huangchung against the rebel Mongols of Kokonor. In 1781 they fought the Salar revolt and in 1784 the Yen Ch'a revolt of the Mohammedans.

During the whole Ch'ing dynasty the descendants of Lu P'ei-tso, in concert with Manchu and t'u-ssu troops of Huangchung and troops of seceders of the T'o Huan clan, quelled revolts and defended the country. Each in succession received the hereditary title of "Assistant Commandant" and an annual salary of 53.4 taels. The Lu P'ei-tso group lived in the country of Hsi Tat'ung and controlled the valleys of Ma Chuang and Yang Fang. It did not control subjects and had no regular soldiers but in time of war its chiefs called on the descendants of the Lu Fu group. It did not have to pay taxes to the Chinese government.[13]

SOCIAL STATUS OF CHIEFS OF GROUPS OF SECEDERS FROM THE CLAN

T'u-ssu are possessors of territories and subjects allotted to them by the emperor, and as beneficiaries of territories, and also the appointed defenders of them have the right to make legal claims against illegal appropriators of their territories. Since subjects are allocated to the t'u-ssu to provide them with defenders of their territories, each t'u-ssu is listed as having a fixed number of regular soldiers. A soldier is not allowed to abandon his chief, a Monguor is not allowed to abandon the t'u-ssu, and it is because the t'u-ssu has to equip his own troops that he is exempt from paying taxes.

By the same reasoning, one who, with his followers, secedes from his t'u-ssu is not legally entitled to either territory or subjects, and ought to be liable to prosecution. Even if he is not prosecuted, he and his group are not exempt from the payment of taxes, because he does not hold a recognized territory, with its attached duties and costs of defense.

---

[13] *Annals* of Kansu **42**: 60a–b.

The emperor himself appoints t'u-ssu and grants their seals and diploma. No officials, even governors, are allowed to appoint t'u-ssu. As an exception, when a new clan splits off from a large clan, a part of the territories and subjects of the clan are granted to the new t'u-ssu by the "old t'u-ssu and the clan chiefs," but in such cases accreditation by the emperor must follow. These facts in the Li and Lu clan have been previously noted. Also every time a new t'u-ssu succeeds to an old one his office must be confirmed by the emperor, with seal and diploma.

It is clear then that the status of a chief of a group of seceders from a Monguor clan is that of a military official, obeying the orders of a Chinese military official, who unlawfully enlisted him and granted him the titles and promotions granted to Chinese officials in the Chinese army; it is not the status of a t'u-ssu. Such a seceding chief and his followers, continuing to live in the territories of the clan, among the loyal subjects of the t'u-ssu, are legally still subject to him, although they have ceased to recognize his authority.

How is it possible for two groups of people to live peacefully together on the territory of a chief, whose authority one of them refuses to recognize? How is it possible to have Chinese officials who do not defend the rights of their subjects to secede from the clan? This paradox was realized in 1645, when the seceders of the T'o Huan clan led by T'u-ssu Lu Tien surrendered to Governor Meng Ch'iao-fang, and had their situation "regularized" by the Governor. A look at the chronicles of the Lu clan helps to clarify this confusing problem.[14]

SECEDERS FROM THE LU CLAN IN 1645

In 1645 Prince Yin of the Ch'ing dynasty arrived to call the people of the two rivers to surrender. He himself, a Manchu, well conversant with the mentality and the social institutions of the Mongols and nomadic peoples, and familiar with conditions in the Lu clan, was so shocked by the disorganization and hatred among the eminent families of the clan, that he ordered the noble Lady Yang, concubine of the killed T'u-ssu Lu Yung-ch'ang in Lien Ch'eng, to write to the emperor a detailed report with "her blood," concerning the disaster of Lien Ch'eng. The report reads: "The subjects of our clan have been divided among traitors, belonging to eminent families of our tribes, our clan properties have been seized and the hereditary lordship over our tribes usurped."[15]

This report is an eye-opener concerning the events of 1644, the confusion existing in the clan and the hatred among the subjects. Reading the report the first impression is that the Lu P'ei-tso group must be rated among the "traitors belonging to the most eminent families of our tribes" and that the territories

of Ma Chuang and Yang Fang had been stolen from the clan, with the people who lived on them. Such were the conditions existing in 1645, the year in which the noble Lady Yang reported to the emperor.

In the accusation sent by Lady Yang to the emperor it is recorded also that T'u-ssu Lu Tien of the Pa-chih-han clan stirred hatred and discord among the eminent families of the T'o Huan clan. Instead of helping save the clan, he aimed at its destruction, at the division of territories and subjects among the eminent families, and the absorption into his clan of more and more territories and subjects, and the patrimony of the abducted legitimate successor of the killed t'u-ssu, Sire Hung.

The resentment against the T'o Huan clan, caused by the forming of the clan of Pa-chih-han and nurtured in the hearts of the successors of the clan t'u-ssu for three centuries, brought the opportunity to take a long awaited revenge. Lu Tien used his influence with Governor Meng Ch'iao-fang to discredit the T'o Huan clan, to secure promotions for the chiefs of the seceding groups, to sow discord in the clan and accelerate its destruction.

At present it is easy to guess that one of the causes of all these troubles was the wrong done by T'o Huan in passing over his oldest son at the time he had appointed his second son as successor and chief of the tribes, and it is easy to believe that this old feud, which had flared up in the period of 1645 and brought the clan to the brink of disaster, is still smoldering in the hearts of the members of both clans.

SECOND GROUP OF SECEDERS

The second group of seceders were members of the same tribe of Lu Chien, the most prominent among the t'u-ssu of the T'o Huan clan. The chief of this second group was Lu Yung. It is noted that, like Lu Fu, he belonged to the nobility of the clan, being a descendant of the founder of the Yuan dynasty. During the Ming dynasty, Lu Chien, Pacificator of the Mongols, achieved his most brilliant successes in his wars against the Mongols in the region of Yu Lin (1448–1488), where his second son Lu Fu and Lu Yung acquired their awards. Lu Yung obtained the title of "general ensign," his son Lu Yu was given the title of "centurion" and during four generations the office of centurion was transmitted to his descendants.

In 1645 Lu Ta-kao, descendant of the seventh generation of Lu Yung, submitted to the Ch'ing and seceded from the clan. The hereditary office of centurion granted to him by the Ming was acknowledged by the Ch'ing. In 1648 he fought the rebel Milayin and in 1675 the rebels Wu San-kuei and Governor Wang Fu-ch'eng, and received the title of major and later that of secretary commandant. Having made an offer of grain to the army, he was made assistant commandant with the hereditary title of commandant. Then during

---

[14] See pp. 89, 101.
[15] See p. 89.

eight generations some members of the group were dignified with the title of commandant and some with that of secretary commandant. During the Ming dynasty the group had never obtained such prominent titles. The group lived in Ku Ch'eng, an annual salary of 73.44 taels was granted to the chief of the group, and the group paid taxes to the government. It controlled seven villages, but no subjects. In time of war the members of the Lu Yung group were used.

A comparison between the social conditions of both groups of seceders is instructive. In group one, during the Ming dynasty, are recorded: one award of secretary commandant, two of assistant commandant, one of captain; in the second group: one of general ensign and six of centurion. According to these titles the social status of group one seems to have been more important during the Ming dynasty than that of group two. During the Ch'ing dynasty in the first group are recorded nine awards of assistant commandant, in the second group are noted the awards of one secretary commandant, of one assistant commandant and of eight commandants. Again the titles of the first group have been more honorable. However, the salary of the chiefs of the second group was 73.44 taels, that of the first group only 53.4 taels. A big difference is that the first group did not have to pay taxes to the government but that the second group had to pay them. It is not easy to find an explanation of the fact that a group of members with higher offices received a smaller salary than members of a group with lower offices. Group one controlled the territories and villages of two valleys, group two controlled seven villages. Neither group controlled subjects but used descendants of their groups in time of war.[16]

It must be noted that during the Ming dynasty both groups of Lu Fu and Lu Yung were submissive and obedient subjects of the dynasty and their t'u-ssu, and that the secession of the first group started in 1645 with the surrender of Lu P'ei-tso to the Ch'ing and that of the second group with the surrender of Lu Ta-kao in 1645. It is worth noting that after the secession from the clan, both groups are recognized by the emperor as its devoted subjects and defenders, notwithstanding that secession is not allowed by the law, and also that t'u-ssu alone are exempt from payment of taxes to the government, and not groups of seceders. There remains the puzzle of how to equip a valuable army without controlling subjects, using only descendants of the founder of the group. Notwithstanding these anomalies, during centuries the "institution" has continued.

GROUP OF LU CHIH-TING, THIRD GROUP OF SECEDERS

Lu Chih-ting belongs to the same tribe of Lu Tien (Pa-chih-han). During the Ming dynasty the office of commandant was granted to him, though it is not

noted in what circumstances or for what reason. However, it was at the very end of the Ming that he formed his group, and that, in 1645, he followed Lu Tien to surrender to the Ch'ing.

In 1648 at the time of the revolt of Milayin he fought the rebel together with Lu Tien and the groups of Lu Fu and Lu Yung and helped recover the lost cities of Kanchow and Liangchow "using his subjects as soldiers." In 1651 his appointment as commandant received from the Ming, was acknowledged by the Ch'ing dynasty.

In 1675 Lu Wen-tu, son of Lu Chih-ting, at the time of the revolts of General Wu San-kuei and Governor Wang Fu-ch'eng, helped recover the lost cities of Lanchow, Ti Tao, etc., in combination with the troops of General Wang of Hsining and those of Lu Ta-kao, of the Lu Yung group, using "his subjects as his troops." In 1677 he was appointed commandant, the same position as that of his father, and eight members of eight generations successively received the same appointment.

The group lived in Ta Yin Wan, and all the chiefs of the group received the honorable title of commandant and a salary of 73.44 taels; however, they had to pay taxes to the government and controlled nine villages.[17] It is not noted that the group controlled subjects, but two times it is noted that it used its own "subjects" as troops, fighting rebels. These are the only times such "innocent" notices are recorded.

The group of Lu Chih-ting seems to have been formed at the very end of the Ming dynasty, at the time he was promoted commandant and so his ancestors are not recorded as chiefs of the group, nor is it recorded that he belonged to the nobility of the Yuan dynasty. However, he is a descendant of Pa-chih-han, eldest son of T'o Huan, who did belong to the nobility.

He is recorded as controlling nine villages, but it is sure that he did not receive the villages from Lu Tien, because Lu Tien possessed only the fourteen villages granted to his ancestor by T'o Huan in 1371. He seceded from the Lu Tien clan and because all the seceders, according to the report of Lady Yang to the emperor, stole subjects and territories from the T'o Huan clan, it is reasonable to suppose that he followed the other seceders in stealing the nine villages from the T'o Huan clan with their subjects.

GROUP OF LU KUO YIN, THE FOURTH GROUP

Lu Kuo-yin is recorded as belonging to the nobility of the Yuan, without a single detail more.

During the Ming dynasty, Lu Kuo-yin, his son and grandson Lu Ta-mu, bore the title of first chiliarch. In 1645, following Lu Tien, he surrendered to the Ch'ing with his group. In 1648 his grandson Lu Ta-mu died on the field of battle, fighting the rebel Milayin.

---

[16] *Annals* of Kansu **42**: 59a–b.

[17] *Annals* of Kansu **42**: 59b, 60a. *Annals* of Chuang Lang 37a.

In 1675 Lu Ta-mu's son Lu Ching-ch'eng, in combination with Major Lu Ta-kao of the Lu Yung group, fought the rebel Wu San-kuei and Wang Fu-ch'eng and recovered Lanchow and other cities and received the hereditary title of first chiliarch. Then members of seven successive generations received the same title during the Ch'ing dynasty.

The group lived in Ku Ch'eng, the chief received a salary of 42.84 taels, controlled the region of Hung Sha Ch'uan but controlled no subjects and at time of war the members of the group were used as soldiers. The group did not pay taxes to the government.

How did the group control the region of Hung Sha Ch'uan and what about the people who lived in the region?

At the time members of the "eminent" families stole territories and subjects from the clan, according to the report of Lady Yang. It is not abnormal, therefore, to encounter members of "less eminent families" belonging to the nobility of the Yuan following their example. The words "members of the nobility of the Yuan" seem to explain the behavior of the founders of groups of seceders.[18]

GROUP OF LU SAN-CH'I, THE FIFTH GROUP

The fifth group of seceders, the group of Lu San-ch'i, is noted as belonging to the imperial family of the Yuan, and to the clan of Tu-ssu Lu Tien.

It is recorded that the father of Lu San-ch'i was Lu P'ang-hsun, who during the Ming had been given the rank of second chiliarch.

In 1645 Lu San-ch'i went to surrender to the Ch'ing with Lu Tien, "to whose tribe he belonged." In 1648 in combination with Lu Tien and others he recovered the cities of Kanchow and Liangchow, occupied by the rebel Milayin. In 1652 his hereditary office of Second Chiliarch granted by the Ming was acknowledged by the Ch'ing. He died in 1671. Then nine members of successive generations received the hereditary office.

The group lived in Ma Chun P'u, controlled no subjects, received an annual grant of 32.64 taels, and did not pay taxes to the government. The descendants of the group fought in time of war.[19]

The group of Lu San-ch'i was the second among the seceders who belonged to the clan of T'u-ssu Lu Tien. Its social status must have been more modest than that of Lu Chih-ting, chief of the first group, because its chiefs had only the rank of second chiliarch while the chiefs of Lu Chih-ting's group held the rank of commandant. This "less eminent" clan family must well have expected to enjoy the same rights enjoyed by the "very eminent" one, and to partake of the division of territories and subjects of the T'o Huan clan, be-

cause it belonged to the same imperial Yuan house as the "very eminent" ones.

There also remains to be mentioned the eminent family of Lu Ch'a-pei who held the rank of centurion, which rank four members of successive generations held during the Ming dynasty. During the Ch'ing dynasty only three members held this rank. However, it is not noted that the group surrendered to the Ch'ing dynasty in 1645 and nothing is said about the relations of the group with the clan of T'u-ssu Lu Tien or with the clan of T'o Huan. It is only said that in 1738 Lu Chou, son of Lu Yuen-nir g, asked to succeed his father but that it was refused. After that there are no more records, so this group of seceders need not be taken into consideration.[20]

The conclusions seem to be that among the five groups of eminent families of the Lu Clans three seceded from the T'o Huan clan and two from the clan of T'u-ssu Lu Tien; that the seceders had been accused by Lady Yang to the emperor in 1645, of having stolen territories and subjects of the T'o Huan clan; that in the records concerning these events the names of the stolen villages and territories are duly noted, but it is positively denied that the five groups controlled subjects. However, it is accidentally noted that the Lu Chih-ting group fought rebels in behalf of the emperor, using genuine soldiers from among his subjects.

THE DISINTEGRATED LU CLAN

In 1645 the Manchu Prince Yin had been so shocked at the sight of the disorganization of the Lu clan and the disgusting hatred among the eminent families of so prominent a clan, that he had ordered Lady Yang to send to the emperor the report "written with her blood" about the conditions existing inside the clan.

What was the answer of the emperor to the report of Lady Yang? What was the redress ordered by the emperor for the injustices endured by the clan?

In 1648, after three full years during which no chief administered the clan and the gap of hatred and aversion between the clan members had deepened appallingly, Lu An, nephew of the killed T'u-ssu Lu Yung-ch'ang, received, with the title of commandant, the decree of appointment and the seal of t'u-ssu ad interim, for so long as the abducted legitimate successor was not discovered. Unfortunately, the t'u-ssu was looked at askance by most of the prominent members of the clan because he was too young.[21]

In the same year the revolt of the Mohammedan Milayin began in Kanchow, cities were lost, troops were hurried to recover the cities and quell the revolt. In the meantime T'u-ssu An waited quietly for the outcome of the revolt.

In 1650 T'u-ssu An was happy at the unexpected arrival at Chuang Lang of Sire Hung, the legitimate

18 *Annals* of Kansu **42**: 60*b*. *Annals* of Chuang Lang, 37*b*.
19 *Annals* of Kansu **42**: 60*b*.

20 *Annals* of Kansu **42**: 62*a*. *Annals* of Chuang Lang 37*a*.
21 See pp. 89, 101.

successor to the incumbency, and he left the distressed city as fast as possible.

From the day of his arrival, misfortunes and hardships awaited Sire Hung, still a boy of sixteen or seventeen years of age. The existence of two factions was instantly manifest: first, the illegal appropriators of clan territories and subjects, who were worried about whether or not they would be allowed to retain possession of the stolen territories and subjects; and second, the loyal and dependable members of the clan. Heated discussions and disturbances between the groups were everywhere evident. It will never be known how many visits were made, or what gifts were offered by each of the groups to the military and civil officials during the discussion of the problem of the conservation or the restitution of the territories and subjects, but after a few weeks the powerful seceders had succeeded in having Sire Hung put in jail for ten years, pouring streams of abuse upon the poor boy, accusing him of not being the genuine son of T'u-ssu Lu Yung-ch'ang. In 1659, after ten years of suffering and humiliation, thanks to the generous efforts of the loyal and dependable members of the clan, the truth became evident and Sire Hung received the appointment and seal of t'u-ssu of a clan rent by discords and hatred for more than twenty years.[22] Sire Hung died after fifteen years, in 1673, at the age of forty.

During the imprisonment of Sire Hung, his wife, Lady Wang, adopted a boy, Ti Hsin, and later bore a boy, Ti Ch'eng. At the death of Sire Hung, both boys being too young, Lady Wang retained the seal and controlled the clan. She had a hard time, suffering humiliation and contemptuous treatment every day from the group of the seceders who called her incapable of controlling the clan.

In 1674 the terrible revolt of the three ministers started, and the city of Lanchow was lost. The clever Lady Wang, hoping for help from powerful officials, sent grain and horses to help the troops and 300 of her soldiers to fight under the command of the general of Hsining. She received a laudatory letter.

In 1683 her son Ti Ch'eng succeeded to the office of t'u-ssu but he died after three years. In 1685 her adopted son Ti Hsin succeeded him.[23] Again the widow and her son endured very painful contumely at the hands of powerful and audacious clan members, as well in private as in administrative matters. This was the more harmful because the financial conditions of the family were at that time less brilliant. The lady had to adapt to her environment as well she could, and bear with fortitude the sad vicissitudes of the time.

In 1699 the Jungar group disturbed the country, and Ti Hsin sent troops to quell the revolt, and grain to groups of troops. Then the Kokonor Mongols invaded the country. Troops arrived from Lanchow to rescue the troops of Hsining, but just at that time the river of Tatung was swollen and the troops were blocked in Lien Ch'eng. Ti Hsin spent thousands of taels to hire carpenters, and using his own wood, he built a floating bridge so that the troops could arrive to save the city of Hsining.

In 1718, at fifty years of age, Ti Hsin asked for retirement and his son Hua Lin succeeded him.[24]

At that time more troops arrived in Huangchung on account of the troubles in Tibet and Turkistan. A Chinese army had been defeated in Tibet and Lhasa taken by the Jungars. In 1720 a new Chinese army marched to Lhasa. Hua Lin, the son of Ti Hsin, leading a strong army, participated in the expedition. The Jungars fled and the new Talai, who had been relegated to Kumbum, was enthroned in Lhasa. Lu Hua Lin, accredited with exceptional achievements, was appointed Lieutenant Colonel of Hsining. The future of the clan seemed to become hopeful.

More troops arrived from Szechwan, commanded by Governor Nien Keng-yao and General Yueh Chung-ch'i, to quell the revolt of the Khoshot Mongols of Kokonor and the lamas and Tibetans of Huangchung. Both officials, not conversant with the countries of Kokonor and Huangchung and the people and tribes, started engaging all the troops of the Monguor t'u-ssu clans of Huangchung.

It happened that the mother of the retired T'u-ssu Ti Hsin, the adopted son of the late Sire Hung, was the noble Dame Yueh, the sister of the father of General Yueh Chung-ch'i. Needless to say, Ti Hsin and his son Hua Lin and the entire family were happy to meet the prominent general and that this happy news was swept across the country among the t'u-ssu.

The general, after a few days, knowing the circumstances of the Lu family, was ready to try to help it out. However, the seceders of the clan still seethed with hatred and avoided contacting the general.

The troops of Lu Hua Lin fought during 1723 and 1724, several times successfully, in combination with the troops of the governor and the general. Hua Lin was promoted colonel in Liangchow. All the t'u-ssu were stimulated to compete with each other in quelling the revolts, and the concord and congeniality among the t'u-ssu and the good understanding with the high officials was unusual.

The eight brutal Tibetan tribes of Hsieh Erh So, living in Cho Tze Shan, the mountainous country of Chuang Lang, had revolted in 1723 and their revolt had been quelled by General Yueh Chung-ch'i after a heavy struggle which had lasted many weeks, and the large country pacified. The many conspicuous achievements of Lu Hua-lin having been reported to the emperor, the emperor awarded him the tribes as subjects. They numbered 453 families totaling 2,365 persons.[25]

[22] See p. 101.
[23] See p. 102.

[24] See p. 102.
[25] See pp. 103, 113.

At the time of the celebration of the victory in Peking, Lu Hua Lin was invited to the capitol to call on the emperor. He received the title of Lieutenant Colonel of Huo Ch'i Ying in Sian, the capital of the Shensi province, and was later transferred to Kanchow as defender of the city and assistant general in Yung Ch'ang.

The Lu clan was flourishing, its honor redeemed, and the clan was again at the crest of its glory. Lu Hua Lin died in 1736.[26]

THE CLAN MEMBERS AND THE SECEDERS

The Lu clan had lost its seceders, but had been granted by the emperor the eight tribes of Hsieh Erh So. But what about the seceders from the clan?

It is a shame that notwithstanding suits lasting during many years, none of the territories and subjects stolen by the seceders had been restored to the clan, and none among the seceders had been punished, nor had any of them come back to the clan. However, after the glorious achievements of Lu Hua Lin, his distinguished promotions, the influence of the honorable family of Yueh Chung-ch'i and the more intimate concord of the Lu clan with all the t'u-ssu of Huangchung, the influence and prestige of the clan had reached its former prominent status in the t'u-ssu society and in that of Chinese officialdom.

The social status of the seceders had decreased in proportion as the social status of the Lu clan had increased. The prestige of a clan depends on the titles and promotions of the clan chiefs, and never had the titles of the seceders been on a par with those of the clan chiefs, even though the troops of the seceders had continued to help quell the revolts in Huangchung. However, the hatred against the Lu clan continued to persist among them with the same bitterness and rancor, and was always ready to flare up at every opportunity, even after so many years.

In the biography of T'u-ssu Fan (t'u-ssu of the fourteenth generation) who died in 1787 after having called on the emperor in 1786, it is noted that his widow and orphan boy suffered vexations and contemptuous treatment from the old foes of the clan. The son being too young to succeed his father, his mother was in a hurry to have the boy appointed in order to avoid difficulties in the succession. In the winter of 1792 she sent a million pounds of fuel to the army which was defending the city of Donkir, and received a fine letter of congratulations and the decree for the succession of the boy to the office of t'u-ssu. That was an old trick used in the clan every time troubles were brewing and the good offices of the emperor were needed.

The same trick was used against the same foes when, in 1826, the clan bought camels for the army fighting in Suchow; in 1857, when the Mint was built and a valuable sum of money was offered to prevent troubles

with the same foes; and again in 1872, at the time of the revolt of the Mohammedans, when the clan built a floating bridge to pass the Tatung River, for the army had to reach Hsining and was blocked at Lien Ch'eng.

The conclusion seems to be that a sword of Damocles swayed above the clan for as long a time as the seceders were alive and assuming an attitude of menacing hostility every time an opportunity would occur.

CONCLUSION

The study ends with the biographies of the ancestors of the most prominent among the clans, the Lu clan, which shed light on the family life of the t'u-ssu and the process of Sinicization in the center of the family.

This section of the Biographies shows the mentality of the chiefs of the clans and their entire families. All the chiefs of the Monguor clans at the beginning of the Ming dynasty were uncouth barbarians, admiring the Chinese civilization, feeling themselves humiliated in the presence of the Chinese. Hence the eagerness in the families of the chiefs of all the clans to learn the Chinese language, to adopt Chinese customs, to have in the family members honored with literary degrees, to see their chiefs dignified with Chinese military titles and promotions. The Chinese knew very well these dispositions and fostered them, granting military titles one after another, even bestowing upon some among them, the title of Duke of Hui Ning and Duke of Kao Yang.

The chiefs of the clans married girls of prominent Chinese officials, and married their girls to important Chinese officials and prominent Chinese families. After a couple of generations the mentality and customs in the family had completely changed. Dinners had become Chinese dinners, clothing Chinese clothing, jewelry Chinese jewelry, furniture in the houses Chinese furniture, and the walls were adorned with Chinese inscriptions and paintings. A hall to the ancestors had been built in the mansion of the chief of the clan where sacrifices were offered according to the Chinese pattern, and rich Monguors liked to display luxury in the Chinese fashion. The introduction of Chinese women into the families of the chiefs of the clan had changed entirely the mind of the family and stimulated its Sinicization. But in China the corners are never wholly square. These Sinicized Monguors profess a Confucianism that allows them to practice, even fervently, lamaism and shamanism, that allows them to burn down and rebuild monasteries, to be proprietors of monasteries and to have sons who become lamas and even Living Buddhas.

The family chronicles of the Lu clan are a great help for the comprehension of the social life of the Monguor clans and also of the attitude of the Chinese administration, related to the policy adopted toward the Mongol and Tibetan brigands on the frontiers.

[26] See p. 103.

In the texts of the imperial orders sent to the t'u-ssu concerning the way of waging war with the Mongol brigands who incessantly for five centuries invaded and plundered the frontiers, abducted and killed people, are encountered continually the words "mobilize the troops and kill the brigands," "exterminate the brigands," "you are capable of doing that," "intercept their roads and kill them," "block their ways and kill them," etc., etc. The rage against and the exasperation caused by the Mongol brigands were uppermost in the minds of the Chinese officials and the frontier people.

It is a pity that the family chronicles of the other t'u-ssu clans are lost, so we miss the texts of the imperial pronouncements at official burials with the three sacrifices and the imperial oration read before the coffin by a high official delegated by the emperor. The first sacrifice was offered and the oration read on the day of the burial. On the anniversary of the death was offered the second sacrifice and there was read a second oration. After the third year, at the end of the mourning period, followed the last sacrifice and the oration. These orations consisted in the glorification of the deceased, of his virtues and merits, and described what the emperor considered to be the virtues and the merits of the officials he used. They always ended with stereotype phrase, "in case your spirits are still conscious and capable to enjoy and breathe the fragrancy of the sacrifice, accept and enjoy it." This last courtesy of the emperor toward the meritorious t'u-ssu, read by a high official, in the presence of the entire clan, created a special atmosphere of devotion among the Monguors toward the emperor. The texts of these orations are always very interesting and instructive.

THE GLORY OF THE T'U-SSU CLANS OF HUANGCHUNG

We have to close the study of the Huangchung Monguors with the list of the names of the Monguor t'u-ssu who died on the field of battle sacrificing their lives for the Ming and the Ch'ing dynasties.

. This is the most glorious page in the history of the Monguors.

DIED ON THE FIELD OF BATTLE

In 1402 T'u-ssu Ch'i Kung-k'o-hsing-chi
In 1403 T'u-ssu Ch'i Tuan-chou
In 1410 T'u-ssu Lu Kung-pu-shih-tieh
In 1426 T'u-ssu Chou-yung
In 1511 T'u-ssu Li Ch'eng's son
In 1536 T'u-ssu Hsin Pao
In 1537 T'u-ssu Yeh Luan
In 1559 T'u-ssu Li Ming-mao
In 1586 T'u-ssu Na Wei-liang
In 1588 T'u-ssu Li Chih-hsien
    T'u-ssu Ch'eng Chih-kang
    T'u-ssu Chao and Wu. With these two t'u-ssu 800 soldiers died.

T'u-ssu Yeh Wei-chien
T'u-ssu Wang Chao
In 1643 T'u-ssu Lu Yung-ch'ang
In 1644 T'u-ssu Li Hung-yuan, his wife and 120 members of his family.
    Wife of T'u-ssu Li T'ien-yu, his concubine, two brothers, three hundred members of the family.
T'u-ssu Yeh Kuo-chi
In 1646 T'u-ssu Ch'eng Kuang-hsien's son
In 1798 T'u-ssu Han Kuang-tsu
In 1864 T'u-ssu Chou Hsieh-chi
    No record existed relating to the number of all the Monguor soldiers who died on the fields of battle during these five centuries.

HONORIFIC ARCHES AND INSCRIPTIONS

Honorific Arch was built and inscription sent by the emperor:

In 1475 for T'u-ssu Lu Chien "During his life he confirmed his faithfulness and probity, incessantly exercised fidelity and zeal."

In 1546 for T'u-ssu Lu Chin "Incessantly practiced faithfulness and justice and was illustrious for his dignity and fame."

In 1568 for T'u-ssu Li Kung "Ch'ing Yun, 'Blue Clouds,' means Bright Intelligence. He was an eminent scholar."

In 1612 for T'u-ssu Ch'i Teh "Honorably favored by Heavenly Grace."

In 1616 for T'u-ssu Ch'i Ping-chung "Served the country, manifested loyalty."

In 1644 for T'u-ssu Li Hung-yuan "Loyal servant and faithful wife, glory of the noble clan."

In 1534 in the city of Hsining was built the HALL OF THE FAITHFUL AND MERITORIOUS OFFICIALS OF HUANGCHUNG.

Four names of t'u-ssu are recorded in the list of these glorious officials. They are:

Li Nan-ko
Li Yin
Ch'eng Chih
Li Ch'ang

IMPERIAL DISTINCTION

After the Hsining troops, seething with hatred against the Mongol brigands of Kokonor, and the son, nephew, and relatives of Altan, had brilliantly demolished the temple in Kokonor, where Altan had met the Dalai Lama, and after two resounding victories had been obtained against these brigands in 1594, reports were sent to the emperor with the names of the meritorious military and civil officials who had contributed to these successful achievements. A delegate of the ministry of war was sent with titles and gifts to reward these officials. Among the names of these meritorious officials we read these of the Monguor t'u-ssu:

> Lu Kuang-tsu
> Li Yu-mao
> Li Hsien-hua
> Ch'eng San-chi
> Ch'i Ping-chung
> Ch'i Teh

STELES ERECTED BY THANKFUL PEOPLE FOR MERITORIOUS T'U-SSU

In 1537 T'u-ssu Yeh Luan pacified the region of Cheng-ch'iang-i and was besieged in the fortress by several groups of Mongol brigands. He fought bravely. Nearly all his soldiers were killed, but he still fought with the courage of despair. Finally he was killed. The thankful people of the country erected a stele in Cheng-ch'iang-i in commemoration of his heroic achievement. The stele still exists.

In 1616 T'u-ssu Ch'i Ping-chung, appointed in Yung-ch'ang, was besieged by the Mongol Yin-ting-ssu-ts'ing and his 1,000 troops. Controlling only 300 soldiers, he fought during two days and nights. When the auxiliary troops arrived, instantly Ch'i Ping-chung pursued the enemy and recaptured the abducted people and stolen animals. The thankful people erected a stele in the city of Yung-ch'ang in commemoration of his glorious performance.

During five centuries the Monguors bore with fortitude the vicissitudes of very hard times, fighting inroads of brigands and revolts of tribes, always on the warpath in their own country and in far-off provinces. A strong factor in buoying their courage was the tie of the clan, which bound them close together in one family, with a t'u-ssu as head of the family.

The appreciation and estimation of their heroic achievements by the emperor and local high officials, the building of Honorific Arches, the favor of official burials and sacrifices, the granting of titles, the names of their chiefs recorded in the City Hall of faithful and meritorious officials, the reports sent to the emperor about their valorous performances, the thankfulness of the Chinese who erected steles to glorify them, were so many stimuli for the Monguors which made life worth living and brought happiness in the clan and in the families.

The last news we have about the Huangchung Monguors is that the Monguor clans are broken up, the t'u-ssu regime is abolished, the ladies are forbidden to wear their distinctive clothes and headdress, the use of their language is prohibited, in every village a school is organized with teachers of the new ideology. Monguors and their wives are enlisted with the Chinese men and women in working groups. The aim is to obliterate the Monguor nation and mix it in the Chinese nation. In a few years from now the Monguors will have disappeared.

INDEX

MEMOIRS

OF THE

AMERICAN PHILOSOPHICAL SOCIETY

————————

TRANSACTIONS

OF THE

AMERICAN PHILOSOPHICAL SOCIETY

Edward T. Cardwell: Peelite. ARVEL B. ERICKSON.
Vol. 49, pt. 2, 107 pp. 1959. $2.00.

Aleut Dialects of Atka and Attu. KNUT BERGSLAND.
Vol. 49, pt. 3, 128 pp., 23 figs. 1959. $3.00.

The Medieval Theories of the Just Price. Romanists, Canonists, and Theologians in the Twelfth and Thirteenth
  Centuries. JOHN W. BALDWIN.
Vol. 49, pt. 4, 92 pp. 1959. $2.00.

The Anatomy of Callimico goeldii (Thomas)—A Primitive American Primate. W. C. OSMAN HILL.
Vol. 49, pt. 5, 116 pp., 77 figs. 1959. $2.50.

Some Assumptions of Aristotle. GEORGE BOAS.
Vol. 49, pt. 6, 98 pp. 1959. $2.00.

Bernard de Fontenelle: The Idea of Science in the French Enlightenment. LEONARD M. MARSAK.
Vol. 49, pt. 7, 64 pp. 1959. $1.50.

Contemporary Japan: The Individual and the Group. Y. S. MATSUMOTO.
Vol. 50, pt. 1, 75 pp. 1960. $2.00.

Studies in Byzantine Astronomical Terminology. O. NEUGEBAUER.
Vol. 50, pt. 2, 45 pp. 1960. $1.50.

The Archaeology of the Lower Tapajós Valley, Brazil. HELEN C. PALMATARY.
Vol. 50, pt. 3, 243 pp., 12 figs., 121 pls., 6 maps. 1960. $5.00.

The Ainu of Northern Japan. A Study in Conquest and Acculturation, by Takakuru Shinichirō. Translated and
  annotated by JOHN A. HARRISON.
Vol. 50, pt. 4, 88 pp., 4 maps. 1960. $2.00.

The Dal Pozzo-Albani Drawings of Classical Antiquities in the British Museum. CORNELIUS C. VERMEULE III.
Vol. 50, pt. 5, 78 pp., 103 figs. 1960. $2.00.

The Paleocene Pantodonta. ELWYN L. SIMONS.
Vol. 50, pt. 6, 99 pp., 18 figs. 1960. $2.50.

Talleyrand: The Cardinal of Périgord (1301-1364). NORMAN P. ZACOUR.
Vol. 50, pt. 7, 83 pp., 3 figs. 1960. $2.00.

The Forming of the Charitable Institutions of the West of England. A Study of the Changing Pattern of Social
  Aspirations in Bristol and Somerset, 1480-1660. W. K. JORDAN.
Vol. 50, pt. 8, 99 pp. 1960. $2.00.

The Nāṭakalakṣaṇaratnakośa of Sāgaranandin, a Thirteenth-century Treatise on the Hindu Theater. Translated
  by MYLES DILLON, MURRAY FOWLER, and V. RAGHAVAN. Introduction and Notes by V. RAGHAVAN.
Vol. 50, pt. 9, 74 pp. 1960. $2.00.

Cultural Sequences at The Dalles, Oregon. A Contribution to Pacific Northwest Prehistory. L. S. CRESSMAN.
Vol. 50, pt. 10, 108 pp., 61 figs., 8 maps. 1960. $3.00.

The Tobacco Adventure to Russia. Enterprise, Politics, and Diplomacy in the Quest for a Northern Market for
  English Colonial Tobacco, 1676-1722.
Vol. 51, pt. 1, 120 pp. 1961. $2.75.

A New Fragment of Xenocrates and its Implications. SHLOMO PINES.
Vol. 51, pt. 2, 34 pp. 1961. $1.00.